Trade and the Industrial Revolution, 1700–1850
Volume I

The Growth of the World Economy

Series Editor: Nick F.R. Crafts
Professor of Economic History
London School of Economics, UK

Trade and the Industrial Revolution, 1700–1850 Volume I

edited by

Stanley L. Engerman

John H. Munro Professor of Economics
and Professor of History
University of Rochester
Rochester, New York, US

THE GROWTH OF THE WORLD ECONOMY

An Elgar Reference Collection
Cheltenham, UK • Brookfield, US

Published by
Edward Elgar Publishing Limited
8 Lansdown Place
Cheltenham
Glos GL50 2HU
UK

Edward Elgar Publishing Company
Old Post Road
Brookfield
Vermont 05036
US

British Library Cataloguing in Publication Data
Trade and the Industrial Revolution,
1700–1850. – (Growth of the World Economy
Series; Vol. 2)
 I. Engerman, Stanley L. II. Series
 382.09033

Library of Congress Cataloguing in Publication Data
Trade and the Industrial Revolution, 1700–1850 / edited by Stanley L.
Engerman.
  p. cm. — (The growth of the world economy ; 2) (An Elgar
reference collection)
 Includes bibliographical references and index.
  1. Commerce—History—18th century. 2. Commerce—History—19th
century. 3. International trade—History. 4. Industrial
revolution. 5. Economic history—1750–1918. I. Engerman, Stanley
L. II. Series. III. Series: An Elgar reference collection.
HF495.T73 1996
382′.09—dc20   95–36557
                                                                                            CIP

ISBN 1 85898 007 0 (2 volume set)

Printed in Great Britain by Galliard (Printers) Ltd, Great Yarmouth

Contents

Acknowledgements

The editor and publishers wish to thank the following who have kindly given permission for the use of copyright material.

Academic Press, Inc. for articles: James F. Shepherd and Gary M. Walton (1976), 'Economic Change after the American Revolution: Pre- and Post-War Comparisons of Maritime Shipping and Trade', *Explorations in Economic History*, **13** (4), October, 397–422; Claudia D. Goldin and Frank D. Lewis (1980), 'The Role of Exports in American Economic Growth during the Napoleonic Wars, 1793 to 1807', *Explorations in Economic History*, **17** (1), January, 6–25; François Crouzet (1980), 'Toward an Export Economy: British Exports during the Industrial Revolution', *Explorations in Economic History*, **17** (1), January, 48–93.

Banco di Roma for articles: Paul Bairoch (1973), 'European Foreign Trade in the XIX Century: The Development of the Value and Volume of Exports (Preliminary Results)', *Journal of European Economic History*, **2** (1), Spring, 5–36; Charles P. Kindleberger (1975), 'Commercial Expansion and the Industrial Revolution', *Journal of European Economic History*, **4** (3), Winter, 613–54.

Cambridge University Press for article and excerpt: Albert H. Imlah (1950), 'The Terms of Trade of the United Kingdom, 1798–1913', *Journal of Economic History*, **10** (2), November, 170–94; Patrick Villiers (1991), 'The Slave and Colonial Trade in France just before the Revolution', in Barbara L. Solow (ed.), *Slavery and the Rise of the Atlantic System*, Chapter 9, 210–36.

Duke University Press for article: Ralph A. Austen and Woodruff D. Smith (1990), 'Private Tooth Decay as Public Economic Virtue: The Slave-Sugar Triangle, Consumerism, and European Industrialization', *Social Science History*, **14** (1), Spring, 95–115.

Elsevier Science BV for article: Peter Temin (1967), 'The Causes of Cotton–Price Fluctuations in the 1830's', *Review of Economics and Statistics*, **XLIX** (4), November, 463–70.

Jacob M. Price for his own article: (1961), 'Multilateralism and/or Bilateralism: The Settlement of British Trade Balances with "The North", *c.* 1700', *Economic History Review*, **XIV** (2), December, 254–74.

Paul Butel for his own article: (1986), 'Traditions and Changes in French Atlantic Trade Between 1780 and 1830', *Renaissance and Modern Studies*, **XXX**, 124–45.

Pinter Publishers Ltd for excerpt: Ralph Davis (1979), 'The Industrial Revolution and British Overseas Trade', *The Industrial Revolution and British Overseas Trade*, Chapter 5, 62–76.

T.M. Devine for his own article: (1976), 'The Colonial Trades and Industrial Investment in Scotland, *c.* 1700–1815', *Economic History Review*, **XXIX** (1), February, 1–13.

W.W. Norton for excerpt: Douglass C. North (1961), 'International Economic Flows – 1815–1860', *The Economic Growth of the United States, 1790–1860*, Chapter VIII, 75–100 and references.

Every effort has been made to trace all the copyright holders but if any have been inadvertently overlooked the publishers will be pleased to make the necessary arrangement at the first opportunity.

In addition the publishers wish to thank the Library of the London School of Economics and Political Science, the Marshall Library of Economics, Cambridge University and the Photographic Unit of the University of London Library for their assistance in obtaining these articles.

Introduction

The period from 1700 to 1850 saw many dramatic changes in the world economy. It was the period of the Industrial Revolution in Great Britain, with the British rise to dominance as an economic and political power, as well as becoming the world's leading trading nation. Modern economic growth emerged elsewhere in Western Europe and in North America, though the British still were the world's richest nation at the end of this period. Political independence was achieved by many nations of North and South America, but political independence from Europe did not mean either economic independence or freedom from the economic policy ideas of the metropolitan powers. This was the period of large-scale movements of labour to the Americas from Europe and Africa, with various combinations of free, convict and indentured servant labour from Europe, and of slave labour from Africa. There were continued flows of labour and trade with Asian nations, and the settlement of Australia by the British began by the end of the 18th century. European nations were frequently at war with each other, on the Continent as well as elsewhere in the world, influencing the timing, if not the ultimate magnitude, of inter- and intracontinental trade, and of labour and capital flows (Kindleberger, Volume I Chapter 1). European exports in the 19th century, after the ending of the Napoleonic Wars, grew at an unusually rapid rate, surpassed only in the years after World War II (Bairoch, Volume I Chapter 2). Based on the New World colonies' production of crops such as sugar, coffee and tobacco, generally with slave labour, as well as tea from Asia, new consumption patterns developed within Europe, with significant impacts on demand patterns as well as the supply of labour, working time, and labour effort (Austen and Smith, Volume I Chapter 3; Pares, Volume I Chapter 9).

There were also a number of dramatic changes in ideas that would influence the basis of trade and factor movements. Over the course of the 19th century the slave trade to the Americas and then slavery there were ended – by legislation in most places, but by slave uprising in French Saint Domingue and the Civil War in the United States. At the same time, serfdom was ended throughout Europe. The basic policies regulating trade, lumped together as mercantilism, emphasizing the competitive nature of international trade and the role to be played by colonies in benefiting the metropolis, came to be revised, particularly among the British, for some combination of economic and ideological reasoning, with the rise of more laissez-faire economic policies and a greater interest in freer trade and free factor flows. International rivalries remained, with concerns about competitive standings and rankings, but with a reduced amount of the direct interference with trade that had characterized the earlier, mercantilistic era.

Britain was the first country to have experienced an Industrial Revolution, although its timing and the magnitude of growth remain debated. Determining its causes, and answering the question of why England and not France, are perennials of historical analysis. Over the first 80 years of the 18th century French foreign trade, with its colonies and elsewhere, had also grown rapidly, only to lose out at the end of the century, with the French and the Haitian Revolutions (Villiers, Volume I Chapter 11; Butel, Volume I Chapter 12). Britain had greatly expanded its international trade, with its colonies and also with Europe, in the 18th century, succeeding in driving other countries out of its colonial trades as a result of the Navigation Acts and related policies. Thus the importance of the growing international trade to the British Industrial Revolution has long been argued for, with the implication that in the absence of such trade the British economy would not have been capable of achieving the full extent (if any) of the development it achieved (Davis, Volume I Chapters 4 and 7; Crouzet, Volume I Chapter 6). An analytically similar argument concerning the importance of exports has been made for the United States in the first half of the 19th century, as well as for its earlier colonial period (Shepherd and Walton, Volume I Chapter 13; Goldin and Lewis, Volume I Chapter 14; North, Volume I Chapter 15; Temin, Volume I Chapter 16). Despite the fact that about nine-tenths of British production went to consumers in the home market, some argue for the more important impact of the dynamic changes due to international demands and profits earned in those foreign transactions. The importance of foreign markets and profits to provide for adequate domestic demand and for capital formation are seen to have arisen from the limitations to demand by British consumers, reflected in the presumed declining standard of living for many within Britain, the latter itself a rather contentious historiographic issue.

In its broadest variant, the focus of the discussion about international trade was placed on foreign markets in general, whether in Europe or elsewhere, as the basis for the necessary external stimulus to British economy. There are also important variants that relate trade patterns with specific areas to British and European growth, often presented with significant moral and political implications. The debates on imperialism gave attention to the growth of Europe at the time of relative, if not absolute, decline in what came to be called the 'Third World', stressing what is described as both unequal political power and unequal exchange (O'Brien, Volume II Chapter 1). Earlier arguments claimed that the Europeans sold exports at high prices and purchased their imports from the less developed world at low prices, and that this European exploitation of the Third World was the basis for the growth of the developed world. A puzzle arose, however, as studies of the terms-of-trade indicated that, particularly in the first half of the 19th century, the British passed on much of the benefit of their productivity improvements to their trading partners in the form of lower prices for its exports (Imlah, Volume I Chapter 8). More recently, however, with the emergence of dependency theory, it was argued that the form of exploitation was different from that earlier argued, with the Europeans selling exports at low prices and paying high prices for imports, thus pushing Third World production into a colonial pattern. On the question of limited Third World growth there are a number of issues similar to those that arise for countries with rapid economic growth: e.g., what was the magnitude of trade relative to GNP, what were the further structural shifts resulting from the initial set of changes, and what was the capacity of the internal economy to adjust to economic changes?

Specific areas have been considered to be the basis of the international connections that led to British and European growth. The so-called 'drain' from India, as well as British trade policy, have often been claimed by Indian scholars and politicians to have had a marked impact upon the expansion of the British economy while leading to the limited growth of the Indian economy (Chaudhuri, Volume II Chapter 6). The argument for a pivotal role of slavery in the Americas for European growth was first made prominent by the Trinidadian historian (and later the first Prime Minister of the newly independent nation of Trinidad and Tobago)

Eric Williams, in his book *Capitalism and Slavery* (Sheridan, Volume II Chapter 3). To Williams, it was the profits from the slave trade and from the exports of slave-produced commodities that helped to finance the capital formation of the Industrial Revolution (Devine, Volume I Chapter 10). Others, arguing for the pivotal role of slavery and the American colonies, stress also the impact of the demands coming from the colonies upon British exports, particularly of manufactured goods, in spurring industrialization.

In examining each of these questions relating to British, European and colonial trades, a certain set of key issues and empirical questions are paramount. Three will be noted here. First, a major question concerns the order of magnitude of foreign trade or of the particular commodity or geographic category of trade being discussed. What was the overall ratio of trade to GNP, and what were the shares of different areas in this trade? How much of the overall change did these trade shares explain? Some effects on the economy no doubt existed, but how does their magnitude relate to the argument concerning relative importance? Of course, economists have developed models in which small shocks generate large effects via dynamic, multiplier or other effects, such as innovation and invention patterns, that differ according to demand source and/or industrial structure, but to establish these magnitudes remains an empirical issue. Further, in evaluating the contributions of merchants' and industrialists' profits from international trade to investment, allowance must be made for the fact that those involved in overseas trade often were involved in trade with numerous countries and also that they had extensive domestic transactions, making it necessary to determine the relative magnitudes of profits from these different sources. Second, it is important to examine the nature of the basic internal economy in responding to external forces in order to evaluate the relative contributions of different forces. Presumably the same foreign demand would have quite different effects depending on the structure of the economy and its ability to adjust to changes. It is clear that in many cases high foreign demands do not get transmitted into rapid economic growth because of the limits of the internal economy and, correspondingly, nations with developed commercial and merchant sectors are generally able to benefit from what might seem to be rather limited foreign opportunities. Were the basic differences between the expanding US economy and the economies of South America and Africa due to differences in the ratio of foreign trade to GNP or in the ability of the internal economy to translate the foreign trade into domestic growth (Eltis and Jennings, Volume II Chapter 2; Leff, Volume II Chapter 4)? Third, another major question for which empirical demonstration is quite difficult concerns the opportunity costs of those resources used in international trade; i.e., the extent to which they had been fully employed prior to their use in producing for foreign markets. If they had been unemployed and not productive, the foreign demand would be seen to have had a more significant impact than if resources had to be shifted from use in producing for home market demands. Even when the conceptual distinction between employed and unemployed resources may seem clear, agreement on what actually existed is seldom so. And once allowance is made for under-employment and leisure (voluntary or involuntary), the problem becomes more complex. The three issues noted in this paragraph reflect the quite different models and counterfactuals that have been used to analyse the relationship between foreign trade and economic growth, and suggest why scholars have often reached different answers to the question.

In addition to the essays on international trade in and among specific geographic areas, there are several essays that deal more generally with topics relating to trade and to the international economy, including trade policy issues, factor (labour and capital) movements, and the institutions of trade (merchants and shipping).

The discussions of policy issues include the examination of debates concerning the impact of trade and trade regulations. There are essays on what has been one of the most debated of trade policy issues, the effects of the British Navigation Acts aimed at restricting the trade of the North American colonies (Harper, Volume II Chapter 7; Sawers, Volume II Chapter 8). In particular, there is an examination of the role the Acts played, as an economic, political or ideological force, in the onset of the American Revolution, as well as of its effect in the development of colonial discontent. Other forces influencing trade patterns and amounts at this time include wartime blockades of military rivals, such as in the Napoleonic Wars, with their dislocations, leading to incentives to divert resources, expanding output in some sectors, but often at the cost of losses due to reduced trade and the movement of resources into less effective uses (Crouzet, Volume II Chapter 10); smuggling, with its political and economic implications for producers, shippers and consumers (Mui and Mui, Volume II Chapter 9); and tariffs on the import of foreign goods and their changes over time, particularly with the general expansion of free trade sentiments and policies in Western Europe in the 19th century (Bils, Volume II Chapter 11). A final essay in this section, dealing less directly with policy, has important implications for the study of British trade policy, stressing the role of the landed classes and providers of services, rather than the manufacturing and industrial interests, in British overseas expansion (Cain and Hopkins, Volume II Chapter 12). This serves as a useful reminder that varying interests, often with different goals and preferred policies, were involved in overseas trade and expansion.

The current interest in 18th century factor movements, particularly of labour, reflects, in some measures, the post-World War II concern with slavery in the Americas. For earlier generations, whose primary focus regarding the development of the British colonies was frequently on the settlement and expansion of New England, immigration to the United States was seen as white, free and in family units. One aspect of the atypicality of this regional pattern has been demonstrated by comparisons of the slave trade from Africa with overall European white migration to the Americas. Down to 1820, probably at least three times the number of African slaves as Europeans crossed the Atlantic, with only the English mainland colonies receiving more whites than blacks. The English Caribbean colonies and those of the other European powers all received more slaves than they did whites. And, in the English mainland colonies, many (probably between one-half and two-thirds) of the white migrants came as indentured servants, not as free voluntary workers. They were trading off, in effect, the borrowing of transport costs for future labouring time. These migrants were predominantly male, and most in the 18th century went to the southern colonies, where, over time, their numbers declined in importance relative to the growing numbers of slaves being brought directly from Africa. Understanding the movements of slaves and servants, and their changing magnitudes, due to economic and/or political factors, informs us about the nature of the settlement process, the benefits to Europe from colonization, and the impact of world expansion upon societies in Africa and elsewhere (Gemery and Hogendorn, Volume II Chapter 13; Menard, Volume II Chapter 15; Galenson, Volume II Chapter 16). Unlike free migration, the movements of slaves from Africa and of indentured servants from Europe also represented commercial transactions, providing revenues and/or goods to those in the supplying regions. The settlement of the New World also involved flows of capital from Europe, while, even in the circumstances of a Europe at war, capital was also able to flow between different European countries in response to economic opportunities and for other reasons (Price, Volume I Chapter 5; Solow, Volume II Chapter 14; Neal, Volume II Chapter 17). Such flows, in peacetime as well as war, could be important to both sending and receiving nations.

The essays dealing with the institutions of trade cover only two of the many possible themes. One of the prominent trends in the period covered was the sharp drop in oceanic freight costs, for goods and for passengers, which served to lower the cost of trade and factor movements and to increase the magnitude and distances covered by these movements (Broeze, Volume II Chapter 5). The analysis of causes of these declines in fares, and whether they were due primarily to institutional or technological factors, is, however, still under debate (North, Volume II Chapter 18; Harley, Volume II Chapter 19). The final essays return to descriptions of the important role played by merchants in British trade with overseas areas, and the changing sizes of their firms in response to market forces and to taxes and regulations imposed by the government (Price, Volume II Chapter 20; Price and Clemens, Volume II Chapter 21). Given the distances and the information problems in long-distance trade, the efficiency of merchants played a major role in the expansion of international trade and in transmitting the benefits from trade into domestic economic expansion.

International trade and factor movements influenced, and were influenced by, the broad movements earlier mentioned, and they had significant economic, political, social and cultural impacts upon changes throughout the world. In the essays included in these volumes the focus is on the economic impacts and the patterns of economic growth due to movements of goods, labour and capital among different nations. Any selection of essays deemed to be interesting and/or important need not, of course, provide a good reflection of the relative quantitative impact of different forces or of their relative contributions to key changes. Little is said in any of these essays about the domestic markets, which generally accounted for at least 80 to 90 per cent of the consumption of domestically produced goods and services. No doubt related to its numbers and its distances, there is more coverage of transoceanic and colonial trades relative to intra-European trade than would be justified on the basis of their shares in European exports and imports. Nevertheless, the broad geographic scope and topical coverage of these essays do provide a most useful examination of the nature of trade and economic growth in Europe and elsewhere in the years of the 18th century and the first half of the 19th century.

Stanley L. Engerman

Part I
The Broad Overview

[1]

Commercial Expansion
and the Industrial Revolution

Charles P. Kindleberger*
Massachusetts Institute of Technology

I

The problem to be examined is the relationship between the commercial expansion of the 17th and 18th centuries and the industrial revolution. In particular it may be asked whether a commercial revolution, i.e., a discontinuously rapid increase in commerce, was necessary to, sufficient for or merely contributed to the industrial revolution. If commercial expansion was not needed in advance of an industrial revolution, was it required as a concomitant? Are different types of merchants needed at different stages of industrial evolution or revolution? In particular, is there a possibility that at a fairly advanced stage of industry, the mercantile function may best be taken over by the industrial firm which undertakes direct buying and direct selling; and continued performance of the middleman function by the merchant community may inhibit technical change by acting as a filter between producer and consumer, blocking communication between them?

* I have been helped in writing this paper by comments and suggestions from Rondo Cameron, François Crouzet, Robert Forster, Donald N. McCloskey, Franklin F. Mendels, Joel Mokyr and R. G. Wilson. They are, however, absolved of all responsibility for errors of fact or judgement.

Charles P. Kindleberger

In the early stages of the industrial revolution, the merchant
has been thought to have contributed to industrialization in various
ways: by extending the market for outputs; by increasing the range
and reducing the cost of available inputs; through capital accumulation; « to some extent » as a source of entrepreneurial ability;
by directly and indirectly increasing purchasing power; by inducing
rationality in business procedures and widening economic horizons
[Minchinton, 1969, p. 51]. Additional points made in other
lists, and somewhat less compelling, are the import of foreign
techniques [Bairoch, 1973, p. 544] and serving as a cause of
growth of large towns and industrial centers [Deane, 1965, p. 68].

The method employed here is to study the role of merchants
in a number of countries which are not widely dissimilar. We first
analyze the activities of merchants in general, and then examine
the ties between commerce and industry in four countries: Holland,
Britain, France and Germany. In particular, we examine the
hypothesis that the commercial revolution produced the industrial
revolution in Britain; a commercial revolution in Holland failed
to lead to an industrialization process; and industrialization occurred
in Germany based on direct selling and buying by industrial firms,
without the need for or the benefit of a flourishing commercial
network; and see which of these general views, if they are
verified, applied in France. Limitations of time and capacity prevent
extending the examination to the Italian city-states with their
commercial expansion of the 12th to 15th centuries, or to Spain
engaged in colonial trade via Seville and Cadiz in the 16th and
17th centuries. Mere mention is made of Swiss experience in
textiles and watches.

Commerce may be foreign, and within foreign, continental
and overseas; or domestic, and within domestic, national, regional,
or local. The term "merchant", moreover, covers a wide spectrum
of individuals engaged in various activities which overlap, but
the central focus of many differs in significant ways. The literature
mentions the great merchant or Merchant Adventurer, the merchant
banker, merchant-shipper, merchant-manufacturer, stapling merchant, wholesaler, retailer. In French, distinctions, not always
identical, are made among *négociant*, *armateur* (ship-outfitter),

Commercial Expansion and the Industrial Revolution

marchand, détailleur, boutiquier; in German among *Grosskauf-mann, Kaufmann, Händler*; in Holland among First Hand, Second Hand, and Third Hand. Differences among various writers in the same country and *a fortiori* between countries make precision about numbers difficult if not impossible. In the main, we are interested in overseas trade on the one hand, and the wholesaler at the national level on the other, and are specifically not concerned with retail shopkeepers.

The functioning of the merchant must of course be specified in historical time since his role has been continuously evolving. N.S.B. Gras traces this evolution from the travelling, unspecialized merchant of the Middle Ages who played a role especially in moving goods as well as financing, buying and selling them, and the sedentary specialized merchant who followed him and who operated from his counting house, and perhaps a warehouse, increasingly specialized by commodities, by function (export, import, shipping, finance, insurance) and by area [Gras, 1939, *passim*]. Specialization by commodities was linked to that by function since when a sedentary merchant was also a shipowner or outfitter, for example, he found it necessary to provide different commodities for both outbound and return voyage, whereas to specialize in commerce without shipping made it possible to deal with limited numbers of products down to one. The specializing merchant, however, was exposed to greater risk as commodity quality changed, or old markets were closed off, leaving his knowledge obsolete and him without a continuing function. After the 18th century, direct buying and selling reduced the roles of merchant and merchant nation.

The mercantile function can be divided analytically into two parts which we may represent by ideal types: the "gains-from-trade" merchant who buys cheap and sell dear in arbitrage fashion, and the "value-added" merchant who concerns himself especially with the quality of goods, and among particular aspects of quality, delivery date or timeliness. The distinction of course is overdrawn, since transport and finance in transit add value to goods in the arbitrage case, and gains from trade are reaped where the merchant is deeply concerned with standardization, quality control

Charles P. Kindleberger

and prompt delivery. Moreover the merchant who brings primary products from the Baltic, Mediterranean, East Indies and America to Amsterdam for stapling in "gains-from-trade" operations generally improves the quality of the goods, refining sugar, curing tobacco, roasting coffee, repacking grain to prevent spontaneous combustion, breaking bulk and the like. The distinction is nonetheless a useful one and runs between joining markets and altering markets by upgrading goods, standardizing them, economizing on inspection and handling. In both cases, the merchant provides information, in the first instance on where goods exist and where they may be needed, in the second of what kinds of goods should be produced to satisfy consumer demand at minimal cost.

Most emphasis in the commercial revolution has been on the "gains-from-trade" merchant who uses his information and courage to obtain large rents when he is successful. The value-added function has perhaps been neglected. To avoid the risk that the goods bought and financed will be rejected by the purchasing merchant or the ultimate consumer, the merchant first inspects, say, textiles closely, not only at the fair or in the cloth hall, but in his warehouse, under strong light, and then undertakes to full, shear, bleach, size, dye or otherwise finish the cloth for the market. New qualities are sought to displace old standards and penetrate new markets.

The distinction between the gains-from-trade and the value-added merchant, while loose, is broadly that between the First Hand in the United Provinces of Holland which dealt, bought and sold goods from overseas, and the Second Hand which sorted them, inspected, arranged for bleaching and dyeing when needed and then repacked. It is not far from Adam Smith's separation between the speculative-merchant who can sometimes acquire a considerable fortune by two or three successful speculations, and the slow accumulator in a single industry who seldom makes a great fortune in consequence of a long life of industry, frugality and attention [Smith, 1776, pp. 113-114]. Adam Smith claimed that the only difference between a competent retailer and a great merchant was the quantity of capital:

Commercial Expansion and the Industrial Revolution

> « Besides possessing a little capital, he must be able to read, write and account, and must be a tolerable judge too of, perhaps, fifty or sixty different sorts of goods, their prices, qualities, and the markets where they are to be had cheapest. He must have all the knowledge, in short, that is necessary for a great merchant, which nothing hinders him from becoming but the want of sufficient capital ». (*Ibid.*, p. 112)

This underrates the qualities which Smith detects in the speculative merchant: boldness and foresight, including the boldness in the "value-added" merchant of urging new varieties of products on producers and consumers.

When the knowledge used by the gains-from-trade merchant has been widely diffused, his contribution is ended. Direct buying and selling replace his intermediary role. Similarly the specialized merchant who develops a particular product for a particular market faces a crisis when a new, better quality displaces his. He many sell the old product in new markets, or more likely a new set of merchants may take over selling the old product in new markets. On this score, the fact that merchants in many societies seek to make a fortune and withdraw from economic life into politics, gentle life or rural pursuits is helpful. Capital accumulated in commerce may be invested in land, government stock, canal, turnpike and later railroad securities, used to build spacious houses or chateaux, and consumed, and hence to be unavailable for industry. Some will be diverted to banking and recycled into other commerce. But the social aspirations of most successful merchants which induce them to withdraw from trade serve an economic and political purpose. Where they continue on, they block economic change and tend to perpetuate oligarchies which may be republican but are not democratic.

II

The commercial revolution for present purposes, ignoring the Hanseatic cities, the Italian city-states and Seville and Cadiz, began in the United Provinces of Holland. Favored by location in the days of sailing ships, at the crossroads of traffic between the

Charles P. Kindleberger

Atlantic (and Mediterranean) and the Baltic, and representing a
« land of cities intimately united by an all-pervading network of
waterways » [Marshall, 1920, p. 33], the Dutch developed colonies, shipbuilding, shipping, herring fisheries and the stapling
trade. The linkage from trade to local production led to shipbuilding, and Dutch success in shipbuilding in the 17th century
gave her an advantage in fishing for herring along the British east
coast in the North Sea. Herring were also bought from Scandinavia,
and packed with salt obtained from Portugal. Baltic grain was
repacked in the stapling ports with Second Hand skill which
prevented it from exploding in the heat of the Mediterranean.
Linens from Europe exchanged against woolens from Britain were
both bought and sold in Amsterdam, after having been finished
at Haarlem with local supplies of acid whey for bleaching along
with seaweed from the Mediterranean and ashes for lye obtained
from many points. The First Hand bought, financed and brought
the goods to Holland, later shipped them on to their ultimate
destination. The Second Hand sorted, inspected, finished, repacked
them. The Third Hand wholesaled them to the hinterland. All
dealt in the highly developed commodity and financial markets
of Holland [Wright, 1955, pp. 1-6].

Dutch shipping is said to have embodied few innovations, but
made effective use of all existing techniques. There was specialization of design between naval and merchant vessels, so that the
latter could be more lightly built — not having to carry cannon —
and could be cheaper and more efficiently sailed. When protection
was needed, as against pirates, they were convoyed. Dutch shipbuilding, it was said, would have provided Adam Smith with a
more striking example of the division of labor than pinmaking
[Haley, 1972, p. 19]. The Dutch *fluyt* was standardized, so that
as many as one a day could be built in the yards of Saardam,
which used labor-saving machinery, especially winddriven sawmills
and great cranes to lift and move heavy timbers. Timber was
imported from the Baltic duty-free, and large inventories were
maintained — for as many as four or five thousand ships [Barbour,
1929-30, pp. 119-24]. With a crew of 10 against one of 30 for
an equivalent English vessel, freight rates in Dutch ships were

one third to one half lower in peacetime than those of any rival. Since it was always easy to find a ship bound for Amsterdam, stapling there was often cheapest even when it was the longest way around [*Ibid.*, p. 132].

Dutch stapling stimulated other industries beside shipbuilding and its related ropemaking, canvas, and naval supplies, and fishing, including herring, cod and whaling. There were cheese and gin, plus the finishing of colonial products and textiles. Haarlem, as mentioned, specialized in bleaching, Leiden in weaving, based on imported wool from Spain, and Amsterdam in silk. The Revocation of the Edict of Nantes in 1685 brought to the Netherlands from France Protestant immigrants estimated by Scoville at 50-75,000. Included among them was a number of entrepreneurs who undertook silk manufacture in Haarlem and Utrecht, as well as production of velvet and linen in the French manner. The stimulus was short-lived, however, as compared with that in commerce and finance, and France recaptured the market for these products after the Peace of Utrecht in 1713 [Scoville, 1960, pp. 341-47].

Dutch successes in the 16th and 17th centuries were not limited to commerce, exploration, shipbuilding, fishing, but extended to public works — especially land reclamation, and not only in Holland but in England, France, Sweden and elsewhere [C. Wilson, 1968, chapter 5] — and to agriculture. The Dutch entrepreneur, workman, farmer, and seaman seems to have been characterized by energy and innovation. This industry and vitality are the only basis that one can make sense of Adam Smith's remark that the « carrying trade is the natural effect and symptom of great wealth, but it does not seem to be the cause of it » [Smith, 1776, p. 354]. Or perhaps a distinction is being made between the carrying trade — shipping — as such, and commerce with large gains from trade. Smith recognized that Holland was the richest country of Europe — though there is some lag here as marks of decline in the Dutch and upsurge of the British were apparent by 1700 and clear by 1730. But in his identification of commerce with manufactures, and merchants with artificers, Smith does not recognize that unlike England, Holland was a country with commerce but not manufactures.

Charles P. Kindleberger

The decline of the Dutch economy after about 1730 is variously explained. Three wars against the British in the 17th century and two against the French in the early 18th were surely a major factor. On narrow economic grounds, these destroyed capital, cut trade routes, raised taxes, which were levied on consumption and thus raised wages. In broader sociological terms, they drained the economy of its energy and innovative capacity. Not only did trade decline, but also shipbuilding, textile production, fishing and agriculture. Dutch industry, sailors, innovators and capital went abroad. Many industries expired without a fight [Wright, 1955, p. 59]. In 1670 the Dutch considered themselves superior to the British in energy and ability as well as capital and material resources. In 1779 a Leiden clothier complained of the general lack of initiative among Dutch industrialists, and a deep-rooted aversion to experimenting with new methods . . . « a lack of initiative and enterprise in many industries and to some extent in agriculture in striking contrast to 100 years previously » [Boxer, 1970, pp. 245, 259]. Cipolla believes this decline in capacity to meet economic challenges is typical of all empires — a three — generations effect which applies to societies as well as to families. « The Dutch of the seventeenth century were great innovators. By the end of the 18th century they were incapable of keeping up with progress taking place outside their boundaries » [Cipolla, 1970, pp. 8-9].

Such sociological explanation is rejected by a recent study of the comparative industrial growth of Belgium and the Netherlands in the first half of the 19th century [Mokyr, 1974a, 1974b], which comes down squarely on the explanation of high wages in Holland as the cause of failure to industrialize [see also Smith, 1776, pp. 826-27, 837]. Other explanations relate to lack of mineral resources, especially coal, inadequate demand, and governmental policy, especially free trade, insisted on by the First Hand as a traditional protector of their gains from stapling [Mokyr, 1974b, chapter 6; Wright, 1955, *passim*]. High wages clearly would make it difficult for Dutch industry to compete in existing industries with existing methods with countries with lower wages, especially if Dutch capitalists provided capital to Dutch and foreign industry at equal rates. But Dutch wage rates were high only in

Commercial Expansion and the Industrial Revolution

the provinces of Holland and Zeeland, and low in Utrecht, Friesland, Overijessel, Gelderland, and Groningen. More fundamentally, the impact of high wages is damaging to industrialization only in a static model. In a dynamic model, high wages stimulate innovation as Habakkuk points out for the United States in the 19th century, and Crouzet for Britain in 18th [Habakkuk, 1962, *passim*; Crouzet, 1966, p. 288]. In the 16th century, the Dutch went into trade for lack of land [Gee, 1729, p. 128, quoted by Smith, 1776, p. 96]. In the early period a dynamic model applies; in the later, a static. The change from the dynamic to the static model may be more significant than parametric shifts in either.

Nonetheless the Dutch experience makes clear that commercial success is not sufficient for industrial success, and that flourishing and highly specialized commerce poses risks while it earns large gains from trade. England set out to challenge Dutch supremacy in trade, with the Navigation Acts and acts of war. Hamburg represented another threat. But the Dutch emporium declined under direct trading even without the aid of mercantile policy. Exeter serges which had first gone via London and Holland to Spain and Portugal cut out first London, and then Holland, after bringing the dyeing and finishing stages to Devon [Hoskins, 1935, pp. 69-74; C. Wilson, 1941, p. 39]. German linens ultimately skipped Haarlem on their way to British ports [C. Wilson, *ibid.*, pp. 55-56]. The proportion of Bordeaux exports which went to the United Provinces bound for Germany and the Baltic declined from 53% in 1717-21 to 21% in 1764-66 while that of exports direct for the "North" rose from 10% to 51% [Crouzet, 1968, p. 256]. From having been the "regulating granary" of Europe in grain, Holland by the 19th century was merely a dumping ground [Wright, 1955, p. 171].

Long-distance trade by sea need have no connection with domestic industry. It is not clear whether this is accidental: « the absence of any large export industry which could form the solid backbone of exports and domestic investment » [C. Wilson, 1941, p. 187] or in the nature of colonial trade. A reviewer of an eight-volume work on Bordeaux notes that « Just like Athens in the classical period, or Carthage in the Roman epoch, or Venice

Charles P. Kindleberger

in the XVIth century or Amsterdam in the XVIIth, Bordeaux found itself operating, in the XVIIIth century, as a center for the deposit and distribution of a flood of goods which passed from one hemisphere (*sic*) to the other . . . left behind by all those ports like London, Le Havre or Marseilles which were connected to the great European industrial centers » [Olivieri, 1973, pp. 454-56]. « A merchant is not necessarily a citizen of any country » said Adam Smith. « It is in a great measure indifferent to him from what place he carries on his trade » [Smith, 1776, p. 395]. Smith's understanding of trade is not always complete: he believed that the merchant employed in exchanging corn from Koenigsberg for wine from Portugal brought both to Amsterdam because he felt uneasy separated from his capital, and wanted to see it enough to compensate for the double charge for loading and unloading [*Ibid.*, pp. 421-22]. This ignores the stapling functions of quality control through grading, packing, storing and the like. But « merchants knew perfectly well in what manner (commerce) enriched themselves. It was their business to know it. But to know in what manner it enriched the country was no part of their business » [*Ibid.*, p. 403].

To the extent that the entrepreneurship thesis is valid, it differs in Holland (and Hamburg and Marseilles) from the formulation applicable in Britain and most of France. Dutch merchants did not withdraw their capital to buy land and enter the nobility as the British and French sought to. There was too little land available for the purpose [C. Wilson, 1968, p. 35; Haley, 1972, p. 49; but for a contrary view see Geyl, 1961, p. 164]. The First Hand closed ranks, formed a tight oligarchy, resisted new entry and moved gradually out of trade into conspicuous consumption and banking. Moreover it was international, not domestic banking, and like Dutch trade unconnected with domestic industry. Charles Wilson overstates the case when he writes that finance became the handmaiden of the industrial revolution in England, but in Holland the mistress of a plundered and bankrupt household [C. Wilson, 1941, p. 188]. Holland's commercial role went into sharp decline by 1750; its financial role, despite crises such as those of 1763

Commercial Expansion and the Industrial Revolution

and 1772, lasted until the Napoleonic Wars. In the long run, finance remains more concentrated, and is slower to cultivate direct relations outside the center than is commerce.

III

In the United Provinces, the commercial revolution was not followed by an industrial revolution. In Britain it was. But the British were not seeking to expand commerce as a basis for industrialization when at the end of the 16th century and throughout the 17th they deliberately set out on mercantilist lines to rival Dutch commerce. On the contrary, they were bent on taking over the Dutch monopoly as Florence had done to Venice [MacNeill, 1974]. The Duke of Albermarle said (later) « What we want is what the Dutchmen have » [Williams, 1970, p. 484]. Sir Josiah Child listed 15 respects in which the English should ape the Dutch [C. Wilson, 1965, p. 40] because with his compatriots he wanted to take over the rents inherent in Dutch gains from trade. To the extent that the commercial revolution in Britain determined the subsequent changes in industry — « perhaps determined » them [Mantoux, 1961, p. 92] it was accidental rather than by design.

Like its Dutch counterpart, the East India Company was established at the end of the 16th century. In 1614 a group of London merchants tried to escape the monopoly of textile finishing by forbidding the export of undyed cloth [C. Wilson, 1968, p. 31]. The effort broke down by 1622. A proclamation of 1615 urging the use of English ships found little favor with Yarmouth, Hull or London merchants [Barbour, 1929-30, p. 114]. Half a century later, however, these policies began to take effect. The Navigation Acts were adopted in 1651, strengthened in 1660, and supplemented in 1663 by the Staple Act which monopolized the carrying trade of the colonies [Williams, 1970, p. 484]. New Amsterdam was exchanged for Surinam after the Second Anglo-Dutch War and rechristened New York. Export restrictions were applied in wool in the time of Edward III and again in 1660; the earliest restriction on export of machinery was that of the stockingframe in 1698.

Charles P. Kindleberger

At the same time measures of protection of British industry were begun (and continued throughout the 18th century) in iron, linen, sailcloth, and to keep out calico in an effort to protect woollens.

A revolution in British trade consisted in the « sudden and rapid growth in re-export trade from negligible to one third of exports in 1699-1701 » [Davis, 1954, p. 94]. In the hundred years after 1660, « the English merchant class was able to grow rich, to accumulate capital, on middlemen's profits and on the growing shipping industry which was needed to carry cheap sugar and tobacco, pepper and saltpeter on the ocean routes. Although re-exports and these imports called for no investment in home industry, but only in trade, this could be called the commercial revolution » [*Ibid.*, p. 95].

As Dutch commercial vitality in colonial products diminished, that of Britain (and France) rose. The initial monopoly of London in the established trading companies and under the Methuen treaty of 1703 with Portugal made the outports restive. The West Coast ports were better located for Atlantic trade; Bristol, Liverpool, Exeter and Glasgow moved into triangular trade with West Africa and the West Indies and American colonies, and direct trade to the American colonies. Glasgow specialized in Virginia and Maryland tobacco, by 1750 outstripping London, Whitehaven, Bristol and Liverpool [Price, 1973, p. 590], and stapling it for Amsterdam and French ports by virtue not of value added in sorting, packaging and the like, but on the basis of the monopoly of British ports conferred by the Navigation Acts.

The great West-Indies merchants like John Pinney [Pares, 1950], or John Gladstone [Checkland, 1971] were "speculative merchants", forced into sugar plantations largely by the necessity to take over the properties of those to whom they sold slaves on credit or advanced funds for other purposes. The record shows little interest in improving such plantations, beyond hiring the most efficient overseer possible. John Gladstone never visited the Indies and John Pinney's "great pride" was "to be considered as a private country gentlemen" [Pares, 1950, p. 141]. Both had more money than they knew what to do with. The Pinney merchant house speculated in cotton and sugar, and once put £ 10,000 into the Great Western Cotton Works [*Ibid.*, p. 331]. For the most part they invested their profits and slave compensation money in English land, government securities, and railway shares [*Ibid.*, p. 319]. John Gladstone supported the industrial revolution to the extent of contributing to the education of artisans and workers through the Mechanics and Apprentices Library [Checkland, 1971, p. 176]. He toyed briefly with the idea of buying a country bank which had suspended payments in Gloucester in 1825 [*Ibid.*, pp. 182-83], but the deal fell through. For a man without pretensions to enter the aristocracy, there were not many investment outlets apart from houses and estates before the railroad boom and limited liability. « He knew little of industry, for the world of a Liverpool merchant prince was distinct from that of factory owner [*Ibid.*, p. 198].

The connections of gains-from-trade commerce with industry were limited. To a small degree Bristol went in for staple-based industries. It had 20 sugar refineries in operation in the middle of the 18th century, glass-making for home demand and exports, tobacco-processing, a chocolate industry established in 1731, and a range of metal manufacture [Michinton, 1969, p. 43]. But the city lost ground in the 18th century for a variety of reasons — delays in modernizing the harbor and the lack of a hinterland caught up in the industrial revolution [Minchinton, 1957b, p. xv]. This reverses the causation from industry to commerce. It savors of understatement to say « not all overseas trade had industrial consequences » [Minchinton, 1969, p. 44]. Glasgow was important in colonial trade and in manufacturing, but there was no connection between the tobacco fortunes and the cotton factories [Campbell, 1964, pp. 17-19]. Merchants became landowners [Devine, 1971, *passim*], bankers, or plantation owners overseas, not industrialists. Minchinton is forced to deny Eric Williams' claim that « profits from West African and West Indian trades provided one of the main streams of accumulation of capital in England which financed the industrial revolution [Minchinton, 1969, p. 47].

Recent research, to be sure, has concluded that the industrial revolution did not need large streams of capital from commerce apart from working capital furnished by merchants. Fixed capital

Charles P. Kindleberger

needs were small, and expansion was financed by plowed back earnings [Crouzet, 1972, *passim*]. As we shall see presently, an exception existed for South Wales in iron and copper, but not in tinplate or coal. For the most part, however, the industrial revolution was not characterized by a discontinuous leap in rates of savings and capital formation, as economic historians have long thought.

At the other end of the analytical spectrum from the Merchant Adventurer seeking large gains from trade in overseas operations was the value-added merchant who operated internally to create a national market within Britain. Bit by bit a mercantile system evolved, starting with a single emporium or relay center, which like Amsterdam in the 17th century world, served as a hub for the system while information was a scarce input and transactions costs high, and gradually was replaced both by direct connections which bypassed the initial pivot, and by the development of new and more efficiently located markets in some commodities, such as Manchester for cotton, cotton yarn, cotton grey-goods and finished cottons.

London was the initial relay, for domestic as for foreign trade. The monopoly in foreign trade was man-made; that in domestic was an evolutionary construct. In 1677, London had 1686 merchants — although it is unclear what this means in the absence of unambiguous definitions. It was the entrepot of England, with the postal system at its inception in the 17th century radiating out along five or more great roads from London, and with one rate charged for a letter to or from London and double that for letters between other parts of the country, on the theory that all letters went to, from or through the capital [Westerfield, 1913, pp. 417, 419].

Trade was local, national and international. In the early stages both national and international trade went through London. International trade separated itself first to the outports [Court, 1938, chapter ix]. The merchants of Leeds and Wakefield finally gained full control of the Yorkshire export trade, and routed it through Hull, rather than London, forty years after 1700 [R.G. Wilson, 1971b, p. 147]. Inland traders were less important than exporters

Commercial Expansion and the Industrial Revolution

in the first half of the 18th century but seem to have used London still to a considerable extent [R.G. Wilson, 1971a, p. 82]. In import-competing goods with no export market, national marketing took place through London merchants, whether in silk as illustrated by Sir Thomas Lombe in London, or ribbons, manufactured in Conventry but sold through 12 merchant-manufacturers with ware-houses in London and Coventry [Prest, 1960, p. 49].

The evolution of the process is seen in detail in cotton. In the first half of the 18th century, London was the center for the greater part of the sale of Manchester goods, home and foreign, and a merchant like Joseph Hague made a fortune in London as both importer of cotton for Lancashire and dealer in cotton goods [Wadsworth and Mann, 1931, p. 237]. The change to Manchester took place more rapidly in cloth than in raw cotton, where London remained the main port until 1795 — a decade after the industry had begun exporting cloth. London lost out in cloth slowly after 1780, and rapidly from 1790 when Liverpool, Manchester and Glasgow merchants took over. Ultimately Glasgow cloth was marketed through Manchester [Edwards, 1967, pp. 107, 151, 171, 176]. At the end, only surplus stock was sent to London [*Ibid.*, p. 181]. In the 19th century there began the movement of some manufacturers into the merchant function — buying cotton in Egypt and the United States, and dispatching cloth to com-mission agents at home and abroad [C. Wilson, 1955, p. 180]. The industry was one, however, in which the merchant system remained powerful and prevented wide development of direct selling. Woolens moved to direct trading [Allen, 1939, p. 260]. In cotton textiles, failure to eliminate the merchant led to an unnecessarily large number of separate qualities of product since the merchant lacked motive to induce the customer to change specifications, however arbitrary, and could transfer orders from one manufacturer to another until he found one who would fill them [Robson, 1957, pp. 92-95]. Like Amsterdam or London as a trading relay, the merchant is efficient at a certain stage of economic development, and disfunctional beyond it. In the func-tional stage, it is important to have trade develop with the scale of industry. Thereafter it helps to have the merchant ready to

Charles P. Kindleberger

withdraw. The speculative merchant finds no difficulty in with-
drawing provided that he is attracted into the high-prestige vocations
of banking, or public service, or the high-prestige avocation of
country life.

Between the pure types of gains-from-trade and value-added
merchants broadly represented by the tobacco importer of Glasgow
and the cotton-yarn specialist of Manchester lay a wide number
who combined both functions. Perhaps the woolen trades provide
the best illustration. In the 17th century Exeter was the scene of
a flourishing export trade in woollens woven in Devon. The dependence of weaver on the merchant is illustrated in Tiverton's action
when a merchant died in 1765 in sending to Exeter for another
[Mantoux, 1961, p. 65]. Exeter first shipped its serges to London
which relayed them to Amsterdam for finishing and distribution
on the Continent. London took the finishing away from Amsterdam.
Then Exeter shipped direct to Amsterdam. Later Exeter took
over the finishing from London and Amsterdam and shipped direct
to Hamburg, Oporto, Cadiz [Hoskins, 1935, chapters 2, 3]. While
these changes were occurring, however, Norwich came up in worsteds
and Devon serges began to decline. As early as 1714 Sir John Elwill,
a leading Exeter merchant, writing to a Dutch client, noted that
« mixt serges (were) not worn by Many Sort of people as formerly ».
In comment, Charles Wilson suggests that it is not altogether
fanciful to seek part of the explanation for failure in the relative
weakness of the link between manufacturer and merchant. In
Devonshire the two functions were often separate; in Norwich
and Yorkshire they were often combined » [C. Wilson, 1955,
p. 177]. After a brief glory, Profesor Wilson notes, Norwich
which had benefited from London merchants gave way to Yorkshire
where the link was most strong (Bowring put the point more
generally in 1872: Exeter's decay he attributed to want of men
of sufficient means and wide views to create new branches of
trade when the old had gone [Hoskins, 1935, p. 53]).

To a considerable extent, however, the Yorkshire experience
has been misinterpreted. A great deal of the difficulty has been
caused by Herbert Heaton's attention to Benjamin Gott, a merchant who went into manufacturing and built Bean Ing, a vast

mill in which all the processes from sorting the wool to packing the finished pieces were carried on under one roof. By 1800 the mill housed a thousand operatives. Heaton called Gott only an Industrial Half-Revolutionary because all his weavers worked handlooms and he supplemented their output by purchasing heavily from small domestic clothiers [Heaton, 1965, p. xix] (Compare Gras, who called Sir Thomas Lombe, a London merchant who financed a silk throwing mill on the Italian pattern on the Derwent river in 1718 the morning star of the industrial revolution, not the rising sun [Gras, 1939, p. 178] because it used waterpower instead of steam). There were others beside Gott who went from merchanting into manufacture, the Luptons [Heaton, 1965, p. xx], John Edwards and Law Atkinson [R.G. Wilson, 1971a, p. 60]. The outcry which this change of profession gave rise to has given a misleading impression. With very few exceptions, merchants did not enter manufacturing. When successful, they put their fortunes into land, annuities, government stock, canals and turnpikes, entered public life or retired to the country. Some like William Denison invested in land but did not retire to the country; he was interested in land for its safe return [R.G. Wilson, 1917b, p. 151]. But the gentlemen merchants of Leeds provided neither capital nor entrepreneurship for the industrial revolution.

They did, however, extend the market, and this by upgrading quality and pushing on delivery dates. Yorkshire's share of British exports of woolens rose from one-fifth in 1700 to one-third in 1772 and three-fifths in 1800. It was accomplished, states R.G. Wilson, by concentrating on the cheap end of the market in both woolens and worsteds and leaving to East Anglia (Norwich) the better worsteds, to the West Country (Cotswolds) the fine broadcloths, and to Devon (Exeter) the serges [*Ibid.*, pp. 6-7]. Cloth was bought in cloth halls, or purchased direct from the clothiers, but in any event was brought to the merchant's workshop after purchase and inspected [*Ibid.*, pp. 56, 75]. No one paid attention to the lead seal testifying to measurements. It was sheared, fulled, dyed and sized by the merchant in his workshop, or on order under his direction. Price was not an issue in exports as compared with quality. « William Denison bullied his clothiers about delays and

Charles P. Kindleberger

inferior workmanship and occasionally threatened withdrawal of his customs, but never attempted to dictate prices » [*Ibid.*, p. 57]. Initially Yorkshire woolens were relayed by way of London, then Amsterdam, then sold direct to Europe. In due course the European market died down and expansion shifted to trans-Atlantic trade with the American colonies, and after interruption from 1770 to 1783 with the United States. As each major shift came in the trade, new merchant houses came to the fore and old either failed or withdrew. The shift from the German and Portuguese trade to America, for example, meant new risks, especially much longer extensions of credit and new names.

Extension of the market underlined by Adam Smith was far from unimportant, but it tended to move parallel to rather than in anticipation of increase in production. Davis claims that the process of industrialization in England from the second quarter of the 18th century relied importantly on colonial demands for « nails, axes, firearms, buckles, coaches, clocks, saddles, handkerchiefs, buttons, cordage and a thousand other things, "goods, several sorts"» [Davis, 1969, p. 106]. In nails, the nailmonger stood between nail-maker and export-merchant, serving especially the colonial trade, grew rich and turned banker [Court, 1938, pp. 199-206]. This did not involve financing industry directly, but rather more trade.

The major systematic provision of entrepreneurship and finance from commerce to industry is found in the iron and copper industry of South Wales. Here the industry was organized from the beginning in large units, and in those branches of industry which started small — coal and tinplate — there was little London and Bristol mercantile capital. In iron, however, the demands of war brought both merchants and their capital — Anthony Bacon to Cyfarthfa Furnace at Methrhy Tydfil in 1765, joined subsequently by the London merchants Richard Crawshay, Alexander Raby, Sir Benjamin Hammett, Henry Smithers, Thompsons, Harfords, Grenfells. John regards the process as an exception to British development. South Wales had raw materials or access to them — coal, iron, copper, tin — but lacked an industrial tradition comparable to that of the Midlands, Lancashire or Yorkshire.

Commercial Expansion and the Industrial Revolution

When war cut off Britain from Russian and Swedish iron ore, an opportunity presented itself with few local resources to take advantage of it. London and to a much lesser extent Bristol merchants brought capital and entrepreneurship. The same opportunities did not present themselves elsewhere [John, 1950, chapters 2, 6].

In frequent other cases trade and industry were linked in the early 18th century, but nothing came of it. At an early non-specialized stage merchants were involved in all kinds of manufacture. The firm of Sutton and Cotesworth started out as tallow-chandlers and corn merchants in Newcastle, traded internationally in grindstones, glass bottles, lead and salt among exports, flax, hemp, madder, whalebone and wines among imports, manufactured candles and sword steel, mined coal and grindstones, and produced salt [Hughes, 1952), pp. 7, 51, 58, 59, 69]. Joseph Pease of Hull invested in trade, shipping, underwriting and whaling, founded a bank, but preferred to think of himself as an industrialist, engaged in oil-seed crushing, white lead, whiting, soap and paint-making, cotton spinning, and through his son-in-law distilling and copper mining. Jackson calls him « one of the great entrepreneurs of the 18th century » [1972, p. 101]. He can hardly have contributed to the industrial revolution.

There were of course revolutionary figures in trade: Strutt who financed Arkwright's patent for the roller spinner and subsequent patents [Fitton and Wadsworth, 1958, pp. 63-64], Robert Owen, David Dale, Samuel Oldknow, but they came from the country draper's shops, not from the merchant princes [Wadsworth and Mann, 1931, p. 239]. In *Fortunes Made in Business* [anon. 1883] only three of 28 industrial fortunes resulted from production of one who had started in trade. Sir John Brown was apprenticed to a cutlery merchant, having wanted to be a merchant as a boy despite family resistance, started to make his own cutlery, and gradually moved into other steel products such as files, and ended up making railway spring buffers. Titus Salt set himself up as a manufacturer to spin alpaca wool after trading in it because he could not induce Bradford spinners to spin that fiber. William Bass was a carrier of beer, then a trader, and finally a brewer. But these connections run between the humblest of value-added

Charles P. Kindleberger

merchants, rather than the merchant bankers, and not at all between the gains-from-trade merchant princes and industry. David Dale who built the New Lanark cotton mills outside Glasgow was not one of the 140 pre-1776 Glasgow merchants making fortunes in tobacco, but started as an apprentice in a silk mercer's house, imported linen yarn, went then into banking and only then into cotton spinning [Fox Bourne, 1866, p. 189].

Trade thus grew with the industrial revolution, rather than starting it, as Bairoch also demonstrates [1973, *passim*]. In fact, it is just as well that merchants who do make great fortunes withdraw from trade. Gains-from-trade merchants have to make a fortune in a few years because their rents are likely to be competed away rapidly. Value-added merchants are usually capable of making only a few major improvements in the organization of trade or a change in product before they settle into a routine. To make a fortune and clear out leaves the coast clear for new families to enter and adjust to evolving conditions. Such new families may not exist, as noted earlier for Exeter.

If then the commercial revolution was the expansion of overseas trade in colonial goods — sugar, tobacco, tea and coffee — the merchant's role was not central to the industrial revolution. The value-added merchant aided industrialization in two ways — by urging improvements and expanding the market, and perhaps in a third way, in the usual case, by removing himself from the economic process after a limited period, and unblocking what would otherwise be a barrier to change. The process of building the market proceeds by stages — first through a relay point like London, and a relay institution like the merchant. As information becomes widespread and change slows down, to maintain the old circuits is inefficient.

IV

French foreign trade expanded somewhat faster than that of the United Kingdom during the 18th century, and trade of some ports — notably Bordeaux, the real exports of which grew at a compound rate of 4.1 percent per year, much faster. Fortunes were

Commercial Expansion and the Industrial Revolution

made not only in Bordeaux, but in Marseilles, Nantes, St. Malo, Rouen, Le Havre among ports, and by the great merchants — *négociants* — of inland cities, Paris, Lyons, Amiens, Beauvais, Le Mans and the like. Much of the trade of the ports, however, like that of Amsterdam, Bristol, Liverpool, Glasgow, was only loosely coupled with domestic production in France and thus had little to do with the industrialization process. Within France there was a commercial and equally an industrial evolution — without the discontinuity one finds in the Britain of the last quarter of the century. The *négociants* reaped large gains from trade and big fortunes. Some went into banking. Many bought *seigneuries* (landed estates) and *offices* (annuities) available from the King, including ennoblement. To a greater extent than in Britain, ports were populated by foreign merchants, or Protestants of French origin, usually nominally converted to Catholicism, whose loyalties ran partly or wholly to fellow-religionists and family members abroad. The internal market developed first through the relay of Paris, and to a lesser extent, Orleans and Lyons, which were finally overcome through direct shipments. Annual and semi-annual fairs gave way in the XVIIIth century to continuous distribution.

French economic historiography has given us a rich detailed picture of the position of the separate ports, and of the textile trades of Beauvais and Le Mans, based on archives and notarial records — Admiralty accounts, rolls for special taxation, and individual marriage contracts, testaments, and bankruptcy proceedings. The prosperity of the ports was due above all to overseas trade. Trade of the Middle Ages in wheat, salt and wine gave away after the middle of the 17th century, and especially in the last quarter, to preoccupation with sugar and slaves, and to a lesser degree coffee, cotton and indigo. Saint Malo and Nantes were deeply engaged in fishing for cod off Newfoundland, which was dried or salted for distribution to the Catholic peasantry of France, as well as, (along with salt beef from Ireland), to slaves in the Antilles. In the course of the 18th century, Bordeaux prospered especially because of her window on the Atlantic and her good relations, based on the ancient trade in wine, with Holland and the Baltic to which excess supplies of sugar, coffee and indigo were relayed.

Charles P. Kindleberger

Nantes (and its neighbor Lorient) had the privilege of the French East India Company (until 1769) and was a center of trade in spices. Its success, most marked in the first half of the century, was owing to its accumulation of capital from the Indian trade, and its three way trade in slaves and sugar. Well placed for the movement of high-value products like spices to the interior, its long-run disability lay in poor road and river connections with Paris [Meyer, 1969, pp. 66, 252]. The salt, cod, sugar, drugs and spices brought to Le Mans from Nantes had to be transhipped from boat to horses and cart at Malicorne [Dornic, 1955, p. 103]. Bordeaux was not much better situated. It could supply planters in Martinique and Saint-Dominique with flour, wines, brandy and salted food, cod transhipped from Brittany or beef from Ireland, but was far from manufacturing centers of France. Crouzet claims this was not important since the biggest export item was textiles and they were not heavy [Crouzet, 1968, p. 210]. Inward shipments were handicapped by high transport costs, administrative and customs obstacles, not to mention low incomes. They consisted of Spanish wool, salt and dried fish, and above all sugar and coffee. Soap, dried fruits, rice, drugs, perfumes and oils came by water from Marseilles [*Ibid.*, p. 275]. Elsewhere Crouzet suggests that if trade is regarded as a superficial phenomenon in France, so was it in the United Kingdom, and that Bordeaux, Nantes and Rouen furnished the colonies with textiles to clothe the slaves, materials for sugar mills, sails, cordage and cannon for ships [Crouzet, 1966, p. 265]. The list seems skimpy. Meyer produces a longer one for Nantes, nearer to the manufacturing centers than Bordeaux — luxury articles wanted by the planters — (furniture, silver, books, clothes) — food for slaves: dried cod from Newfoundland, salt beef and butter from Ireland and Brittany; food for the planters: flour, grain, wine, brandy; construction materials: bricks, lime, wood; cheap cloth for the slaves, etc. and calls them of "mediocre" or "feeble" value [Meyer, 1969, pp. 164, 225]. Commercial expansion was not a strategic factor in the growth of industry, nor did the international conjuncture spread to the peasantry — whose economic life was rather dominated by the state of the harvest well into the nineteenth century.

Commercial Expansion and the Industrial Revolution

If overseas commerce did not help greatly with demand, there remains the question of capital formation. Fortunes were made at Nantes and Bordeaux in 10 to 15 years, Arthur Young said [quoted Meyer, 1969, p. 207]. Many of these were consumed in purchases of seigneuries and the building of chateaux. Others found their way into banking. Some went abroad. Foreign merchants never completely dominated the merchant communities of France, but they frequently led them. Bordeaux was a melting pot, and at the top of society were foreign merchants, living assembled at Chartrons and connected through the "Protestant international" to Huguenots and other Protestants not only at other French ports but at Amsterdam, London, Geneva [Poussou, 1968, p. 345; Crouzet, 1968, pp. 213-24]. Not all foreigners were Protestants; among them were Irish and English Catholics, themselves religious and political refugees as the Huguenots were from France. As the total number of *négociants* recorded by Carrière in Marseilles rose from 275 at the beginning of the 18th century to 750 near the end on the eve of the French Revolution, the proportion of foreigners went from 10 to 18 percent, and those of French from the Languedoc and Dauphiné, largely Protestants if nominal converts, from 9 to 28 percent [Carrière, 1973, p. 280]. Some Huguenot capital was exported from France following the Revocation of the Edict of Nantes and particularly in the waves of penalties against failure to abjure Protestantism begun 10 years before 1685 and lasting as late as 1730 [Scoville, 1960, chapter 2]. It was easy for merchants and shippers to export gold, silver, jewelry, furniture. Van Harzel, a Dutch Protestant, who possessed the second largest fortune in Nantes in 1715 — 400,000 livres — escaped in 1730 with his entire wealth [Meyer, 1969, p. 173]. Contemporaries and later scholars made a great deal of this loss, and of the dependence on Marseilles and even Nantes merchants on Swiss funds of the "Protestant diaspora" [Dermigny, 1960, p. 209], but this is denied [Carrière, 1973, pp. 930ff]. The Protestant infusion of the *négoce*, however important, owes a great deal to the movement of Protestants excluded from charges and *offices* and with inhospitable farmland, off the southern slopes of the Central Massif, to Bordeaux and Marseilles [Cavignac, 1967, p. 30, Carrière, 1973,

Charles P. Kindleberger

p. 279]. Foreigners took part when a port failed to maintain representatives abroad — as Marseilles, not deeply engaged in Northern trades, let Swiss, German, British, Dutch agents buy, rather than itself sought to sell [Carrière, 1973, p. 274] or in some views filled a vacuum left by French disdain for commerce [Mathorex, 1919, chapter II, section 1]. Or it could possibly be regarded as a supply response, with excess German potential merchants, limited by the closed ranks of the Hanseatic cities, and anxious to join the race for fortunes, finding a place in French ports and even in the West Indian islands. Jean-Jacques Bethmann (*sic*) was the richest shipowner and one of the greatest merchants in Bordeaux, of Frankfurt-am-Main origin, and there were many others [Cavignac, 1967, p. 30; Thésée, 1972, p. 10]. Spanish and Portuguese Jews expelled from their countries were not numerous, but some of them were among the most prominent. Abraham Gradis had many friends in high places, was owed money by the Marshall of Richelieu and the Duke of Lorges, and died, some years after a loss of 2,700,000 livres tournois, with a fortune of 10,000,000, second only to that at 15 millions in 1791 of the Languedocian, François Bonaffé, a Protestant who married a Creole in Guadeloupe [Poussou, 1968, pp. 349-50].

As in Britain, there are a few examples of close connection between commerce and industry. The Dolle brothers, originally from the Dauphiné, made money in commerce with the Antilles, via the fair of Beaucaire, and moved to buy plantations in the Islands, rather than land in France. In 1787 they explored the desirability of going into linen weaving in Grenoble to assure a supply of cloth for their slaves [Léon, 1963, p. 87]. This conveys a hint of market failure, that adequate supplies would not be available at appropriate times and prices when needed, although perhaps it is nothing more than an outlet for surplus funds. More apposite, but also more debated, is the Huguenot ship-owner, Antoine-Jean Solier, who took funds from his correligionists in the calico printing (*indiennes*) trade, whether in Switzerland to which they had been expelled by the Revocation of the Edict of Nantes, or after their return to France in the Oberkampf plant at Jouy [Dermigny, 1960, *passim*]. Solier et Cie was a *négociant* in general as well

Commercial Expansion and the Industrial Revolution

as a specialist in import of undyed calico from India, and it is not certain that Swiss participation in this last trade was more significant than any other.

One odd connection between trade and comerce led through land. The merchant retired to the country on an estate, but then entered industry as a *maître de forge* on the basis of iron discovered on the property and woods available for charcoal. Le Nicolais of Laval was a *négociant blanchisseur* who acquired the forge of Aron in this way [Dornic, 1955, p. 171]. Another was Narcisse L., associated with his father in the wine trade in Paris who, in 1833, took on interests in mines and blast furnaces [Daumard, 1970, p. 368]. The equivalent in Glasgow was the tobacco merchant whose land turned out, or was known in advance, to bear coal, and led its owner into the coal, salt or iron business [Price, 1973, p. 587; Hughes, 1952, chapter ii].

Rouen and Le Havre were more closely connected with industry, and Rouen more than Le Havre which participated in the colonial trade. Woolens and linens of Northern France were sold at fairs at Caen and Guilbray and shipped over Rouen when exported. More important was the growth of the cotton-textile industry, based on cotton imported from the Islands, and the putting-out system operated by Rouen merchants. "Siamoises", a mixture of linen and cotton patterned after the dress worn by the ambassador of Siam and the members of his suite in 1684, were one speciality. Total production rose rapidly in Rouen and its parishes from 50,000 pieces in 1717 to 489,000 in 1767, and were exported as well as sold within France [Dardel, 1966, p. 119]. As Britain mechanized, Rouen tried to follow suit, with the aid of British workers, merchants and manufacturers. Fortunes were perhaps made more quickly in the colonial trade either directly, or via Cadiz, than by industry, and in banking, which was closely associated with Paris. Rouen was more like Liverpool, Bordeaux like Glasgow, except that Liverpool was associated with an innovative textile center, Rouen with an imitative. It was badly hurt by the Eden treaty of 1786 which lowered duties on English textiles and earthenware.

Charles P. Kindleberger

Apart from Rouen, the *grand négoce* of the ports had a limited connection with the industrial evolution of France. The same was not true of the great merchants of inland cities, insofar as they have been studied. France is a hexagon, closed against the outside world, but connected internally by a communication network. Until the 18th century, this operated commercially with Paris as the entrepot, pivot, or relay. In the sixteenth century the brightly colored cloths of Paris and Rouen were being sold in the Languedoc by merchants travelling to fairs [Le Roy Ladurie, 1966, pp. 123-26]. At the end of the 17th and beginning of the 18th century, Paris began to be eliminated by direct selling. In 1650, Beauvais sold its linens two thirds to Paris and Lyons, with the rest local or exported over Rouen. In 1690 exports had gained at the expense of Paris, and direct relations had been established by Beauvais merchants with Montpellier, Toulouse and other inland cities. By 1730, the role of Paris had shrunk to very small proportions. Lyons sustained its trade. In the early period it had been a relay point for the south. Later it served as a stapling place for exports to Switzerland and Italy [Goubert, 1959, maps, pp. 29, 71, 103]. Over the eighty years and throughout the rest of the 18th century exports grew to a preponderant position because of the competition at home from cotton cloths. The high quality *demi-Hollandes* of the seventeenth century became an export staple because of the loss of home demand. By diverting the existing supply to new outlets, the Danse, Motte and other mercantile dynasties relieved the pressure on Beauvais manufacturers to keep up with technological change, and thus contributed indirectly to their fossilization and ultimate decline.

Paris remained the relay longer for the newer goods in greater demand. While Oberkampf at Jouy (after 1759) sold no *indiennes* in export markets, it used Paris as a center of consumption and for redistribution to distant points. Alongside this network, however, there developed marketing directly through the established textile centers: Abbeville, Amiens, Beauvais, Troyes, etc. and the establishment of depositories who handled shipments to fairs [Bergeron, 1973, p. 19]. There was of course specialization. One Parisian *indienneur*, Dubois, sold four-fifths of his output in the provinces; another, Jarry, mostly in Paris [*Ibid.*]. In silk, another high-grade product, as well as in printed cottons, Lyons sold through Paris throughout the century, apart from export sales. Two thirds of domestic sales went through the relay of Paris, rather than directly and the « overpowering superiority of Paris limited the direct intervention of Lyon *négociants* in the rest of the country » [Garden, 1973, p. 20]. Even in silk, however, Paris was a rival but did not dominate [*Ibid.*, p. 24].

There were some interesting features in the trade in *etamines*, a loosely woven light woolen cloth in which Le Mans and the surrounding cities specialized. The numbers of *négociants* in Le Mans engaged in this product was seven in 1712, a dozen toward the middle of the century [Dornic, 1955, pp. 45, 59]. It is stated these *négociants* followed the extension of the master manufacturers « or at least did not precede it », but became the masters of the trade by buying, finishing and shipping the cloth [*Ibid.*, p. 53]. Le Mans and its surrounding towns specialized in *etamines* dyed black, which was sold in large quantities to monks and nuns within France and to Italy as well. Domestic sales through fairs were handled largely by merchants from Paris or other towns, rather than by the *marchand/drapier mercier* of Le Mans who existed in large numbers or the Le Mans *négociants* [*Ibid.*, pp. 1, 43, 100, 105]. Like *demi-hollandes etamines* lost out to cotton textiles, and also suffered from the deterioration in the quality of wool. Paris merchants dropped out of the trade, leaving the great merchants of Le Mans only with overseas trade.

The account of textiles in Maine provides a footnote on Paris as a relay in the « curious commercial circuit » in linens. The Abbey of Le Beauvais in Le Mans bought linen for shirts, underpants and stocking from Alençon, 30 kilometers to the north and slightly west, each year from 1713 to 1730. These were delivered at the end of January or beginning of February, like other linens bought from Rouen for surplices, table linen and handerchiefs, by a certain Marigner, wholesale cloth merchant of Paris, 100 kilometers to the east of Le Mans [Dornic, 1955, p. 109]. Dornic suggests that the explanation lies in the state of the local roads in winter. Another possibility is that until direct selling took over especially

Charles P. Kindleberger

in the declining products which lost out in the French luxury market, the relay of Paris remained critical. In foodstuffs, of course, it continued at Les Halles in Paris until the market was moved to Orly in the 1960s.

By the middle of the 18th century, Paris, like London and Amsterdam, was shifting from trade to finance. It continued to invest in trade, through the trade of the ports. One scholar states bluntly that Paris in the 18th century was a financial not a commercial city [Cavignac, 1967, p. 132], but this presumably would apply more fully to the second than to the first half of the century. But the funds were invested but little in industry. Le Couteulx, Paris banker and Rouen merchant, invested in textile manufactures in Rouen, but mainly trafficked in Spanish piastres through his Cadiz branch [*Ibid.*]. Paris was a relay for money which went back to the ports and to foreign trade, when it was not used to buy privileges from the court, rather than into industry. At the same time, the commercial network within France, if not the superficial but profitable trade of the ports, evolved side by side with the progress in production.

V

Germany has been characterized as an economy without highly developed commerce, and one which sprang directly from traditional society to industrialization without passing through an extended commercial development [Borchardt, 1971, pp. 89-90, 145-46; Kocka, 1974, p. 9]. In the early 19th century, a British observer characterized Münster as having « little commerce », claimed that the « commerce of Hanover (is) inconsiderable despite the connection of Bremen » and further that:

> « A body of merchants and manufacturers, who by their capital give employment to numerous workmen, and who like country gentlemen are too rich to be dependent on the smiles or frowns of the court, is not to be found in Prussia [Jacobs, 1820, pp. 94, 116, 225].

Bavaria was marked by a lack of a considerable group of great merchant families and great long-distance trading houses [Schremmer

Commercial Expansion and the Industrial Revolution

1970, p. 594]. In Baden, merchants were mistrusted as swindlers and speculators and the task of industrial development (*Gewerbefoerderung*) was to protect and strengthen the middle class against them [Fischer, 1962, p. 79].

This picture is perhaps one-sided, leaving out as it does the Hanseatic cities — Cologne, Bremen, Hamburg, Lübeck — the Rhineland, and Frankfort-am-Main, in which merchant communities were highly developed. Cologne had sunk back from a leading position in international commerce as Antwerp and Rotterdam proved better located for stapling. In its turn, Lübeck, the site of Thomas Mann's novel of a merchant dynasty, *Buddenbrooks* [1901], lost out to the better-located Hamburg and Bremen. These cities, however, developed their own merchant dynasties, with Hamburg especially strengthened by displaced Huguenots in the early 17th century and by refugees from the French Revolution at the end. Hamburg specialized in short-haul trade to the Baltic and above all London. It became known as the « English city ». Bremen developed long-distance traffic, especially trans-atlantic, in tobacco, cotton and rice. Hamburg dominated in sugar, coffee, hides, tropical wood and wines. Bremen complained that it lacked an export product, as Hamburg had grain and the Baltic ports grain and wood [Rauers, 1913, pp. 13-15]. Frankfurt was the gateway for British goods to southern German states.

Frankfurt and Hamburg differed profoundly in social and political ways. Frankfurt was a creation of the Prussian king, who established the Frankfurt fair there, at the major crossing on the east-west trade route of central Europe. When the Zollverein was formed under Prussian leadership, Frankfurt found membership irresistible. Hamburg was republican, oligarchic, devoted to trade, shipping and finance to the exclusion of all else. The leading merchants associated but little with bureaucrats from government, refused to accept titles, and frowned on intermarriage with Prussian officers [Eckardt, 1910, I, p. 200]. In contrast to Augsburg whose merchants were anxious to be ennobled, the city not only forbade ennoblement as a strict rule as early as 1276, a regulation renewed in 1658 and practised throughout the 17th century, but stated on the earliest of these occasions that no knight could live in the

Charles P. Kindleberger

city [Schramm, 1969, p. 82]. Hamburg was a miniature Holland, populated by gains-from-trade merchants stapling commodities produced for the most part at a distance. It resisted incorporation in the Zollverein and the Reich, until the patriotic surge of 1870, and even then it remained a free port, rather than an integral economic member of the Empire, for another decade and half. Within Frankfurt, moreover, there was a difference of view between the patrician merchants who wanted to stay out of Zollverein, and the new group who succeeded in winning adherence [Böhme, 1968, *passim*]. The difference corresponds roughly to the gains-from-trade leading merchants, interested in overseas trade and especially British goods, and value-added men concerned with developing the local market.

Limited economic development in most of the German states, and especially poor transport connections among them, and political separation, led to stunted commercial growth outside the Hanseatic states, Frankfurt and the Rhineland. The Rhineland and Westphalia were different from the other German states even before guild restrictions were eliminated by Napoleon at the end of the century. Merchant networks large and small were much more fully developed. Barmen and Elberfeld concentrated in textiles, and especially bleaching and dyeing, with the former emphasizing production, the latter marketing. What is impressive about Barmen and Elberfeld is their capacity to shift as comparative advantage was lost— from linens to cottons and then to ribbons and embroidery. When high wages and English competition with machine-made cottons made it necessary, a plant was moved across the river to Gladbach-Rheydt. By the end of the 18th century, the mercantile elite with customers throughout Europe, and especially France, the Netherlands and London, was a close-knit oligarchy, cut off from the aristocracy as the English and French were not, and turned inward into a life of luxury — horses, servants, fiinishing schools for daughters, wine, jewelry and speaking French. Of 300 mercantile houses in Frankfurt, 240 were of German origin and in 1776 some 50 to 60 of them were from Barmen and Elbertfeld [Kisch, 1972, pp. 347, 363, 383, 387]. Similar mercantile towns existed in Krefeld and Münster, not to mention Cologne.

Commercial Expansion and the Industrial Revolution

Silesia was otherwise. The linen trade flourished from the 16th century only when Dutch and English merchants by-passed the guilds because they could not adjust to the requirements of foreign markets [Kisch, 1959, p. 543]. By the late 17th, early 18th century Silesian linen dominated the world, and produced a class of wealthy merchants, who loaned out their profits in mortgages of the aristo-cracy and, when they could, acquired estates [*Ibid.*, p. 552]. When linen lost its overseas market to cotton, the only response was lower wages and fraud and adulteration [Blumberg, 1960a, p. 99].

The merchant class in the Rhineland seems to have furnished entrepreneurs for industry, but the petty merchant class rather than the *Grosskaufmänner*. A study of Rhenish and Westphalian entrepreneurs notes that many of them in the 19th century came from merchant families of the previous century [Zunkel, 1962, chapter 11]. The author comments that whereas in Britain entre-preneurs came largely from artisans, in Germany merchants played at least an equal role [*Ibid.*, p. 25]. These small merchants, *Kaufmänner* rather than *Grosskaufmänner* of the sort found in Hamburg, went from putting-out into manufacturing, like J.G. Brugelmann who built the first mechanised cotton-spinning works at Ratingen near Düsseldorf in 1783, five stories high, with 1600 spindles, and partly but not entirely waterpowered [Adelmann, 1970, p. 86]. Until 1830-50, foreign trade and financing of foreign trade were largely in Dutch hands. Krupp, Stinnes, Haniel, Liebrecht, Ehrenbold also moved from trade to pro-duction in iron and coal in the first half of the 19th century [Wutzmer, 1960, pp. 148-50]. Mannesmann at Remscheid was a printer and merchant who started a file factory in competition with British imports [Zunkel, 1962, p. 26]. « It was not the successful handworker who made it big, but his son, who, converted from being a powerfully capitalized merchant, used the corporate form, and hired a technical man who remained in the second rank » [Aycoberry, 1968, p. 518]. On the other hand, in Switzerland in the textile industry, factory pioneers were technical people, not financial, trade or managerial [Braun, 1965, p. 78]. Elsewhere, however, Braun noted that the north of the Alps there formed a local stationary class of merchants united in guilds parallel to the handwork guilds of the city, who were interested in innovation, achievement-oriented, and busy not only in trade, traffic and finance but also in production. He cites the Geneva watch industry along with the Zurich textile industry, as linked to city merchants, who, once the restrictions of the ancient regime were lifted, put forth a tremendous burst of energy [*Ibid.*, pp. 263-64].

There is some slight evidence of merchants investing in industry. A table of professions of the founders (original stockholders) of 61 companies in Prussia in the 1850s, covering 480 individuals, showed 32 percent merchants, 14 percent manufacturers, 12 percent state officials, 11 percent bankers, 7 percent large landowners and 1.3 per cent military. The representation of merchants in mining in Silesia was lower than for Prussia as a whole, dominated by the Rhineland [Blumberg, 1960b, p. 196]. In one Cologne cotton spinning and weaving plant, 29 merchants, 8 bankers, 2 manu-facturers, one mine-owner, one newspaper publisher and 2 state officials were investors; and in a Silesian mine, 3 mine-owners, 13 merchants, 13 mine officials, 22 independent artisans and trades-men, 8 officials, 4 millowners, 2 teachers, 2 doctors, 2 innkeepers, 1 "investor", 1 printshop owner and eight other persons [*Ibid.*, p. 201]. The Stinnes coal and iron complex in 1850 had 41 living stockholders in Cologne consisting of 14 merchants, 7 bankers, 7 rentiers, 1 mine-owner, and one each of the occupations of director, building inspector, major general, chief accountant, judge, privy councillor, inspector, lawyer, doctor, lady, widow [Zunkel, 1962, p. 52]. The evidence is available only for the period after our primary interest, and is highly fragmentary. It suggests, however, that merchant wealth provided one of the major sources of company capital. It is assumed that these were the value-added type of merchant rather than gains-from-trade overseas traders.

The explanation given for underpresentation of merchants in Germany as contrasted with Britain and France has various elements: first, the late unification of the country and the failure at an early stage to build an entrepot or relay pivot apart from the fairs of Frankfurt and Leipzig; second, the disdain with which German social values regarded commercial pursuits, holding the merchant in lower status than the industrialist, in contrast with Britain where the opposite ranking obtained; and third, the early bureau-cratization of the firm, with direct buying and selling combined with production in a single business entity.

The low standing of commerce in Germany (outside the Hanseatic cities and Frankfurt-am-Main) contrasted with the higher status of the nobility and the military of course, and of industry as well. Merchants were scorned as tradespeople, *Händler* as opposed to heroes, in Sombart's book *Helden und Händler*, contrasting the Germans and the British. The term contained anti-semitic prejudice as well as a sense of economic and social inferiority *vis-à-vis* the British [Kehr, 1965, p. 153]. The three-generations-from-shirtsleeves-to-shirtsleeves did not apply in Germany nor was there opportunity to gain acceptance in an open aristocracy [Zunkel, 1962, p. 13]. Purchase of land in Prussia was forbidden to all but the nobility until 1807 [Ucke, 1888, pp. 8, 11] although there was brisk trade in land along the coastal lands such as Mecklen-burg and Holstein. After 1807 there is evidence of rich merchants buying estates [Kisch, 1959, p. 552] and farms which had been in the same family for two or three hundred years changing hands three, four or six times in ten to fifteen years [Abel, 1962, p. 304]. Sartorius von Waltershausen is quoted to the effect that in the 1820-1830 agricultural crisis 80 percent of aristocratic landlords lost their estates [Bramsted, 1964, p. 54], and presumably not all were broken up and sold off piecemeal to land-hungry peasants. Later estates were purchased. But the rule broadly held: while bourgeois were permitted to purchase estates after the Stein-Harden-berg reforms, and aristocrats to enter trade, for the most part th old barriers to social integration held.

Industrialization on a significant scale in Germany came in the middle of the 19th century, and relied on direct buying and merchants. There is some debate as to when German industrial "take-off" occurred [Hardach, 1972, pp. 67ff] but for our purposes the difference of 20 years is inconsequential. In mining, distribution of coal was regulated by the state, subject to price control, and did not need to rely on a mercantile structure [Jankowski, 1973, pp. 718ff]. Railroads were large-scale and so, quickly, were iron and steel producers. In the earliest stages of getting started, when

Charles P. Kindleberger

the firm consisted of 35 workers, Albert Poensgen, of the steel tubing plant of Poensgen & Schoeller, took over all mercantile activities of the firm personally, especially supervising the routine purchasing of inputs by two employees after Dutch merchants failed to perform what he had expected from them [Hatzfeld, 1966, p. 204].

In the electrical and chemical new industries, bureaucratic organization took place from the beginning. Siemens and Halske was started by a military engineer, Werner Siemens, and quickly acquired a manager in another military man, Wilhelm Meyer. Initial sales were of telegraphic installations for the military forces of Prussia, and the Russian government. By 1872, Werner Siemens noted the necessity to write to customers in advance of undertaking production. « Only thus can our fabrication constructions be very cheap, good, and quickly delivered » [Kocka, 1969, p. 126]. The middleman was eliminated before he had taken hold in an effort to speed up technical progress. Kocka observes that the monopoly in education which the merchant class had had earlier was eroded by general universal education, and that rather than rely on a mercantile network, large companies enforced standardization, undertook communication of goods and prices, delivered goods to inventories of shops, sold by sending samples over distances, undertock direct contact between buyer and seller [*Ibid.*, p. 165]. Dye companies initially marketed abroad through export firms in the developing countries, and through wholesale firms in Europe and the United States. These agents were allowed, however to carry only one firm's lines. After 1885, they went to direct selling [Beer, 1959, p. 95]. The chemical industry requires intimate contact between producer and consumer to ensure proper use of frequently dangerous materials, but in any case products which must be employed in exact ways to achieve efficient results [Hohenburg, 1967, pp. 127ff].

Did the absence of a well-knit system of markets hurt? Political reality more than the absence of mercantile connections was responsible for the fact that prior to *Zollverein* and the railroad, Germany was not one country but a juxtaposition of a number of half-closed economies. With *Zollverein* and the railroad, a large German market quickly substituted for inumerable local markets [Benaerts, 1933, pp. 121-22]. It has frequently been claimed that Germany was poor in capital prior to 1950. Sombart observed that great fortunes were rare, and the man with a mere half-million talers regarded as rich [*Ibid.*, p. 123]. Hamburg at mid-century is said to have had 100 millionaires in mark banco (equivalent to 500,000 talers) as opposed to only seven or eight in Cologne [Aycoberry, 1968, p. 515]. But as Borchardt has made clear in a classic article, it is hard to give content to the widely held view that German's lag behind Britain in the early 19th century was the result of lack of capital. Capital markets, like goods markets, were fragmented and underdeveloped, but banking institutions (and foreign credits) responded quickly to the demand for capital for such large projects as railroads and iron foundries, and once started, they proceeded on reinvested profits [Borchardt, 1961, *passim*]. The so-called Germany way to industrialization may have been delayed by the absence of an antecedent capital market built on mercantile credit but not for long.

VI

No attempt has been made to compare numbers of merchants at various periods in Holland, Britain, France or Germany, or to evaluate such statements as that England in 1721 had two-thirds the numbers of merchants of all Europe put together, though Amsterdam in 1671 handled 10 times as much trade as London with one-twentieth of the retailers [Westerfield, 1915, p. 412]. The secondary sources are weak on the merchant communities of London and Paris because of their great size and complexity, and because of the destruction of the Paris archives in 1871 [Daumard, 1970, p. 8]. A few qualitative conclusions can perhaps be drawn, however.

The widely-held view of contribution of the merchant to industrialization seems clearly exaggerated insofar as the profits of "gains-from-trade" commerce are concerned. These fortunes are neither necesary nor sufficient to stimulate industry. They are typically consumed, invested in non-industrial outlets, including banks which finance primarily trade or foreign governments, and in land, government stock, annuities, *offices*. When industry

Charles P. Kindleberger

catches hold, it largely uses trade credit, finances itself with ploughed back profits. In large-scale industry — South Wales iron and German joint-stock companies — one can find investor contributions from merchants and — especially in the latter case — banks. They are the exception.

Nor do merchants typically become manufacturing entrepreneurs, unless one limits the discussion to the putters-out of the proto-industrialization period. Again there are exceptions like Benjamin Gott among the "value-added" merchants. The great majority of merchants who made fortunes moved out of business into banking, politics or rural pursuits. Where there was no aristocracy to ape — perhaps the agriculture of the area did not produce a surplus which needed to be guarded, or which could be expropriated by the landed aristocracy and military — merchant oligarchies formed, tended to dig in, and ultimately lead to mercantile decay. The moving off of successful merchants served the economic function of removing what might otherwise have developed into a block to change.

The value-added merchant is a unit in an information network. In the early stages, information is needed to see what can be produced and what is needed or sought, and where. Surveillance of quality and delivery timeliness is one aspect of information control. Division of labour between producer and his intelligence-gathering collaborator permits maximum efficiency.

With success comes fossilization, at which stage the merchant network is a barrier to change, with the result that it is helpful to have him ready to retire. Where he clings to the old ways, decay ensues.

One general force reducing the role of the merchant was universal education. The rents earned by both types of merchants were initially based on his monopoly of calculation and languages. Apprenticeship was expensive and consisted in instruction at home and in the offices of associates abroad. Money and opportunity costs limited entry. But the spread of education brought down the rents of merchants through competition. With information cheap, direct connections rendered the middleman obsolete when he was not disfunctional.

Commercial Expansion and the Industrial Revolution

BIBLIOGRAPHY

GERHARD ADELMANN, *Structural Change in the Rhenish Linen and Cotton Trades at the Outset of Industrialization*, in F. Crouzet, W.H. Chaloner and W.M. Stern, eds., « Essays in European Economic History, 1789-1914 », New York, St. Martin's Press, 1970, pp. 82-87.

G.C. ALLEN, *British Industries*, London, Longmans Green, 2nd ed. 1939.

ANON., *Fortunes Made in Business*, Vols. I, II, III, London, no publisher stated, 1883.

PIERRE AYCOBERRY, *Probleme der Sozialschichtung in Köln im Zeitalter der Frühindustrialisierung*, in W. Fischer, Hgbr., « Wirtschafts- und sozialgeschichtliche Probleme der frühen Industrialisierung », Berlin, Colloquium Verlag, 1968, pp. 512-28.

PAUL BAIROCH, *Commerce international et genèse de la revolution industrielle anglaise*, « Annales, Economies, Sociétés, Civilisations », XXVIII, 3 (mars-avril 1973), pp. 541-71.

VIOLET BARBOUR, *Dutch and English Merchant Shipping in the Seventeenth Century*, « Economic History Review », Vol. II reprinted in Warren C. Scoville and J. Clayburn La Force, eds., « The Economic Development of Western Europe », Vol. II, The Sixteenth and Seventeenth Centuries, pp. 108-37.

JOHN JOSEPH BEER, *The Emergence of the German Dye-Stuffs Industry*, Urbana, University of Illinois Press, 1959.

PIERRE BENAERTS, *Les Origines de la grande industrie allemagne*, Paris, Editions F.H. Turot, 1933.

LOUIS BERGERON, *Paris dans l'organization des échanges intérieurs à la fin du XVIIe siècle*, a paper presented to the Colloque National de l'Association Française des Historiens Economistes at Paris, 6 October 1973, entitled « Aires et structures du commerce français au XVIIIe siècle ».

HORST BLUMBERG, *Ein Beitrag zur Geschichte der deutschen Leinenindustrie von 1834 bis 1870*, in Hans Mottek, Hgbr., « Studien zur Geschichte der industriellen Revolution », Berlin, Akademie-Verlag, 1960a, pp. 65-143.

HORST BLUMBERG, *Die Finanzierung der Neugründungen und Erweiterungen von Industriebetrieben in Form der Aktiengesellschaften während der fünfziger Jahrhunderts in Deutschland, am Beispiel der preussischen Verhältnisse erläuert*, in Hans Mottek, Hgbr., « Studien zur Geschichte der industriellen Revolution in Deutschland », Berlin, Akademie Verlag, 1960b, pp. 165-208.

HELMUT BÖHME, *Frankfurt und Hamburg*, Das Deutsches Reiches Silber- und Goldloch und die Allerenglishste Stadt des Kontinents, Frankfurt am Main, Europäische Verlagsanstalt, 1968.

KNUT BORCHARDT, *Zur Frage des Kapitalmangels in der ersten Hälfte des 19. Jahrhunderts in Deutschland*, in « Jahrbücher für Nationalökonomie und Statistik », Bd. 173 (1961), pp. 401-21.

C.R. BOXER, *The Dutch Economic Decline*, in Carlo M. Cipolla, ed., « The Economic Decline of Empires », London, Meuthen, 1970, pp. 235-63.

ERNEST K. BRAMSTED, *Aristocracy and the Middle-Classes in Germany: Social Types in German Literature, 1830-1900*, rev. ed., Chicago, University of Chicago Press, 1964.

RUDOLF BRAUN, *Sozialer und Kultureller Wandel in einem ländlichen Industriegebiet im 19. und 20. Jahrhundert*, Erlenbach-Zurich, Eugen Rentch Verlag, 1965.

Charles P. Kindleberger

R.H. CAMPBELL, *An Economic History of Scotland in the Eighteenth Century*, « Scottish Journal of Political Economy », XI, 1 (February 1964), pp. 17-24.

CHARLES CARRIÈRE, *Négociants Marseillais au XVIIIe siècle*: Contribution à l'étude des économies maritime, Marseilles, Institut Historique de Provence, 1973.

S.G. CHECKLAND, *The Gladstones, A Family Biography, 1764-1851*, Cambridge, Cambridge University Press, 1971.

CARLO M. CIPOLLA, *Editor's Introduction*, « The Economic Decline of Empires », London, Methuen, 1970.

W.H.B. COURT, *The Rise of the Midland Industries, 1600-1838*, London, Oxford, 1939.

FRANÇOIS CROUZET, Book II on *Economie et société (1715-1789)*, in François-George Pariset, ed., « Bordeaux au XVIIIe siècle », Bordeaux, Federation historique de Sud-Ouest, 1968, Vol. VI.

FRANÇOIS CROUZET, *Croissances comparées de l'Angleterre et de la France au XVIIIe siècle, Essai d'analyse comparée de deux croissances économiques*, « Annales, Economies, Sociétés, Civilisations », XXI, 2 (mars-avril), 1966, pp. 254-91.

FRANÇOIS CROUZET, ed., *Capital Formation in the Industrial Revolution*, London, Methuen & Co., 1972.

PIERRE DARDEL, *Commerce, industrie et navigation à Rouen et au Havre au XVIIIe siècle*, Rivalité croissant entre ces deux ports, Rouen, Société libre d'émulation de la Seine-Maritime, 1966.

ADELINE DAUMARD, *Les Bourgeois de Paris au XIXe siècle*, Paris, Flammarion, 1970.

RALPH DAVIS, *English Foreign Trade, 1660-1700*, « Economic History Review », Second Series, VI (1954), reprinted in W.E. Minchinton, ed., « The Growth of English Overseas Trade in the 17th and 18th Century », London, Methuen, 1969, pp. 78-98.

RALPH DAVIS, *English Foreign Trade, 1700-1774*, « Economic History Review », Second Series, XV (1962), reprinted in W.E. Minchinton, ed., « The Growth of English Overseas Trade in the 17th and 18th Century », London, Methuen, 1969, pp. 99-120.

PHYLLIS DEANE, *The First Industrial Revolution*, Cambridge, Cambridge University Press, 1965.

T.M. DEVINE, *Glasgow Colonial Merchants and Land, 1770-1815*, in T. Ward and R.G. Wilson, eds., « Land and Industry », The Landed Estate and the Industrial Revolution, New York, Barnes and Noble, 1971, pp. 205-65.

LOUIS DERMIGNY, *Cargaisons indiennes, Solier et Cie, 1781-1793*, Paris, S.E.V.P.E.N. Tome I, Text, Tome II Documents, 1960.

FRANÇOIS DORNIC, *L'industrie textile dans Le Maine et ses débouches internationaux (1650-1815)*, Le Mans, Editions Pierre-Belon, 1955.

JULIUS V. ECKARDT, *Lebenserinnungen*, Leipsig Verlag S. Hirzel, Bands I, II, 1910.

MICHAEL M. EDWARDS, *The Growth of the British Cotton Trade, 1780-1815*, Manchester, Manchester University Press, 1967.

THOMAS ELLISON, *The Cotton Trade of Britain*, first impression 1886, new ed. New York, Kelley, 1968.

WOLFRAM FISCHER, *Der Staat und die Anfänge der Industrialisierung in Baden, 1800-1850*, Berlin, Duncker u. Humblot, 1962.

Commercial Expansion and the Industrial Revolution

H.R. Fox Bourne, *English Merchants*, Memories in Illustration of the Progress of British Commerce, London, Richard Bentley, 1866.

R.S. Fitton and A.P. Wadsworth, *The Strutts and the Arkwrights, 1758-1830*, A Study of the Early Factory System, Manchester, Manchester University Press, 1958.

Maurice Garden, *Le commerce lyonnais au XVIIIe siècle*, a paper presented to the Colloque National de l'Association Française des Historiens Economistes at Paris, 6 October 1973, entitled « Aires et structures du commerce français au XVIIIe siècle ».

Joshua Gee, *Trade and Navitagtion of Great Britain Considered*, London, 1729.

Pieter Geyl, *The Netherlands in the Seventeenth Century*, Part One, *1609-1648*, New York, Barnes and Noble, 1961.

Pierre Goubert, *Familles marchands sous l'Ancient Regime: les Danse et les Motte de Beauvais*, Paris, S.E.V.P.E.N., 1959.

N.S.B. Gras, *Business and Capitalism*, An Introduction to Business History, New York, F.S. Crofts, 1939.

H.J. Habakkuk, *American and British Technology in the Nineteenth Century*, Cambridge, Cambridge University Press, 1962.

K.H.D. Haley, *The Dutch in the Seventeenth Century*, London, Thames and Hudson, 1972.

Lutz Hatzfeld, *Kaufmannische Probleme der Rohrenfabrik Poensgen & Schoeller, 1844-1850*, in Karl Erich Born, Hgbr., « Moderne deutsche Wirtschaftsgeschichte », Köln-Berlin, Kiepenheuer & Witsch, 1966, pp. 203-13, from Lutz Hatzfeld, « Die Begründung der deutschen Röhrenindustrie durch die Fa. Poensgen & Schoeller, Manuel, 1844-1850 », Wiesbaden, Franz Steiner Verlag, 1962, pp. 60-75.

Karl W. Hardach, *Some Remarks on German Economic Historiography and its Understanding of the Industrial Revolution in Germany*, in « Journal of European Economic History », Vol. 1, No. 1 (Spring 1972), pp. 37-99.

Herbert Heaton, *The Yorshire Woollen and Worsted Industries*, Oxford, Clarendon Press, 2nd ed., 1965.

Paul M. Hohenberg, *Chemicals in Western Europe, 1850-1914*: An Economic Study of Technical Change, Chicago, Rand McNally & Co., 1967.

M.A. Holderness, *The English Land Market in the Eighteenth Century: The Case of Lincolnshire*, « Economic History Review », Second Series, XXVII, 4 (November 1974), pp. 557-76.

W.G. Hoskins, *Industry, Trade and People in Exeter, 1688-1800*, With Special Reference to the Serge Industry, Manchester University Press, 1935.

Edward Hughes, *North Country Life in the Eighteenth Century*, Vol. I, *The North-East, 1700-1750*, London, Oxford University Press, 1952; Vol. II, *Cumberland and Westmoreland, 1700 1830*, London, Oxford University Press, 1965.

Gordon Jackson, *Hull in the Eighteenth Century*, A Study in Economic and Social History, London, Oxford University Press for the University of Hull, 1972.

William Jacob, *A View of the Agriculture, Manufactures, Statistics and Society in the State of Germany and Parts of Holland and France*, Taken during a Journey through those Countries in 1819, London, John Murray, 1820.

Manfred D. Jankowski, *Law, Economic Policy and Private Enterprise: The case of the Early Ruhr Mining Region, 1766-1865*, « Journal of European Economic History », II, 3 (Winter 1973), pp. 688-727.

Charles P. Kindleberger

A.H. JOHN, *The Industrial Development of South Wales, 1750-1850*, An Essay, Cardiff, University of Wales Press, 1950.

ECKHART KEHR, *Der Primat der Innenpolitik*, Gesammelte Aufsätze zur preussissch-deutschen Sozialgeschichte im 19. und 20. Jahrhundert, H.-U. Wehler, Hgbr., Berlin, Walter de Gruyter & Co., 1965.

HERBERT KISCH, *The Textile Industries in Silesia and the Rhineland: a Comparative Study of Industrialization*, « Journal of Economic History », XIX, 4 (December 1959), pp. 591-64.

HERBERT KISCH, *From Monopoly to Laissez-faire: The Early Growth of the Wupper Valley Textile Trades*, « Journal of European Economic History », I, 2 (Fall 1972), pp. 298-407.

JÜRGEN KOCKA, *Unternehmungsverwaltung und Angestelltenschaft am Beispiel Siemens, 1847-1914*: Zum Verhältnis von Kapitalismus und Bürokratie in der deutschen Industrialisierung, Stuttgart, Ernst Klett Verlag, 1969.

JÜRGEN KOCKA, *Expansion, Integration, Diversifikation: Wachstumstrategien industrieller Grossunternehmen in Deutschland vor 1914*, comment on Theme 2 of the Sixth International Congress on Economic History, Copenhagen, 1974, A.D. Chandler, Jr. and Herman Daems, « Investment Strategy in Europe, the United States and Japan », unpublished version, pp. 1-23 plus 1-10 of footnotes.

EMMANUEL LE ROY LADURIE, *Les Paysans de Languedoc*, Paris, S.E.V.P.E.N., 1966.

PIERRE LÉON, *Marchands et speculateurs dauphinois dans le monde antillais du XVIIIe siècle*, Les Dolle et les Raby, Paris, « Les Belles Lettres », 1963.

PAUL MANTOUX, *The Industrial Revolution in the Eighteenth Century*: An Outline of the Beginnings of the Modern Factory System in Britain, New York, Harper & Row Torchbooks, rev. ed., 1961.

ALFRED MARSHALL, *Industry and Trade*, A Study of Industrial Technique and Business Organization, and of Their Influences on the Conditions of Various Classes and Nations, London, Macmillan, 1920.

PETER MATHIAS, *The First Industrial Nation*: An Economic History of Britain, 1700-1914, London, Methuen, 1969.

J. MATHOREZ, *Les Étrangers en France sous l'Ancient Régime*, Histoire de la population française, Tome I, Paris, Edouard Chapinon, 1919.

WILLIAM H. MCNEILL, *Venice*: The Hinge of Europe, 1081-1797, Chicago, University of Chicago Press, 1974.

JEAN MEYER, *L'Armement Nantais dans le deuxième moitié du XVIII siècle*, Paris, S.E.V.P.E.N., 1969.

W.E. MINCHINTON, *The British Tinplate Industry*, A History, Oxford, Clarendon Press, 1957a.

W.E. MINCHINTON, ed., *The Trade of Bristol in the 18th Century*, Bristol, Record Society's Publication, XX, 1957b.

W.E. MINCHINTON, *The Merchants in England in the Eighteenth Century*, « Explorations in Entrepreneurial History », X (December 1957c), pp. 62-71, reprinted in Hugh G.J. Aitken, ed., « Explorations in Enterprise », Cambridge, Mass., Harvard University Press, 1965, pp. 278-95.

W.E. MINCHINTON, *Editor's Introduction*, in W.E. Minchinton, ed., « The Growth of English Overseas Trade in the 17th and 18th Centuries », London, Methuen & Co., 1969.

Commercial Expansion and the Industrial Revolution

JOEL MOKYR, *Industrial Growth and Stagnation in the Low Countries, 1800-1850*, doctoral dissertation, Yale University, 1974a, to be published by Yale University Press.

JOEL MOKYR, *The Industrial Revolution in the Low Countries in the First Half of the Nineteenth Century: A Comparative Case Study*, « Journal of Economic History », XXXIV, 2 (June 1974b), pp. 365-91.

ANGELO OLIVIERI, *An Urban Case History: Bordeaux*, « Journal of European Economic History », II, 2 (Fall 1973), pp. 447-56.

RICHARD PARES, *A West-India Fortune*, Longmans Green, 1950, reprinted New York, Archon Books, 1968.

J.-P. POUSSOU, *Demographic and Social Structures*, Chapter V in François-George Pariset, ed., « Bordeaux au XVIIIe siècle », Bordeaux, Fédération historique de Sud-Ouest, 1968.

JOHN PREST, *The Industrial Revolution in Coventry*, London, Oxford University Press, 1960.

JACOB M. PRICE, *France and the Chesapeake*, A History of the French Monopoly and of its Relationship to the British and American Tobacco Traders, Ann Arbor, University of Michigan Press, 1973, 2 vols.

FRIEDRICH RAUERS, *Bremer Handelsgeschichte im 19. Jahrhundert*, Bremen, Franz Leuwer, 1913.

R. ROBSON, *The Cotton Industry in Britain*, London, Macmillan, 1957.

PERCY ERNEST SCHRAMM, *Hamburg und die Adelsfrage (bis 1806)*, « Zeitschrift des Vereins für Hamburgische Geschichte », Bd. 55 (1969), pp. 81-93.

ECKART SCHREMMER, *Die Wirtschaft Bayerns vom hohen Mittelalter bis zum Beginn der Industrialisierung*: Bergbau, Gewerbe, Handel, München, Verlag C.H. Beck, 1970.

WARREN C. SCOVILLE, *The Persecution of Hugenots and French Economic Development, 1680-1720*, Los Angeles, University of California Press, 1960.

ADAM SMITH, *An Inquiry into the Nature and Causes of "The Wealth of Nations"*, Cannan ed., New York, Modern Library (1776), 1937.

FRANÇOISE THÉSÉE, *Négociants bordelais et colons de Saint-Domingle*, Liaisons d'habitations, La Maison Henry Romberg, Papst et Cie, Paris, Société française de histoire d'outre-mer, 1972.

RAY B. WESTERFIELD, *Middlemen in English Business*, Particularly between 1660 and 1760, New Haven, Yale University Press, 1915.

E.N. WILLIAMS, *The Ancien Regime in Europe*, Government and Society in the Major States, 1648-1879, New York, Harper & Row, 1970.

CHARLES WILSON, *Anglo-Dutch Commerce and Finance in the Eighteenth Century*, Cambridge, Cambridge University Press, 1941.

C. WILSON, *The Entrepreneur in the Industrial Revolution in Britain*, « Explorations in Entrepreneurial History », VII, 3 (February 1955), pp. 229-5, reprinted with omissions in Barry E. Supple, ed., « The Experience of Economic Growth »: Case Studies in Economic History, New York, Random House, 1963, pp. 171-88.

CHARLES WILSON, *England's Apprenticeship 1663-1763*, New York, St. Martin's Press, 1965.

CHARLES WILSON, *The Dutch Republic and the Civilisation of the Seventeenth Century*, London, Weidenfeld and Nicholson, 1968.

Charles P. Kindleberger

R.G. WILSON, *Gentlemen Merchants*, The Merchant Community of Leeds, 1700-1830, Manchester, Manchester University Press, 1971a.

R.G. WILSON, *The Denisons and Milneses: Eighteenth Century Merchant Landowners*, in J.T. Ward and R.G. Wilson, eds., « Land and Industry », The Landed Estate and the Industrial Revolution, New York, Barnes and Noble, 1971b, pp. 145-72.

H.R.C. WRIGHT, *Free Trade and Protection in the Netherlands, 1816-30*, Cambridge, Cambridge University Press, 1955.

HENIZ WUTZMER, *Die Herkunft der industrielle Bourgeoisie Preussens in den vierziger Jahren des 19. Jahrhunderts*, in Hans Mottek, Hgbr., « Studien zur Geschichte der industriellen Revolution in Deutschland », Berlin, Akademie-Verlag, 1960, pp. 145-63.

FRIEDERICH ZUNKEL, *Der Rheinische-Westfälische Unternehmer, 1834-1879*, Ein Beitrag zur Geschichte des deutsche Bürgertums im 19. Jahrhundert, Köln und Opladen, Westdeutscher Verlag, 1962.

[2]

European Foreign Trade in the XIX Century: The Development of the Value and Volume of Exports (Preliminary Results)

Paul Bairoch

University of Geneva

GENERAL INTRODUCTION.

The aim of this article — which contains some results of our projected reconstruction of the development of foreign trade in the XIX century [1] — is, above all, to provide an approximate estimation of the growth of European foreign trade in the XIX century that is more accurate than those that have been available hitherto. Paradoxical though it may seem, the data used in tracing the development of the value of European exports have all until now relied, directly or indirectly, on calculations made by statisticians at the end of the XIX century, and especially on estimations made by

---

[1] This study is part of a group of four articles based on similar topics: « Geographical structure and trade balance of European foreign trade from 1830 to 1910 » (which will appear in a later issue of this review), « Foreign trade of the Third World in the XIX century », to appear shortly and « World foreign trade: development of the value, volume and geographical structure of exports from 1800 to 1970 (preliminary results) » in preparation.

[2] M. G. MULHALL, in his 1880 study (« *The Progress of the World* ») attempted an initial assessment of the development of the trade of various countries for 1830 and 1878 (pp. 45-46 and 534). But the basic material most often used is the table in his *Dictionary of Statistics* (4th edition, London 1898, p. 128) which shows the development of the value of combined imports and exports for the major countries and for Europe as a whole (also for the world).

Paul Bairoch

Mulhall[2] and Von Neumann-Spallart.[3] These estimations formed the basis of the calculations made by the League of Nations[4] and they became, to a great extent, the most important source for the study of word trade for the period between 1876 and 1913.

The fact that the basic data derive from calculations made at the end of the XIX century does not in itself imply that they are invalid. But their analysis reveals that some estimations were rather imprecise, while a certain number of countries (of little importance, it is true) were omitted. On the other hand, there have been until now no estimations available of European exports alone before 1870. Our work has involved making completely new calculations according to the data for individual countries, (see the methodological appendix) and tracing the series of figures back to 1800, or at least until 1830.

As regards the volume of European exports, Kindleberger's calculations[5] have provided us with a reasonably reliable estimate. However his calculations go back only to 1870, while several new indices of export prices have been published between 1955 (the date of Kindleberger's calculations) and the present, and these permit a more complete and accurate analysis of the subject. Lastly, Kindleberger's index is deliberately restricted to industrialized Europe. So here too we decided to go back to the beginning and construct an index of prices of European exports (see the methodological appendix).

The methodological appendix at the end of this article shows the unreliability of some data (especially those from the first half of the XIX century) — the reader is referred to it. Here we shall merely warn readers not to place too much confidence in the figures we propose and point out that the geographical definition of Europe

---

2 See note on previous page.

3 F. X. von NEUMANN-SPALLART, *Uebersichten der Weltwirtschaft 1880*, Stuttgart 1881 and subsequent editions. The latter were continued by F. von JURASCHEK and edited in Berlin.

4 *Industrialization and Foreign Trade*, Geneva 1945.

5 C. P. KINDLEBERGER, *The Terms of Trade. A European Case Study*, New York 1956; and *Industrial Europe's Terms of Trade on Current Account 1870-1953* in « The Economic Journal », March 1955, pp. 19-35. These data were included and extended to 1960 in the study by A. MADDISON, *Growth and Fluctuation in the World Economy 1870 1960*, in « Banca Nazionale del Lavoro Quarterly Review », June 1962.

followed in this study includes Russia (also Asian Russia), but excludes European Turkey (by its 1913 borders). Lastly we should note that the problem posed by the effect of the creation of new trade deriving from the foundation of a certain number of states (especially in the Balkans) has been resolved by postulating for these countries (and for the period before their foundation) a development in exports approximating to that of other European countries with similar characteristics.

As the essential aim of this article is to present the results of our calculations and estimates, the accompanying analysis will be very limited. No attempt has been made to analyse the causes of the evolution nor to interpret the consequences of the development of foreign trade on economic activities as a whole, or, in particular, on the process of development. We have tried to provide a solution to some of these problems in our recent study — « Commerce extérieur et developpement économique de l'Europe au XIX siècle », which will appear in 1974.

A) *Evolution of European exports in current values.*

This section will be devoted firstly to the development of exports in Europe as a whole, and secondly to the development of the respective importance of the various European countries. The data referring to the volume of exports will be presented and analysed in section B of this article.

1) *Exports of Europe as a whole.*

Table 1 sums up the results of our calculations of the growth of the current value of total European exports during the XIX century. Following the well justified tradition, we have included in the XIX century the years of the XX century up to the outbreak of the World War. The data are given in current dollars, therefore in dollars of the gold parity in existence before the 1934 United States devaluation, in what are generally termed « old gold dollars ».[6]

---

[6] The devaluation of 31st January 1934 was 41% in relation to gold.

Paul Bairoch

TABLE 1

EUROPEAN SPECIAL EXPORTS, IN CURRENT VALUES, 1800-1913
(pre-1933 gold dollars; territorial boundaries of 1913; three year annual averages, except 1913)

	Total exports		Per capita exports	
	Value (millions of dollars)	Annual rate of growth (%)	Value (dollars)	Annual rate of growth (%)
1800	(670)		(3.3)	
1810	(680)	*	(3.2)	*
1820	(680)	*	(3.1)	*
1830	655	*	2.7	*
1840	875	2.9	3.4	2.1
1850	1200	3.2	4.4	2.6
1860	2160	6.0	7.5	5.4
1870	3260	4.2	10.4	3.6
1880	4050	2.2	11.8	1.3
1890	4630	1.3	12.1	0.3
1900	5490	1.7	13.0	0.7
1910	8650	4.7	18.2	3.6
1913	10550	6.8	21.3	5.6

* Not significant.

Note: The slight rounding off of the figures does not imply a corresponding margin of error, especially for the pre-1850 figures. The rates of growth have been calculated from figures that were not rounded off at all.

Sources: Our calculations, see text and methodological appendix.

The margin of error in these figures (see the methodological appendix) is very small, not to say negligible for the period 1880 to 1913, when valid statistics provide 100% of the data. For the period 1860 to 1870 valid statistics provide 75% of the data, while 23% derive from estimations containing a small margin of error. For 1850 the rates are 61% and 37% respectively. This amounts to a margin of error that is on the whole fairly small. On the other hand, for 1840 the proportion of very reliable figures is no more than 55%, and for estimations with a small margin of error, 30%. These rates fall to respectively 53% and 11% for 1830. From 1800 to 1820 the development is based on relatively reliable statistics and estimations concerning countries where foreign trade must have represented about 50% of the European total. It is obvious that the margin of error of even those statistics considered as valid is much more important for the first than for the second half of the XIX century. As a general rule the data with wide margins of error will appear in brackets.

From 1800 to 1900 the value of European exports rose from just below 700 million dollars to 5,500 million, and even reached 8,700 million in 1910, representing an increase in the ratio of 1 to 13 in one century (1810-1910). From 1830 (from which year the data become more reliable) to 1913 the ratio of increase was 1 to 16. Compared with the previous century (and very probably to previous centuries), these are extremely rapid increases. Still in terms of value European exports probably did not improve during the XVIII century in ratios above 1 to 3 or 1 to 4.[7] Of course, as we shall see later, the ratios of the XIX century were relatively modest compared with contemporary times.

If the first thirty years of the XIX century are excluded — and they are not significant, given the margins of error of the figures, the troubled nature of the years 1800-1815 and the very strong drop in prices — four main periods can be distinguished in the rhythm of the growth in value of European exports in the XIX century. The first, which lasted till 1850 or, more precisely, until 1846-47, if yearly data are used as a basis,[8] was marked by relatively moderate growth in exports, of about 3% per year. The second period, covering the years 1846-47 to 1865-68, showed a sharp acceleration of growth (the expansion rate exceeded 5%). The third period, lasting until the years 1896-97, is a phase of very slow growth, the annual rate being below 2%. The last period which ends with the begin of the war was marked by a very strong increase in the value of exports, of about 5%, the growth being particularly rapid from 1903 to 1907 and from 1909 to 1913.

Although the data relating to the volume of trade are more important, we should note that the analysis of the development of value of exports is of definite interest. In fact they were the only data available, especially during the XIX century, and the analysis of the development of foreign trade was almost exclusively based

---

[7] In England this increase was 1 to 5 but in France only 1 to 3.

[8] Until 1870, based on the data for individual countries; after 1870, based on MAD-DISON's data (*Growth and Fluctuation...*, op. cit.) for Western Europe.

Paul Bairoch

on these figures. In this context the acceleration of trade after 1846, that is after the repeal of the Corn Laws in Great Britain, must be stressed. This rapid expansion in trade was certainly not unrelated to the success of free-trade ideas on the Continent, just as the slackening in the expansion of the value of exports from 1865-68 was not unrelated to the protectionist reaction in Continental Europe. Although this article is not intended to be analytical, we shall return to this problem at greater length when studying the development of the volume of foreign trade.

As the population of Europe more than doubled during the XIX century, growth in terms of per capita exports[9] was more moderate, although still very rapid in comparison with previous centuries. Between 1830 and 1913 per capita exports rose from about three dollars to more than twenty-one dollars.

In Table 2 we have placed the XIX century data in a wider historical context, by comparing them with the increases recorded in the course of the XX century. We should immediately point out that the figures for the current value of European exports until 1913 have been corrected in order to make them more or less comparable with contemporary data. The correction involved addiing an arbi-

---

9 We have calculated the data used for the growth of the population of Europe on the basis of the most recent estimations available for the different countries. For Russia we have decided to increase the figures in the data from before 1870. Below are the results of these calculations (the population of Europe not including European Turkey;* Russia: including her Asian territories; in millions):

	Europe	Russia	Europe total
1800	151.5	50.0	201.5
1810	158.0	52.0	210.0
1820	167.5	55.0	222.5
1830	180.5	59.0	239.5
1840	193.0	63.5	256.5
1850	203.5	68.5	272.0
1860	215.5	74.0	289.5
1870	228.5	84.5	313.0
1880	245.0	97.5	343.0
1890	265.0	118.0	382.5
1900	288.0	133.0	421.0
1910	313.5	161.0	474.5
1913	324.5	168.5	493.0

* The population of European Turkey (1913 boundaries) was 1.9 million in 1913. It must have been about 1 million around 1800 and about 1.5 million around 1880.

trary estimated value of the extra trade brought about by the creation of new political entities after the First World War to European exports up to 1913.[10]

TABLE 2

EUROPEAN SPECIAL EXPORTS IN CURRENT VALUES, 1830-1970

(territorial boundaries of 1970 [a]; 1830 to 1890: three year annual averages)

	Total exports		Per capita exports	
	Value (millions of dollars)	Annual growth rate (%)	Value (dollars)	Annual growth rate (%)
1830	685		3	
1860	2260	4.0	8	3.3
1890	4840	3.9	13	1.6
1913	11025	3.6	22	1.9
1929	16050	2.4 *(b)*	30	1.9 *(b)*
1953	35220	3.3 *(b)*	60	2.8 *(b)*
1970	167970	9.6	238	8.4

(*a*) European Turkey is not included: see text for corrections to make date for 1830 to 1913 more or less comparable with those that follow.

(*b*) If an arbitrary period of six years is omitted from the calculation to account for the effects of the war, the annual rate rises to 3.8% for total exports and 3% for per capita exports from 1913 to 1929, and to 4.5% and 3.8% respectively for 1929 to 1953. The 1934 revaluation however makes all these rates insignificant for the period from 1929 to 1953.

Note: The slight rounding off of the figures does not imply a corresponding margin of error. The rates of growth have been calculated from figures which were not rounded off at all.

Sources: 1830-1913 see Table 1 and text; 1929-1970 based on publications of the League of Nations and the United Nations

We shall restrict our analysis of this table to the most essential points, as we shall return to this problem when examining the more important data concerning the growth in the volume of exports. But as we have noted above, the data in current values are nevertheless important for the very reason that they are very often used. The important points to note at this stage are the irregularity of

---

10 On the basis of the world trade network in 1928 (*The Network of World Trade*; League of Nations, Geneva 1942, appendix III) we have calculated the importance of additional exports resulting from reciprocal trade between Russia and the U.K. on one hand and the countries which previously formed part of these political entities on the other hand. In 1928 the total of these exports represented 4.3% of total European exports or 4.5% of total European exports minus this trade. This rate of 4.5% has been applied to the figures for exports between 1830 and 1913. We have decided to correct the old data rather than recent ones in order to enable readers to up date the recent figures, when this becomes necessary.

Paul Bairoch

XX century development compared with that of the XIX century, and the very rapid expansion of recent years.

The irregularity of development in the XX century had basically been due to the effects of the great crisis in the 1930s which took the form of a drastic slump in both world and European trade. The combined effect of a reduction in the volume and prices of exports brought the value of European exports from a peak of 16.1 thousand million dollars in 1929 to 13.4 thousand million in 1930 and 5.9 thousand million in 1933. This movement had reached a bottom in 1935 with an amount of 5.5 thousand million old dollars.[11] But because of the dollar devaluation of January 1934, European and world trade increased, in statistical terms, by 70%, due to this alone (although in fact everything remained the same otherwise). A slump of such proportions never took place in the XIX century (at least not between 1820 and 1913). In the same way the expansion recorded since the end of the Second World War is also an entirely new phenomenon if we consider its pattern and duration. We shall return to this aspect of the problem in the section devoted to the volume of trade.

Before going on to examine the relative share of the individual countries in total European trade, we should point out that the

---

[11] The following shows the development of European exports (Europe including Russia, but excluding Turkey) for the period between the two World Wars and the post-war period after the 1939-1945 war, in millions of current dollars:

1913	11025 (a)	1931	9660	1950	24370
		1932	6530	1951	33330
1925	13710	1933	5920	1952	34400
1926	13520	1934	9450 (b)	1953	35220
1927	14780	1935	9340	1954	38310
1928	15240	1936	9820	1955	42910
1929	16050	1937	11230	1956	47700
1930	13350	1938	10210	1957	51550
				1958	51920
				1959	56820
				1960	64210

(a) Made roughly comparable with the later data.

(b) After this year they are expressed in dollars according to the new parity after the devaluation of January 1934; expressed in old gold dollars, they would be 5580 million dollars for 1934. The conversion rate used by the statistics services of the League of Nations was one new dollar = 0.5906 old dollars.

Sources: Our calculations based on the « Statistical Year-book » and the « Memorandum on Trade and Balances of Payments », League of Nations, and U. N. statistics.

European share in total world trade developed in roughly the following way.[12]

1800	70%	1913	57%
1830	67%	1929	60%
1850	66%	1953	43%
1870	68%	1960	50%
1900	60%	1970	54%

The decline of the European share in world trade in the course of the XIX century and especially after 1870 was due primarily to the extremely rapid expansion in the exports of non-European developed countries — North America, Australia, Japan — whose relative share in world trade grew from some 8% in 1830 to 20% in 1913. From this it can be concluded that the share of the developed countries as a whole in world trade was practically the same in 1830 as in 1913. However these rates do not take into account the diverging development of prices, which led to a perceptible variation in these rates. Unfortunately we cannot examine these issues more closely in the framework of this article.

2) *The relative shares of individual countries.*

The great increase in the value of European trade was accompanied by a substantial modification in the relative shares of the different European countries in total exports. As regards the three major trading powers — the U.K., France and Germany — which together accounted for more than 60% of European trade, this was shown particularly in the rapid advance of Germany, which overtook France as early an 1880 and practically caught up with the U.K. at the end of the period (in 1913, Germany accounted for 23% of European exports, against 24% for the U.K.). For the U.K. the XIX century can be divided into two distinct phases.

---

[12] For more details see our article « Le commerce extérieur mondial: évolution de la valeur, du volume et de la structure géographique des exportations de 1800 à 1970 »; in preparation.

Paul Bairoch

TABLE 3

RELATIVE SHARE
OF EUROPEAN COUNTRIES' EXPORTS IN THE EUROPEAN TOTAL, 1830-1970
(percentages; on the basis of three year annual averages, except 1970)

	1830	1860	1880	1890	1900	1910	1970 (a)
Austria-Hungary	(4.7)	5.8	7.4	6.5	7.0	5.6	3.0 (c)
Belgium	(2.9)	4.0	5.9	6.1	6.7	7.3	6.9 (e)
Bulgaria	—	—	0.1	0.1	0.2	0.3	1.2
Denmark	—	0.9	1.1	1.1	1.4	1.5	2.0
Finland	—	0.2	0.4	0.4	0.7	0.6	1.4
France	(15.9)	19.2	16.3	15.3	14.4	13.4	10.6
Germany	—	18.4	18.2	17.4	19.6	20.4	22.8 (b)
Greece	—	0.2	0.2	0.3	0.3	0.3	0.4
Italy	—	5.1	5.3	3.8	4.9	4.5	7.9
Netherlands (f)	—	1.6	2.1	3.2	4.1	4.0	7.0
Norway	—	0.7	0.7	0.7	0.8	0.8	1.5
Portugal	(1.6)	0.7	0.6	0.5	0.6	0.4	0.6
Romania	—	—	1.1	1.1	1.2	1.3	1.1
Russia	(7.9)	5.6	6.7	8.3	6.6	8.9	7.6
Serbia	—	—	0.2	0.2	0.2	0.2	1.0 (g)
Spain	(2.3)	2.3	2.9	3.4	2.1	2.2	1.4
Sweden	(1.2)	1.0	1.4	1.8	1.8	1.8	4.0
Switzerland	(4.0)	3.6	3.6	2.9	2.9	2.6	3.1
United Kingdom	(27.5)	29.8	26.0	26.6	24.7	23.7	11.3 (d)

(a) Data not stricly comparable with those of previous periods.
(b) Total for the two Germanys (excluding trade between them).
(c) Total for Austria and Hungary (exluding trade between them).
(d) Total for Great Britain and Ireland (excluding trade between them).
(e) Belgium and Luxembourg.
(f) Very approximate percentages; see appendix for reservations about statistics for the Netherlands.
(g) Yugoslavia.

Sources: See text.

The first, lasting until about 1870, showed a constant increase
in the country's share in European trade; about 27% in about 1800
to approximately 31% in about 1870. From this time there was
a continuous, although irregular, decline. And if, on the eve of
the First World War, the U.K. was still the foremost trading
power of Europe (and of the world, closely followed by the U.S.A.),
as early as the post-war years it was supplanted by the U.S.A.,
joined, in 1930, by Germany. However we should point out that
because of the very great importance of the re-export trade, the
U.K.'s relative share in world trade was more important than her
share measured by domestic or special exports alone suggests. Thus

in 1900, from the point of view of total imports, the U.K. still accounted for 31% of the European total, as against 25% for special exports. And in this respect the U.K. remained the foremost power in world trade until the eve of the Second World War and did not yield second place to Germany until 1965.[13] This shows how slowly the processes of readjustment take place in the network of world trade.

TABLE 4

RANK OF THE 10 LEADING EUROPEAN TRADING POWERS (a)

(on the basis of total of special exports)

Rank	1830	1860	1910
1	United Kingdom	United Kingdom	United Kingdom
2	France	France	Germany
3	Germany	Germany	France
4	Russia	Austria-Hungary	Russia
5	Italy	Russia	Belgium
6	Austria-Hungary	Italy	Austria-Hungary
7	Switzerland	Belgium	Italy
8	Belgium	Switzerland	Switzerland
9	Spain	Spain	Spain
10	Portugal	Sweden	Sweden
Share of the 10 countries (a)	89%	96%	93%

(a) Not including the Netherlands because of the uncertainty of its trade statistics. In 1830 and 1860 the Netherlands would probably occupy 9th or 10th place, in 1910 probably 7th or 8th.

For the other countries the most significant changes concerned Belgium, Portugal, Switzerland and Italy. Belgium is the country whose relative share in European exports grew most rapidly. Belgium went up from eighth place in 1830 to fifth in 1910. On the other hand Portugal — which was, around 1800, still the fifth or sixth most important trading power in Europe (it is true that at that point its exports had reached a rather exceptional peak) — fell to eighth or ninth position as early as 1830, and was in seventeenth place in 1910. Only Serbia and Bulgaria had a lower export figure. Switzerland and Italy both fell back in relative terms but to a less extent than Portugal (see Table 3).

---

[13] Without taking into account the territorial changes in these two countries.

Paul Bairoch

As a general rule it can be stated that trade development was more favourable than the European average in countries located north of a line passing roughly through the centre of France, while the opposite was true for the countries situated south of this line. However in the framework of this article we cannot obviously undertake an analysis of the causes of those diverging trends.

Table 5 shows the changes in the per capita exports for certain periods. These statistics are of twofold interest. Firstly, and this is not specifically related to the fact that the figures given are for the XIX century, they reveal the rather divergent patterns of demographic growth and territorial changes, thus providing certain comparative growth processes with a better perspective. This is the case especially with Germany and France. Due to the combined effect of the loss of Alsace-Lorraine coupled with very slow demographic growth, France was clearly outstripped, as we have seen, as the second European trading power in terms of total exports. But translated in terms of per capita exports the picture alters radically, because in this case France's exports increased relatively faster than those of Germany.

The second reason which makes these per capita export figures interesting is that in view both of the absence of reliable national accounting data for many of the countries, and of the lesser differences between levels of development in the XIX century, these figures provide a rough picture of the differences in export rates in relation to the national product of the different economies.

The great disparity between the individual countries as regards per capita exports will be noted. Thus for 1860 the margin between the group of countries with a low per capita export rate (comprising especially Russia, Spain, Italy, Austria-Hungary, Greece etc.) and the group with a high export rate (U.K., Switzerland, Belgium) is of the order of 1 to 6. Although some countries with low export rates experienced a more rapid growth in exports than the average, and were thus promoted to an intermediate group, the gap between the two groups still increased and reached 1 to 11 in about 1910. The coefficient of variations (for the 16 countries reported both in 1860 and 1910) increases from 8.3% to 45.7%.

European Foreign Trade in the XIX Century

TABLE 5

PER CAPITA SPECIAL EXPORTS
OF INDIVIDUAL EUROPEAN COUNTRIES, 1830-1970
(current dollars; three year annual averages, except 1970)

	1830 (*a*)	1860	1880	1900	1910	1970 (*e*)
Austria-Hungary	1	4	8	8	9	285 (*g*)
Belgium	5	19	43	55	85	1058 (*h*)
Bulgaria	—	—	2	3	5	236
Denmark	6	12	20	29	45	681
Finland	1	3	8	14	18	492
France	3	11	15	20	29	349
Germany	3	11	16	19	27	488 (*f*)
Greece	—	2	2	3	5	73
Italy	2	4	7	8	11	246
Netherlands (*d*)	5	10	21	43	59	903
Norway	4	9	15	19	29	633
Portugal	3	4	5	6	6	99
Romania	—	—	9	10	17	91
Russia	1	2	3	3	5	53
Serbia	—	—	4	5	7	82 (*i*)
Spain	1	3	7	6	9	71
Sweden	3	6	13	19	28	844
Switzerland	12	31	50	48	60	820
United Kingdom	8	22	30	33	48	323 (*i*)
Europe as a whole	3 (*b*)	7	12	13	18	238
Europe-Russia	3 (*c*)	9	15	18	25	336

(*a*) The data are approximate for most of the countries.
(*b*) About 2.8.
(*c*) About 3.3.
(*d*) Very approximate data: see appendix for reservations about statistics for the Netherlands.
(*e*) Data not strictly comparable with those of previous periods.
(*f*) Total for the two Germanys (excluding trade between them).
(*g*) Total for Austria and Hungary (exluding trade between them).
(*h*) Belgium and Luxembourg.
(*i*) Total for Great Britain and Ireland (excluding trade between them).
(*j*) Yugoslavia.
Sources: See text.

As has often been remarked with reference to contemporary figures, the importance of per capita foreign trade in the XIX century was in general in inverse proportion to the size of the country but in proportion to the level of development. It is therefore not surprising to find Switzerland, the U.K. and Belgium at the top of the classification table (see Table 6). The extremely high level attained by Switzerland results from factors stated above — to which can

Paul Bairoch

be added a rather low rate, for the period, of locally produced food (whence the necessity arose to sell other products in order to balance trade) — and from the policy of industrialization in the textile sector, which relied partially on the import of cotton yarn (relatively little especially before 1850 came from local spinning-mills) and on the export of highly elaborated goods. But as Belgian exports increased much more quickly, Belgium snatched first place from Switzerland an early as 1890.

TABLE 6

CLASSIFICATION OF THE 10 LEADING EUROPEAN COUNTRIES IN TERMS OF PER CAPITA EXPORTS (a)

Rank	1830	1860	1910
1	Switzerland	Switzerland	Belgium
2	United Kingdom	United Kingdom	Switzerland
3	Belgium	Belgium	United Kingdom
4	Denmark	⎧ Denmark	Denmark
5	⎧ Germany	⎨ France	⎧ Norway
6	⎪ France	⎩ Germany	⎩ France
7	⎨ Norway	Norway	Sweden
8	⎪ Portugal	Sweden	Germany
9	⎩ Sweden	⎧ Portugal, Italy	Finland
10	Italy	⎨ Austria-Hungary	Romania

(a) Excluding the Netherlands because of the uncertainty of its trade statistics. In 1830 the Netherlands would probably occupy a rank before Italy, in 1860 before Norway and in 1910 a place close to that of Denmark.

For the entire XIX century the U.K. remained leader of the major countries by a long way in terms of per capita exports. In this field the most important changes have taken place in recent decades. At present both Germany and France have outstripped the U.K. in this field; Germany did so, decisively and some time ago, while France has surpassed the U.K. only narrowly, and a short time ago.[14] Moreover, while in 1910 the per capita exports of the U.K. exceeded those of Continental Europe (without Russia) by

---

[14] These figures are scarcely changed if corrections are made to take Ireland's independence into account.

about 100%, in 1970, for the first time for at least two centuries, the per capita exports of Continental Europe (without Russia) exceeded those of the U.K.

B) *Growth in the volume of European exports.*

As we have already noted, the preliminary nature of the conclusions presented here becomes more marked for data on volume than for those concerning current values.[15] In order to reduce the text the reader is referred to the appendix for methodological problems and other issues of the same kind (sources, margins of error etc.). Here, apart from presenting and analysing the data, we shall only refer to problems of methodology in the briefest terms. This section, as the previous one, will be devoted first to the growth in the volume of trade of Europe as a whole, then to that of individual countries.

1) *Development of the volume of exports from Europe as whole.*

Table 7 contains the essential findings concerning the development of prices and the volume of European exports. The price index which we have drawn up here is a weighted average between the various indices available. The statistical coverage is relatively good until 1880 (about 75%). Before this date, calculations on a national basis were extremely rare and before 1830 the index only in fact consisted of the average between U.K. and French prices. But

---

[15] However one should not place too much faith in the potential modifications made possible by improved data. Thus the differences between Kindleberger's index of export prices (see introduction) and the index we have calculated are relatively minor, in spite of the fact that for some countries the basic data have been revised meanwhile and that our index includes a greater number of countries. Thus, on the same 1900 =: 100 basis, the two indices (three years annual average around the year quoted) are as follows.

	Kindleberger index	Our index	Differences
1870	133.1	132.0	+ 0.8%
1880	113.4	118.6	— 4.4%
1890	100.0	103.8	— 3.7%
1910	105.9	105.3	+ 0.6%

Paul Bairoch

because of the structure of their exports these two countries are fairly representative of the whole of Europe (especially with the corrective we employed: see appendix). For the period from 1840 to 1870, for which there is no price index for German exports, we have drawn on a valid estimate of the volume of German exports, (see appendix).

TABLE 7

EUROPEAN SPECIAL EXPORTS VALUE, EXPORT PRICES
AND VOLUME, 1800-1913

(three year annual averages; except 1913)

	Current value (millions of dollars)	Export prices 1899-1901 = 100	Exports in constant values 1899-1901		
			Millions of dollars	Index 1899-1901 = 100	Annual growth rate (%)
1800	(670)	(312.0)	(216)	(3.9)	*
1810	(680)	(310.0)	(219)	(4.0)	*
1820	(680)	(229.3)	(297)	(5.4)	(3.1)
1830	655	150.9	434	7.9	3.9
1840	875	137.0	645 (a)	11.7	4.0
1850	1200	124.3	936 (a)	17.0	3.8
1860	2160	141.4	1516 (a)	27.6	4.9
1870	3260	132.0	2509 (a)	45.7	5.2
1880	4050	118.6	3415	62.2	3.1
1890	4630	103.8	4461	81.2	2.7
1900	5490	100.0	5490	100.0	2.1
1910	8650	105.3	8215	149.6	4.2
1913	10550	110.8	9525	173.5	5.1

* Not significant.

(a) For these dates the volume of exports does not derive solely from the correction of value by the price index; see text and appendix.

Note: The slight rounding off of the figures does not imply a corresponding margin of error. The rates of growth have been calculated from figures which were not rounded off at all.

Sources: Our calculations; see text and appendix.

As export prices dropped greatly the growth in the volume of exports during the XIX century was much more rapid than the increase in their value. From 1830 to 1910, the growth in volume was about 1 to 38, against 1 to 13 in value, and in terms of annual growth rates 3.4% and 2.4% respectively. There was a very rapid acceleration in the growth rate compared with the previous century (and most probably with previous centuries). It can be held that during the XVIII century European exports grew at an annual rate of about 0.7%-1.4%.

In the XIX century four phases can be distinguished in the pattern of growth in the volume of exports. The first, which probably began in about 1815-1820 and lasted until 1845-47, showed a relatively rapid growth in the volume of European exports, about 3%-4% per year. To a certain extent this must have been a process of recovery, for the period from 1796-1815 was disturbed by wars. Although the available data are not very reliable, it is likely that the level of European foreign trade around 1815 was no higher than in 1790.[16] However the principal cause of the rapid expansion of trade lay in the effects of industrialization — increased demand for raw materials, the initial reductions in transport costs and rapid population growth[17] all promoted international trade.

The second phase, from 1845-47 to 1873-75, was marked by an extremely rapid expansion in the volume of European trade. The annual rate of growth was about 4.5%-5%. In all probability a similar medium term period of such rapid expansion in European foreign trade — and consequently, given the dominant role of Europe, in world foreign trade — had never occurred before. In the course of these 28-29 years the volume of European exports multiplied fourfold. Of course the policy of free trade adopted by the U.K. from 1846 (especially with the repeal of the Corn Laws) was a vital factor in this rapid increase in international commerce. Liberalisation of trade had an increasing role when, after the success of the British (between 1846 and 1856 the value and volume of U.K. exports doubled) almost all the European countries, led by France, freed their tariff systems after 1860. But it must be stressed that the rate of trade expansion slackened before the protectionist reaction in Europe, whose outset can be placed in 1879 when German legislation was modified.[18] Indeed, from 1873-75 a slacken-

16 However it should be noted that for the U.K. this period was marked by a rather rapid increase in exports. But this was offset where total European figures are concerned by a fall in the volume of trade of the Continental European countries (especially France, Germany and Italy).

17 Where it is generally estimated that the population of Europe grew at an annual rate of about 0.5%-0.6% during the second half of the XVIII century, according to our calculations this rate would have reached approximately 0.8% from 1810 to 1850.

18 For the history of customs tariffs in Europe and especially the effects of liberalism on the European economy, we refer the reader to our book: *Commerce extérieur et développement économique de l'Europe au XIXe siècle* (chapter II) to appear in 1974.

ing in the annual rate of expansion was evident and in the period
from 1873-75 to 1900 the average annual rate of growth of the
volume of exports fell to 2.5%, almost half that of the previous
decades. As Table 7 shows, from 1890 to 1900 the rate was even
nearly as low as 2%, which in terms of per capita increase was
little more than a mere 1% (see Table 8).

In contrast, the 13-14 years preceding the First World War were
marked by a very rapid expansion in the volume of European
exports. From 1900 to 1910 the annual growth rate in volume
was 4.2%, and even reached 5.1% between 1910 and 1913; that
is an annual average rate of 4.3% from 1900 to 1913. If this rate
is not exceptionally high in comparison with expansion registered
during the XIX century (it was even lower than the probable rate
for the decade from 1850 to 1860), it is worth pointing out, however,
that it is only in the contemporary period that a similar rate of
expansion was to be equalled, or even exceeded. In fact, (see
Table 8) even laying aside the great crisis of the 1930s, characterized
by a slump in the volume of European and world exports which
was unprecedented in contemporary history,[19] it must be emphasized
that the very rapid expansion in the volume of foreign trade in
Western Europe in the years 1921-1929 (annual rate 11%) was to
a great extent the result of a process of recovery after the depression
caused by the war and the crisis of reconversion; European exports
did not recover their 1913 volume until 1927.

On this subject it should also be noted that after the Second
World War the 1937-39 volume of exports for Western Europe had
again been attained as early as 1950's and the 1929 level by 1951.
Consequently the extremely high rate of growth in the volume
of foreign trade which has taken place from 1953 until the present
has little to do with a recovery process.[20]

---

[19] From 1928 to 1932 the volume of exports from Western Europe fell by 36% and
world exports by 27%. And, what is even more exceptional, even in 1937, which was
the best year of the '30s in economic terms, the volume of European or world trade had
not yet reached the 1928 level. (See A. MADDISON, *op. cit.*, and « Statistical Yearbook
1969 United Nations », New York 1970, p. 54).

[20] Even in terms of per capita volume, the 1953 level of exports exceeded that of
1937 by 43%.

European Foreign Trade in the XIX Century

TABLE 8

VOLUME OF EUROPEAN SPECIAL EXPORTS,[a] 1800-1970

(1800-1900: three years annual averages; at prices of 1899-1901)

	Total exports			Per capita exports		
	Millions of dollars	Index 1899-1901 = 100	Annual rate of growth (%)	Dollars	Index 1899-1901 = 100	Annual rate of growth (%)
1800	(226)	(3.9)		(1.1)	(8.2)	
1840	674	11.7	*	2.6	20.0	*
1860	1583	27.6	4.4	5.5	40.1	3.7
1880	3569	62.2	4.1	10.4	76.3	3.2
1890	4662	81.2	2.7	12.2	89.4	1.6
1900	5737	100.0	2.1	13.6	100.0	1.1
1913	9953	173.5	4.3	20.2	148.1	3.1
1929 (a)	11143	194.2	0.7 (b)	21.1	154.8	0.3 (b)
1953 (a)	12974	226.1	0.6 (b)	22.0	161.1	0.2 (b)
1970 (a)	53494	932.4	8.7 (c)	75.9	556.8	7.6 (c)

* Not significant.

(a) The data for 1800 to 1913 have been corrected in order to make them relatively comparable to those that follow (see text preceding Table 2). The development of the volume of exports from 1913 to 1970 is based on the index of export prices for Western Europe (that is, 82% of total European exports), an index which has been applied to the total of European exports (sources: A. MADDISON, *op. cit.*, and « Statistical Yearbook » and « Monthly Bulletin of Statistics » of the U. N.; various nos.).

(b) If a period of six years is excluded arbitrarily from the calculation to account for the effects of the war, the annual rate for 1913 to 1929 rises to 1.1% for total exports and 0.4% for per capita exports; for 1929 to 1953 it is 0.8% for total exports and just over 0.2% for per capita exports.

(c) From 1970 to 1972 the annual rate of growth has been 7.5% for the volume of total exports and 6.5% for per capita exports.

Note: The slight rounding off of the figures does not imply a corresponding margin of error. The rates of growth have been calculated from figures which were not rounded off at all.

Sources: Our calculations; see text and appendix.

The speeding up of the rhythm of growth in the volume of exports which started in the first years of the XX century occurred at a time when most European countries (but not the U.K.) were still strengthening the protectionist aspects of their tariff legislations. In addition to the factor of economic growth, which is always decisive in explaining changes in the development of foreign trade, the influence of the rapid expansion of trade with what is now called the Third World must be stressed in order to account for the rapidity of this growth. While it can be estimated that from 1870 to 1900 the volume of European exports to the Third World grew at an annual rate of about 3.0%, from 1900 to 1910 the rate was 5.6%.[21]

---

[21] In both cases this is an approximate estimate of the volume; we have arbitrarily assumed that prices of exports to the Third World had developed in an identical way to the prices of the total exports.

Paul Bairoch

In addition to this relative independence of tariff policies, as shown in the preceding analysis, it should also be mentioned that changes in the growth rate of the volume of exports also took place place independently of price movements. Phases of speeding up or slackening in the pace of growth occur in time of both increasing and decreasing price. Thus, among the four decades where trade volume increased the most rapidly, two of those occur when prices were decreasing (the 1840's and the 1860's) and two when they were increasing (the 1850's and the 1900's) The same point may be made for Europe as a whole with regard to the growth of foreign trade in relation to demographic growth. It is true that in this field the differences are less marked, for the variations in demographic growth rates occured within rather narrow limits (from 0.6 to 0.9% per year).

Furthermore it is because of milder variations in the demographic rates (and also, because of the relatively modest expansion in per capita exports, at least in certain period) that the variations in the growth rates of the volume of per capita exports are much more marked than for the total exports. Thus (see Table 8) the annual growth rate in the volume of per capita exports from 1840 to 1860 was about 4.4%, while it fell to 1.3% from 1880 to 1900, and then almost recovered the previous rate from 1900 to 1913. 1913 to 1953 was a period of near stagnation, for the 1913 level was not reached again until 1952, almost half a century later. On the other hand the annual rate of growth climbed to 7.6% from 1953 to 1970, that is more than double than any previously achieved over a medium term period.

If we examine the development on a medium or long-term basis, the XIX century as a whole was distinguished by a rapid expansion in the volume of foreign trade, in comparison not only with previous centuries but equally with the period from 1913 to 1950. While the volume of European exports grew 3.9% per year from 1830 to 1913, from 1913 to 1950 this rate was only 0.4% owing to the effects of the two World Wars and the crisis of the 1930s. On the other hand, the past twenty-five years have been truly unique in history. During the quarter century between 1948 and 1973 the annual rate of growth in the volume of exports in Western Europe has been around 8.5%. From 1946 to 1973 it was even above 9%, which brought about a ninefold increase in the volume of per capita exports. It should be noted that the inclusion of the Eastern European countries would not essentially affect these rates. As was the case in the XIX century, (see below), this extremely rapid expansion in foreign trade during the last few decades has not affected all the European countries equally. Without examining individual examples, we can point out that the volume of exports of the Common Market countries (in its pre-1973 form) increased from 1953 to 1970 by 10.5% per year, while the corresponding rate for the E.F.T.A. countries (in its pre-1973 form) was only 6%.

2) *Development in the volume of exports of individual countries.*

The scarcity of data for the period before 1860 and the greater margin of error has led us to concentrate on the second half of the XIX century. However it should be pointed out that for the first first half of the XIX century the expansion in volume of exports was markedly more rapid in the U.K. than in France.

TABLE 9

ANNUAL RATE OF GROWTH IN THE VOLUME OF SPECIAL EXPORTS FOR *SOME EUROPEAN COUNTRIES*

(on the basis of three year annual averages; percentages)

	1860-1870 (a)	1870-1880	1880-1890	1890-1900	1900-1910	1860-1910
Belgium (d)	6.4	3.5	2.1	2.2	5.6	4.3
Denmark	—	—	2.2	3.3	4.2	3.6 (b)
Finland	5.6	3.9	1.6	3.9	3.7	3.8
France	5.7	3.0	1.7	1.7	2.6	2.9
Germany	6.7	2.3	2.2	4.2	5.7	4.2
Italy	5.5	2.0	— 0.7	3.7	3.4	2.6
Norway	—	2.9	3.0	1.1	4.6	2.9 (c)
Sweden	7.3	3.4	3.6	1.8	3.0	5.0
United Kingdom	3.8	2.6	2.7	1.0	3.8	2.8
Europe	5.2	3.1	2.7	2.1	4.2	3.4

(a) Finland 1861-1870; Italy 1862-1870.
(b) 1875-1910.
(c) 1865-1910.
(d) Respectively from 1861 to 1873; 1873 to 1883; 1883 to 1893; 1893 to 1902; 1902 to 1913; and 1861 to 1913.

Paul Bairoch

Although the rates of growth differed appreciably from one country to another, it should be noted that the fluctuations in the rate of growth were fairly uniform, in particular during the thirty years from 1860 to 1890 and in the decade from 1900 to 1910 (in comparison with the previous decade). In practically all European countries the decade from 1860 to 1870 — the first of the free trade period — was marked by a rapid expansion in the volume of exports. However it should be pointed out that growth did not speed up in all cases in the countries for which we have data for the previous decade as well. In two instances (Belgium and the U.K.) there was a slackening in growth, in one case (France) there was no change, and in two cases (Germany and Sweden) an increase. The second decade of the free-exchange period was distinguished by a general falling off in the rhythm of growth in the volume of exports. The decade 1880 to 1890 was less uniform but was general marked by a new drop in expansion.

A strong revival expansion in sales from protectionist Germany from 1890 to 1900 (in fact from 1893) contrasted with a new slow down in sales from the free trade U.K. Indeed this decade saw the smallest growth in the volume of British exports ever recorded for the whole period from 1790 to 1910. This contrast between British and German development intensified the controversy between the supporters and opponents of modification in British tariff policy.

From the period from 1860 to 1910 as a whole the growth in volume of sales was very rapid in Sweden, Germany and Belgium. On the other hand it was fairly slow in France, the U.K. and especially in Italy. As far as Denmark and Norway were concerned the rates of growth were probably between 4.5% and 5.0% and 3.5% and 4.0% respectively for the entire period.

For those countries for which there are no statistics available for the development of the volume of trade, on the basis of both the data referring to the increase in the value of exports and the approximate indications of the prices, it can be concluded that, for the period from 1860 to 1910, the growth in the volume of exports was certainly more rapid than the European average in the following countries: the Netherlands, Russia, Bulgaria, and probably also in Greece. On the other hand it was probably slower in Portugal, Serbia and Switzerland. In Austria-Hungary, Spain and Romania the growth must have been fairly close to the European average.

International differences in the rates of demographic expansion in general tend to reduce noticeably the differences in growth rates in terms of the expansion of per capita exports. The following are the annual growth rates in the volume of per capita exports for the period from 1860 to 1910:

Belgium	3.3%
Denmark	(3.0 - 4.0%)
France	2.7%
Germany	3.1%
Italy	1.9%
Norway	(2.5 - 3.0%)
Sweden	4.3%
United Kingdom	2.0%
Europe	2.4%

Of these the only country distinctly different from the others was Sweden, whose growth in per capita foreign trade was almost double than the average for the other European countries. France — which in terms of total growth in exports was below the European average — exceeded this average in terms of per capita growth. Compared with the contemporary period the disparity between the growth rates in the volume of per capita exports was smaller in the XIX century.

SUMMARY.

As the aim of this article is essentially to present the results of our calculations on the development of European exports in the XIX century, the analysis accompanying the table has been deliberately restricted. The most important data for these calculations are to be found in Tables 1 and 7, which indicate respectively the development of the total and per capita exports of European in current values from 1800 to 1913, and the development of prices and the volume of European exports for the same period.

In *current* values the exports rose from less than 0.7 thousand million dollars in 1830 (the dates from which the statistics are more reliable) to 10.6 thousand million in 1913, that is an increase of the order of approximately 1 to 16, or 2.4% per year. Per capita exports rose from less than three dollars in 1830 to just over 21 in 1913. As regards the pace of growth of the value of exports, the period from 1830 to 1914 can be divided into four phases: 1830-1846/47: annual growth rate 3%; 1846/47 - 1865/68: 5%; 1865/68 - 1896/97: 2%; and 1896/97 - 1913: 5%.

Throughout all the XIX century the U.K. remained the foremost trading power in terms of total exports. Moreover her share in the total European exports continued to grow until 1870, rising from 27% in 1800 to 31% in 1870. From 1870 she fell back steadily, — and in 1913 Germany, which had overtaken France in 1880, almost caught up with the U.K. (22.8% and 24.2% respectively). For the other countries it appears that in general foreign trade expanded more rapidly than the European average in countries located north of a line passing roughly through the center of France, while the opposite was true of the countries lying to the south of this line.

As is generally the case for contemporary statistics, the importance of per capita foreign trade was, in the XIX century, in inverse proportion to the size of the country, and in proportion to the level of development of the country. The disparity between the different European countries in terms of per capita exports, which was already pronounced at the beginning of the XIX century, became even more strongly marked (see Table 5). Between 1860 and 1910 the coefficient of variation of exports per capita increased from 8.3 to 45.7%.

As export prices on the whole fell during the XIX century. European exports expanded much more rapidly in *volume* than in value. From 1840 to 1910 the volume of exports expanded at an annual rate of about 3.6%.

As regards the pattern of growth in the volume of exports, the XIX century can be divided into four phases. From 1815/20 to 1845/47 the annual rate of growth was about 3%-4%. To some extent at least this must have been a period of recovery. From 1845/47 to 1873/75 growth was very rapid; 4.5%-5.0%. It is very likely that such a medium term rapid expansion in European trade — and in consequence, given the dominant role of Europe, world trade — had never occurred previously. The free trade policy (practised by the U.K. already since 1846 and by other countries manly after 1860) contributed greatly to this acceleration. But it must be stressed that the slackening of pace in trade expansion (between 1873/75 and 1900 the annual rate fell to 2.5%) preceded the protectionist reaction in Europe which can be traced to 1879 at the earliest. The relative independence of the rates of expansion of foreign trade in relation to developments in commercial policies is also confirmed in the fourth phase. Between 1900 and 1913, when protectionism was gaining ground in practically all Continental European countries, a new period of rapid growth took place — and the volume of exports grew by 4.2% per year.

The rate of expansion of European foreign trade was equally independant of the main trends in prices. Taking Europe as whole, the same can be said of the relationship with demographic expansion.

For the period from 1860 to 1910 the growth in the volume of exports was very rapid in Sweden, Germany Denmark, Norway and Belgium. On the other hand it was relatively slow in France, the U.K., Switzerland and especially in Portugal and Italy. Despite these differences the fluctuations in the rate of growth of the volume of exports were fairly uniform; the phases of speeding up and slowing down coincide very well in practically all countries.

If the growth rates recorded in the volume of European exports during the XIX century are placed in a wider historical context, two essential conclusions emerge. In comparison both with previous centuries and with the following fifty years the XIX century is clearly distinguished by a very rapid expansion in the volume of international trade. However the three decades since the end of the Second World War have been truly unique in economic history; the volume of European exports has grown during this period by 9% per year, that is by more than double any growth previously experienced in a period of comparable length.

Paul Bairoch

METHODOLOGICAL APPENDIX AND SOURCES.

The reader will find here below information on the methods which have been used and on the principal sources. We have deliberately reduced this section to a minimum.

Current value of exports.

The evolution in current values of European exports was calculated by starting from the series of statistics available for the individual countries, and then completed by estimates in cases of missing data (see below). The figures in local currency have been converted into dollars according to the rates of exchange in force for each of the periods under consideration.

For a certain number of cases and for certain periods (particularly before 1850) the only series available are in constant values. In these cases we have converted such data into current values, using a local index of export prices, when available (this was the case for France, particularly for the pre-1850 statistics), or, where there is no such information, by using approximate information based on the movement of prices in other countries. It should be noted that the additional margin of error caused by this lack of statistics is of little importance for the period from 1850 to 1913, the exports involved representing less than 5% of the total. For the Netherlands, apart from the problem of constant values, there was also the problem that a valid series of special exports before 1913 was not available; we have accepted, following Svennilson[22] and Maddison,[23] the correction that a third of so-called 'special' exports were in fact re-exports.

The basic data used for the calculation of the European total can be separated into three groups; the first comprises the various regular statistical series; the second estimates of various authors; and the last our own extrapolations. The relative importance of each of these sources obviously varies greatly. From 1880 to 1913 the statistical coverage is practically 100%. For 1870 statistics

---

22 I. SVENNILSON, *Growth and Stagnation in the European Economy*, United Nations, Geneva 1954.
23 A. MADDISON, *op. cit.*

represent some 78% of the total, estimates (with a very narrow margin of error) 21%, and the extrapolations only 1%. For 1860 those figures were respectively 72%, 26% and 2%, and for 1850 61%, 37% and 2%. The proportion of actual statistics for 1840 falls to 55%, that of the reasonably valid estimates to 30% and the extrapolations are 15%. For 1830 they were 53%, 11% and 36% respectively. For the earlier periods these proportions were not greatly changed, but the margin of error of each of the three series of data increased very appreciably.

The extrapolations that we made were of two kinds. The first were figures for the countries whose political creation took place during the period under consideration — in particular in the Balkans. In these cases we made the arbitrary assumption that their exports during the period before their foundation had developed similarly to countries with a comparable economic structure. The second group concerned countries for which, as far as we knew, there were neither statistical series nor valid estimations; in this case we estimated the increases in exports arbitrarily, taking as a basis the general economic development of these countries (see below for discussion of the margins of error).

Finally we should note that, except for the data for 1913 and the years after 1913, figures are based on the annual average for the three years around each given date.

Index of export prices and volume of exports.

The price index calculated in this article is a weighted average drawn from the various indices of exports prices available for the individual countries. The relative importance of the exports of each country for the period under consideration was used as weight. In other words it is a Paasche type index.

Apart from the price indices for the total exports of the different countries, we have also incorporated the French and German indices for the prices of food-stuff exports, in order to compensate for the lack of indices for certain countries whose exports consisted mainly of agricultural products. We have arbitrarily assigned to the average of these two indices a weighting of some 7% of the total.

Paul Bairoch

For the period from 1880 to 1913, the indices relating to individual countries account for a volume of exports of about 76% of the European total (not including the partial index of food-stuff products). This proportion was about 60% for 1870 and 55% for 1860. Between 1810 and 1830 the proportion was only about 47% (U.K. and France). But for the period from 1840 to 1870 the calculation of the volume of exports was improved by the introduction of the German series (see below).

The volume of European exports was obtained by applying the index of export prices to the data for current values. However from 1840 to 1870 — a period for which there were no available indices on German export prices — we took into account the availability of valid estimates of the development of the volume of exports of that country. To the figures in constant dollars between 1898 and 1901 for exports from Europe excluding Germany, we have added an extrapolation in constant dollars of German exports, which were derived from the index of the volume of these exports. Finally an average was made of the series thus obtained and the series obtained by the traditional method.

Margins of error of the data.

First we shall examine the series of exports in current values. The margin of error can be considered to be very low, almost negligible, for the data for the period from 1880 to 1913. In fact, as we have just seen, the statistical coverage for this period was 100%. Certainly, as in the contemporary period, official series of statistics on foreign trade contained a margin of error varying in magnitude from one country to another. But it is fairly probable that this margin was not much greater around 1880 than it is today. For the data from 1860 to 1870, owing to the absence of certain statistics, the *additional margin of error* as regards the European total must probably be below 5%,[24] even by deliberately over-

---

[24] We have assumed arbitrarily (rather a high estimate as this concerns not an individual country but a group of countries) a margin of error of 25% for the extrapolated data and 10% for the reliable estimates.

estimating this margin. This additional margin of error must have been about 6% for 1850[25] and 11% for 1840,[26] and 17% for 1830.[27] For the pre-1830 data (and to some degree for those between 1830 and 1850) the greater margin of error of the statistics themselves must be borne in mind. Smuggling was certainly of greater statistical importance (although it is true that it had greater influence on import figures). It can be estimated, again quite arbitrarily, that the margin of error of these figures for the period from 1800 to 1820 might have reached 20% to 25%.

With regard to the volume of European exports, the additional margin of error introduced by the price indices must be borne in mind, together with the absence of such indices for some countries in certain periods (see above). However the relatively uniform growth in prices somewhat reduces the effects of this deficiency. It is very difficult to estimate the size of the additional margin of error for the data on volume in comparison with the margin of error of the data on current values. For the period from 1870 to 1913 it must have been very narrow, and quite narrow from 1840 to 1830. On the other hand, for the data from 1810 to 1830, as we have seen, are dealing only with the weighted average of the French and British indices, which are perhaps not sufficiently representative of the development of the rest of Europe, although they represent about 50% of European exports.

The preliminary nature of the results.

We have termed the results presented here 'preliminary' in the sense that we wish to continue our researches and reduce the margin of error of the figures which we have put forward. In the field of current values the improvement could only be made at the

---

25 We assume a margin of error of 30% for the extrapolated data and 15% for the reliable estimates.

26 We assume a margin of error of 35% for the extrapolated data and 20% for the reliable estimates.

27 We assume a margin of error of 40% for the extrapolated data and 25% for the reliable estimates.

Paul Bairoch

cost of a vast amount of research, which is impossible for an isolated researcher to contemplate. As an illustration we can add that the time taken just to assemble the basic data .presented here was between six to eight months, and that in order to halve the margin of error in the data for before 1860 about thirty to fifty months' work would probably have to be devoted to reconstructing the missing series or improving those that are unreliable.

However, in the field of export prices, and thus of the volume of exports, we expect to be able to present improved series by about 1975. We are planning to elaborate an entirely different index of export prices for the European countries as a whole: instead of aggregating indices of export prices of countries we plan to aggregate export prices indices of a wide range of commodities. The weighting will be based on calculations we hope to make on the development of the comodity structure of European and world exports.

Geographical coverage.

Europe, as defined in this study, comprises the whole of Europe including Russia, but excludes the European part of Turkey (in its 1913 boundaries). The impossibility of separating validly, for many periods, the exports of the Asian part of Russia, together with their slight importance, have led us to include this region in Europe both for trade and population statistics. This is, however, a fairly common practice.[28] The exclusion of European Turkey is justified by the impossibility of separating the exports of this area from those of Turkey as a whole. It is worth pointing out here that in comparison with the population of Europe in 1913 (as it is defined above), which was about 493 million, the European part of Turkey had a population of only slightly less than two millions, and Asian Russia some 25 millions, out of about 173 millions for Russia as a whole.

---

[28] Especially by the statistics office of the League of Nations and those of the United Nations and so by almost all the various statistics offices.

European Foreign Trade in the XIX Century

SOURCES.

A) *Exports in current values.*

It is impossible to quote here in full all the sources we used. In fact, for each country concerned our research has followed the three following phases:

1) Where available, historical statistical abstracts.

2) Statistical abstracts for the periods under consideration (general statistical abstracts and statistical abstracts of foreign trade).

3) Studies on the historical development of foreign trade.

This whole process of data collecting necessitated the consultation of more than 200 volumes or texts representing more than 100 titles.

This systematic research was completed by making use of the international sections of certain statistical abstracts, notably those of France and Germany, and a series of secondary sources, listed below:

Foreign Commerce Yearbook (US Department of Commerce), various years, Washington.

J. R. McCulloch, *A Dictionary of Commerce and Commercial Navigation,* London 1844.

Mouvement général du commerce et de la navigation des principaux pays étrangers (« Annales du commerce extérieur », from 1888), Paris.

M. G. Mulhall, *A Dictionary of Statistics* (4th edition), London 1899.

F. X. von Neumann Spallart, *Uebersichten der Weltwirtschaft 1880,* Stuttgart 1881 and subsequent editions.

Statesman's Year-Book (from 1864 et seq.), London.

Statistical Abstract of Foreign Countries (US Department of Commerce), Washington 1909.

Statistical Abstract for the Principal Foreign Countries (from 1873), London.

Paul Bairoch

B) *Indices of export prices and volume of exports.*

These are the sources from the various countries used to construct our index of export prices for Europe as a whole, and for the data on the development of the volume of exports.

Germany: W. G. HOFFMANN, *Das Wachstum der Deutschen Wirtschaft seit der Mitte des 19. Jahrhunderts*, Berlin 1965.

Belgium: S. CAPELLE, *Le volume du commerce extérieur de la Belgique 1830-1913* in « Bulletin de l'Institut de Recherches Économiques », Louvain, November 1938, pp. 15-56.

Denmark: A. ØLGAARD, *Growth, Productivity and Relative Prices*, Amsterdam 1968.

Finland: E. PIHKALA, *Finland's Foreign Trade 1860-1917*, Helsinki 1969.

France: M. LEVY-LEBOYER, *L'héritage de Simiand: prix, profits et termes d'échanges au XIXe siècle* in « Revue Historique », No. 493, January-March 1970, Paris, pp. 77-120.

Italy: P. ERCOLINI, *Documentazione Statistica di base* in G. FUA (editor). « Lo sviluppo economico in Italia », vol. III, Milan 1969, pp. 380-460.

Norway: J. BJERKE, *Langtidslinger I Norsk Økonomi 1865-1960*, Oslo 1966, and *Nasjonalregnskap 1900-1929* (National Accounts 1900-1929), Oslo 1953.

Portugal: *Estatisticas do comercio externo 1968*, vol. I, Lisbon 1969.

United Kingdom: A. H. IMLAH, *Economic Elements in the Pax Britanica*, Cambridge (Mass.) 1958.

Sweden: G. FRIDLIZIUS, *Sweden's Exports 1850-1960. A Study in Perspective* in « Economy and History », vol. VI, Stockholm 1963, pp. 3-10.

[3]

Private Tooth Decay as Public Economic Virtue: The Slave-Sugar Triangle, Consumerism, and European Industrialization

RALPH A. AUSTEN & WOODRUFF D. SMITH

The only group of clear gainers from the British trans-Atlantic slave trade, and even those gains were small, were the European consumers of sugar and tobacco and other plantation crops. They were given the chance to purchase dental decay and lung cancer at somewhat lower prices than would have been the case without the slave trade. [Thomas and Bean 1974: 914]

ALTHOUGH the quotation above represents a radical departure from earlier economic assessments of the Atlantic slave trade, it shares with them an almost universal assumption: that the real significance of the Atlantic sugar triangle lay in its contribution to the productive capacity of Europe. Thus, concluding that only consumers "benefited" is tantamount to reducing the slave trade to economic triviality. This view of import trades has informed

Ralph A. Austen is professor of African history at the University of Chicago and author of *African Economic History* (1987) as well as articles on the Islamic slave trade out of Africa, the history of coastal Cameroon, and African heroic/antiheroic narrative.

Woodruff D. Smith is professor of history at the University of Texas at San Antonio. His research interests include European imperialism, modern Germany, the history of social and cultural science, and early-modern European economic history. He has published articles on the European side of the seventeenth-century East India trade. His most recent book is *The Ideological Origins of Nazi Imperialism* (1986).

Social Science History 14:1 (Spring 1990). Copyright © 1990 by the Social Science History Association. CCC 0145-5532/90/$1.50.

historical understanding not only of the factors leading to industrialization in Europe but also of those apparently retarding similar development in the Third World, including Africa and the West Indies (Bairoch 1975: 198–99).

In the present article we suggest that the slave and sugar trade (along with the importation of other "colonial goods") was essential to European industrial development precisely because it stimulated and ultimately reshaped the entire pattern of Western consumer demand. We will review the role assigned to "luxury" consumption in the literature on industrialization, suggest some ways in which this factor can be better understood, and conclude with comments about sugar-based and related consumerism in later stages of modern economic history.

The simplest measure of the relationship between sugar and industrialization, employed both by Thomas and Bean and by Eric Williams (1944), is the profitability of the Atlantic triangle, which is then linked to protoindustrial capital accumulation. A more sophisticated argument, advanced by several contributors at a recent conference dedicated to the "Williams thesis," is to reevaluate the share of the Atlantic triangle(s) in overall British trade during the seventeenth and eighteenth centuries (Inikori 1987; Richardson 1987). Even more complex is the argument that efforts to maintain large-scale long-distance trade in exotic goods, no matter what its immediate economic value was, created new institutional capacities for lowering transaction costs, which were then adaptable to the more productive undertakings of an industrial economy (Austen 1987: 110; North forthcoming). At a more basic level, Immanuel Wallerstein (1974) has contended that the caloric content of imported sugar was critical to the labor capacity of early-modern Europe.

In all of these arguments, the attraction of sugar as a nonessential consumer item in Europe is either explicitly or implicitly treated as negative. For Thomas (1968) and Coelho (1974), the Atlantic triangle was a positive misallocation of resources inspired by the mistaken notions of mercantilist economics. Wallerstein and others go to great lengths to emphasize that the importance of sugar lay in its linkages with the production of other commodities, in part because they do not regard consumption as significant in itself.[1] Thomas and Bean's allusion to the physical harm resulting from sugar consumption is consistent with Sidney Mintz's (1985) view of sugar as a drug disguising real deteriorations in British popular diet. However, Mintz (ibid.: 180ff.), in the most challenging account we have of consumerism in the development of European capitalism, insists that it was precisely through their negative nutritional qualities that "sugar and other drug foods" contributed to industrialization; "by provisioning, sating—and, indeed, drugging—farm and factory workers, [these items] sharply reduced the overall cost of creating and reproducing the metropolitan proletariat."

The literature dealing more generally with European economic history on the eve of the industrial revolution (Mokyr 1977, 1984) has given greater attention to consumption issues—even when they systematically deny that demand factors are autonomously relevant to such change—than most historians of overseas trade have.[2] However, the explanations for evidently very dramatic rises of domestic European consumption standards from the late seventeenth century are usually framed outside the process of consumption itself and linked instead to changes in agricultural productivity and demography.[3] Imports of sugar and related goods become, in these arguments, mainly indicators of increased European effective demand rather than causal factors in new patterns of consumption.

Without denying either that the Atlantic sugar triangle had some role in the development of European productive capacity or that independent changes in that capacity were necessary conditions for consuming new imports, we are convinced that the significance of sugar in the protoindustrial economy can be better understood if we take more seriously its function in the transformation of European consumerism. Our assumption here is that consumption of a commodity like sugar is not a given of human nature, merely waiting for incomes and prices to reach the proper equilibrium, but that consumption systems are social and cultural constructs, linked to broader historical factors no less vitally than production systems are. The importation of large quantities of sugar and the closely related beverage commodities, cocoa, coffee, and tea, in the early-modern era had a decisive role in changing not only the patterns but also the organization and meaning of consumption in Europe. These changes can be seen in the levels and distribution of sugar consumption, in the economic and social institutions linked to this increased consumption capacity, and in the conceptions of economy and society provoked by the contemplation of entirely unprecedented experiences of consumption.

MEASUREMENT: SUGAR AS A MASS-CONSUMPTION COMMODITY

Measurement is the aspect of sugar consumption which has been most carefully studied by previous historians. There is a consensus in the literature that per capita consumption rose markedly from the latter 1600s. What we need to know more fully and precisely, however, is the rate at which such consumption rose before industrialization set in. To what degree did it extend beyond the elite and reach what could be called a "mass market"? Existing studies are ambivalent or even negative upon this point, mainly because the industrial revolution made possible an acceleration of mass consumption on a scale far greater than anything that had appeared before.[4] However, it is our argument that the qualitative break from elite to mass consumption took place before the industrial revolution and thus was as much its cause as its effect. Quantitative evidence does not suffice to identify the new form of consumerism we seek to define, but it is nonetheless important to examine carefully the relevant numbers and anecdotal evidence indicating how much was consumed in the protoindustrial era and by whom.

Table 1 is drawn mainly from a historian, Sheridan (1973), who has already argued strongly for the role of sugar (and its accompanying beverage, tea) as a major element of expanding consumption in Britain before the industrial revolution. From the rising rate of per capita consumption implied by the retained import statistics, we see that this increased use of sugar must have extended well beyond the elite (however defined) into the middle and even lower strata of society. Sheridan, Mintz, and others have provided ample anecdotal evidence to support such a view. It would be useful also to know something about the urban versus the rural distribution of sugar consumption. If, as naive logic (and the French case, discussed below) would lead us to suspect, a disproportionate part of this consumption did take place in urban areas, then the probability of "mass," that is, wide lower-class, consumption would rise, since the per capita figures within the urban population would be considerably higher. This last issue is even more important in the French situation (Table 2).

Slavery, Sugar, and Industrialization 99

Table 1   British sugar consumption, 1698–1775

	Net import (1,000s cwt.)	Growth (%)	Population (1,000s)	Pounds consumed per capita	Growth (%)
1698–1700	280.7	—	6,122	4.6	—
1701–5	262.4	−6.5	—	—	—
1706–10	300.5	14.5	6,352	4.7	3.1
1711–15	342.5	13.9			
1716–20	473.1	38.1	6,253	7.6	59.9
1721–25	571.9	20.8			
1726–30	686.2	19.9	6,183	11.1	46.7
1731–35	741.7	8.0			
1736–40	720.1	−2.9	6,153	11.7	5.5
1741–45	678.4	−5.7			
1746–50	761.5	12.2	6,336	12.0	2.7
1751–55	892.9	17.2			
1756–60	1,102.1	23.4	8,000	13.8	14.6
1761–65	1,063.6	−3.4			
1766–70	1,379.2	29.6	8,500	16.2	17.8
1771–75	1,542.9	11.8			
Net growth		449.7	—	—	253.9

Sources: Net imports, Sheridan 1973: 22; population, Mitchell 1962: 5. We have taken the highest of the England and Wales population series given here and added approximations from the one figure given for eighteenth-century Scotland.

A comparison of Tables 1 and 2 reveals that during the eighteenth century French sugar imports generally equaled, and sometimes exceeded, those of Britain. However, a far lower proportion of French sugar was retained for domestic consumption: France was obviously more committed to mercantilist policies of export balances than to internal consumer demand. Given the much larger French population, this means that per capita consumption was far lower than in Britain and, even within its absolute limits, subject to a much less sustained pattern of growth.

These data appear to support the observations of Sheridan (1973: 24–25) and others, based on literary evidence and more limited statistics, that France did not experience the same sugar

Table 2   French sugar consumption, 1730–90

	Total import (1,000s cwt.)	Retained import (1,000s cwt.)	Retained growth (%)	Population (1,000s)	Pounds consumed per capita
1730–34	590	240	—	23,000	1.0
1735–39	860	260	8.3	23,800	1.1
1740–42	900	380	46.2	24,200	1.6
1743–45	1,000	400	5.3	24,500	1.6
1750–52	900	400	.0	24,600	1.6
1753–55	1,200	450	12.5	25,000	1.8
1767–70	1,200	500	11.1	26,500	1.9
1770	1,640	800	—	27,066	3.0[a]
1771–73	1,400	650	30.0	27,200	2.4
1774–78	1,200	400	−38.5	27,700	1.4
1784–87	1,600	550	37.5	28,300	1.9
1788–90	1,850	600	9.1	28,560	2.1
Net growth			213.6		1.1 = 110%

Sources: Stein 1980: 5–6; Dupâquier et al. 1988: 64–68.
[a] This is the only single year for which Stein (1988b: 163–64) gives fairly precise import retention statistics. We have corresponded with him, but he is no longer able to supply us with the tabular import data which went into his 1980 published graphs.

and beverage consumer explosion as Britain. Indeed, French sugar consumption at its eighteenth-century high point (1770–73) did not match the level of Britain in 1698–1700.[5] Moreover, we know that even in the consumption of more basic domestic staples, France had not achieved Britain's security by the 1780s, a decade in which bread shortages remained a major factor in the French national economy (Rogers 1980).

In short, high levels of imported luxury food consumption appear to be linked to other indicators of economic growth pointing toward industrialization, in which France has always been assumed to have lagged considerably behind Britain. However, just as comparisons of French and British economic growth have lately undergone considerable revision, so the role of sugar consumption in these two societies may not be contrasted as simply as national statistical comparisons suggest.[6]

Much less research has been done on sugar consumption in eighteenth-century France than in Britain. However, Robert Stein (pers. com., 1988a; 1988b: 164) has discovered evidence of the distribution of sugar within France which suggests that per capita consumption in Paris during the 1780s may have been as high as 50 pounds and in Marseilles in 1755, nearly 10 pounds. Moreover, sugar shortages were the immediate cause of the popular Paris riots, which led in 1792 to the final overthrow of the French monarchy.[7] Thus, by the late eighteenth century sugar was sufficiently accessible to populations in the best-supplied centers of France as to be an established article of mass consumption.

Obviously, we need to know a good deal more about the role of sugar in eighteenth-century French commerce and industry as well as about consumption patterns before we can draw any definitive conclusions about its prominence in comparison to the more evident British case. What the French quantitative evidence does suggest is that the emergence of mass sugar consumption is not primarily created by the labor needs of an emerging industrial economy.[8] But does such a shift in consumption represent anything more than a "natural" response to cheaper commodities entering an invisible-handed market?

CONSTRUCTING A COLONIAL-GOODS MARKET

The measurement of European consumption of sugar and other colonial products allows us to establish the existence of greatly extended markets for such goods by the eighteenth century, but in itself such an exercise does not explain the structures of the markets, the extent to which their formation was related to major institutional and cultural changes, or the connection (if any) between enhanced colonial-goods consumption and the expansion of industrial production in the eighteenth century. An overview of the issues involved in these matters is possible if one thinks in terms of active construction of a broader European market for overseas goods in the seventeenth and eighteenth centuries, construction in the sense both of establishing institutions which promoted certain consumer behavior patterns and of assigning new meanings to colonial commodities in European conceptions of the economy.

The structural outlines of the seventeenth-century European market for overseas products are well known. It consisted of a network of interconnected urban markets arranged in a roughly concentric pattern, with Amsterdam (and, by the eighteenth century, London) at the center. The European marketing system was linked to its suppliers in a variety of ways, but most notably, for a wide range of Asian products, through large, bureaucratic, and more or less monopolistic companies. Smith (1982) has argued that an entirely new approach to marketing evolved from the peculiar circumstances of the Dutch East India Company. The company imported large quantities of new or previously rare goods for buyers who themselves sold on a continental scale. The bureaucracy in Asia which supplied these commodities (often in the form of "surprize" cargoes) represented a huge overhead cost, was only partly controllable from Holland, and, at best, required an unprecedentedly long lead time for orders. To deal with this situation, the Dutch East India Company (and its English rival) instituted a series of innovations in planning, research, and advertising that were later adapted to selling the output of industrial factories.

To what extent was sugar a part of all this? Sugar was, of course, distributed within Europe through the same general marketing structure as the other overseas products, but it was not really a new commodity, and it was never controlled by semimonopolistic organizations such as the East India companies. And, although it was a subject of considerable public discussion on the grounds of its possible effects on personal and national well-being, there seems to have been relatively little advertising or large-scale promotion of its use.[9] The expansion of sugar consumption was thus in some sense "invisible," quite literally so when sugar was incorporated into the preparation of other food and drink, such as pastries, puddings, and punches.

And yet, indirectly, sugar also participated in the institutional restructuring of consumer-goods markets, because its consumption came to be tied to that of tea, coffee, and cocoa, the first two of which were introduced in large quantities by the East India companies. The process by which it became a necessary complement to these items changed the nature of demand for sugar at the end of the seventeenth and the beginning of the eighteenth centuries. As Mintz (1985: 78, 108–50) explains, sugar became a "sweetener" more than a medicine, spice, decorative material, or preservative.[10] The markets for sugar in the latter forms, although dynamic in the seventeenth century, were limited compared to the tea-coffee-cocoa-sugar complex, which grew explosively in the eighteenth. So it was not by itself but as part of a broader and more complex consumption pattern, one actively expanded by new commercial institutions, that sugar came to have the immense impact that it did.

But how did sugar come to play so central a role? In the areas from which the "bitter" beverages were imported, they were seldom taken with sugar, nor were they originally so consumed in Europe. There is little evidence for a deliberate institutional promotion of the sweetening habit until it had already appeared.[11] In any case, the extent to which early-modern institutional marketing could actually create new consumption patterns, as opposed to exploiting opportunities presented by current fashions, was quite limited. It is obviously necessary to take into account the interaction between the set of items of which sugar was a part and sociocultural changes in Western Europe within which the consumption of those items had meaning. We can only point to a few features of this interaction here.

The actual process by which sugar became attached to tea and coffee consumption is not wholly known, but it may have started in the last quarter of the seventeenth century, not in order to sweeten those beverages but rather to encourage the use of tea as a medium for consuming sugar, whose negative effects on teeth and the body were becoming apparent, in a healthy way.[12] However it happened, sometime around 1700 tea and sugar, like coffee and sugar, became part of the daily routine that increasing numbers of Europeans, especially in Britain, practiced in their homes. Previously, the consumption of exotic beverages, usually without sugar, had taken place in aristocratic gatherings or in coffeehouses and teahouses. Much of the increase in coffee consumption in England between 1660 and 1700 had been due to the central role which coffeehouses had come to play in urban social, commercial, and political life. By 1700, the taking of tea and sugar with other foods in the morning and late afternoon had become a central domestic ritual in Britain and some other parts of Western Europe.[13] It was the generalization of this ritual that sustained the growing demand for tea and sugar throughout the eighteenth century. It also created the institutional and cultural framework within which the tea-and-sugar custom became a source of true mass consumption by the end of the eighteenth century, as tea prices continued to fall and people at lower levels of income adopted the custom.

The significance and impetus of these rituals have been debated. Chandra Mukerji (1983) suggests that they were related to similar developments in dress, which in turn arose from an increasing "materialism" in European social perceptions in the early-modern era. This materialism emerged out of the interaction between new printing technologies and the changing dynamics of European society. The new consumption patterns created a demand for printed Asian textiles which, by engendering competition between importers and domestic textile producers in Britain, helped stimulate technical innovation among the latter and therefore the industrial revolution. One could, in fact, demonstrate a similar linkage between the widespread adoption of the sugar-and-tea ritual and innovations in the pottery industry, but clearly textiles were far more important to early industrialization than "china." [14] More significant is Mukerji's linking of demand to social perceptions through rituals of consumption. But where did the rituals come from?

Many scholars have emphasized the effects of "bourgeois" imitation of elite dress and behavior in the seventeenth and eighteenth centuries. It is argued that, like most fashions, the taking of sugar by itself and with exotic beverages started as an elite custom and then "trickled down" to a "rising" bourgeoisie anxious to ape its betters (Freudenberger 1963).[15] When the trickle became a flood in the course of the eighteenth century, as yet poorer classes imitated *their* immediate superiors, mass consumption arose. Reductions in price, due to economies of scale in production and (in the late eighteenth century) lower duties on tea, sugar, and the like, obviously played a role as well. The "emulation" theory presupposes an ongoing change in class structure, with luxury consumption a sign of the rising importance of the middle class and accelerating individual social mobility, not an autonomous factor contributing actively to social restructuring.

There are several weaknesses in this sort of explanation. The reason that the emulation process continued for a century and a half—long after sugar and its associated beverages had ceased to be distinctively elite luxuries—is difficult to explain. Mintz (1985: 180–83) is undoubtedly on the right track in indicating that each social group that adopted the sugar-coffee-tea ritual in fact interpreted the meaning of the ritual in its own way, which limits the trickle-down explanation to the initial introduction of a commodity to a new group of potential users. Second, the explanation tends to ignore the fact that the mode of taking sugar, tea, and so on and the links to other social behavior actually changed markedly several times over the space of a few generations, and not always because of innovations introduced at the apex of society. The movement of coffee and tea use (at different times) from aristocratic parlors to public establishments to domestic houses shows this, as does the convergence of sugar taking with these forms of consumption. Each form had, for example, different political associations: with inner-elite politicking, with the primary system for clearing political and commercial information (in the coffeehouses), and, finally, with a domestic context in which public affairs were relatively insignificant.

In our opinion, the relationship between the sugar-tea-coffee-cocoa consumption complex and the broader culture of the immediate preindustrial period centered primarily on the phenomenon of respectability.[16] Respectability was not simply a matter of emulating elite fashions, although that was of course part of it. It was a distinctive cultural pattern, incorporating rather strict guidelines for individual and group behavior and an elaborate system of moral legitimation, that evolved in several European countries in the seventeenth and eighteenth centuries. Its emergence appears to have been connected to an array of economic changes, probably including a degree of income redistribution to the "middling" classes in an expanding commercial economy, but the connection was not an automatic or in every respect a direct one. Such a redistribution does not necessarily produce a particular, clearly defined cultural pattern; a rise in income among a group of people does not automatically mean that they will decide to spend a substantial part of it on sugar and tea. Economic factors fit themselves into broader patterns of thought and action that have immediate meaning to the participants, while deep coherence (such as the connection of respectability to the growth of a commercial middle class) is often the result of later rationalization. Material objects are also fitted into the same sort of pattern, to be manipulated, often in ritual fashion, to produce meaning. From this standpoint, the use of commodities such as sugar, coffee, and tea is not simply a sign of more "real" or "basic" socioeconomic changes but an active process of cultural construction in itself. As signs of deeper social phenomena, tea, sugar, printed cottons, and the like could easily have been interchanged with other products without much effect; indeed, if their consumption had simply been a matter of fashion, they almost certainly would have been.[17] But they persisted, apparently because the nature and the interpretation of these particular commodities came to play a significant role in shaping the rituals of respectability and thus of respectability itself.

In very-late-seventeenth- and early-eighteenth-century England, the consumption of sugar with tea and, to a lesser extent, with coffee became one of a number of significant elements of a cultural pattern that had meaning because it both signified and constituted the respectability of the people who participated in it. In a functional sense, one could say that respectability centered on a demand on the part of certain people for respect from people above them, below them, and at the same level in their society —respect that was to be manifested in different ways, depending on the social position from which the respect was to come. In this sense, taking tea and sugar in certain ways, with the proper implements, at the proper times of day, was connected to a wider array of cultural practices such as wearing fashionable clothes, following the now-generalized rules of "polite" behavior, and so forth. All of these things constituted a demand for respect. Most were tied to modes of moral justification for the respect demanded. Tea was especially significant in this regard, because it was consciously presented as a substitute for alcoholic drink and therefore not only symbolized but also was an aspect of respectable sobriety and concern for health (Short 1750: 28–33). Taking sugar in tea, as opposed to other forms of using it, such as in sugared decorations for foods, displayed and constituted similar qualities. Sugared food decorations symbolized exactly the aspects of aristocratic fashion that respectable people (regardless of their official or conventional social standing, which could in fact encompass nobility) rejected: immoderation and wastefulness, not to mention excessive ornateness. Consuming sugar in tea symbolized contrasting virtues, but it also was an alternate form of behavior that could be seen to have beneficial social consequences (by stimulating commerce without waste and, as part of the tea ritual, sociability without inebriation).[18]

That the tea-and-sugar pattern was fitted into the larger cultural pattern of respectability was of course of immense importance to Britain's overseas trade, especially as respectability became an increasingly significant element of British life after 1700. The lesser importance of the domestic market for sugar and tea in France may have been due in part to the evolution of alternate patterns and rituals of respectability (which featured unsweetened wine rather than tea, one suspects)—although the behavior of the revolutionary mob noted above may indicate that some of the same pattern appeared at the petit-bourgeois level even of French society.

The relationship between the sugar trade and eighteenth-century industrialization, seen from the demand side, is thus an extremely complex one. The rituals of respectable consumption of sugar and its related products did directly stimulate some industrial demand, especially in the pottery industry. But more important was the effect that the availability of commodities like sugar, tea, calicos, chinaware, and the like had on the formation of the rituals themselves and on the way those rituals were related to the social perceptions, political aspirations, and moral expectations that came to be seen as respectable. Respectability was one of the main sources of demand for the products of the early industrial revolution (cottons, tableware, etc.). Respectability is not a general condition of human social life but a very specific cultural pattern that developed in the period immediately preceding industrialization. Much more work on this subject needs to be done, but we can say that to the extent that sugar played a role in the construction of respectability, it contributed to the conditions that made industrialization historically possible.

TOWARDS A WORLD OF (EVER-EXPANDING) COMMODITIES AND CONSUMERS

It is widely recognized that eighteenth-century economic thinkers such as Adam Smith failed entirely to recognize the incipient industrialization whose posthumous ideologues they were to become (Caton 1985). What did capture the attention of economic discourse in the seventeenth and eighteenth centuries, however, was the spread of luxury consumption beyond the limited boundaries of elite society.

In the specific cases of sugar and tea, this discussion encompassed concern for the medicinal value frequently claimed by sellers of these commodities. In the late seventeenth century, evidence of the damage to physical, including dental, health that sugar could inflict was increasingly cited in opposition to the proponents of sugar. As we have seen, the habit of taking sugar in tea may have arisen out of an attempt to reconcile these perceptions.[19] However, the more significant issue was not the effect of hitherto rare or unknown foodstuffs on individual bodies but the social consequence of making such goods available cheaply enough that large numbers of people could consume them.

It is not necessary to explain at length the contradiction between these new conditions and traditional "sumptuary laws" (class-specific restrictions on various forms of consumption) as well as theories about backward-bending labor supply curves (assertions that cheaper consumer goods would decrease incentives to work). The intellectual confrontation between continuing belief in such restrictions and the expanding early-modern consumer market took place very publicly during the period itself and has been widely noted by economic historians (De Vries 1976).

The most serious form of this confrontation came in the debates over doctrines and policies generally referred to as mercantilism. Whether or not a self-defined ideology ever existed under this name, European states did systematically seek to maximize balances of trade and bullion accumulation by encouraging reexport rather than domestic consumption of colonial goods such as sugar. Mercantilist writers were driven not only by their belief in the correctness of these policy goals but also by the interplay of government revenue needs and the wishes of economic interest groups. Sugar importers and plantation owners, like the importers of Asian products, took an active part in the politics of mercantilism in Britain and France, inconsistently over time and frequently in conflict with other, similar interests. On the whole, however, the importing interest tended to argue against the idea that widespread consumerism endangered society and the economy. This position ultimately contributed to the nonzero-sum view of consumerism as public economic virtue advanced in Smith's *Wealth of Nations*, which thus, even without its author's foreseeing industrialism, became the canon of liberal economics. [20]

Among the forms of individual self-interest thus vindicated, sugar consumption is quite prominent, if for no other reason than that it grew so rapidly and conspicuously despite the prevalence of anticonsumerist doctrine in the first half of the eighteenth century. To see the economic role of sugar in these terms is to stand a major portion of the Williams thesis upon its head. Williams argued that the sugar-slave triangle and mercantilism were bonded together as an aspect of "primitive" capital accumulation, to be dispensed with once industrialism and free trade had triumphed. If instead we associate sugar with free trade and consumerism, we can appreciate its importance to industrialization independently of capital accumulation. This change in the evaluation of the products of West Indian slavery parallels our new understanding of slave labor itself, not as an inefficient anachronism of the ancien régime but as a precursor of industrial capitalist production. Even in the late eighteenth century, despite Adam Smith's denunciation of the inefficiency of bonded workers, other free-trade economists, such as Turgot, recognized the rationality of slave plantations under southern New World conditions (Davis 1975: 132–33).

Viewed from a cultural perspective, the very overvaluation of colonial trade by mercantilist theorists can be understood to have had a positive impact on the development of capitalist culture, whatever it may have done for or against the attainment of maximal monetary returns on available eighteenth-century capital. As students of political culture in eighteenth-century France and of contemporary U.S. election campaigns have noted, the outcome of any public debate may depend less on which side wins specific points than on which set of terms becomes the basis for subsequent discourse. Colonial commodities and their consumers, because of their visibility, gave rise to a debate about economics which, though temporarily won by the mercantilists, assured the eventual triumph of a position fully based upon a world of commodities and consumers. Mukerji (1983), with her emphasis upon media of communication and intraclass demonstration effects, addresses aspects of early-modern culture necessary for full communication of market information and propaganda. But more critical to the substance of modernism in this era is contemplation of the market itself as the central object and model of discourse for both economics and broader social issues.

CONSUMERISM, UNDERDEVELOPMENT, AND A ZERO-SUM UNIVERSE

Not the least appealing element of the Williams thesis was the connection it made between the anguish of slavery and what is regarded in both Marxist and liberal terms as the core of capitalist development. Slaves and proletarians may be victims of capitalism, but if industrialization is essentially based upon the material fruits of their labor, they remain part of its consciousness and may ultimately, as Marx promises, become its heirs. The present consumerist argument implies an alienation for third world primary producers far more cruel than what Marx ascribes to industrial workers. If the capitalism "constructed" from their efforts is essentially a cultural entity, its reality exists only for those who participate in the central arena. It is only the commodities and those who consume and exchange them, not the primary producers (despite the new construction of blacks in Africa and the New World by the abolitionist movement), who are visible and can visualize.

Within the mercantilist version of protoindustrial capitalism, Africans and West Indian slaves were valued as consumers of goods manufactured in Europe. However, as Eric Williams painfully noted, the triumph of liberalism brought a decline in concern for markets which lacked the dynamism of the Europeans' own world. Nonetheless, in absolute terms, Africa and the West Indies received far larger quantities of consumer goods from Europe and North America in the nineteenth century and afterwards than they had during their era of mercantilist prominence. Initially, these goods were mainly textiles, but eventually sugar/beverage consumption ("coca-colanization") played its role in this process.

The result of this kind of consumerism has not, however, been the replication of European industrialization processes in the tropics. Instead, economists have pointed to a negative demonstration effect in which a few import-substitution industries fail to close the gap between heightened consumption expectations and limited local productivity (Felix 1974).[21] Moreover, the experience of integration into the world market has not only failed to transplant "modernization" into third world culture but (at least in Africa) directly encouraged an economy of patron-client practices and witchcraft beliefs, based upon zero-sum visions of the material and social world (Berry 1985; Austen 1986).

Slavery, Sugar, and Industrialization   III

The orthodox response to this problem among development economists is to recommend that third world countries place more emphasis on production and in particular adjust food pricing and other policies so as to stop favoring urban consumers over rural producers (World Bank 1981). However, it has been argued recently, on the basis of successful industrialization in Asia, that the formula for economic development in the Third World should include the encouragement, or at least endorsement, of mass consumerism, with all its emphasis on urbanization, nonessential commodities, and advertisement (McGee 1985).[22] The relevance of earlier European experience for contemporary issues thus remains ambiguous.

Clearly, a study of consumerism in the pre-nineteenth-century connections between Africa, Europe, and the slave plantations of the New World cannot claim to resolve twentieth-century debates over worldwide development and underdevelopment. However, in revising our models for the international dimensions of the first industrial revolution, we can at least expand the intellectual, moral, and practical vision with which we contemplate the dilemmas of the present.

NOTES

1   The theoretical basis for this evaluation among dependency theorists such as Wallerstein is Sraffa 1960; however, similar arguments can be found in liberal economic literature following the less pretentious "linkage" arguments of Hirschmann (1958). In more empirical terms, this kind of argument does establish important links between *Asian* "luxury" trade and industrialization, since European tastes for both Chinese pottery and, more importantly, Indian cottons eventually led to the development of innovative import-substitution industries. However, this is not true for sugar, which inspired (at least within protoindustrial Europe) only the proliferation of small-scale food-processing enterprises. The affinity between the New World sugar plantation and the European industrial factory has often been remarked upon, but without any demonstration of an influence of the former upon the emergence of the latter; the influence suggested here came through the marketing and cultural assimilation of mass-produced consumption goods.
2   The major exceptions to this statement are Mintz (primarily an anthropologist rather than a historian) and the excellent, although essentially descriptive, chapter on British sugar and tea consumption in Sheridan 1973: 18–35.
3   This is the central argument of the very valuable chapter on consumption in De Vries 1976: 176–209; see also Eversley 1967. A more autonomous role for consumption is postulated by Jones (1973).

4   See Ewen 1976, Fraser 1981, and Zaretsky 1976; for a useful discussion of recent historiography on preindustrial consumerism, see McCracken 1988: 1–30.

5   This point holds even if we accept the maximum consumption figure of four pounds per capita given in Stein 1988b: 164.

6   For a review of studies closing the "development gap" between Britain and France see Cameron and Freedeman 1983.

7   For an indication of the kind of public discourse on sugar consumption which arose from these events and might form the basis of a fuller investigation of the French case, see Mathiez 1927: 29ff.

8   Mintz (1985: 188ff.) is thus unjustified in his self-righteous lipsmacking over the relative absence of sugar in the superior cuisine of France and China, as opposed to that of the drugged victims of industrialism and imperialism in Britain and the Third World.

9   Sugar, though retailed through the same channels as other colonial goods, appears to have been either omitted from marketing campaigns or incorporated into them as a "loss leader" (McKendrick et al. 1982: 93–94); however, there is one example of a folded and illustrated German handbill advertising sugar during the first half of the eighteenth century (see Baxa and Bruhns 1967: 48–49). Normally, however, sugar appears in British handbills as an element of trade policy under debate, as in the 1698 publication "On the State of the Sugar Plantations in America" (Goldsmith's Library 1698).

10 Ongoing research by Smith indicates that the British domestic fashion of drinking tea with sugar probably took hold widely between 1695 and 1700.

11 Unlike sugar, tea and coffee were regularly advertised in Britain in the late seventeenth and early eighteenth centuries (McKendrick et al. 1982: 146ff.; Cranfield 1962: 211: "The ordinary necessities of life were rarely advertized in these newspapers. . . . The only goods advertized with any frequency were luxury goods such as millinery from London, tea, coffee and chocolate, and wines and spirits"). See also the career of John Houghton, "Father of Publication Advertising" and seller of "coffee, tea, chocolate and other commodities" in late-seventeenth-century England (Presbrey 1929: 56ff.).

12 This possibility and the dating of the process to the end of the seventeenth century are based upon Smith's ongoing research in contemporary British literature and family account books.

13 On coffeehouses and teahouses see Ukkers 1935, 1: 38–43. The importance of domestic consumption of tea with sugar is emphasized in Short 1750: 32, 40.

14 See McKendrick et al. 1982: 99–145 on Josiah Wedgwood.

15 McCracken (1988: 11–16, 93–103) pushes the fashion changes back to Elizabethan England and refines the "trickle-down" theory of fashion changes.

16 For an indication of the complex relationships which might have existed between social identity and consumption in early-modern Europe, see Schama 1987: 130–220.

17 This apparently happened in France during the late seventeenth century,

Slavery, Sugar, and Industrialization   113

when the coffee and tea fashion was simply displaced (Dufour 1685: 27–40).

18 "Then consider the many sober Companies it [tea drinking] assembles both in Coffee-houses (which in London are only about six hundred) and private Houses. Observe we further the Business, Conversation and Intelligence it promotes, the Expence and Debauchery it prevents. Nor is its consumption of Sugar, which is a great Encouragement to our American Colonies to be forgot" (Short 1750: 32).

19 Baxa and Bruhns (1967: 44–46) cite treatises from as early as 1693 indicating potential damage to the teeth from sugar; the earliest such statement known to us is Blankaart 1683: 39–43.

20 The above argument has been developed most strongly by Appleby (1978); for a critique of Appleby's entire opus (which does not, in our opinion, diminish its value for the present argument), see Winch 1985.

21 For a Marxist version of this view, with special attention paid to the negative effects of mass-marketing culture, see Langdon 1981.

22 McGee not only counters the austerity doctrines of development economists but also suggests a productive role for "informal sectors," as opposed to the views of Berry (1985).

REFERENCES

Appleby, J. O. (1978) Economic Thought and Ideology in Seventeenth-Century England. Princeton: Princeton University Press.

Austen, R. A. (1986) "The criminal and the African cultural imagination: Normative and deviant heroism in precolonial and modern narratives." Africa 56: 385–98.

——— (1987) African Economic History: Internal Development and External Dependency. London: James Currey.

Bairoch, P. (1975) The Economic Development of the Third World since 1900. Berkeley and Los Angeles: University of California Press.

Baxa, J., and G. Bruhns (1967) Zucker im Leben der Völker: Ein Kultur- und Wirtschaftsgeschichte. Berlin: A. Bartens.

Berry, S. (1985) Fathers Work for Their Sons: Accumulation, Mobility, and Class Formation in an Extended Yoruba Community. Berkeley and Los Angeles: University of California Press.

Blankaart, S. (1683) Die Bogerlyke Tafel: Om lang gesond sonder ziekten te leven. Amsterdam.

Cameron, R., and C. E. Freedeman (1983) "French economic growth: A radical revision." Social Science History 7: 3–30.

Caton, H. (1985) "The pre-industrial economics of Adam Smith." Journal of Economic History 45: 833–53.

Coelho, P. R. D. (1974) "The profitability of imperialism: The British experience in the West Indies, 1768–1772." Explorations in Economic History 10: 253–80.

Cranfield, G. A. (1962) The Development of the Provincial Newspaper, 1700–1790. Oxford: Clarendon.

Davis, D. B. (1975) The Problem of Slavery in the Age of Revolution. Ithaca: Cornell University Press.

De Vries, J. (1976) The Economy of Europe in an Age of Crisis, 1600–1750. Cambridge: Cambridge University Press.

Dufour, P. S. (1685) Traitez nouveaux et curieux du café, du thé, et du chocolat. The Hague.

Dupâquier, J., et al. (1988) Histoire de la population française. Vol. 2, De la Renaissance à 1789. Paris: Presses universitaires de la France.

Eversley, D. E. C. (1967) "The home market and economic growth in England," in E. L. Jones and G. E. Mingay (eds.) Land, Labour, and Population in the Industrial Revolution. London: Arnold: 206–59.

Ewen, S. (1976) Captains of Consciousness: Advertising and the Social Roots of the Consumer Culture. New York: McGraw-Hill.

Felix, D. (1974) "Technological dualism in late industrializers: On theory, history, and policy." Journal of Economic History 34: 194–238.

Fraser, W. H. (1981) The Coming of the Mass Market, 1850–1914. Hamden, CT: Archon.

Freudenberger, H. (1963) "Fashion, sumptuary laws, and business." Business History Review 37: 37–48.

Goldsmith's Library (1698) "On the state of the sugar plantations in America." Broadsheet Collection, vol. 1, no. 87. London: Goldsmith's Library.

Hirschmann, A. O. (1958) The Strategy of Economic Development. New Haven: Yale University Press.

Inikori, J. E. (1987) "Slavery and the development of industrial capitalism in England." Journal of Interdisciplinary History 17: 739–93.

Jones, E. L. (1973) "The fashion manipulators: Consumer tastes and British industries, 1660–1800," in L. P. Cain and P. J. Uselding (eds.) Business Enterprise and Economic Change. Kent, OH: Kent State University Press: 198–226.

Langdon, S. W. (1981) Multinational Corporations in the Economy of Kenya. New York: St. Martin's.

McCracken, G. (1988) Culture and Consumption. Bloomington: Indiana University Press.

McGee, T. G. (1985) "Mass markets, little markets: Some preliminary thoughts on the growth of consumption and its relationship to urbanization: A case study of Malaysia," in S. Plattner (ed.) Markets and Marketing. Monographs on Economic Anthropology, No. 4. Lanham, MD: University Press of America: 205–33.

McKendrick, N., J. Brewer, and J. H. Plumb (1982) The Birth of a Consumer Society: The Commercialization of Eighteenth-Century England. London: Europa.

Mathiez, A. (1927) La vie chère et le mouvement social sous la Terreur. Paris: Payot.

Mintz, S. W. (1985) Sweetness and Power: The Place of Sugar in Modern History. New York: Viking.

Mitchell, B. R. (1962) Abstract of British Historical Statistics. Cambridge: Cambridge University Press.

Mokyr, J. (1977) "Demand versus supply in the industrial revolution." Journal of Economic History 37: 981–1008.
——— (1984) "Demand versus supply in the industrial revolution: A reply." Journal of Economic History 44: 806–9.
Mukerji, C. (1983) From Graven Images: Patterns of Modern Materialism. New York: Columbia University Press.
North, D. C. (forthcoming) "Institutions, transaction costs, and the rise of merchant empires," in J. D. Tracy (ed.) The Rise of Merchant Empires, vol. 2. Cambridge: Cambridge University Press.
Presbrey, F. (1929) The History and Development of Advertising. Garden City, NY: Doubleday, Doran.
Richardson, D. (1987) "The slave trade, sugar, and British economic growth, 1748–1776." Journal of Interdisciplinary History 17: 739–93.
Rogers, J. W., Jr. (1980) "Subsistence crises and political economy in France at the end of the ancien régime." Research in Economic History 5: 249–301.
Schama, S. (1987) The Embarrassment of Riches: An Interpretation of Dutch Culture in the Golden Age. New York: Knopf.
Sheridan, R. B. (1973) Sugar and Slavery. Baltimore: Johns Hopkins University Press.
Short, T. (1750) Discourses on Tea, Sugar, Milk, Made-Wines, Spirits, Punch, Tobacco, Etc. London.
Smith, Woodruff (1982) "The European-Asian trade of the seventeenth century and the modernization of commercial capitalism." Itinerario 6: 68–90.
Sraffa, P. (1960) The Production of Commodities by Means of Commodities. Cambridge: Cambridge University Press.
Stein, Robert (1980) "The French sugar business in the eighteenth century: A quantitative study." Business History 22: 3–17.
——— (1988a) Personal communication, November.
——— (1988b) The French Sugar Business in the Eighteenth Century. Baton Rouge: Louisiana State University Press.
Thomas, R. P. (1968) "The sugar colonies of the old empire: Profit or loss for Great Britain?" Economic History Review 21: 30–45.
———, and R. N. Bean (1974) "The fishers of men: The profits of the slave trade." Journal of Economic History 34: 885–914.
Ukkers, W. H. (1935) All about Tea. 2 vols., New York: Tea and Coffee Trade Journal Co.
Wallerstein, I. (1974) The Modern World System, vol. 1. New York: Academic.
Williams, E. (1944) Capitalism and Slavery. Chapel Hill: University of North Carolina Press.
Winch, Donald (1985) "Economic liberalism as ideology: The Appleby version." Economic History Review 38: 287–97.
World Bank (1981) Accelerated Development in Tropical Africa. Washington: World Bank.
Zaretsky, E. (1976) Capitalism, the Family, and Personal Life. New York: Harper and Row.

Part II
Great Britain

[4]

English Foreign Trade, 1700—1774[1]

By RALPH DAVIS

Eighteenth-century Englishmen were less troubled about the mercantile future of their country than their forefathers had been. The doubt which had nagged for so many decades at men's minds, whether England could successfully meet Dutch competition, faded unperceived during the long wars between 1689 and 1713 in which the rivals fought side by side. The newer commercial threat from the France of Louis XIV appeared less menacing after the military defeat of the French and the accessions made to England's colonial territories. As in every age, there were propagators of gloom and prophets of catastrophe; but the general atmosphere was one of optimism. Yet widespread optimism was little better founded than the pessimism it replaced. The bounding growth that had characterized English overseas trade before these wars – at the very time when fears of Dutch competition were most intense – was not resumed when the wars were over; though the return of peace saw a quick recovery of the wartime drop in trade, there succeeded a long period in which development was painfully slow. Although overseas trade did eventually break through into another spell of headlong expansion, the eighteenth century was by no means the long success story for English merchants that its predecessor had been. It was a century of realignment of trade – geographically and in terms of commodities – and not until towards mid-century could the swelling tide be seen unmistakably rolling in again.

This study of English trade up to the time when American Independence and Industrial Revolution fundamentally changed the conditions in which it was carried on, is based in the main on the trade figures for 1699–1701, 1722–4, 1752–4 and 1772–4, which are summarized in the Appendix.[2] It attempts to

[1] I am grateful to Dr A. H. John for valuable criticisms. A version of this paper was read to Prof. Habakkuk's seminar in Oxford and to Dr John's seminar in London in December 1961, and its present form shows, I hope, the benefit of the discussion and criticism it met on those occasions.

[2] These are derived from the Inspector-General's returns in the Public Record Office (Customs 3). Some doubt has been thrown by historians on the value of these statistics, but I do not believe the revision of them, if it were possible, would very seriously alter the general picture shown here. Much error in important detail is evident, and some of the necessary modifications are indicated below; but the most serious (and most carefully studied) errors in the statistics arise from the sharp advance in the general price level which affects only the last decade or so of the century. Prof. T. S. Ashton has a lucid and temperate discussion of their use and weaknesses in his introduction to E. B. Schumpeter, *English Overseas Trade Statistics, 1697–1808* (Oxford, 1960), pp. 1–9.

This paper deals only with *English* trade. Despite the Union with Scotland in 1707, the customs records of Scotland were kept separately, and Scottish statistics are available regularly and in orderly form only from 1755. At that time, they show Scotland's trade as having about 5 per cent of the value of England's. Large quantities of Scottish goods were sent to London for export, and appear, therefore, only in the English trade statistics.

In analysing the statistical records a number of arithmetical errors have been discovered, and the

show which were the lagging and which the dynamic elements in English trade, and to suggest their relation to general economic development.

No year is 'normal', but these groups of three, with slightly irregular intervals, avoid war and major convulsions and contain reasonably mixed conditions. 1699–1701 was a period of growth in renewed peace towards good trade, though not of high boom. 1722–4 saw emergence into fair prosperity from the slump which followed the South Sea Bubble. 1752–4 was marked by a turn down towards depression from a beginning in high prosperity. 1772–4 spans a very brief if intense commercial crisis, but compensates for this by including good years on either side. None of these periods shows unrelieved depression or unclouded prosperity; [1] their comparison should give a fair illustration of the long-term development of trade, but it is not suggested that the intervening years saw uninterrupted and even processes of change.

For many centuries England's export trade consisted almost entirely of wool or woollen manufactures, and as late as 1700 the latter made up the sole considerable export of England's own produce. Supplemented during the later seventeenth century by growing re-exports of colonial and Indian wares, the constantly increasing export of woollens had with their help paid for more imported manufactures (chiefly linens) from the industrial areas of Europe, for more wine, fruit, sugar and tobacco from southern Europe and the Americas, and for a rising volume of industrial raw materials.[2] The English sheep had for so long carried most of the burden of English trade expansion on its back that at the opening of the eighteenth century its continuing success in this role (when the return of peace should permit) was taken for granted as the essential basis of English prosperity.

Yet woollen exports had already lost their momentum of growth, and they did not recover it. This is the more surprising when we observe the general tendency for the price of wool to fall, from the Restoration until far into the eighteenth century; [3] the great extension of production of cloth in such low-wage areas as Devonshire, Lancashire and Yorkshire; [4] and the exploitation, in the first two of these areas at least, of the extraordinarily cheap wool and spinning labour of Ireland. There were strong reasons, even in the absence of technical innovation, why many grades of English cloth should have been produced much more cheaply around 1720 or 1750 than half a century earlier. Nevertheless the European market, which took 92 per cent of the woollen goods exported in 1699–1701, showed almost complete stagnation. The rapid

---

figures here consequently differ from the Inspector-General's totals and others derived from them. The most important of these errors are: over-addition of London exports to Spain, 1752, by £100 thousand; under-addition of London exports to Virginia and Maryland, 1773, by £100 thousand; under-addition of London imports from Russia, 1773, by £161 thousand.

[1] T. S. Ashton, *Economic Fluctuations in England, 1700–1800* (Oxford, 1959), pp. 140–60.

[2] R. Davis, 'English Foreign Trade, 1660–1700', *Econ. Hist. Rev.* n.s. VII (1954).

[3] See J. R. McCulloch (ed.), *Early Tracts on Commerce* (1856), p. 321; *House of Commons Journals, 1737–42*, p. 357; *A Short View of the Rise, Progress and Establishment of the Woollen Manufacture* (1753).

[4] This intense industrial activity ultimately contributed to rises in wages both in Devonshire and in the north of England; but for some decades these areas had advantages over, for example, East Anglia.

ENGLISH FOREIGN TRADE, 1700-1774 287

advance of export to Spain and Portugal, which did continue, was balanced by decline elsewhere; so the total of woollens exported to Europe remained almost unchanged (apart from short-term fluctuation) until 1750, and the brief burst of increased activity in the fifties was followed by decline. The growing contribution of other manufactured exports to the total English trade with Europe was on too small a scale to compensate for this failure of the one great traditional product.

Industry was being developed and diversified rapidly not only in England but also through much of western and central Europe, to such a degree that for a time the effect was to discourage rather than stimulate mutual trade in manufactures. Industrial self-sufficiency was increasing; and neither England nor continental states had much chance of selling the products of new or small industries, without special cost advantages, across national frontiers and against the barriers of transport costs, customs duties and the national ties of merchants. At the same time, national self-sufficiency was checking international trade even in those manufactured textiles, produced by large highly-specialized industries, which had long circulated throughout Europe.

English woollen merchants, baffled by the effects of this general tendency towards self-sufficiency, might have seen illustrations of it on their own doorstep, in their own importing habits. The total English import of manufactures from Germany, Holland, Flanders and France fell from £1,015 thousand to £471 thousand per annum during the first three-quarters of the eighteenth century. Two groups of government measures contributed to bringing this about. The action taken by the ministers of Louis XIV to build up French political and economic power had produced a series of English responses in the mercantile field; prohibition of trade with France between 1678 and 1685 and again in wartime after 1689, and the imposition in 1693 and 1696 of special tariffs on French goods, virtually prohibitive so far as manufactures were concerned, which remained effective until the signing of the Eden Treaty in 1786. A wide variety of manufactures had been imported from France, many of them fine goods of which the coarser varieties were made in England. Quantities of them were still smuggled in; but behind the tariff barrier, with the aid of the technical skills of Huguenot refugees, industries were built up which went far towards replacing them.

Among manufactured imports, however, the most important category was that of coarse linens from Holland and Germany. Imports had grown fast in the seventeenth century, for England had no considerable industry to compete effectively or to clamour loudly for protection. In the new century the general heightening of tariff barriers in England was accompanied by steps which encouraged the bringing in of coarse linens from England's dependencies rather than from the continent. The import of linen wares from Ireland was aided by the removal of duties on them in 1697, while the Union of 1707 threw down all tariff barriers between England and Scotland. There were further measures to advance the Irish and Scottish linen industries; the abolition of the Irish export duty in 1705, the creation of a Board to encourage the growing of flax and the training of weavers and spinners in Scotland in 1727, and the provision in 1742 of a bounty on Scottish and Irish linen exported from England. With their natural advantages of cheap labour and lands suited to flax cultivation, their preference over continental goods in the English market, and presently the export bounty, the Irish and Scottish linen industries grew with mounting speed in the second and third quarters of the century; [1] by 1774 most of the linen used in England and her colonies came from within the British Islands and the import from Germany and Holland had been cut in half. [2]

Meanwhile continental development towards self-sufficiency nibbled in the same way at the market abroad for English woollens. France, of course, had built up her woollen industry and closed her gates to imports in the seventeenth century, and was becoming a serious competitor in south European markets. The growth of the German industry threatened many of the oldest English markets in central Europe, and it began to receive some measure of protection from the Imperial government. [3] English merchants engaged in the Hamburg trade never tired of explaining how the reduction of English linen imports caused a corresponding decline in woollen exports. [4] Sweden put a heavy duty on imported woollens to protect her infant industry, and thereby practically ended their import from England. Even Spain and Portugal which, against the general European trend, took increasing quantities of English woollens throughout the first half of the century, began to foster their own industries in the fifties and sixties, and their demand for English manufactures at last slackened and fell away. [5]

English commercial relations with Europe were in fact becoming less and less concerned with its industrialized north-western corner and increasingly with the Baltic and Mediterranean lands; a geographical shift associated with a long-term change in the character of English demands – not only with the declining demand for manufactured goods, but even more with the rising English need for raw materials for her growing industries. With every decade the imports of flax and hemp, textile yarns, iron, dyestuffs, oil, silk, timber and cotton showed a rise; and most of these things came from the Baltic or Scandinavian coasts or from the shores of the Mediterranean. [6]

---

[1] Excellent accounts of these industries are C. Gill, *The Rise of the Irish Linen Industry* (Oxford, 1925); H. Hamilton, *The Industrial Revolution in Scotland* (Oxford, 1932), chap. IV. There is no history of the English linen industry.

[2] A growing import of cheap Russian linen partly accounts for the decline of import through Hamburg or Amsterdam; but the total coming from continental sources was falling sharply by mid-century, and was already quite outstripped by Scottish and Irish supply.

[3] See the long report on the German industry and the prospects for Anglo-German trade (1716) in the papers of the Board of Trade in the P.R.O. (C.O. 388-18-68).

[4] Petitions in *House of Commons Journals, 1702–04*, p. 498; *1711–14*, p. 426; *1718–22*, p. 295; *1737–41*, p. 121; *1741–45*, pp. 631, 817.

[5] R. Herr, *The Eighteenth Century Revolution in Spain* (Princeton, 1958), pp. 123–44; A. Christelow 'The Economic Background of the Anglo-Spanish War of 1762', *Journ. Mod. Hist.* XVIII (1946), pp. 22–36; V. M. Shillington and A. B. W. Chapman, *The Commercial Relations of England and Portugal* (1908), pp. 260–4, 277–9.

[6] In these analyses trade with Turkey is included as 'European'. It was a branch of the Mediterranean trade, altogether distinct from the other Asian trade carried on, via the Cape of Good Hope, by the East India Company.

ENGLISH FOREIGN TRADE, 1700–1774   289

Imports from Europe (excluding Ireland)
(thousands of £s)

	1699–1701	1722–4	1752–4	1772–4
Manufactures:				
linens	846	922	853	594
other	339	220	100	101
Foodstuffs	864	843	659	1,141
Raw materials	1,507	1,748	2,200	2,834

In the seventeenth century there had been an approximate balance between the three classes of imports – manufactures, foodstuffs and raw materials – but this was now being tipped sharply, in European trade, towards the last of these.[1]

If English manufactures failed to expand their European market significantly, why did they need this fast-growing supply of raw materials? In part it was to replace some imported goods by their counterparts made at home. Moreover, the demand for manufactured goods was growing as the English became more prosperous or, more accurately, had an increasing surplus of money to spend during a half-century in which basic foodstuffs were becoming cheaper.[2] Expanding fleets, naval and mercantile, required great quantities of imported 'naval stores'. But to a significant degree English industrial growth now served an entirely new field of overseas trade – the demand for manufactures from the fast-multiplying population of the Americas.

The spreading of industry on the continent of Europe had set limits to the expansion of English cloth markets there. No such limits yet existed to the demand for all kinds of English goods on the other side of the Atlantic. In the northern colonies land was endless and men were few; the wage-earner could command very high payment, and only those craftsmen whose work had to be carried out on the spot were employed in large numbers. English artisans were reluctant to go to the slave islands of the Caribbean, and the essential workmen were attracted only in small numbers and by high wages. Until almost the end of our period the colonies had little industry of their own apart from some household production of coarse woollens and linens; and this not because of repressive measures of the home government, but simply because colonial labour costs were far higher than those in England. Only in such a case as that of shipbuilding, where local needs were great and an abundance of cheap raw materials set off the high wages, was local industry able to exclude English products. The colonists had to import their requirements of manufactures; and they were accustomed by long habit, as they were compelled by the Navigation Acts, to deal with English merchants and to take their imported requirements from England. Nearly all these goods were made in England, Scotland or Ireland; German and Dutch linens were the only important exceptions, and they were being replaced from British sources by mid-century. Moreover,

[1] The growth of smuggling modifies the picture presented by these statistics, since it was chiefly concerned with wine, brandy and fine manufactured goods.
[2] A. H. John, 'Aspects of English Economic Growth in the first half of the Eighteenth Century', *Economica*, XXVIII (May, 1961), pp. 181–7.

colonial population, small as it was by comparison with that of European countries, was growing at a tremendous pace, from a few hundred thousand in 1700 to approach three millions in 1774, and wealth and income were evidently growing faster. The protected Anglo-Scottish market of some eight or nine million people in 1774 had acquired a very useful colonial supplement.

The principal dynamic element in English export trade during all the middle decades of the eighteenth century was, therefore, colonial trade. This is well known. More than this; colonial trade introduced to English industry the quite new possibility of exporting in great quantities manufactures other than woollen goods, to markets where there was no question of the exchange of manufactures for other manufactures. At last in these protected markets outlets were appearing for English metalwares, Scottish linens, and a host of other things, in quantities which by the eve of the American Revolution had come to rival the whole export of the woollen industry itself. Moreover, so rapidly was American expansion proceeding after mid-century that even woollens began to go to the colonies in a volume that usefully supplemented the declining European demand. The process of industrialization in England from the second quarter of the eighteenth century was to an important extent a response to colonial demands for nails, axes, firearms, buckets, coaches, clocks, saddles, handkerchiefs, buttons, cordage and a thousand other things; a variety of goods becoming so wide that the compilers of the Customs records tired of further extending their long schedules of commodities and lumped an increasing proportion of these exports under the heading of 'Goods, several sorts'.[1] I have taken it for granted that these were nearly all manufactures. In the iron and brass industries and all the metal-working crafts dependent on them, colonial demands made an important supplement to those of the growing home market, and must have played a considerable part in encouraging the new methods of organization, the new forms of division of labour and the improved techniques, through which the metal industries were to make a major contribution to industrial revolution in England. Other industries, smaller and with less familiar histories, may well have been similarly affected.

The colonial market was only one – though much the most important one – of a group in which English goods had special advantages of a character they could not secure in continental Europe. Ireland was very much a dependency of the British crown. Its trade with Europe, though substantial, was limited by the ban on the export of Irish woollen cloth; its colonial trade was restricted by the Navigation Acts; the combination of these measures with the strong personal and political connexions with England ensured that Ireland looked to England for nearly all its imported manufactures. In the course of the eighteenth century this Irish connexion became of very great importance. Ireland's recovery from the extreme depression into which it had been beaten

[1] For this reason the totals of particular kinds of trade in E. B. Schumpeter, *op. cit.* cannot be used in this kind of analysis. Mrs Schumpeter listed and totalled the values of some of the more important commodities, but her selected commodities form a rapidly declining proportion of non-woollen exports. Thus of manufactured goods exported, other than woollens, she covers some two-thirds (in value) in 1699–1701, and some one-third of the much greater total of 1772–4. The table in A. H. John, *op. cit.* p. 178, is therefore not comparable with the figures used in this paper.

by the military campaigns of 1689–92 was at first very slow, but towards mid-century a rapid economic expansion was under way – in which the export trade in linen goods and livestock products played a great part – and the Irish market began to absorb considerable imports from England.[1] Like the American colonies, Ireland was ready to take a wide variety of manufactured goods. The strength of the native woollen industry made it impossible to sell English woollens in any quantity until the new West Riding products made their impact in the fifties; but metalwares, silks, hats and other goods went in great and fast-growing volume. A new view of Ireland, not as a rival but as an aid to English expansion, began to appear. 'If we consider (apart from pre-judices and particular interests) how greatly we are already Gainers by the Trade and Industry of that Country, poor as it is, we shall perhaps . . . begin to think that the Wealth and Prosperity of Ireland is not only compatible with that of England, but highly conducive also to its Riches, Grandeur and Power.'[2] Further afield, West African demand for English goods grew rapidly in the forties, providing a useful stimulus to the cotton industry in particular; a demand ultimately derived, of course, from the colonial import of slaves for the plantations. In Asia, the English merchant settlements which had always paid out great quantities of silver for the goods which they bought for England now began to develop a demand for English manufactures. The growth of military establishments and the securing of a firm grip on Bengal and Madras, with the trend towards English political dominance and all that this meant in terms of local revenue, was accompanied by a big expansion of English exports of all kinds to India, reaching substantial proportions after 1748.

Exports of Manufactures from England
(thousands of £s)

	1699–1701	1722–4	1752–4	1772–4
Woollen goods:				
Continental Europe	2,745	2,592	3,279	2,630
Ireland and Channel Islands	26	19	47	219
America and Africa	185	303	374	1,148
India and Far East	89	72	230	189
Other manufactures:				
Continental Europe	456	367	647	987
Ireland and Channel Islands	60	40	168	280
America and Africa	290	376	1,197	2,533
India and Far East	22	15	408	501

The principal dynamic element in English trade expansion during the second half of the seventeenth century had been the re-export of colonial goods. This branch of trade continued to be of great importance in the new century, kept its place with a little over a third of the growing total of exports throughout the period, still providing an important element in overall growth though now

[1] On the growth of Irish prosperity from about 1725 onward, see D. MacPherson, *Annals of Commerce* (1806), III, 181, 289; A. Dobbs, *An Essay on the Trade and Improvement of Ireland* (Dublin, 1729).
[2] *A Collection of Tracts concerning the Present State of Ireland with respect to its Riches, Revenue, Trade and Manufactures* (1729), p. 25.

quite overshadowed in the *pace* of its expansion by the miscellaneous manufactures. Indeed, the rate of growth of the re-export trade slowed markedly in
the early part of the century and was never fully recovered.

One other branch of export trade must be briefly mentioned. Not only was
England nearly self-sufficient in manufactures; for a long time all needs of
basic foodstuffs were produced at home. The appearance of corn surpluses
late in the seventeenth century led to a system of bounties to encourage their
export,[1] and this export reached a peak in the years round 1750 when it
contributed quite significantly to the total English export trade. The new
growth of population which was then beginning, while providing the labour
force for accelerated industrial expansion, quickly absorbed the food surpluses
and turned England in two decades from a large corn exporter to a substantial
importer – the sharpest, most sudden large change in England's trading
situation in our period. Legislation was introduced to discourage export and
facilitate the import of corn, while the barriers which had long before been
erected against the import of Irish meat and dairy produce were dismantled.[2]
Despite the apparent panic over food supplies in the sixties, however, the
deficit was for a long time only a marginal one, as the surplus had been.

The sketch of export trade more or less explains developments in imports as
well. By mid-century, more variegated foodstuffs came from the colonies, more
raw materials from Europe; the growing surplus of colonial foodstuffs over
English needs went to Europe to pay for the rising purchases of raw materials,
while America itself – to complete the circle of trade – was satisfied for her
increasing supplies by receiving in exchange a deepening and extending
stream of English manufactures.

Summary Table of English Foreign Trade
(percentages of total exports and imports)

	Total		Europe *		Asia, Africa and America	
	1699–1701	1772–4	1699–1701	1772–4	1699–1701	1772–4
EXPORTS						
Woollen mfrs.	47·5	26·7	43·2	18·2	4·3	8·5
Other mfrs.	8·4	27·4	3·5	6·2	4·8	21·2
Foodstuffs	7·6	3·7	6·7	2·7	·9	1·0
Raw materials	5·6	5·1	5·3	4·7	·3	·4
Total exports	69·1	62·9	58·7	31·8	10·3	31·1
Re-exports	30·9	37·1	25·9	30·5	5·0	6·6
Total of exports and re-exports	100·0	100·0	84·6	62·3	15·3	37·7
IMPORTS						
Manufactures	31·7	16·9	22·1	10·7	9·5	6·2
Foodstuffs	33·6	50·9	15·5	12·0	18·1	38·9
Raw materials	34·7	32·2	30·5	24·7	4·3	7·5
Total imports	100·0	100·0	68·1	47·4	31·9	52·6

* In this table, Ireland and Turkey are both included in 'Europe'.

[1] See D. G. Barnes, *A History of the English Corn Laws* (1930), chaps. I and II.
[2] *Ibid.* pp. 31–45.

The general pattern of English export trade between 1700 and 1774 has been indicated. To understand its meaning, however, we must briefly adopt a wider perspective. The export trade had been growing for centuries, but its development had not been smooth. It had gone forward in a series of spurts, each touched off by some new factor which operated violently for a time and then lost its initial force. The first of these which is relevant to this discussion is the change in the nature of woollen cloth exports which had its origin late in the sixteenth century. The political troubles which at that time caused havoc in the cloth-finishing industries of Brabant, and destroyed Antwerp's international trading position, drove English merchants to seek a new centre to replace Antwerp as their chief market, and to sell cloth directly to many customers formerly supplied through Antwerp. During much the same period, Spanish and Mediterranean markets began to present new openings to English cloth, not merely because of Antwerp's troubles but also by reason of the increasing costs of Italian and Spanish production. So the English woollen industry expanded the value of its exports in two ways. It developed the dyeing and finishing branches in association with its traditional products,[1] so that the proportion exported in a finished and dyed state went up, in the course of the seventeenth century, from about one-third to almost 100 per cent.[2] The slowly declining number of these cloths of traditional type exported during the century therefore provided, until near its end, an increasing value in export trade.[3] Secondly, it created alongside the old industry a new one, chiefly engaged in the making of worsteds of various kinds, which found that its products could be sold in great and rapidly growing quantities in Spain and Portugal, and to a lesser extent in Italy.[4] With the older branch of the industry slowly increasing the value of its export, and a new branch burgeoning so vigorously that it soon out-rivalled the old, cloth exports as a whole were rapidly expanding during most of the seventeenth century. But difficulties began to appear. In the third quarter of the century, the export of the old types of cloth reached a position in which nearly all were going out dyed and finished, and as their numbers were slowly decreasing their total value began to fall well before the end of the century. Woollen industries were developing on the continent, and in some cases secured tariff protection against English competition.[5] A tendency was appearing for replacement of even the lightest woollens by cottons, linens and silks; above all, the use of Indian textiles in Europe leaped forward at an astonishing pace from the 1670's. Though their

[1] The export to Antwerp had been principally of undyed, unfinished cloths, which were dyed and dressed there.

[2] The figures for the first decade of the seventeenth century can be found in A. Friis, *Alderman Cockayne's Project and the Cloth Trade* (Copenhagen, 1927), pp. 61–8.

[3] The value added to a cloth by dyeing and dressing varied, according to the dye used, between about 30 and 100 per cent.

[4] For general discussion of these developments, see F. J. Fisher, 'London's Export Trade in the Early Seventeenth Century', *Econ. Hist. Rev.* n.s. III (1950); R. Davis, 'England and the Mediterranean, 1570–1670', *Essays in the Economic and Social History of Tudor and Stuart England*, ed. F. J. Fisher (Cambridge, 1961).

[5] See p. 288 *supra*, and C. Wilson, 'Cloth Production and International Competition in the Seventeenth Century', *Econ. Hist. Rev.* n.s. XIII (1960).

cheapness secured these Indian fabrics new customers who would not have bought the dearer woollens in the same quantity, it is certain that they made some inroads on the demand for woollen fabrics at home and abroad. In 1708 Defoe could write – no doubt with his customary exaggeration: 'Almost everything that used to be wool or silk, relating either to the dress of the women or the furniture of our houses, was supplied by the Indian trade.' [1] These various influences were combining, towards the end of the seventeenth century, not indeed to reduce woollen exports, but to give a check to their constant expansion. And the momentum once lost could not be recovered; the woollen export neither advanced nor retreated – it hung fire.

The export trade as a whole was not, however, destined to languish in these last decades of the seventeenth century. Its total was carried forward on the crest of another wave, this time of the re-exports of colonial and Indian goods. Before the Civil War, re-exports were trivial; by the sixties they were making a notable addition to English native exports; by the end of the century they added to that total no less than 50 per cent. In this new spurt forward, cheapness was the factor that made possible the growth of trade. Tobacco and sugar produced under plantation conditions could be sold at prices that brought them within the reach of most of Europe's population, and calicoes were cheap because of the low earnings of their Indian producers. The explosive initial rate of expansion could not have been continued indefinitely; but in fact the trade in each of the three chief re-export commodities met special difficulties in the early eighteenth century. First, sugar. The French development of the island of Hispaniola (present day San Domingo), which they acquired from Spain in 1697, faced the small British West Indian islands and their over-cropped soils with competition at prices they could not meet outside the protected British market. Sugar re-exports to continental Europe fell away to negligible proportions in less than two decades after the Peace of Utrecht; only the Irish market remained. Tobacco re-export continued to grow fast, but for some decades after 1707 its increase was channelled through Glasgow, and until this port had fully worked up the trading possibilities which the Act of Union gave it, the *English* tobacco trade could make little progress. The re-export of Indian textiles was checked by the prohibitions and discriminations against them set up by nearly every European government in the years round 1700, though the trade still expanded slowly. In the first quarter of the new century, therefore, the total of tobacco, sugar and calico re-exports, which had been growing so fast, remained virtually stable. [2]

Both the dynamic factors in seventeenth-century trade expansion – first the woollen export and then the new re-export – were therefore losing strength around 1700. The onset of war in 1689 brought a sharp check to all trade, but this merely crystallized at a particular point of time the ending of a phase. The long, rapid, exhilarating rise in English trade was at last steadying down, under a variety of influences. Two great waves of progress had nearly spent their force, and it was this fact, not merely the long wars of 1689–1713, that slowed

[1] Defoe's *Review*, 3 January 1713.
[2] R. Davis, 'English Foreign Trade, 1660–1700', *Econ. Hist. Rev.* n.s. VII (1954).

the overall expansion of trade for nearly half a century. There had to be a pause, for the next wave had not yet gathered its strength. Such buoyancy as remained in the export trade in the first half of the eighteenth century, indeed, came from returning prosperity in Spain and Portugal; in the interval before they, too, developed autarchic ambitions, their growing demand for English manufactures offset the decline in export to other parts of Europe. But it did no more; the products of English industry in its old form had very nearly reached the saturation point in their European markets.

The third leap forward, as we have seen, resulted from the expanding demand for manufactured goods of all kinds, coming from the growing colonial population. It was a most vigorous leap, which carried forward the total of exports very strongly right up to the Industrial Revolution. Even before 1700, though still in an embryonic stage, this trade had been developing fast; its growth accelerated in the late twenties and thirties, and was then halted by the onset of war. Indeed, the war of 1739–48 appeared to nip in the bud unmistakable signs that exports as a whole were beginning to gather way once more. Wars always imposed painful setbacks upon foreign trade, and this one was no exception, but there were significant differences in the way trade responded to such handicaps. During 1689–1713 the state of war concealed a weakening of England's foreign trading position that would have occurred anyway, war or no war. In 1739–48, on the other hand, the armed conflict was holding back trade that had great expansive potentiality, damming up demand that waited hungrily to be fed. The peace of 1748, therefore, found England ripe for an extraordinary increase in the volume of export trade. The major and continuing influences were the now violently accelerating growth in the export of miscellaneous manufactures to the colonies, Ireland and India, which had brought their total to very large proportions. It was reinforced by the growth to maturity of new re-export trades; in mid-century Carolina rice and China tea were being sent out from England in very large quantities, and they were soon to be reinforced by West Indian coffee. The re-export trade, which had languished for so long, grew very fast during the third quarter of the century. Significant additions to the total of exports were made, during the first years after the peace of 1748, by more temporary influences: the release of Spanish demand which had been pent up by nine years of war with England, and the export of surplus corn which reached its peak in the years round 1750. All these factors working together pushed English exports forward at a tremendous pace before the onset of new war in 1756.

Trade expanded slowly in the early part of the century because there was cessation or slowing of growth in some directions without the emergence of important counterbalancing forces elsewhere. In the third quarter of the century, however, decline in certain branches did not prevent a rapid expansion of total exports. The corn export ceased abruptly in this period; trade with the Iberian peninsula – the one branch of European woollen export which had always retained some vigour – turned downward as the ministers of Spain and Portugal strove to encourage and protect their home industries. Yet the continuing rise of colonial, Irish and Indian markets for manufactures, which now outstripped those of Europe, supported by renewed advance in re-export trade, were by now more than enough to outweigh these depressive effects.

It remains to draw attention to a doubt about the healthiness of the sharp rise in exports to America. The period of most rapid growth was the Seven Years' War itself; it was most marked in relation to the colonies which were the principal bases of military operations. Clearly, it represented in some degree the private shipments by contractors of army stores,[1] the supply of goods to meet the demands made from the pay of officers and soldiers sent out from England, and the spending on English-made goods of local earnings from supply and service to the armies. War conditions may be set aside as exceptional; but it may be wondered how much of the enhanced export to America in the post-war years resulted from the demands of the garrisons which were main-tained on a much larger scale than before the war in the colonies; garrisons whose pay and provisions were paid for in England, drew funds from the pocket of the English taxpayer, and so artificially replaced a home demand for goods by one which drew the goods across frontiers at which Customs officers stood guard, noting them all down and so turning them into International Trade. The buoyancy of Anglo-American trade after 1783 suggests we should not overstress the importance of this; but it cannot be ignored in discussion of the last years of colonial trade.[2]

The seventeenth-century Navigation Laws, which were not seriously modified before 1786, gave English merchants and shipowners an almost complete monopoly of trade with the colonies. The overall effect of these laws has been the subject of much discussion, but it can hardly be doubted that if the colonies had been free, from the beginning, to send their products direct to their ultimate markets in the cheapest ships available, a good deal of the trade would not in fact have been carried on with English ports, nor in English ships. English goods secured their fast-growing sales in colonies which were politically directed from England in ways intended to serve English (and to some extent colonial) as opposed to foreign interests. The colonies had to send their most considerable export staples to England, whatever the ultimate destination; when a new colonial commodity was found to be acquiring a useful European market, it was promptly added to the list of these 'enumerated commodities'. The colonies took their requirements from England or from each other, in the first place, because the laws compelled them to earn pounds sterling rather than pieces of eight, rix dollars, livres or ducats from the sale of their own goods; and because the Navigation Acts required that goods be brought to them only from English ports. They bought British rather than continental goods in the early decades of colonization because (except in the case of linens) continental goods could not bear the price of re-shipment plus the small part of English customs duties that was not refunded on re-

---

[1] Goods sent out by government departments themselves do not appear in the Customs records.
[2] The trade with India similarly expanded when the English military forces were increased in the forties, and no doubt this accounts for some of the rise in exports. But these forces were not, like the army in America, paid for by the English taxpayer.

export. The restrictions imposed by law were vitally important to England in the early decades of colonial development; they excluded, as they were designed to exclude, the exercise of Dutch commercial, financial and maritime skills which were well fitted to engross a large part of transatlantic trade. In time, changing conditions reduced the practical importance of the Navigation Laws, for they moulded the infant colonial trade so effectively that it developed the required character, and eventually matured in a form which was largely independent of the legal strait-jacket. Most of the colonial population, and nearly all the well-to-do of the merchant and planter and professional classes, were of British origin. The merchant houses, if they were not simply agencies of Liverpool and Glasgow firms, were English or Scots. Generation after generation the population of the colonies had become accustomed to take manufactures from British sources and sell through British factors. If a demand arose in Boston or Savannah or Kingston for new commodities – military buttons or musical boxes – the traders turned first to England to meet it. The force of habit was, by the mid-eighteenth century, even stronger than the force of law in maintaining the Anglo-American commercial connexion. Moreover, English industry which colonial demand had helped to foster had evolved, in many of its branches, new organization with greater efficiency and more advanced techniques, so that by 1774 some English manufactures probably had real advantages in cost over their European rivals. Finally, as wealth grew in England, her own market became particularly important to some colonial producers; the West Indian islands, above all, gained far more from the English tariff preferences for their sugar than they lost by being prevented from selling it directly in the savagely competitive markets of Hamburg or Amsterdam.

Nevertheless, right down to the American Revolution the Navigation Acts did impose some distortion on the pattern of trade. This is clearly illustrated by the records of the tobacco trade. In the years 1771–5 inclusive, England imported 278 million lb. of tobacco from America, and re-exported 230 million. In the years 1786–90 inclusive, an independent United States sent only 203 million lb. to England, of which 110 million lb. were re-exported.[1] Released by war from the bonds of the Navigation Acts, Americans at once began a large direct tobacco trade with their continental customers. On the other hand, the large tobacco trade which was still – in spite of the temper of the times – carried on through English intermediaries, is eloquent of the extent of America's continuing dependence on old ways.

It was only in the very long run that the United States broke completely free from this economic dependence; but from 1783 Americans did trade directly with continental Europe, on an increasing scale. If they had found there manufactures which outclassed England's in quality or price, it is unlikely that old habits would have ruled for long; but in fact English manufactures were, at this very point in time, beginning to acquire a genuine superiority. In 1783, however, this was not clearly apparent as it is now, and a serious loss of Ameri-

---

[1] E. B. Schumpeter, *op. cit.* Table XVIII.

can trade appeared to face English industry. The West Indies, Canada, a growing Indian dominion and Ireland remained in the English sphere. But the health of the West Indian economy was likely to be undermined by the ending of their special relation with the former northern colonies, while Ireland had already seized the opportunity of the American war to force great commercial concessions from the English government, and was in a state of ferment which seemed likely to lead to the breaking of this connexion too.[1] The prospects for trade based on privilege and non-economic influences were becoming gloomy indeed during the last quarter of the eighteenth century.

All this time, at England's doorstep there lived a population of 200,000,000 Europeans (as compared with 3,000,000 Americans across the Atlantic). They were England's traditional customers, and until recently her only ones. Yet it was only the old woollen industry that seriously carried on – as it had always done – the 'hard sell' on the continent; the newer industries cut their teeth on easier, privileged markets, mostly far away. The privileges could not be held for ever. They did not need to be. By the time privilege was threatened, towards the end of the century, England's cotton and metal industries had transformed themselves out of all recognition; they were poised ready to invade not only the European but all other markets with their irresistible bundles of products of the Industrial Revolution. Our period, which had opened full of false hopes for the future of trades already doomed to stagnation, closed with equally unreasonable fears at the loss of artificial aids which English commerce had already outgrown.

The University, Hull

---

[1] Ireland attempted in 1780 to use the very weapon with which the American colonies had struck their first serious blow — the non-importation of English manufactures. See D. B. Horn (ed.), *English Historical Documents, 1714–83* (1957), p. 694.

ENGLISH FOREIGN TRADE, 1700–1774   299

Note to the Tables

The areas are constituted as follows:

North-west Europe: Germany, Holland, Flanders, France.
Northern Europe: Norway, Denmark, Iceland, Greenland and the Baltic.
Southern Europe: Spain and Portugal and their islands, the Mediterranean
     including Turkey and North Africa.
British Islands: Ireland, Channel Islands.
America: North America, British and foreign West Indies and Spanish
     America, West Africa.
East India: all lands bordering the Indian and Pacific Oceans.

RALPH DAVIS

English Foreign Trade, 1699–

	Total				North-west Europe				Northern Europe			
	1699–1701	1722–4	1752–4	1772–4	1699–1701	1722–4	1752–4	1772–4	1699–1701	1722–4	1752–4	1772–4
IMPORTS												
Linens	903	1,036	1,185	1,246	798	838	684	415	48	84	169	179
Calicoes	367	437	401	697								
Silks and mixed fabrics	208	208	112	82	18	11	1					
Metalwares	72	39	7	7	63	39	7	7	9			
Thread	79	40	11	14	79	40	11	14				
Miscellaneous	215	123	107	111	57	71	42	35	2		1	5
Total manufactures	1,844	1,883	1,823	2,157	1,015	999	745	471	59	84	170	184
Wine	536	573	378	411	42	36	18	15				
Spirits	10	23	88	205	6	17	18	41				
Sugar	630	928	1,302	2,364								
Tobacco	249	263	560	519								
Fruit	174	135	117	159	9	4	3	5				
Pepper	103	17	31	33								
Drugs	53	60	179	203	7	13	23	34	2		5	7
Tea	8	116	334	848								
Coffee	27	127	53	436								
Rice	5	52	167	340								
Corn				398				204				119
Miscellaneous	174	156	191	561	44	60	55	70	7	7	6	10
Total foodstuffs	1,969	2,450	3,400	6,477	108	130	117	369	9	7	11	136
Silk, raw and thrown	346	693	671	751	1		2	2			5	
Flax and hemp	194	182	397	481	8	22	20	25	185	159	376	453
Wool	200	114	74	102		5		9	2			
Cotton	44	49	104	137				11				
Textile yarns	232	221	250	424	141	60	46	193	3	3	16	21
Dyes	226	318	386	506	41	39	139	69				
Iron and steel	182	212	293	481	8	22	11	14	149	170	267	452
Timber	138	157	237	319	26	31	27	23	96	113	120	181
Oil	141	122	130	162	1				4		9	
Tallow	85	15	4	131				5	1			93
Skins and hides	57	66	72	164	10	12	1	1	2		1	
Miscellaneous	191	276	362	443	59	39	64	50	73	55	68	79
Total raw materials	2,036	2,425	2,980	4,101	295	230	310	402	515	500	862	1,279
Total imports	5,849	6,758	8,203	12,735	1,418	1,359	1,172	1,242	583	591	1,043	1,599

ENGLISH FOREIGN TRADE, 1700–1774   301

74 *(thousands of £s)*

Southern Europe				British Islands				America				East India			
1699-1701	1722-4	1752-4	1772-4	1699-1701	1722-4	1752-4	1772-4	1699-1701	1722-4	1752-4	1772-4	1699-1701	1722-4	1752-4	1772-4
				57	114	332	652					367	437	401	697
83	51	15	6									107	146	96	76
28	8	23	34	50	21	28	17				1	78	23	13	19
11	59	38	40	107	135	360	669				1	552	606	510	792
92	528	328	363	2	8	21	16		1	11	15				2
4									6	70	163				
							4								
							1								
								630	928	1,302	2,360				
								249	263	560	518				
65	131	114	152												
24	17	51	67					6	22	55	55	103	17	31	33
												14	8	45	40
18	4									3	414	8	116	334	848
5								52	167	340		9	123	50	22
							1				51				
							23								
39	26	38	48	44	7	2	347	40	49	82	82		7	8	4
47	706	531	636	46	15	23	387	925	1,321	2,250	3,998	134	271	468	951
102	643	570	593					1				42	50	94	156
1					2										
73	41	56	91	122	66	18	2					3	2		
20	4	48	38					23	45	56	88	1			
37	47	21	15	47	111	167	195					4			
92	124	149	267					85	152	97	167	8	3	1	3
24	19	9	5	1	1	1				5	10				
1										1					
17	96	78	69					14	13	90	114				
								19	26	43	93				
				84	15	4	33								
5	4	3	5	17	16	21	47	23	34	46	111				
25	40	94	67	5	20	26	33	17	88	97	187	12	34	13	27
97	1,018	1,028	1,153	277	230	238	311	182	358	434	770	70	89	108	186
655	1,783	1,597	1,829	430	380	621	1,367	1,107	1,679	2,684	4,769	756	966	1,086	1,929

English Foreign Trade, 169

	Total				North-west Europe				Northern Europe			
	1699–1701	1722–4	1752–4	1772–4	1699–1701	1722–4	1752–4	1772–4	1699–1701	1722–4	1752–4	1772
EXPORTS												
Woollens	3,045	2,986	3,930	4,186	1,354	863	1,177	847	190	123	148	11
Linens		25	211	740			3	4				
Silks	80	78	160	189	14	13	51	9	1	2	4	
Cottons, etc.	20	18	83	221	2		1	1	1		1	
Metalware	114	181	587	1,198	9	18	53	100	3	5	15	1
Hats	45	125	248	110	4	4	15	1	2	1		
Miscellaneous	279	371	1,131	1,843	52	84	90	151	5	14	25	6
Total manufactures	3,583	3,784	6,350	8,487	1,435	982	1,389	1,113	202	145	193	19
Grain	147	592	899	37	105	351	444	5	9	40	12	
Fish	190	138	145	70	92	15	12	5	2	1		
Hops	9	72	161	136			4				1	
Miscellaneous	142	84	213	329	35	14	46	28	18	7	4	2
Total foodstuffs	488	886	1,418	572	232	380	506	38	29	48	17	2
Lead	128	113	149	182	70	56	79	81	9	14	13	2
Tin	97	67	129	116	46	37	63	45	10	2	25	2
Coal	35	98	177	333	14	45	65	133	1	5	9	2
Miscellaneous	102	94	194	163	62	34	50	58	4	2	14	
Total raw materials	362	372	649	794	192	172	257	317	24	23	61	7
Total exports	4,433	5,042	8,417	9,853	1,859	1,534	2,152	1,468	255	216	271	30
RE-EXPORTS												
Calicoes	340	484	499	701	239	419	434	478	2		4	
Silks, etc.	150	354	281	501	116	202	181	245	1	1	2	
Linens	182	232	331	322	3		9	4				
Miscellaneous	74	46	34	38	21	3	2	5				
Total manufactures	746	1,116	1,145	1,562	379	624	626	732	3	1	6	1
Tobacco	421	387	953	904	232	287	813	736	56	17	36	7
Sugar	287	211	110	429	255	151	9	9	6	12		
Pepper	93	44	104	110	29	8	34	50		1	5	
Tea	2	267	217	295	2	237				1		
Coffee	2	151	84	873	2	144	60	778		2	1	4
Rice	4	63	206	363	4	53	176	321		2	10	1
Rum				199				9				
Drugs	48	30	102	132	34	26	50	91	1		1	
Miscellaneous	84	107	159	237	26	60	70	54	5	6	12	
Total foodstuffs	941	1,260	1,935	3,542	584	966	1,203	2,048	68	41	65	15
Dyestuffs	85	83	112	211	57	56	41	95	4	1	17	3
Silk	63	39	70	125	51	16	7	13				
Miscellaneous	151	216	230	378	92	86	44	118	5	3	3	1
Total raw materials	299	338	412	714	200	158	92	226	9	4	20	5
Total re-exports	1,986	2,714	3,492	5,818	1,163	1,748	1,921	3,006	80	46	91	21
Total of exports and re-exports	6,419	7,756	11,909	15,671	3,022	3,282	4,073	4,474	335	262	362	51

ENGLISH FOREIGN TRADE, 1700–1774   303

774 (thousands of £s)

	Southern Europe				British Islands				America				East India			
	1699–701	1722–4	1752–4	1772–4	1699–1701	1722–4	1752–4	1772–4	1699–1701	1722–4	1752–4	1772–4	1699–1701	1722–4	1752–4	1772–4
	201	1,606	1,954	1,667	26	19	47	219	185	303	374	1,148	89	72	230	189
		3	14	43			3	6		22	189	681			2	6
	10	17	33	11	19	8	11	31	36	38	60	133			1	3
	1			6		3	4	37	16	15	78	176				
	7	35	76	6	12	7	28	52	73	107	331	755	10	9	84	148
	12	81	154	128	1				24	38	59	93	2	1	20	10
	43	90	113	146	28	22	122	154	141	156	480	995	10	5	301	334
	274	1,832	2,344	2,007	86	59	215	499	475	679	1,571	3,981	111	87	638	690
	23	138	261	8	2	55	160	8	8	8	21	14			1	1
	80	95	128	62	7	9	3		9	18	2	3				
					9	72	156	135				1				
	25	10	16	11	24	23	64	124	38	29	78	132	2	1	5	7
	128	243	405	81	42	159	383	267	55	55	101	150	2	1	6	8
	35	31	40	48	4	6	4	8	2	2	5	7	8	4	8	9
	35	25	37	46	6	2	4	2						1		
		1	4	7	20	45	97	161		2	2	12				
	12	9	49	22	16	29	38	43	7	20	28	26	1		15	10
	82	66	130	123	46	82	143	214	9	24	35	45	9	5	23	19
	484	2,141	2,879	2,211	174	300	741	980	539	758	1,707	4,176	122	93	667	717
	36	14	24	116	18	6	5	15	45	45	32	85				
	5	22	10	24	14	12	12	18	14	117	76	210				
	13	8	15	33	9	2	6		157	222	301	285				
	10	4	2	3	4	3	5	7	36	36	23	16	3		2	7
	64	48	51	176	45	23	28	40	252	420	432	596	3		2	7
	41	18	16	33	91	63	85	45		2	3	19	1			1
	5	5			21	43	110	411				1				
	63	31	58	44		3	2	4	1	1	5	7				
			20	39		24	104	213		5	113	82				
		6	16	21		5	3	7		1	3	7				
				8		1	1	1				37				9
								134								
	7	2	18	14	2	2	4	4	1		5	12	3		24	10
	5	7	31	42	11	9	13	13	32	19	19	108	5	6	14	12
	21	69	159	201	125	150	322	832	34	28	148	273	9	6	38	32
	16	13	23	35	8	13	19	31			1				11	11
	4	1	2	4	8	22	60	107			1	1				
	19	45	50	37	7	30	58	97	26	39	45	102	2	13	30	13
	39	59	75	76	23	65	137	235	26	39	47	103	2	13	41	24
	324	176	285	453	193	238	487	1,107	312	487	627	972	14	19	81	63
	708	2,317	3,164	2,664	367	538	1,228	2,087	851	1,745	2,334	5,148	136	112	748	780

[5]

Multilateralism and/or Bilateralism: the Settlement of British Trade Balances with 'The North', c. 1700

BY JACOB M. PRICE

During 1949–51, Mr Charles Wilson and the late Professor Heckscher in a number of articles in this journal exchanged views on the relative importance of the mechanisms through which trade balances were normally settled in 'the period commonly described as "mercantilist"'. [1] The discussion or controversy centred on two questions: (a) to what extent were coin and bullion shipments rather than bills of exchange used to settle international accounts; and (b) were trade balances ordinarily settled bilaterally or multilaterally. The general drift of the argument associated bilateral settlement with specie shipments and multilateral settlement with the exchange mechanism. Abstractly, of course, this association is not necessary. The bilateral use of the exchange mechanism, however convenient to individual merchants, could not of course redress a trade imbalance between two nations; but specie transfers might be multilateral. Country A having an unfavourable trade balance with country B, a merchant in A, with debts to pay in B and unwilling to take the characteristic loss by the exchange, orders his correspondent in C to ship specie to B, reimbursing that correspondent either by specie shipment from A, by exchange, or by goods in trade. Though such multilateral specie shipments can be conceived of abstractly (and actually occurred, as will be shown below), it was convenient for Mr Wilson to associate specie shipments with bilateral settlements inasmuch as he used, in his original article, the actual necessity for bilateral specie settlements as a justification or explanation of the advocacy by many mercantilist publicists and policy makers of the necessity of individually balanced trades (as distinct from the liberal satisfaction with an overall national balance of trade).

Mr Wilson and Professor Heckscher based their argument in very great part on contemporary controversial literature with supporting references to modern scholarship and contemporary statistics and estimates. Evidence was used from the sixteenth to the eighteenth centuries, suggesting that the normal modes of settlement had remained essentially the same for at least several centuries. Since there has never been any question in modern scholarship about the heavy use of coin and bullion in European trade with the East Indies, argument centred on the degree to which such shipments were used in settling English trade mbalances with Scandinavia and the Baltic – a classic area of deficit

---

[1] Charles Wilson, 'Treasure and trade balances: the mercantilist problem', *Economic History Review*, 2nd ser. II (1949), 152–161; Eli F. Heckscher, 'Multilateralism, Baltic trade, and the mercantilists', *ibid*. III (1950), 219–228; Charles Wilson, 'Treasure and trade balances: further evidence', *ibid*. IV (1951), 231–242.

trade. The purpose of this note is not to re-open the question generally at the many levels suggested by Mr Wilson and Professor Heckscher but rather to examine narrowly the *actual procedures* used by British merchants in the generation or so after 1689 to settle their debts in 'the North' (the useful contemporary term embracing Scandinavia, Russia, Poland and most of the Baltic litoral, but excluding Germany from Stettin west). No use will be made either of the hitherto much used contemporary controversial literature or of contemporary estimates of trade and payments. The evidence used will instead be confined primarily to that obtainable from official statistics and contemporary merchants' accounts. The argument to be adduced from such evidence applies only to the years covered and should not be applied to any earlier period without the greatest caution.

As even some schoolboys perhaps know, English trade ran a chronic deficit with the countries of the North during most of the seventeenth and eighteenth centuries. The record is quite explicit after the start of official English trade statistics in 1696 (Table 1):

Table 1. *Annual averages of English exports to and imports from the North, etc., 1697–1730, at official values (in £000's).*[1]

		1697–1700	1701–1710	1711–1720	1721–1730
Russia [2]	Imp.	104	124	182	191
	Exp.	44	132	88	43
	Bal.	−60	+9	−94	−149
East	Imp.	177	140	127	198
Country [3]	Exp.	146	115	75	120
	Bal.	−31	−25	−52	−78
Sweden	Imp.	204	189	132	167
& Finland	Exp.	52	56	35	35
	Bal.	−152	−133	−96	−132
Denmark	Imp.	78	75	86	100
& Norway	Exp.	49	43	80	71
	Bal.	−30	−31	−7	−29
Germany [4]	Imp.	584	605	613	681
	Exp.	589	971	889	1087
	Bal.	+5	+366	+276	+406
Holland	Imp.	549	588	538	571
	Exp.	1,547	2,147	2,020	1,876
	Bal.	+998	+1,559	+1,482	+1,305
All	Imp.	4,973	4,558	5,680	6,951
Countries	Exp.	6,035	6,512	7,767	10,236
	Bal.	+1,062	+1,954	+2,087	+3,285

[1] Sir Charles Whitworth, *State of the trade of Great Britain in its imports and exports, progressively from the year 1697* (London, 1776), part ii, 5, 7, 15, 17, 29, 35. Cf. Heckscher, *loc. cit.* 227. Whitworth's '1697' and '1698' end at Michaelmas; his other years at Christmas. He omits the quarter Mich. – Christmas 1698.

[2] Archangel, St. Petersburg, Narva.

[3] Baltic ports from Reval to Danzig inclusive. Even after Livonia and Estonia passed into Russian hands, English customs continued to classify the ports from Reval to Riga inclusive as in 'East Country', not Russia. Narva was properly considered in Russia, even when in Swedish hands, because it lay within the trading monopoly of the Russia Company. This may not have been strictly observed. Cf. PRO C.O. 390/5, fo. 125.

[4] In effect, Emden to Stettin.

256   J. M. PRICE

England, it is obvious, had an unfavourable trade balance not only with the North as a whole, but also with every part of it. There was very little that English statesmen or merchants could do about these imbalances in the short run. They rested firmly upon the coincidence of restricted local demand for English goods (based on poverty, high import duties and Dutch competition) and an unrestricted, growing English demand for the raw materials of the region: Swedish iron, Finnish pitch and tar, Russian hemp and later iron, Riga hemp and masts, Danzig and Königsberg linen and grain on occasion, Norwegian timber and masts, etc. It was not until almost 1720 that the bounties adopted in 1705 created for Britain in North America a real alternative supply of great masts, pitch, tar, and turpentine. For smaller masts, hemp, coarse linens, and iron, however, all Britain still remained dependent on the North.[1] Table 1 suggests, however, that, in her favourable balances with Germany and Holland, England at least had close at hand ostensible resources more than adequate to meet her Northern deficits.

It is generally recognized that we cannot accept too uncritically the absolute data (particularly the value data) we get from the ledgers of the Inspector-General of Imports and Exports. Freight, for example, was automatically included in the price of imported goods, but not of exported goods; official values, reasonable in the 1690's, grow less dependable with each succeeding decade; exporters may have systematically overentered and overvalued goods not subject to export duties.[2] Many of these defects, of course, balance each other out. Nevertheless, with all due caveats registered, there is no evidence extensive enough to challenge the reasonableness of the general picture of the Northern trade provided by the official statistics.

So much granted, then, the immediate problem becomes the extent to which the imbalances arising from England's Northern trade might have been redressed by shipments of coin and bullion. Since 1663, the export of bullion and foreign coin had been permitted by statute. Since 1672, the Treasury had further permitted the export of plate as bullion without export duty.[3] We have no data on imports of gold and silver but we do have official statistics on their export. Such statistics cannot include English coin smuggled out, but logically there was little reason to risk smuggling out any *great amount* of English coin when it was not current abroad and when it was so much easier to melt it down and export the bullion legally.[4] An examination of Table 2 will reveal what coin and bullion were actually exported to the areas under consideration.

---

[1] PRO C.O. 390/6, pp. 223–42; C.O. 390/8/H.
[2] [Sir] G[eorge] N. Clark, *Guide to English commercial statistics 1696–1782* (London, 1938), pp. 33–42.
[3] 15 Car. II c. 7 s. 9 (*Statutes of the Realm*, V, 451); *Cal. T. B.*, III, 1084, 1259; PRO T.1/24/53.
[4] The only northern country where English coin seems to have been in current use was Norway, at least ca. 1751–1761. Cf. H. S. K. Kent, 'The Anglo-Norwegian timber trade in the eighteenth century', *Economic History Review*, 2nd ser. VIII, 1955, 73. There are numerous references to melting down English coin: e.g. Sir Isaac Newton (1702) in William A. Shaw, *Select tracts and documents illustrative of English monetary history 1626–1730* (London, 1935), p. 138. Even if abstractly such bullion could be converted into current coin in Holland or Hamburg at a cost trivial compared to the risks of smuggling, too much should not be made of such shipments. Silver bullion formed a trifling part of English exports of precious metals: e.g. during the three years Michaelmas 1704–1707, silver bullion formed less than 3% of total English exports of precious metals (and also of exports to Holland) while foreign silver coin formed over

MULTILATERALISM   257

Table 2. *The value of English exports of foreign coin and bullion to Holland, Germany, and the North, Christmas 1698–Christmas 1719.*[1]

	Russia	East Country	Sweden/ Finland	Denmark & Norway	Germany	Holland
1699	£948	—	£ 421	£ 473	—	£ 3201
1700	5208	£486	1375	—	—	3332
1701	435	—	165	677	£ 14	6618
1702	990	75	—	146	900	20,411
1703	6901	—	—	25	—	12,291
1704	10,360	—	—	—	—	51,535
1705	4158	—	—	—	—	13,960
1706	3694	—	—	—	—	25,665
1707	4578	—	—	—	—	9287
1708	1798	—	—	—	—	40,278
1709	3052	—	—	—	9680	185,675
1710	1214	—	—	—	—	164,841
1711	3873	—	—	—	—	122,480
1712	—	—	—	—	—	440,257
1713	—	—	—	213	115	66,200
1714	—	125	—	—	—	1210
1715	431	—	10	—	—	11,888
1716	—	—	—	—	1300	103,948
1717	—	—	—	—	—	32,761
1718	425	—	—	500	—	953,272
1719	462	—	—	1125	—	275,890

Bullion and coin played a very large part in English overseas trade – almost £13 million being exported in the twenty-one years 1698–1719. But 70 per cent of this went to the East Indies.[2] A glance at Table 2 quickly reveals that there is no significant correlation between gold and silver exports and the areas of trade deficit revealed in Table 1. Sweden, the East Country, Denmark and Norway received virtually no specie from England. Russia did get some, but perversely received most in the decade 1701–1710 when its trade was balanced with England and virtually none in the next decade when the trade balance moved in its favour. The greatest European shipments always went to Holland with whom England had a most favourable balance. Some of this, of course, came back. (The greatest European shipments after Holland were in peacetime those to France with whom England also had a most favourable balance of trade.) Had we no other evidence than that supplied by Tables 1 and 2, we could only conclude: (1) that ca. 1698–1719 gold and silver were exported

90% of exports. PRO C.O. 388/11/17 (I.14). Though foreign silver coin declined somewhat in relative importance in succeeding years as gold coin and bullion became more important, silver bullion remained of trivial importance. In the ten years following the devaluation of the guinea in December 1717, gold accounted for almost half of total English coin and bullion exports, but predominated in shipments to Europe. Such silver bullion as was exported went almost entirely to the East Indies. PRO C.O. 390/5, ff. 19–19v (1710–1717) and T. 64/276B/391 (1717–1727).

[1] [Henry Martin], 'An essay towards finding the ballance of our whole trade annually from Christmas of 1698 to Christmas 1719' in Clark, *Guide*, pp. 77–9. Martin's figures for Christmas 1698 to Christmas 1715 can be verified in PRO T.1/194/10 or C.O. 390/5, ff. 26v–27. His later figures cannot be exactly verified. This creates a problem, for the figures given for the individual countries in 1717 come to almost £300,000 less than the total given for that year. For ascription of authorship to Martin, see T. S. Ashton in Elizabeth Boody Schumpeter, *English overseas trade statistics 1697–1808* (Oxford, 1960), p. 3.

[2] Clark, *Guide*, pp. 77–9.

from England for reasons other than the bilateral settling of trade balances;[1] and (2) that, since England's trade deficits with the various Northern states could not have been settled by bilateral movements of precious metals, they must have been settled by some multilateral mechanism.

There is nothing peculiar about the twenty-one years covered by Martin's account (Table 2). Other data available on the following eight years, 1719–1727, are fully consistent: substantial coin and bullion exports only to Holland; negligible exports (none at all in five years out of eight) to the North (Russia, East Country, Sweden/Finland, Denmark and Norway).[2] Exports in the 1720's were almost entirely from London, rather than the outports, suggesting that they were more financial than commercial in character.[3] It has been suggested that if 'the figures for bullion export to the Baltic area are in fact small', it is because 'the exchange had been favourable during the period with which [Martin] ...was concerned'.[4] There is in fact no evidence that the exchange was particularly favourable at this time except through the inference that because the exchange mechanism was widely used the rate must have been favourable.[5] Actually the twenty-nine years here considered (1698–1727) are quite mixed in character, including years of general war, regional war, rumours of war, even total peace, as well as times of boom, crisis, depression, high prices, low prices, etc., etc. None of these vagaries, though, seems to have had much impact on the movement of coin and bullion between England and the Baltic.[6] There were numerous occasions on which merchants complained that the exchange was quite unfavourable, but still bore it.[7] More fundamentally, before we advance such an argument, ought we not to ask whether the exchange rate can be regarded as an independent variable governing the use of bills of exchange, rather than as a most dependent variable, itself governed by multilateral balances of trade and the multilateral supply of and demand for bills. Specifically, then, should the use of bills (inferred here from the absence of specie movements) be regarded as a result of a favourable bill rate, rather than as a likely cause of a deteriorating bill rate?

So much for statistical speculation. To understand the problems involved in shipping money, we must look at the quality as well as the quantity of the money shipped. From contemporary commercial handbooks down to modern

---

[1] Contemporary explanations of the upsurge of specie and bullion exports to Holland and France, ca. 1718, stress speculation and do not consider reshipment to the North. PRO T.1/214/67.

[2] PRO T.64/276B/391.

[3] PRO T.64/276B/392,393.

[4] Wilson, 'Further evidence', *loc. cit.* 237.

[5] It is not quite clear just what 'exchange' or exchanges are meant here. For the exchanges at Stockholm, see Table 3 below. For the Copenhagen exchange, see Astrid Friis and Kristof Glamann, *A history of prices and wages in Denmark 1660–1800* (Copenhagen, 1958), I, 66–77. For the rates at Amsterdam, see Nicolaas Wilhelmus Posthumus, *Inquiry into the history of prices in Holland* (Leiden, 1946), I, 594–8. For some London-Amsterdam rates, see James E. Thorold Rogers, *The first nine years of the Bank of England* (Oxford, 1887), pp. 165–8. For London-Hamburg rate, see Thomas S. Ashton, *An economic history of England: the 18th century* (London, 1955), p. 253.

[6] For price data, cf. Posthumus, Friis and Glamann, as in previous footnote. For prices of naval stores, the principal English import from the North, see William [lord] Beveridge, et al. *Prices and wages in England* (London, 1939), I, 670–80.

[7] Cf. below pp. 266–8, 271–2.

MULTILATERALISM 259

'standard accounts',[1] the literature has always recognized that the Dutch in the seventeenth and eighteenth centuries were the mintmasters of the North, that is that large numbers of coins minted in the United Provinces were exported to the North where they circulated widely, being at the very least as acceptable for commercial purposes as the local currencies. This has never been in controversy. However, with the diminution of silver arrivals from Spanish America after 1660, hard money became progressively tighter in Europe till past the turn of the century. This was reflected in the downward tendency of prices in peacetime.[2] It was also reflected in the silver shortage in the United Provinces, ca. 1691–1707, noted by Mr Wilson.[3] (The shortage was ultimately relieved by Brazilian gold after 1710.) Now, whereas Mr Wilson interpreted the exceptions made for the Northern trade during the Dutch bans on silver exports after 1691 as proof of the importance of money *vis-à-vis* bills of exchange in that trade, one might also wonder whether the ability of this (and indeed of all) trades to expand during decades of increasing tightness in specie supplies does not in itself suggest increasing use of alternative methods of payment.[4]

We are, however, not concerned here with Dutch but with English settlements with the North.[5] The very fact, however, that the North imported and used so much Dutch coinage made it more not less difficult for the English to clear their deficits there by direct bilateral specie shipments. The coins the North would readily accept were not readily available in Britain.[6] A London merchant writing to a correspondent in Hull in 1700 about the newly opened Archangel trade describes it as 'chiefly driven in barter but you may be sure that either Specie Rixdollars or duchatts will be very acceptable'.[7] A Scottish merchant in Stockholm writing a few months later to his brother in Glasgow suggested in view of the unfavourable exchange that his brother try sending '2 or 300 Bank Dollers ... [explaining that] all with the spread eagle save they with the Bear, all with the Sword tho wanting the Belgick Lyon & all of equall weight with Bank excepting Cross Legs & ffrench are equal in value'.[8] But his brother never sent any, for Dutch 'Bank dollers' etc. though well enough known in Scotland, could not be spared for remunerative export.

In other words, the coins most readily acceptable in the North were Dutch coins and, as such, were not available in Britain in sufficient quantity ca. 1700

[1] E.g. J. G. Van Dillen, 'Amsterdam, marché mondial des métaux précieux au XVIIe et au XVIIIe siècle', *Revue historique*, CLII (1926), 194–200; —, 'The Bank of Amsterdam', *The history of the principal public banks* (The Hague, 1934); Violet Barbour, *Capitalism in Amsterdam in the seventeenth century* (Baltimore, 1950), ch.2.

[2] E.g. Posthumus, *Prices in Holland*, diagrams I, II; p. ci.

[3] Wilson,,'Further evidence', *loc. cit.* 232, 240.

[4] Cf. Ruggiero Romano, *Commerce et prix du blé à Marseille au XVIIIe siècle* (*Monnaie-Prix-Conjoncture*, III) (Paris, 1956), pp. 29–30.

[5] One may well argue, of course, that Dutch specie shipments to the North supported English bill operations there. This may be little more than saying that in a multilateral settlement complex, all transactions affect each other. We lack all quantitative data on the volume of Dutch specie shipments to the North, and on the proportion that might have been on English account.

[6] Cf. [Pierre Daniel Huet], *Mémoires sur le commerce des Hollandois* (Amsterdam, 1717), p. 63.

[7] PRO C.111/127, Henry Phill letterbook: to Wm. Crowle, 21 Mar. 1699/1700.

[8] Mitchell Library, Glasgow, Adam Montgomerie letterbook, p. 37, 25 July 1700.

for bilateral export to the North. If British merchants required them in the North, they could only get them there by commercial, monetary or exchange operations via Amsterdam. All this is most explicitly demonstrated in an experience of the Russian Tobacco Company, the group of English merchants that enjoyed the Russian tobacco monopoly during 1698–1700 and which remained active in the Russia trade through at least 1713.[1] There is some evidence that the company's agent in Russia may have drawn bills for ordinary commercial purposes, but it is not certain. The company's tobacco remittances to Russia provided it with virtually all of the cash it needed for ordinary commercial purposes there. Government demands, however, obliged it to get Dutch coins as best it could. Some export duties in Russia had for years been paid in Dutch coin.[2] About the time of the start of the Great Northern War in 1700, the Russian government adopted further regulations by which Russian inland traders selling hemp, flax, tallow or leather to foreign merchants at Archangel were obliged to exchange Dutch coins at the treasury for local 'coyne of a base alloy' at a rate prescribed by the government: e.g. two rixdollars for every berquet of hemp and tallow or every pude of leather sold. Since there was absolutely no way for the Muscovite inland traders to come by the rixdollars, foreign buyers like the tobacco company were 'obliged either to take those sums upon themselves, or to quit the market'. In addition, the Russian state in granting monopolies for the export of masts, pitch, tar, etc. frequently insisted on partial or total payment in foreign currency or exchange. Such was the case of the potash export agreement of 1702 made by the tobacco company's agent in Russia. Finally, the Russian government on occasion brought pressure on the larger firms to supply it with foreign bill remittances. Such was the 20,000 rixdollar bill on Amsterdam supplied by the tobacco company's agent in 1702 to help pay Peter's subsidy to King Augustus of Poland.[3] The currency demands of the Russian government brought on a crisis in 1703. Up to that time, the tobacco company had apparently been able to meet its currency needs in Russia by purchases of rixdollars made by their agent in Amsterdam (who reimbursed himself by drawing on them in London) and shipped thence to Archangel. Up to that year the company would seem to have been unimpeded by Dutch currency regulations. In 1703, however, there was a total ban on the export of specie from both Holland and (nominally) Hamburg.[4] In its predicament the company applied to the English govern-

---

[1] The following paragraphs are based primarily on the author's study of this company, *The Tobacco Adventure to Russia* (Transactions of the American Philosophical Society, L 1, pt. 1), Philadelphia, 1961.

[2] Cf. V. Barbour, *Capitalism in Amsterdam*, p. 48.

[3] Some of the greatest international monetary movements, ca. 1689–1713, were of course governmental in character. The English government remitted enormous sums for continental subsidies and the support of its troops abroad. Dr John Sperling promises a detailed study of this soon. Since such remittances were seldom directed towards the Baltic, I have no intention of going into them here. However, Professor Caroline Robbins has called to my attention an interesting report in PRO S.P. 75/22, ff. 113 *et seq.* H. Gregg to Warre, 8 Sept. 1689, on the mechanism of remitting a payment from London to the King of Denmark for the hire of Danish mercenaries to serve in Ireland. It was handled by a bill operation via Hamburg.

[4] British Museum Add.MS. 37,352, ff. 213–213v; Add.MS. 37,354, ff. 80, 102, 104, 147, 213–14; PRO S.P.91/4.

ment. The government was sympathetic and instructed the English minister at The Hague:

> The Contractors for the Exportation of Tobacco into Russia, haveing occasion to Carry Thirty Thousand Dollars out of Holland to Arch Angell desire you will please to be assisting to Mr. Abraham Romswinckell their Agent with your good offices for obtaining a Licence of the States to that Purpose.[1]

The envoy applied twice for this privilege, first in his own name, then 'as by her Majesties recommendation'; he 'received a flat refusal'. The Dutch would not make exceptions for English traders which they had denied their own subjects.[2]

The tobacco company, unable to get any dollars, eventually satisfied the Russian government by giving it bills of exchange on Amsterdam, but at the rate fixed by the Russians. This 'extortion' remained for several years a great English grievance. As the English minister in Moscow explained in 1705:

> As to the returning of Bills, the English have allways and are till ready to do it at the ordinary course of exchange [N.B.] between Dollars and Russ money; but they ware oblig'd to make over those Dollars at a much lower rate than the courrant price, and therefore the disadvantage . . . was wholly to them.[3]

When the tobacco company could not get permission to export dollars from the United Provinces in 1703, why didn't it ship them 'bilaterally' from London? There was in fact a rise in English specie exports to Russia in 1703 and 1704; but rixdollars were not available in London at that time in the quantities required by the trade. (Total English specie and bullion exports to Russia in 1703 came to less than the 30,000 rixdollars needed by this single firm.) The tobacco company was hardly inexperienced or uninfluential in financial circles. Its shareholders included two ex-governors of the Bank of England and ten persons who were then serving or had served within the preceding five years as directors of the Bank of England, plus nine current directors of the new East India company and six managers of the joint East India trade. It could bring pressure at the highest diplomatic levels, but it couldn't find 30,000 rixdollars in London. If it couldn't, private Russian and Baltic merchants are unlikely to have had any more luck.[4] Bilateral monetary movements are hardly feasible when the currency units in demand are not readily available in the would-be exporting centre.[5]

---

[1] PRO S.P.104/69, fo. 241, Hedges to Stanhope, 25 June 1703.
[2] PRO S.P.84/224, fo. 463, Stanhope to Hedges, 30 June/10 July 1703.
[3] British Museum Add.MS.37,354, ff. 202–203; PRO S.P.91/4.
[4] Some London merchants who contracted with the Navy Board to supply hemp in 1703 had even less luck than the tobacco company when they tried to get special permission to export from Holland 2000 rixdollars to Archangel and 2000 to the Baltic. PRO S.P.104/69, ff. 242–242v, Hedges to Stanhope, 2 July 1703.
[5] The specie export ban may have had something to do with the decline in the number of ships passing the Sound in 1703. But, if Dutch traffic was down at the Sound and at Archangel, English traffic was unaffected at the Sound and was up at Archangel. S. Van Brakel, 'Statistische en andere gegevens betreffende onzen handel en scheepvaart op Rusland gedurende de 18de eeuw', *Bijdragen en mededeelingen van het historisch genootschap (gevestigd te Utrecht)*, XXXIV (1913), 394; PRO C.O.388/9/F.3; BM Add.MS.15,898, fo.141.

With the possibility of specie shipments thus limited both by quantitative and particularly by qualitative inadequacies of supply, the only alternative available was of necessity the bill market, however punitive the exchange rates. Even in Russia, the remotest, most backward and least typical part of the Northern market, this had to be so. Though trade with the petty Russian inland merchants might be carried on in great part by barter, foreign merchants resident in Russia ca. 1700, in their dealings among themselves, with the Russian government and with their correspondents in the west, were accustomed not only to multilateral specie movements but also to complex bill operations.[1] Just because rates on Archangel, Moscow and Narva do not appear in the Amsterdam (and London) price-currents at this time does not mean that there were not regular bill operations between those points and Amsterdam and London. The price-currents do not contain rates on Riga, Stockholm, Copenhagen or Königsberg either.[2] All that this means is that there was no regular supply *at* Amsterdam or London of bills on those places. But there was a plenteous supply in all of those places of bills on Amsterdam (and sometimes London) and there were regular market quotations of exchange rates on the western centres in most of them.[3]

Neither Russia, with its artificial government demand for cash, nor the oversized, politically involved Russian Tobacco Company was typical of English trade to the North. For a surer picture of the normal remittance mechanism between England and the North, we must look at the records of more characteristic middling firms trading to more conventional markets. Among the Chancery Masters' Exhibits in the Public Record Office are the papers of Henry Phill, a member of both the Eastland and unreformed Russia companies, active as a merchant at Riga and at London.[4] The papers include his letterbook (1692–1700) started when he was resident at Riga and continued after he returned to London in January 1694/5, as well as his London ledger and journal for 1698–1706. The letterbook for the Riga years contains frequent references to bill business. He regularly quotes the rates on Amsterdam and Hamburg, but not on London. Thus, we are not surprised to find that his normal way of settling balances with his London correspondents was to draw on an agreed intermediary at Amsterdam who redrew on London to cover the bill.[5] It will be more useful for our purposes, however, if we focus our closer

---

[1] Examples of bill drawing from Russia, ca. 1700 (in addition to those mentioned above) will be given below in the discussion of H. Phill's affairs. For further examples of drawing bills from Russia, ca. 1710–1720, see the Heathcote & Dawsonne letterbook in the Heathcote of Hursley MSS., Hampshire Record Office, Winchester.

[2] For the Amsterdam price-currents and rates of exchange, see Posthumus, *Prices in Amsterdam*, Introd. and pp. 579–97; for London, see J. M. Price, 'Notes on some London price-currents, 1667–1715', *Economic History Review*, 2nd ser. VII (1954), 244. The best source for exchange rates at London is the bi-weekly *Course of the Exchange*. A good set from 1698 exists in the library of the London Stock Exchange. There are microfilm copies of it in the Goldsmiths' Library, University of London, and the Kress Library, Harvard Business School.

[3] For Copenhagen rates on London and Amsterdam, ca. 1696–1748, see Friis and Glamann, *Prices in Denmark*, I, 66–74. For Stockholm rates, ca. 1700, see Table 3 and discussion below of Adam Montgomerie's business. For rates quoted at Riga, Koenigsberg, and in Russia, cf. note 1 above.

[4] PRO C.111/127.

[5] E.g. to Chitty & Peacock (Amsterdam), 17 Nov. 1692. Phill draws on them with instructions to redraw on John Cary (a great Virginia and Baltic merchant of London) who, he assures them, will cover. PRO C.111/127.

analysis of Phill's affairs on his years in London, years for which we have his journal and ledger and years in which his business was more revelatory of the whole structure of the Northern trade.

Henry Phill's London business was based squarely upon the Baltic. His ledgers show some eight accounts at Riga, five at Danzig, three at Königsberg, plus one each at Narva, Moscow, Stockholm and Copenhagen. Outside the Baltic, he had four correspondents at Amsterdam, two at Hamburg, one each at Dunkirk, Setubal, Livorno, etc. Those with whom he dealt most frequently he termed his factors. His usual business was the consignment of cloth and other English merchandise to Riga in particular, but also to the other Baltic centres. In addition he on occasion sent a ship to Setubal in Portugal or to the Mediterranean for salt shipped thence straight to the Baltic. The proceeds of the sale of the salt and the English goods rarely covered the costs of the full cargoes of hemp, etc. returned by his correspondents. The usual method of settling accounts was by drawing. Thomlinson & Norris, the correspondents at Stockholm, drew directly on London. (That is, to get cash they sold in Stockholm bills on Phill made payable to the buyers' nominees in London.) At all the other Northern centres, the drawing was not directly on London, but indirectly on Amsterdam (usually) or Hamburg. The precise route was left to the correspondent's own discretion. Thus, Phill gave Abraham Hoyle in Narva 'leave to draw on de Vries at Amsterdam or Peter Grieve att Hamb[urg] the best you can for my interest eithere there directly or any way else'.[1] Usually, the factor or correspondent in Riga, Danzig, Königsberg, Narva or Moscow would draw on one of a limited number of houses in Amsterdam or Hamburg who in turn then redrew on Phill in London. A typical journal entry might read: 'Benjamin Benson [factor at Königsberg] D[ebto]r to Chitty & St Quintin [Amsterdam] for sundry summs of mo[ney] dr[awn] on my acc[oun]t' – followed by a list of seven bills drawn by Benson on Chitty & St. Quintin with the exchanges from Königsberg guilders into Dutch guilders or Flemish pounds. An equally typical entry would be 'Dirck de Vries D[ebto]r to Isaac Navarro per bill pay[ab]le to him at 34s 7 1/2d flem: w[i]th Banck mo[ney] 51/8 per Ct. ... f 873 : 11 ... £80'. That is, in order to recoup himself for sums expended in meeting bills drawn on Phill's account from the North, Dirck de Vries, Phill's principal correspondent in Amsterdam, drew a bill on Phill payable to Isaac Navarro in London for £80 sterling or 873 guilders 11 stivers at an exchange rate of 34 shillings 7 1/2d Flemish to the pound sterling (6 guilders making a Flemish pound) with 51/2 per cent difference between current money in which bill transactions took place and bank money in which accounts were kept.

Such bill transactions fill Phill's ledger and journal, up to ten bills being included in a single journal entry. By contrast, transactions involving the movement of specie are relatively infrequent. The only regular ones are for the Russia trade. Ottwell Meverell, Phill's factor in Moscow, drew on Dirck de Vries fairly regularly. He also depended on de Vries in Amsterdam for cash. In April 1700, de Vries sent him 1,600 rixdollars *per mare* (probably to Archangel);

[1] Letter-book: to A. Hoyle, 5 April 1700, PRO C.111/127.

and 6,335 more in January 1700/01, 2,400 in January 1701/02 and the equivalent of 1,835 rubles in December 1702. (It is hard to imagine what route they followed at that time of year, though the ledger says *per mare*).[1] From 1703 to 1706, Phill's factor in Moscow was William Ballam. For some of the sums he needed, he drew on Chitty & St. Quintin in Amsterdam; but cash had also to be sent to him for the Russian duties, etc. In 1703, when the export of coin was banned in the United Provinces, Phill's correspondent in Hamburg, Peter Grieve, was able to circumvent local regulations and send Ballam 1000 rixdollars (approx. £250) via Archangel in July. A year later, in July 1704, Grieve sent another thousand rixdollars from Hamburg to Ballam in Archangel.[2] Three thousand rixdollars were also sent to Ballam *per mare* in 1706.

Although the only substantial, regular monetary movements shown in Phill's ledger and journal are those to Russia, there are some other minor ones. For example, in 1699, his correspondent at Copenhagen, Alexander Ross, sent his factor at Riga, Thomas Waller, some £30 : 18 : 9 worth of rixdollars and Danish crowns. In February 1699/1700, Samuel Wordsworth, Phill's factor at Danzig, sent Waller & Bindon at Riga 1100 rixdollars in two shipments. There was a substantial loss on this transaction. In the summer of 1700, Captain Rounsivill, master of a salt ship from the Mediterranean, brought several thousand dollars from the Mediterranean which were distributed among Phill's factors in Danzig, Königsberg and Riga. In 1704, a large sum seems to have been sent to Abraham Hoyle in Narva. All in all, however, it seems unlikely that all the coin shipped directly or indirectly by Phill to his correspondents in the North averaged as much as a thousand pounds sterling a year. One day's entry of bills drawn by a single correspondent frequently came to more.

Thus, as far as Henry Phill's records are any guide, it would seem that trade balances between London and the Eastland ports were normally met by the correspondents at Riga, Königsberg, etc. drawing via Amsterdam or Hamburg.[3] Specie in modest amounts was sent fairly regularly to the factors in Russia, occasionally to correspondents in the Baltic. It might be obtained in Holland, Hamburg, the Mediterranean, even in the North itself, but never in England.

The one country within the Baltic for which Phill's records are particularly thin and uninformative is Sweden. His dealings there were infrequent and only experimental. Fortunately, there exists in the Mitchell Library, Glasgow, the contemporary letterbook (1699–1702) of a Scots merchant, Adam Montgomerie, resident in Stockholm about the same time Phill was active in

---

[1] Two hypotheses suggest themselves: (1) coin sent by sea to Archangel in the summer reached Meverell in Moscow in December or January after the overland sleigh route was opened; (2) de Vries, foreseeing trouble in getting the necessary coin, bought it several months in advance of the opening of the shipping season to Archangel.

[2] It was usual for the English merchants in Moscow to go to Archangel in the late summer to meet the fleet and to return to Moscow in the early autumn after the fleet had sailed for home. In PRO S.P.82/20 fo.107 there is reference to five or six ships bound from Hamburg to Archangel in July 1703 with severall thousand Rixdollars on board.

[3] There are a few minor cases of more roundabout drawing, e.g. Königsberg on Danzig on Amsterdam on London, but they are not quantitatively important.

London.[1] (Some firms are mentioned in both sets of records.) Montgomerie went out from Glasgow to Stockholm in the fall of 1699 to act as general factor for any Glasgow merchant that might care to trust him. He attracted a fairly wide patronage from Glasgow, plus occasional business from Edinburgh, Linlithgow and Belfast. He also hoped for business from London but got very little of that in the two and a half years covered by the letterbook except an occasional iron purchasing order from his cousin and London correspondent, William Brown. Competing with him at Stockholm were several English and at least one other Scots house. He was not unsuccessful. Though starting with very little capital, he was able in 1701, after meeting all business and personal expenses, to increase his meagre stock by £250 sterling for the year.

Montgomerie acted as factor or commission agent for sales and purchases. A firm in Glasgow, etc. would charter a vessel or portion thereof (so much 'lastage' it was usually termed) and ship out the full freight chartered in herring to Montgomerie in Stockholm to be sold by him. For returns, he was usually instructed to load the consigning firm's full lastage in iron, or in a mixture of iron (preponderantly), deals and occasionally tar.[2] Though Glasgow or Clyde herring was preferred over its Dutch and Forth competition,[3] prices realized were (except for the fall of 1701) disappointingly low. This was blamed on, among other things, the good harvest of 1700 (with local provisions cheap, people ate less imported herring), on the removal of the military garrisons (good customers for bulk purchases) from Stockholm at the start of the Great Northern War, and, in 1702, on the small size of the fish. Montgomerie also received minor shipments of raw wool (surreptitiously) of disappointing quality,[4] plus some stockings and cloth.[5] Regardless of the year or the commodity, the iron returned always seemed to come to more than the Scots goods sent out (primarily herring). (The only notable exceptions were in the fall of 1701 when a few accounts were more than balanced by high herring prices.) Such a trade then normally left substantial balances to be settled. In addition, Montgomerie received a number of orders from pin manufacturers in Glasgow, etc. for brass wire. Not being merchants, they consigned no goods to cover these orders, leaving the entire cost of their wire as a balance to be settled. The only consistent exception to the general unfavourable balances produced by these trades came through the shipment of tobacco via Whitehaven or London. A given lastage of Virginia tobacco sold in Stockholm was expected to realize more than was needed to load the same lastage home in iron.[6]

[1] I am indebted to Mr A. G. Hepburn, now deputy-librarian, for bringing this volume to my attention in 1952.

[2] Even before the opening of the Northern War in 1700, tar was difficult to get. With the war and the Russian invasion of Finland, it disappears from Montgomerie's correspondence. On one occasion (Letterbook, p. 16) he wrote that he had been able to get tar when needed only because he had been recommended from London to an eminent merchant who was a director of the monopoly Tar Company.

[3] Letterbook, pp. 45, 63.

[4] For some interesting references to the surreptitious export of wool from Scotland, see Letterbook, pp. 14, 24, 25, 29, 142, 226, 228, 235–6, 284–7, 308, 322, 334–6, 367.

[5] For an attempt to sell Scots woollens in Sweden, see Letterbook, pp. 142, 149.

[6] Adam Montgomerie's tobacco business is discussed in detail in the author's *Tobacco Adventure to Russia*, ch. 1.

A further complication for Montgomerie was the conditions of sale usual in Stockholm. Not only did herring frequently sit months on his hands before it was sold, but herring, wool, etc. even tobacco, had to be sold on long credit. Iron and brass, on the other hand, could only be bought at competitive prices when bought for cash. This was particularly true in the late summer (August-September) when scores of ships had to be loaded quickly as 'the fleet' hurried to be out of the Baltic while 'the open water' lasted. The masters too had frequently to be supplied with small sums in cash. All this put a great seasonal financial strain on the Stockholm factor who had to be in funds for purchases before he was fully recompensed from his sales.

Despite his great need for cash and despite the fact that Glasgow was very awkwardly situated for bill transactions, there is not one mention in the several hundred letters that fill his letterbook of Adam Montgomerie's having received a single shipment of coin or bullion. On one occasion, mentioned above,[1] he asked his brother and principal correspondent in Glasgow, James Montgomerie, jr., to send him about 300 Dutch dollars if he could spare them – but none were forthcoming. Adam may have brought some cash with him, but it could only have been for his personal needs, for we know he came with £1300 sterling in letters of credit, and drew as soon as his first ships arrived.[2] Earlier in the century Scots merchants may have exported specie to the Baltic.[3] By 1700, it would appear, their descendants were able to conduct their affairs entirely by bill operations.

Adam Montgomerie was of necessity flexible in drawing on his Glasgow correspondents. If the amount due him was trifling (say, under £10 sterling), Montgomerie wrote asking informally that it be paid to his brother James in Glasgow. For middling sums (from £120 to £360 Scots, or £10 to £30 sterling), he almost always drew a regular bill of exchange payable to his brother James in Glasgow. For larger sums, he sometimes drew payable to his brother in Glasgow; at other times, he drew payable in sterling in London either to his correspondent, William Brown, or more commonly to the nominee of the person to whom he sold the bill in Stockholm.

There was no market rate on Scotland at Stockholm, and in drawing bills payable in Glasgow, Adam Montgomerie had to calculate the exchange from copper-dollars (in which accounts were kept in Stockholm) to Scots pounds on the basis of the current Stockholm rate on London plus what he understood the London-Scotland rate to be at last report. He frequently found such calculations to be very risky indeed. Nor were they always understood by his correspondents. When the exchange on London was 'at par' at Stockholm (which it never actually was at this time), i.e. 27 to 27 1/2 copper-dollars to the pound sterling, the copper-dollar was worth only about 9d. sterling – or 9s. Scots at the par between English and Scottish currency. When, however, the London rate at Stockholm was down to 24 1/4 or 1/2 as it was in 1700 (see

---

[1] See above, note 8, p. 259.
[2] Letterbook, p. 1.
[3] S. G. E. Lythe, *The economy of Scotland in its European setting 1550–1625* (Edinburgh, 1960), pp. 139–41, 161–5, 184–6.

MULTILATERALISM   267

Table 3, the copper-dollar was worth near 10*d.* sterling or 10*s.* Scots. A high
or disadvantageous rate between London and Scotland could further enhance
the exchange value of the copper-dollar to as much as 11*s.* Scots.[1] Thus,
although the copper-dollar was nominally worth about 9*d.* sterling or 9*s.*
Scots, Adam Montgomerie, in drawing on Scotland for payment in Scotland,
usually made conversion at between 10*s.* 3*d.* and 11*s.* Scots per copper-dollar.
This took a lot of explaining.

Table 3. *Exchange rates at Stockholm on London, Amsterdam and
Hamburg (selected quotations), May 1700–May 1701*

1700	London (copper-dollars per pound sterling)	Amsterdam (copper-marks per rixdollar current)	Hamburg (copper-marks per rixdollar banco)
8–16 May	25–3/4		
30 ,,	25–1/2	23–1/8	24–3/8
5 June	25		
15 ,,	25	22–15/16	23–5/8
4 July	25	22–15/16	23–13/16
7 ,,	25	22–9/16	23–11/16
22 Aug.		22–1/2	23–1/2
1 Sept.	24–3/8	22–1/4	23–3/8
· 5 ,,	24–3/8	22–1/4	23–1/2
29 ,,	24–1/4		
24 Oct.	24–9/16	22–3/4	23–3/4
31 ,,	24–7/8	23	24–3/16
10 Nov.	25–1/8	23–1/8	24–3/8
24 ,,	25–1/16	23–1/8	24–1/4
28 ,,	24–15/16		
8 Dec.	24–3/4		
12 ,,	25		
15 ,,	24–7/8	22–7/8	24
22 ,,	24–7/8	22–7/8	24–1/8
1701			
12 Jan.	24–7/8	22–13/16	24
26 ,,	24–5/8	22–3/4	24
13 Feb.	25–1/2	23–1/8	24–1/4
13 Mar.	25–1/2	23–1/4	24–3/4
23 ,,	25–1/4	23–1/4	24–3/8
6–10 Apr.	25–3/4	23–1/4	24–3/4
17 ,,	26		
1 May	25–7/8	23	

Drawing a bill from Stockholm on Scotland payable in Scotland was hardly
a full-fledged or complete utilization of the exchange market, for such a bill
could not normally be sold in Stockholm for cash. Thus, when his brother in
Glasgow had collected the sums due on the bills remitted, there still remained
the problem of forwarding the money collected to Stockholm where it was
needed. Sometimes Adam Montgomerie let this money sit in his brother's
hands, trusting James to forward it to London at his convenience and 'as
opportunity offered' – that is, as he was in cash and as good bills on London
were available at reasonable rates. At other times, despite his brother's bitter
complaints, he was forced to draw on him in Scotland payable in London.

[1] Cf. Letterbook, pp. 64–5.

Adam Montgomerie's policy on whether to draw payable in Scotland or in London changed several times in the two and a half years covered by his letterbook. At first, to oblige his correspondents, he almost always drew payable in Scotland. This, however, early led him into significant losses, for, once having drawn, the ultimate remittance was 'on his own account' and at his own risk. Neither his brother in Glasgow nor his cousin in London informed him regularly enough about the London-Scotland rate. Moreover, with the Stockholm-London rate declining (depreciating the pound) during the spring and summer of 1700 (see Table 3), the rates at which he originally calculated when drawing on Scotland were not the rates prevailing when his money actually came to be remitted from London to Stockholm. For example, exchange on London at Stockholm fell from 25-3/4 on 16 May to 25 on 3 June – a loss to Adam Montgomerie on any bills drawn on 16 May of 3 per cent before the bills were even paid in Scotland. He reminded his brother how easy it was to lose more by exchange than he gained by commission.[1] Such losses by exchange could be hedged against by drawing simultaneously on London whenever one drew on Scotland with the expectation that remittances from Scotland would arrive in London in time to satisfy the London bills when due. This was very difficult because London bills, to sell at par, had to be drawn at one usance, i.e. made payable one month after sight (presentation), while bills on Scotland might be drawn payable anywhere from twenty days' sight to two months after date. Even where hypothetically possible by the calendar, in practice too little time was allowed for making remittances from Glasgow to London to make this method of covering feasible.[2] Thus, starting in September 1700, Adam Montgomerie felt himself forced to disoblige his Scottish correspondents and make all bills drawn on them for sums over £30 sterling payable in London. (He covered himself against fluctuations in exchange usually by selling the bill in Stockholm, or alternately by drawing on London a few days later and selling that bill. His bills on Scotland payable in London were, like London bills, ordinarily payable at one month's sight.) He continued this practice till April 1701 when a temporary cloud over his credit induced him to revert for the time being to his earlier practice of drawing payable in Scotland.[3] The favourable and steady rates on London prevalent at Stockholm in 1701 encouraged him to continue this arrangement until the end of the letters in 1702.

Whether drawing immediately on his correspondents in Glasgow, etc. or, at a second stage, on his brother, the bills Adam Montgomerie drew on Scotland payable in London could be sold in Stockholm as London bills, and thus be turned immediately into cash. The buyer in Stockholm named the London payee; the acceptor or drawee in Scotland named the London house at which

---

[1] Cf. Letterbook, p. 17.

[2] One method used by Adam Montgomerie occasionally to cover himself against fluctuations in the London-Scotland rate was to draw on Scotland payable in Scotland *in sterling*. This meant usually that the drawee/acceptor paid when due in Scots currency at the rate prevailing that day between Scots money and sterling. This experiment didn't solve the problem of the Stockholm rate and was dropped after a short try. Letterbook, pp. 17, 18, 20, 21.

[3] Letterbook, pp. 158–63, 170–2, 187, 227.

the bill would be paid. Montgomerie, the seller, having given due notice to the drawee, had his money and was quits of the bill unless it should be protested (refused) somewhere along the line. He had only 1/4 per cent broker's fee to pay in Stockholm in selling the bill. Thus, when Glasgow bills payable in London were at a par with ordinary London bills, Montgomerie understandably preferred to sell such bills in Stockholm for cash, rather than send them home for collection by his London correspondent, William Brown. However, in the winter, when the bill market was slack in Stockholm, Montgomerie found 'bills on Scotland payable in London are much scrupled because of the loss of tyme & Expenses thereon' in sending to Scotland for acceptance.[1] Persons desiring to remit funds to London then became 'somewhat shy of takeing bills on Scotland payable in London unless at 1/8 or 1/4 per lb Sterling under the Current Course'.[2] One-quarter copper-dollar per pound sterling amounted to a discount of 1 per cent. Montgomerie felt he could not sell at such a discount 'which as it would be Ungrateful to my friends soe can I never thinke of doing, what May any way Reflect on my own Credit'.[3] Rather than compromise his reputation by accepting a 1 per cent discount under the current rate on London, Montgomerie then sent his Scotland/London bills to his cousin Brown in London for collection.

Brown need not be thought of as a philanthropist. He normally collected 1 per cent in commissions and charges on all money passing through his hands – to compensate for the trouble and expense of sending the bills to Scotland to be accepted, collecting the money in London and ultimately remitting it to Sweden. Adam Montgomerie had avoided sending much money through Brown's hands in the 1700 shipping season, and thus avoided Brown's London charges. In 1701, however, as previously mentioned, the exchange on London was more favourable and he employed Brown more. Brown was annoyed and suggested 3 per cent as a suitable commission for collecting bills on Scotland payable in London. He claimed this was the practice when Londoners handled bills drawn in France on Scotland. Montgomerie rejected the request as unheard of and inconsistent with his reputation, pointing out that there were other routes by which one might draw on Scotland from Sweden.[4]

Adam Montgomerie's money thus came into William Brown's hands in London in three ways: (1) James Montgomerie in Glasgow might buy London bills and send them to Brown for collection; (2) Adam might draw on his brother or his correspondents in Scotland and send the bills (rather than sell them at a discount in Stockholm) to Brown for collection in London; and (3) Brown might be authorized to draw on James Montgomerie as needed. (These last bills were usually sold in London, but might be held for collection, depending on the quickness with which the money was needed.) At the beginning, Adam Montgomerie usually moved such funds from London to Stockholm by drawing bills on Brown for sale in Stockholm. Adam was very careful that funds

---

[1] Letterbook, pp. 117–18. Cf. pp. 118, 120.
[2] *Ibid.* p. 115.
[3] *Ibid.* p. 122. Cf. p. 123.
[4] *Ibid.* pp. 20, 199.

from Scotland should be in Brown's hands before any bills drawn on him became due. When in doubt, he instructed his brother to make remittance a few days before due so as not to pinch cousin Brown. Nevertheless, on certain occasions Brown was 'in advance' for Adam Montgomerie and complained bitterly. Though Montgomerie authorized him to charge interest in such cases, it wasn't missing three or four day's interest that angered Brown so much as being 'pinched' and having his freedom of action restricted. Hence his petulance in asking for the 3 per cent commission.[1]

So much for the usual channels. During the height of the shipping season when his business was most active and his need for money most acute, Adam Montgomerie could not follow normal procedures blindly. He had to watch the daily shift in rates between Stockholm, Hamburg, Amsterdam, and London, and between London and Scotland. During his first year, his complaints were almost incessant about the falling prices he got selling London bills in Stockholm.[2] (Cf. Table 3.) The Amsterdam rate was better, if only slightly; the Hamburg best of all. 'I find daily', Adam Montgomerie wrote on 1 August 1700 to Brown in London, 'Current Course on Hamburgh and ordinarily proves 1 per % or upwards better then to Amsterdam and 11/2 better then to draw directly on London tho all of them are very Low at present.'[3] In subsequent years he reported the advantage in drawing via Hamburg rather than direct on London as at something between two and three per cent. Understandably then, Montgomerie frequently urged Brown and his Glasgow correspondents to take advantage of any chances that came their way to remit money to Hamburg, or even to Amsterdam. Neither Brown in London nor brother James and his other 'friends' in Scotland were too co-operative, but they did on occasion remit to Amsterdam – though never to Hamburg.[4] Much more frequently, Adam Montgomerie himself took the initiative and drew (sold bills in Stockholm) on correspondents in Hamburg and Amsterdam, reimbursing them either by sending them bills on Brown or authorizing them to draw their own bills on Brown in London. In either case, they could sell the London bills locally before Adam's bills on them from Stockholm became due.[5] When he had no funds at Brown's, this involved triple drawing: e.g., he drew on Hamburg, authorizing his correspondents there to draw on Brown for reimbursement, while simultaneously he drew on his brother in Glasgow payable to Brown in London to put Brown in funds before the bill on him from Hamburg became due. Allowing for all expenses, Adam Montgomerie estimated at times that this still saved 2 per cent over direct drawing on London or via Amsterdam.[6]

1 Letterbook, pp. 101–2, 199.
2 On occasion, Adam Montgomerie preferred to borrow money in Stockholm (paying interest, he claimed, for the first time in his life) in anticipation of the receipt of money from his herring sales rather than draw on Britain at rates too disadvantageous to his correspondents. He paid 9 per cent interest and said others paid 12 per cent, although the legal rate was only 6 per cent. Letterbook, pp. 17, 25.
3 Letterbook, p. 39.
4 E.g. *ibid.* pp. 47, 108–9, 121, 125–6, 150, 180. James Montgomerie once agreed with a Scots merchant going to Amsterdam for the latter to deposit 1200 guilders to Adam's account there.
5 Letterbook, pp. 133, 151.
6 *Ibid.* pp. 142, 144, 152.

With this marked differential, Adam Montgomerie not unnaturally saw an opportunity for some rather safe operations in arbitrage. If only Brown would let him overdraw, he might get cash in Stockholm by selling bills on Hamburg (covered by Brown in London) and use that cash to buy good bills on London to be remitted to Brown 'sometimes with 2. or 3 per cent advantage'.[1] It was all perfectly safe, but Brown apparently didn't have the resources, or in lieu thereof the nerve, to back such operations. There were however much greater houses in Stockholm and London than Montgomerie and Brown and some of them must have engaged in just such arbitrage operations [2] – else the London rate at Stockholm could not have moved so consistently parallel to the Hamburg and Amsterdam rates.

With the passage of time, the unattractive Amsterdam rate led Adam Montgomerie to use that channel less and less frequently (except for insurance after the start of the French war in 1702).[3] He turned instead more and more to Hamburg. Lacking Scots connexions there, he had through the good offices of the great Stockholm and London houses of Mitford and Joy been introduced to the prestigious Hamburg house of Stratford and Free (Francis Stratford the elder was governor of the Hamburg Company). They were prepared to allow him quite extensive liberty to draw as long as Brown in London assumed responsibility.

Adam Montgomerie also used Hamburg and Amsterdam when he had occasion to transfer money within the Baltic. For example, 702 guilders owing him in Königsberg in 1700 were remitted by exchange to Amsterdam, whence he realized them in Stockholm by selling an Amsterdam bill.[4] A sum in Danzig in 1701 was similarly realized in Stockholm by drawing operations through Hamburg.[5] When he had occasion to reimburse the agent in Elsinore who paid the Sound tolls on the various ships consigned to him in Stockholm, Montgomerie sent a bill on Hamburg.[6]

On infrequent and uncharacteristic occasions, Adam Montgomerie was obliged to remit money back to Scotland. With only two Scots factors in Stockholm, there was no such thing as a market in bills on Scotland. Each of them handled such situations privately, drawing on such of his correspondents in Scotland as owed him money to reimburse those whom he owed. Such informal procedures could be slow. If a firm in Scotland wanted its money more quickly, it was asked to name a house in London or Amsterdam to whom remittance could and would be made promptly.[7]

Throughout Adam Montgomerie's correspondence, the rate of exchange looms as an awesome, uncontrollable, if sometimes predictable deity. It was lowest in the late summer and early autumn as the iron ships were loading. Everyone

[1] Letterbook, p. 150.
[2] That they were in fact is indicated by the frequency with which the name Mitford appears as the London payee of bills sold by Montgomerie in Stockholm. John Mitford (ancestor of the lords Redesdale) was a Baltic merchant of London whose eldest son William was his factor in Stockholm.
[3] Letterbook, p. 236.
[4] Ibid. pp. 41–2.
[5] Ibid. p. 179.
[6] Ibid. pp. 212–13.
[7] Ibid. pp. 245, 258, 295, 302–4, 324–5.

then, of course, knew it would rise, but it was 'hardly like to do [so] untill the English have done shipping Iron which they do entirely by bill'.[1] It recovered somewhat in the late autumn, but the cessation of most foreign business in the winter hindered a full recovery. (See Table 3.) It was highest in the spring, when the Baltic became open again and Swedish vessels hurried westward. There is little reason to think that Swedish merchants (or foreign merchants domiciled in Sweden) needed exchange on Amsterdam or London primarily to cover purchases in the United Provinces or England. Presumably, they wanted such credits so that their factors in France, Spain and Portugal could draw on Amsterdam or London to cover purchases of salt and wine, etc. For the likes of Adam Montgomerie, however, the knowledge that exchange would be higher in the winter and early spring was little consolation in August and September. He needed cash then for his iron purchases and was forced to draw and sell bills and make his correspondents pay the loss by exchange. After he had been in Stockholm a while, Montgomerie took all this for granted; at the beginning, though, he suffered a thousand torments lest his 'friends' in Glasgow think the 'miserable Low' exchange was due to his carelessness.

Even in his greatest perplexity, however, Adam Montgomerie thought entirely in terms of the exchange mechanism. Aside from the one occasion when he weakly and futilely suggested that his brother send a few hundred Dutch dollars, the 'gold point' or 'silver point' hardly seems to have existed for him. He wrote to one Glasgow correspondent:

> But though the money [you paid in Glasgow] lyes now at London I cannot without 5 per % Loss draw it in again so that I must wait to see if the exchange grows better els at the present Course I'll lose double the provision besides wanting the use of it but *theirs no preventing such rubbs* [italics mine] for the Course of exchange here is very variable & I must take my Chances.[2]

To another he explained:

> The last money I drew on you & some other ffriends Lyes yet att London & I cannot draw it in without 5 or 6 per Cent loss the Chief occasion is the Custome of Woolens from England & elsewhere proves so high that ffew goods is imported & much of the product (or most rather) of this Countrey shipt for England or Holland & their reimbursement taken by bills . . .[3]

Glasgow represents a rather extreme case. It lay far from the main travelled routes of the 'map of commerce' of 1700; for all practical purposes, it was even

---

[1] Letterbook, p. 50. Cf. p. 52. The seasonal pattern here discussed, which the letters describe as typical, is confirmed by the exchange quotations for 1700 and 1702 but not for 1701, when the late summer slump in the London rate was minimal and the fall recovery very rapid. (The Letterbook gives only London quotations between May and Oct. 1701.) Several reasons for the stability of the London exchange at Stockholm in 1701 suggest themselves: (1) the adverse visible balance of trade between England and Sweden was only £119,703 in 1701 compared to £141,357 in 1700 and £188,636 in 1699; (2) the Swedish government may have been remitting funds to its armies and allies on the continent via the exchanges – keeping the Hamburg rate high and supporting via arbitrage the London and Amsterdam rates; (3) the price of herring was up in the latter part of 1701.

[2] Letterbook, p. 44.

[3] *Ibid.* p. 46.

further from the principal financial centres where exchange was current and rates were fixed. Yet even at Glasgow the exchange mechanism was made to work – at a cost – to cover almost exclusively the imbalances in the Swedish trade. If the exchange mechanism could be made to work there, is it not likely that it could be made to work at comparable cost at almost any significant port in northern or western Europe?

* * *

In his second article, Mr Wilson very aptly sums up the issues remaining unsettled between Professor Heckscher and himself.[1] Even after conceding 'that the use of precious metals as a medium of international payment constitutes one kind of multilateral settlement', he observes, 'I cannot help feeling that there remains a difference of conception as to the normal pattern of international trade and payments in the mercantilist age. Professor Heckscher appears to me to suggest too small a *role* for bullion, too large a *role* for the bill of exchange. Was the world of Thomas Mun *really* as much like the world of Alfred Marshall as Professor Heckscher suggests?' This present paper has been concerned neither with the world of Thomas Mun, nor with that of Alfred Marshall, nor even with the economic 'world' at all – but merely with the payments mechanism in a specific trade (British-Northern) at a specific moment in time, some half century or more after Mun's death in 1641. If the author of such a limited exercise may be permitted a more general observation, it does seem that one weakness in the discussion hitherto has been an imprecise historicity. Neither circumstance nor practice was static during the several centuries of 'the period commonly described as "mercantilist"', least of all in the last decades of the seventeenth century. The bill of exchange came into wide use amongst the more important commercial centres in the later Middle Ages not simply to avoid the dangers and costs of specie transfers, but in part to compensate for the relative scarcity of currency.[2] By contrast, in the century or so before 1660, silver became available in unprecedented quantities in north-western Europe. This not only had the so oft emphasized effect on prices; it also made possible the expansion of trades inside and outside of Europe hitherto limited by the shortage of specie. (The European East India trade of 1740 could not have been carried on with the money supply of 1540.) The bill mechanism did not disappear during the silver glut. It simply was supplemented by specie flows of unprecedented volume. After 1660, however, there was a contraction in the supply of new silver. During the next two generations, prices in Europe declined generally in peacetime. But almost all branches of

---

[1] Wilson, 'Further evidence', *loc. cit.* 233.

[2] For the earlier history of the bill of exchange, see the following works of Raymond de Roover: *L'Evolution de la Lettre de Change, XIVe–XVIIIe siècles* (*Affaires et gens d'affaires*, IV), Paris, 1953; *Gresham on foreign exchange* (Cambridge, Massachusetts, 1949) and 'What is dry exchange? a contribution to the study of English mercantilism', *Journal of Political Economy*, LII (1944), 250–66. On p. 261 of the last cited, and elsewhere, de Roover stresses 1650 as the approximate turning point between the older inflexible bill market confined to non-negotiable foreign bills and the modern market made much more flexible through the development of negotiability, discount and the domestic bill.

trade continued to expand regardless of their state of balance.[1] Such expansion in the face of diminished money flows could only have taken place through the relatively greater use of the multilateral exchange mechanism – or in some cases by greater commodity flows to balance the trade. (For example, after ca.1708, the Marseilles Levant trade reacted to the silver shortage by exporting more woollens.) [2] In the North, however, local customs duties and Dutch competition made it impossible for the English or Scots to expand commodity exports sufficiently to balance their trade. Therefore, of necessity, the exchange mechanism had to be more heavily used. Whatever may have been the state of affairs half a century earlier,[3] by the 1690's multilateral exchange operations had become the characteristic, indeed almost the exclusive instrument for settling British trade balances with the North. The only partial exception was Russia where government regulations created an artificial demand for specie. English merchants met this demand not bilaterally, but by indirect shipments from Holland or Hamburg.

The University of Michigan

---

[1] If some branches of shipping through the Sound never reached after 1660 the levels they had reached before 1618, this must be ascribed not to contractions in western demand, but to contractions in local supplies. Danzig grain shipments never recovered during 1660–1750 their pre-1618 levels.

[2] Ruggiero Romano, *Commerce et prix du blé à Marseille au XVIIIe siècle* (*Monnaie-Prix-Conjoncture*, III) (Paris, 1956), pp. 29–30. M. Romano ascribes the chronic credit crisis in Marseilles after 1675 less to the silver shortage than to failure of the conservative Marseilles merchant community to make more extensive use of bills of exchange and other forms of commercial credit.

[3] Professor Supple is of opinion, for ca. 1600–1640, 'that even in the abnormal situation of regular exchange operations, these would not have helped English exporters; and that generally, and specifically during a slump, a chronic payments deficit with the Baltic market placed the existence of such a system entirely out of the question'. B. E. Supple, *Commercial crisis and change in England 1600–1642* (Cambridge, 1959), pp. 83–5. Mr Hinton would seem to concur, ca. 1620–40; after 1660, it is his opinion that the export of silver was still necessary to Norway, but not to Sweden. R. W. K. Hinton, *The Eastland trade and the common weal in the seventeenth century* (Cambridge, 1959), pp. 22–3, 42–3, 115–16.

[6]

EXPLORATIONS IN ECONOMIC HISTORY 17, 48–93 (1980)

Toward an Export Economy: British Exports during the Industrial Revolution

FRANÇOIS CROUZET

University of Paris–Sorbonne

The term "the Export economy" has been applied by S. B. Saul to Britain during the period 1870–1914, which saw the peak of influence of foreign trade in the economy, at least in a purely statistical sense, the ratio of foreign trade to national income having been at its maximum in the 1870s and 1880s and falling only moderately thereafter.[1] The origins of this peculiar position of the British economy have never been investigated in depth, while recent work, especially by A. H. John, D. E. C. Eversley, and P. Bairoch, seems to have established that during most of the 18th century (up to ca. 1780) exports played only a marginal role in the growth of the British economy, which received its main impetus from the home market.[2] This implies that important changes took place at some time after 1780 in the relationship between the progress of exports and national economic growth.

This is the problem with which the present paper is concerned; it will cover the period from the 1780s to 1873, when Britain had definitely become an "export economy"—though some incursions in the early and mid-18th century have been deemed necessary—and it will investigate four main points: (a) the periodization of the growth of British exports, in

---

[1] S. B. Saul, "The Export Economy, 1870–1914," *Yorkshire Bulletin of Economic and Social Research,* **17,** No. 1, May 1965, p. 5; also P. Deane and W. A. Cole, *British Economic Growth 1688–1959* (Cambridge, 1967), 2nd ed., pp. 28, 311.

[2] A. H. John, "Aspects of English Economic Growth in the First Half of the Eighteenth Century," *Economica,* N.S. **28** (1961), pp. 176–190; D. E. C. Eversley, "The Home Market and Economic Growth in England, 1750–1780," In E. L. Jones and G. E. Mingay (Eds.), *Land, Labour and Population in the Industrial Revolution* (London, 1967), pp. 206–259; P. Bairoch, "Commerce international et genèse de la révolution industrielle anglaise", *Annales E.S.C.,* **28,** No. 2 (1973), pp. 541–571. For a different view, see: W. E. Minchinton, *The Growth of English Overseas Trade in the Seventeenth and Eighteenth Centuries* (London, 1969), pp. 36–52; K. Berrill, "International Trade and the Rate of Economic Growth," *Economic History Review,* N.S. **12,** No. 3 (1960), pp. 351–359.

48

order to ascertain the stages by which Britain became an "export economy"; (b) the changing commodity structure of exports, in order to find out what kind of products were mainly responsible for the increase in exports; (c) the changing geographical distribution in exports, in order to specify the leading markets on which those goods were sold; (d) finally, the growth of exports will be confronted with the available data on national income and industrial production.

This study will be primarily descriptive, rather than analytical and will be concerned only with *domestic* exports, the reexports of "colonial and foreign goods" being left out. It faces familiar problems in its quantitative sources. The only statistics of English (and later British) exports, which are available up to the last years of the 18th century were computed by the Customs according to the system of "official values" (O.V.), i.e., at constant prices; historians generally agree, though, that they provide rough, but reliable indices of the volume of exports.[3] Moreover, during most of the 18th century, when average prices were stable, there was probably not much difference between the official values of exports and their market values.[4] On the other hand, the sharp advance in the general price level and the upheaval in the price structure, which started in the 1780s, created a serious gap between official and market values and made the former a source of inaccuracies, especially for analyzing the commodity structure of exports.[5] Fortunately, from 1796 onward, annual totals of the "declared" or "real," i.e., current values of exports (C.V.), based on the declarations of exporters, become available, and, after 1814, they are complemented by detailed figures by commodities and countries of destination, which have been extensively utilized.[6] Moreover, the late Ralph Davis had been kind enough to allow us to use, before their publication, the results of his research project on "The Industrial Revolution and Overseas Trade," and especially a series of tables in which exports are revalued at current prices for a group of 3 years in each decade, from 1784/1786 to 1854/1856, with a breakdown among the main

[3] G. N. Clark, *Guide to English Commercial Statistics. 1696–1782* (London, 1938), pp. 37–39; A. H. Imlah, *Economic Elements in the Pax Britannica* (Cambridge, Mass., 1958), pp. 20–23; B. R. Mitchell and P. Deane, *Abstract of British Historical Statistics* (Cambridge, 1962) (cited infra: *Abstract*), p. 275; T. S. Ashton, Introduction to E. B. Schumpeter, *English Overseas Trade Statistics. 1697–1808* (Oxford, 1960), pp. 4–6; P. Deane, *The First Industrial Revolution* (Cambridge, 1965), p. 62; Deane and Cole, pp. 42–45, Appendix I, pp. 315–317.

[4] J. F. Shepherd and G. M. Walton, *Shipping, Maritime Trade and the Economic Development of Colonial North America* (London, 1972), pp. 177–184, Appendix II; also R. Davis, "English Foreign Trade, 1700–1774," *Economic History Review, N.S.* **15**, No. 2 (1962), p. 285, note 2; Minchinton, p. 15, note 3.

[5] *Abstract*, p. 276; Ashton, in Schumpeter, pp. 4–5; Deane and Cole, pp. 15, 317, Table 84. From 1804 onward, the gap between C.V. and O.V. began to narrow.

[6] Imlah, pp. 23–24, 26, on the validity of those statistics.

50   FRANÇOIS CROUZET

areas of destination and the major commodities.[6a] We have also used A.
H. Imlah's volume series for exports from the United Kingdom from 1796
onward, and some other volume series which have been computed with
his index of the price of exports as deflator.[7]

These time series have been processed by computer to calculate their
mean rates of growth per year for various periods or subperiods. These
calculations have been made between bench-mark years *by exponential
adjustment,* so that all the values between those years are taken into
account.[8] Absolute and relative deviations from the long-term trend of
each series have also been systematically calculated and they have been
used to pinpoint accurately the turning points between the periods of
acceleration and deceleration.[9]

I. THE STAGES OF GROWTH

The 18th century, taken as a whole, did not see a remarkably fast
growth of English exports: from 1697 to 1800, their mean rate of growth
per year is only 1.5%. But, a most interesting feature is the existence of
five fairly distinct periods (about 20 years long) of alternating growth and
stagnation or decline. This alternation, which had been pointed out by
Deane and Cole,[10] is confirmed by the analysis of the deviations from
trend and by the calculation of exponential rates of growth between the
turning points which they reveal (cf. Table 1). It was only during the last
of those phases, starting in the 1780s, that British exports underwent a
really fast and sustained growth, a well-known fact that this paper can
only confirm.

(A) From 1697 to 1714, despite (or because of) the war of Spanish
succession, the rate of growth is markedly higher than for the whole

---

[6a] R. Davis, *The Industrial Revolution and British Overseas Trade* (Leicester, 1978), pp.
94–101, Tables 41 to 48. Except for these tables, this book (and other recent literature) has
not been used in the present article, which was completed in 1975.

[7] A list of the various time-series, which have been used, and of their sources is given in
appendix; so detailed references to them are not supplied.

[8] All rates of growth quoted in this paper have been computed by this method. So the
position in the business cycle of the first and last years of the periods for which they are
calculated has no serious influence on the growth rate.

[9] The writer expresses his warmest thanks to Professor M. Barbut and to M. Auffray, of
the Department of Applied Mathematics and Computer Science, at the University of Paris–
Sorbonne, for their help in these calculations.

[10] Deane and Cole, p. 47, also Table 14, p. 48. J. W. Wright ("British Economic Growth,
1688–1959," *Economic History Review, N.S.* **18,** No. 2, August 1965, p. 399) maintains
that, if adjustments for war were made, all we could have might be a smoothly accelerating
growth; but it would be artificial, even if it was possible, to take into account only the
relatively short (between 1739 and 1815) periods of peace and it is wiser to consider the
course of exports as it actually took place.

BRITISH EXPORTS, 1783–1873   51

TABLE 1
Mean Rates of Growth per Year of Exports from England and Wales

Year	%
1697 to 1714	2.8
1714 to 1744	0.9
1744 to 1760	3.0
1760 to 1781	−1.5
1781 to 1800	5.1

century; deviations from trend are mostly positive and increasing to a peak in 1714.[11]

(B) Then comes a 30-year period of much slower growth and even stagnation of exports, which fluctuated around £ 5 million. From +26.7% in 1714, deviations fall, irregularly but clearly, to −20.3% in 1744 and are negative for a majority of years. If the declining trend which had developed from 1714 to 1727 was interrupted by a rather strong recovery from 1728 to 1738, this upsurge was cut short by the outbreak of war with Spain in 1739 and, in the early 1740s, up to 1744, exports were depressed.[12]

(C) In 1745, exports started to recover and they rose very fast up to 1750, when official values were 75% above their 1744 level, and the deviation from trend was +27.9%. Though exports declined afterward to 1755, they rose later to new record figures in 1759/1761 and in 1764, when for the first time their official value exceeded £ 10 million. Deviations from trend are constantly positive from 1748 to 1768 (except in 1755), but they reach their peak in 1760 (+28.2%) and then start to decline.[13] The period from 1745 to 1760 was thus one of relatively marked progress for exports.

Deane and Cole have attributed much importance to the turning point of the mid-1740s and to the "dramatic increase" in exports which followed; they have maintained that the period 1745–1760 witnessed an advance almost as spectacular, if not nearly as regular, as after 1780.[14] There was indeed a significant change in the pace of British exports, but, if the jump from 1744 to 1750 was very sharp (at a rate of growth per year of 9.8%), it

[11] Deane and Cole, p. 48; P. Mathias, *The First Industrial Nation. An Economic History of Britain, 1700–1914* (London, 1969), p. 98; A. H. John, "Agricultural Productivity and Economic Growth in England, 1700–1760," In E. L. Jones (Ed.), *Agriculture and Economic Growth in England, 1650–1815* (London, 1967), p. 180.

[12] Deane and Cole, p. 48; Ashton, in Schumpeter, p. 13; Ashton, *Economic Fluctuations in England, 1700–1800* (Oxford, 1959), pp. 58–60; Minchinton, pp. 14–16; John, in Jones, pp. 180, 190.

[13] This is why we have chosen 1760 as the turning-point.

[14] Deane and Cole, p. 48; also Davis, "English Foreign Trade . . .," p. 295. But these views have been mitigated in W. A. Cole, "Eighteenth-Century Economic Growth Revisited," *Explorations in Economic History,* 10 (1973), pp. 328, 331, 333.

52   FRANÇOIS CROUZET

was short-lived and the growth from 1750 to 1760 was much slower (1.4% per year); this jump was more an end-of-war and postwar recovery and boom, resulting from the release of foreign pent-up demand and also from exceptional sales of grain abroad,[15] than the beginning of a sustained growth of exports, while the high level of overseas sales in 1759/1761 is related to the special circumstances of the Seven Years War.[16] Anyway, the rate of growth of exports from 1744 to 1760 is markedly lower than from 1781 to 1800 and most of the progress which had then been achieved was cancelled by the depression which followed.[17]

(D) After the end of the Seven Years War, English exports reached, in 1764, a record figure of £ 11.5 million, which was not to be exceeded before 1788, but they declined in the following years up to 1769 and, if they recovered somewhat in 1770 and 1771, they suffered in the 1770s an almost uninterrupted fall which brought them in 1781 to £ 7 million, i.e., lower than in any year since 1745. Deviations from trend decreased sharply after 1760, to reach eventually the low level of −39.4% in 1781. From 1760 to 1781, the rate of growth per year of exports is negative, at −1.5%. These 20 years not only of stagnation, but of actual decline in the volume of exports, are quite unique in the history of British trade in the 18th and 19th centuries; but their importance has been often overlooked, though they are a strong argument for those scholars who stress the role played by the home market in British economic growth at the beginning of the Industrial Revolution.[18] Though difficulties in European markets played a part at first,[19] the main cause of this depression was the conflict with the 13 colonies, starting with their boycott of British goods and culminating in an unsuccessful war against America, France, Spain, and Holland.

(E) After the trough of 1781, exports rose very fast and unceasingly until 1792, with only a slight setback in 1785 and some slowing down from 1784 to 1787; exports from Great Britain (O.V.) increased by 141% from £ 7.6 million in 1781 to £ 18.3 million in 1792 (see Table 2).[20]

[15] Ashton, *Fluctuations*, pp. 46, 183, Table 3; Ashton, in Schumpeter, p. 12; Minchinton, pp. 25, 27, 43, 63, Table 7; John, in Jones, p. 179; id., review of Deane and Cole, in *Kyklos*, 17, No. 2 (1964), pp. 278–279; Cole, p. 338.

[16] Ashton, *Fluctuations*, pp. 60–61; Davis, "English Foreign Trade . . .," pp. 295–296; Minchinton, pp. 14–16; Cole, pp. 329 sqq., 339.

[17] See also Deane and Cole, p. 48, Table 14; P. Deane and H. J. Habakkuk, "The Take-Off in Britain," In W. W. Rostow (Ed.), *The Economics of Take-Off into Sustained Growth* (London, 1964), p. 81, Table 3.

[18] Eversley, pp. 209, 236, 247–249; Bairoch, p. 558.

[19] Ashton, *Fluctuations*, pp. 46, 61; Ashton, in Schumpeter, p. 14; Minchinton, p. 17; M. W. Flinn, *The Origins of the Industrial Revolution* (London, 1966), p. 58.

[20] With Davis' current values, the rise would be faster (except at the end of the period), because of the increase in prices: from 1784/86 to 1794/96: +76% (O.V.: +54%); from 1794/96 to 1804/06: +72% (O.V.: +46%); from 1804/06 to 1814/16: +16% (O.V.: +53%); *The Industrial Revolution . . .*, pp. 94–97.

TABLE 2
Mean Rates of Growth per Year of Exports

	Year	%
From England and Wales (O.V.)	1781–1792	7.0
	1792–1800	5.0
From Great Britain (O.V.)	1781–1792	6.9
	1792–1802	5.9
	1802–1814	3.1
From the United Kingdom (O.V.)	1802–1814	3.2
Imlah's volume series	1796–1814	1.9
	1802–1814	2.0
Current values	1796–1814	1.7
	1802–1814	0.7

However, several writers have pointed out rightly that part of this upsurge of exports was a rebound from the artificially low level to which they had been forced by the War of American Independence, a result of the cessation of hostilities and of the backlog of export orders accumulating in markets which had been cut off from Britain during the war: the low starting point of 1781 (or even 1783) exaggerates the steepness of the growth curve.[21] These views can be supported mathematically: first, despite the fast growth from 1781 to 1800, the rate of growth of English exports for the century 1697–1800 (1.5%) is slightly lower than for 1697–1760 (1.6%), so that the post-1781 gains did not quite cancel the losses suffered during the depression of the 1760s and 1770s; second, the deviations from trend, though recovering from their 1781 low point, remain negative until 1789; it was only from 1790 onward that the "recovery" gave way to a new growth.

Moreover, the fact that the American war had not been victorious helped to make this postwar rebound more pronounced and sustained than after earlier successful wars. Instead of having to hand back enemy territories which she had occupied, British recovered some colonies which she had lost; there was no cessation of subsidies to allies (which had stimulated exports during the Seven Years War), as she had fought alone; the enemy markets which reopened were much larger than formerly: not only Spain and France, but also Holland and the United States.[22]

Even so, the truly spectacular and unprecedented character of the upsurge of exports in the 1780s must not be underestimated; it was "both more rapid and sustained than in any previous period" and there was

[21] Deane and Habakkuk, p. 78; Deane, *First Industrial*, p. 66; Flinn, p. 60.
[22] However, see Cole, pp. 341–342.

54   FRANÇOIS CROUZET

TABLE 3
Percentage Increases between the Quinquennial Average
Official Values of Exports from Great Britain

Years	%
1783/87 to 1788/92	+35
1788/92 to 1793/97	+ 9
1793/97 to 1798/1802	+45
1798/1802 to 1803/07	+ 2
1803/07 to 1808/12	+23

undoubtedly during those years a decisive change of momentum in the course of British exports, which entered an entirely new stage.[23] Moreover, their fast growth was sustained for another decade.

The uninterrupted upsurge of British exports came to an end in 1793, when the outbreak of war with France brought about a serious slump. The peak figure of 1792 was not exceeded before 1796 and the average official value for the 5 years 1793–1797 was only 9% higher than for the preceding quinquennium (cf. Table 3). But there was a new and very sharp upsurge of exports from 1798 to 1802, so that the rate of growth of British exports from 1792 to 1802 (5.9%) is only one percentage point lower than from 1781 to 1792, a difference which cannot be interpreted as a sign of deceleration; the continuous increase, without any cyclical fluctuation, which had taken place after 1781, was obviously exceptional and, war or no war, a more normal pattern, involving some years of recession, was bound to reappear. It would be absurd to project the 1781–1792 trend to find out the export figures which would have been reached if the war had not broken out. The 1790s and early 1800s are clearly a prolongation of the 1780s and, taken together, these 20 years are one of the major leaps forward in the history of British exports.[24]

However, the growth rates in Table 2, the figures in Table 3, and the deviations from trend show that there was a definite slowing down in the progress of exports after 1802, a year which was a new turning point in the fluctuations of British exports growth rates.[25]

The deviations from trend of the various time-series reach peak positive figures between 1799 and 1802, but they tend to decline from 1803 onward, a movement which was to go on after the end of the wars. The volume of exports drifted downward from 1802 to 1808 and, despite the new peak figures which it reached in 1809, 1810, and 1814, its recovery during the

[23] Deane and Cole, p. 47; Deane and Habakkuk, pp. 77–78; also Ashton, in Schumpeter, p. 14; Mathias, p. 98.
[24] This is stressed by Deane and Habakkuk, pp. 78–79.
[25] M. M. Edwards, *The Growth of the British Cotton Trade, 1780–1815* (Manchester, 1967), p. 74, writes that, after 1803, the export effort for cotton goods resembled a gigantic dumping operation.

later years of the Napoleonic war was far less pronounced than the upsurge it had known around 1800.[26] As for the current values, their growth rate from 1802 to 1814 is extremely low. After the fast growth of exports from 1782 to 1802, came therefore a phase of much slower growth, which actually extends astride the Napoleonic war and the post-war years.

It is obvious that the short-run fluctuations of British exports during the French wars were largely influenced by military and political developments abroad, but the impact of the wars on the long-run growth of exports and on the movements which have just been delineated is far less clear.

Two factors are often quoted as having strongly stimulated British exports during the wars: hostilities crippled Britain's major competitors on the Continent and gave to the British Navy effective control of oceanic routes, so that Britain alone could take full advantage of markets enhanced by growing population and incomes in Europe and America.[27] However, the impact of those factors must not be overestimated.

There is no doubt that the Revolution and the war seriously harmed French industry during the 1790s, that its output and its exports more or less collapsed. Moreover, they interrupted for some time the attempts which had been made in France in the 1780s to introduce British innovations and, as technology was progressing rapidly in Britain, the gap between the two countries widened.[28] But, as the rise of British exports in the 1790s and 1800s resulted mainly from the spectacular upsurge of cottons exports, the French competition which was crippled by Revolution and war was a *potential* much more than an actual competition, as the pre-1789 French cotton industry was not competitive with the British and did not export much.[29] The other industrial areas of the Continent suffered far less than France from internal disturbances and wars, and the difficulties of the cotton industries of Saxony and Switzerland came mostly from British competition enhanced by British technological superiority (from which they were actually saved by the Continental Blockade after 1806). It is thus difficult to see which of Britain's competitors in cottons were really crippled by the wars.[30] Other British manufactured goods, how-

[26] With Imlah's volume figures, there is a decrease of 2% from 1798/1802 to 1803/07 and an increase of only 14% from 1803/07 to 1808/12.

[27] Deane and Habakkuk, pp. 78–79; also Flinn, p. 60.

[28] M. Lévy-Leboyer, *Les banques européennes et l'industrialisation internationale dans la première moitié du XIXe siècle* (Paris, 1964), pp. 23, 27–32.

[29] And the "crippling factor" ought to have had its strongest impact during the early years of the Revolutionary war, when the French economy was collapsing; actually, from 1792 to 1797, British exports to Europe fell sharply and total exports did not increase much.

[30] Though, after 1807, the Continental cotton industries suffered from the shortage and high price of cotton wool, which resulted from the British Orders in Council and the American Embargo.

56   FRANÇOIS CROUZET

ever, possibly did displace French articles which either were no longer competitive or could no longer reach their former markets. A test-case might be linens and silks, two French specialities which, before the Revolution, were very competitive with similar British goods. Actually, exports of British linens did increase very slowly during the 1790s and 1800s, while exports of silks rose somewhat up to 1796, but declined markedly afterward.[31] In both cases, the substitution of British for French products does not seem to have been significant. However, linens and silks everywhere then were suffering from the competition of cottons and such French products might have been replaced, not by similar British goods, but by British cottons—and there is evidence, though at the end of the wars period, that this actually happened.[32]

As for Britain's ascendancy at sea, it was not before the later years of the Napoleonic war that it was both absolute and fully used, through the enforcement of the Orders in Council of November 1807, to favor British trade by cutting off competitors from overseas, i.e., American markets, and giving Britain a monopoly there. Previously, the Continentals were not prevented from exporting to the United States or to the French or Spanish colonies.[33] It is true that they did not make much inroad into the United States market, but this had nothing to do with the war: the French had discovered to their disappointment during the peace years after 1783, that they could not compete there with the cheaper goods and better trading organization of the British. However, the greatest gain to British trade from 1808 onward came from the opening of Brazil and of the Spanish colonies, which was a consequence of the political and military events in the Peninsula in 1807 and 1808, much more than a benefit accruing directly from sea power.[34]

British sea power did, however, make easy the conquest of a number of enemy colonies, which henceforth were supplied by Britain rather than by the Continentals. This gave to the British, during the later years of both wars, new markets, which were not insignificant: during the 4 years 1798–1801, the "Conquered West Indies" received 5.3% of total British exports (O.V.).[35]

---

[31] See Table 5. Deviations from trend, after a maximum in 1792 for linens and in 1796 for silks, fall rather sharply.

[32] Edwards, pp. 56, 60.

[33] But exports from enemy countries to their colonies had to make a "circuitous" voyage, which increased their cost and this was a stimulus to the smuggling trade from the "Free ports" in the British West Indies to the enemy colonies.

[34] Part of the trade which was thus carried directly with those territories was only a substitute for a former circuitous or illegal trade.

[35] In 1808, their share was 4.8%; we do not have separate figures for those territories after 1808; see also Table 9. There were other conquests in Africa (the Cape of Good Hope) and the East Indies. The slaves' revolt in San Domingo—an indirect effect of the French Revolution—also favored British trade.

Another factor, which has been mentioned as a stimulus to British exports, is the unrequited capital export by the government in wartime both for the maintenance of British troops abroad and as loans or subsidies to allies. However, such expenditures did not become really heavy before 1808.[36]

To sum up, the wars brought about some trade diversion to the benefit of Britain and to the detriment of the Continentals, but this diversion does not seem to have been very large,[37] except for the opening of the Latin American market, from 1808 onward, but a large part of the additional exports thus engendered only offset the loss of the markets in Europe and the United States at the same time. On the other hand, such redirection does not seem to have played the dominant part in the export boom of 1798 to 1802, when there was more trade creation than trade diversion, thanks to the fall in the prices of cotton goods. Moreover, the boom in exports to the United States, which was responsible for a large share of the increase in total exports during the 1790s, was only stimulated marginally by the war: insofar as American national income and foreign purchasing power were pushed upward by the profits of the neutral and indirect carrying trades. The main factor was the increase in demand from the American home market.

On the other hand, the wars also had some serious negative impact upon exports, through the sudden closures of markets, when European countries joined France against England or were occupied by the French armies. In particular, the Continental Blockade, which, despite extensive smuggling and the ingenuity of British merchants in finding new trade routes and new outlets, was pretty effective at times in closing most European markets to British goods, and the dispute with the United States from 1807 onward, culminating in the war of 1812, were undoubtedly instrumental in the slowing down of the growth of British exports during the Napoleonic war.[38] It is also possible that the impoverishment of European countries by protracted warfare and the stagnation in Britain of consumption per capita, which affected imports and therefore the purchasing power of foreign countries, had deleterious effects upon British exports. On the whole, and in the long run, the French wars seem to have been either slightly unfavorable or simply neutral toward British ex-

---

[36] A. D. Gayer, W. W. Rostow, and A. J. Schwartz, *The Growth and Fluctuations of the British Economy, 1790–1850* (Oxford, 1953), II, p. 647. The calculation of those foreign expenditures by J. L. Anderson, "A Measure of the Effect of British Public Finance, 1793–1815," *Economic History Review*, N.S. 27, No. 4 (1974), p. 618, Table I, shows that they exceeded £ 4 million per year only in 1794–95 and from 1808 to 1815.

[37] And the various factors of diversion were not effective with a continuous intensity. The situation is quite different for reexports.

[38] cf. F. Crouzet, *L'économie britannique et le Blocus Continental, 1806–1813* (Paris, 1958, 2 vols.).

58   FRANÇOIS CROUZET

TABLE 4
Mean Rates of Growth per Year of Exports from the United Kingdom

	Imlah's volume series (%)	Current values (%)
A. 1814–1846	4.3	1.1
1846–1873	4.7	5.7
1814–1873	4.8	3.4
B. 1802–1826	2.5	−0.5
1826–1848		2.7
1848–1873		5.6
1826–1856	5.6	
1856–1873	3.8	

ports,[39] and the ubiquitous military and political factors might conceal the influence of some purely economic forces.[40]

The progress of British exports after the French wars is shown in Table 4.

The periodization in part B of the table has been suggested by the deviations from trend. Their decline, which had started during the Napoleonic war, after 1802, goes on after the peace, to a nadir in 1826, both for volumes and values. But, after 1826, deviations in the volume and the value series behave differently. Deviations in volume rise progressively to reach a peak (+25.6%, against −28.2% in 1826) in 1856, after which they tend to fall again.[41] After the fast growth of export volume from 1782 to 1802, there was thus a phase of markedly slower growth up to 1826, followed by a period of acceleration and fast growth from 1826 to 1856 and a deceleration thereafter—despite the boom of the late 1860s and early 1870s. On the other hand, if the periods considered are those delimited by "political" changes (the end of the wars, the triumph of Free Trade), the rates of growth of volume are quite close and seem to have been just a little higher for 1814–1846 than for 1781–1814.[42]

As for the current values, their deviations from trend fall sharply from 1802 to 1826, but their curve is U-shaped, with its bottom from 1826 to 1848, where they fluctuate around a low level, and it is only from 1849 onward that they rise very sharply to a peak of +74.5% in 1872. Moreover, unlike the volume figures (which do not cease to rise on trend,

[39] The fact that the early years of the two wars saw only a modest increase of exports over the preceding period suggests that the state of war per se was not favorable to British exports.

[40] As the deceleration which started after 1802 went on after the war, it might be part of a long-term fluctuation, independent from the influence of political and military developments.

[41] They have a minimum in 1864 (−5.1%) and then rise, but to +17.3% only in 1871.

[42] It is difficult to be definite, because Imlah's volume series starts in 1796, and the rate of growth for 1781–1814 must be calculated on the different official values series.

despite the postwar slumps), the current value of British exports, after a very slow growth from 1802 to 1814, tends to fall from 1815 to the late 1820s and only starts to rise again clearly in the late 1830s.[43] There is therefore during the first half of the 19th century, not only a different periodization in the course of volumes and values, but also a contrast between the fast growth of the volume of exports and the much slower growth of their values.[44]

This contrast resulted from a marked fall in the prices of exports during this period; cotton yarn and cloth had the sharpest fall and its impact was aggravated by the growing proportion of cotton textiles in total export volume. Those falling prices resulted mainly from increasing mechanization and higher productivity, so that they must not be interpreted as a sign of "economic adversity," inasmuch as the volume of exports grew rapidly.[45] But, L. G. S. Sandberg has also shown that there was a substantial and (after 1830) continuous decline in the average quality of British cottons exported, as an increased share of them was shipped to low-income countries (especially India), which bought only low-quality goods.[46]

However, from 1852 onward, the average prices of exports rose, so that the contrast between the rates of growth of volume and of value disappears for the period 1846–1873, when actually export values grew faster than volumes.

On the other hand, the rate of growth of export volume from 1846 to 1873 is only slightly higher than from 1814 to 1846 and this raises doubts about Imlah's views on "the failure of the British protectionist system," i.e., its alleged retardative impact upon industrial output and exports, and the "success of British Free Trade policy," which he makes largely responsible for a phenomenal and unprecedented growth of exports after 1842.[47] Imlah argued that the Corn Laws restricted the expansion of the

[43] As is shown by their averages for quinquennial periods in Imlah, pp. 37–38, Table 2.

[44] This differential manifested itself from the turn of the century (cf. Table II); the index of the average price of exports, which has been computed by Imlah (p. 94, Table 8) has its peak

[44] This differential manifested itself from the turn of the century (cf. Table 2); the index of British industrial prices reaches its peak in 1814: G. Hueckel, "War and the British Economy, 1783–1815: A General Equilibrium Analysis," *Explorations in Economic History,* **10** (1973), p. 388, Table 3.

[45] Imlah, pp. 93, 100, 102–109.

[46] L. G. Sandberg, "Movements in the Quality of British Cotton Textile Exports, 1815–1913," *Journal of Economic History,* **28,** No. 1 (1968), pp. 1, 7–9, 13, 19–20. This fall does not mean that specific types of cloth had deteriorated, but that there is a shift toward cheaper cloth.

[47] Imlah, pp. 115, 117, 123, 125–128, 132, 156–157, 163–167. Actually, Imlah has made a serious mistake in calculating his rates of growth of exports: he gives them as 11% per year in volume from 1842 to 1873 (against 7% from 1816 to 1842) and 14% in value (against 1.5%). But he has computed them between the first and last years of these two periods; as 1842 is a year of depression and 1873 a year of boom, the rate of growth is heavily overestimated.

FRANÇOIS CROUZET

British home market and the purchasing power of foreign countries, especially in Northern Europe, while the import of grain was a spasmodic, emergency trade, paid for in part by gold, so that the additional purchasing power which it brought to foreign countries did not result in an immediate or equivalent response in their buying of British goods; otherwise there was a high degree of export–import dependence in British trade with many areas, with exports being the dependent variable.[48] However, there is much good sense in J. H. Clapham's older views that up to the 1840s, Britain did not need large regular imports of grain and that freer importation of the other articles which were kept out by protection (foreign timber, sugar, and coffee, French wines, German linens) would not have had much influence upon exports; and that "no amount of tariff manipulation or reciprocity could have opened very much wider the European markets," given the decidedly protectionist policy of France, Austria–Hungary, and Russia (a fact which Imlah overlooks) and the existing reasonably open channels for British goods through the Low Countries and various German states.[49] If British protectionism slowed down the growth of British exports, it cannot have done so by much; that the growth of export *volumes* accelerated from 1826 to 1856, to slow down later, seems independent of tariff policy.

This survey of the course of British exports during the 18th century and the first three quarters of the 19th century shows that the alternation of periods of growth and stagnation or decline in the *volume* of exports, which Deane and Cole observed in the 18th century, seems to have existed also in the 19th, with the difference that there was no period of actual decline (like the 1770s), but only an alternation of phases of faster (1782–1802, 1827–1856) and of slower (1803–1826, 1857–1873) growth. In the long run, the growth of British exports would display a "cyclical" pattern, with long fluctuations in its rate of 40 to 50 years.[50] The growth of export values was a function of both volume and prices. From the time ca. 1790 when the price stability of the 18th century came to an end, the fluctuations in the rate of growth of export values are quite pronounced, with two periods of fast growth (when both volume and prices of manufactured exports rose together), from 1782 to 1802 and from 1849 to 1873, and

[48] This is confirmed by R. C. O. Matthews, *A Study in Trade-Cycle History: Economic Fluctuations in Great Britain, 1833–1842* (Cambridge, 1954), pp. 43 sqq., for trade with regions others than the USA and Northern Europe.

[49] J. H. Clapham, *An Economic History of Modern Britain*, Vol. I (Cambridge, 1939 edition), pp. 479–481; R. G. Wilson, *Gentlemen Merchants. The Merchant Community in Leeds (1700–1830)* (Manchester, 1971), pp. 113, 116, on the impact of *foreign* protection on British woollens exports.

[50] We put cyclical between inverted commas, because we do not want to imply that there was a self-generating movement like in the short-term business cycle. The volume series of exports for the main products display the same "cyclical" pattern in their rates of growth, from the mid-18th century onward, but with different turning points.

TABLE 5
Mean Annual Rates of Growth per Year, Principal British Exports
(Official Values)[a]

Product	1697–1760	1760–1783	1783–1792	1792–1802	1802–1814	1783–1814
Woolen and worsted manufactures	0.9	−2.2	4.9	4.9	−1.4	1.8[b]
Cotton yarn and manufactures	2.8	2.9	10.7	17.3	8.4	12.3
Linens	6.6	−1.6	6.4	0.5	2.6[c]	2.2[c]
Silks	1.2	−2.2	0.8	−0.7	−0.7	−1.1
Iron and steel, unwrought and wrought	3.5	−0.3	9.6	3.1	1.4	2.3
Nonferrous metals and manufactures	1.5	0.8	6.9	1.9	−4.9	−0.5
Total exports	1.6	−1.4	6.0	5.9	3.1	4.1

[a] Exports are from England and Wales up to 1791, from Great Britain later. Calculated by exponential adjustment, and expressed in percentage.
[b] The data used stop in 1808; woollen hats are included, except for 1802–1814.
[c] The data used stop in 1812.

in-between periods of slower growth or even decline. This will have an important impact upon the relationship between exports and national product.

II. THE SECTORS OF GROWTH

During most of the 18th century—up to the 1760s, exports of woollens and worsteds grew at a slow pace (0.9% per year between 1697 and 1760 or 1772, against 1.6% for total English exports; see Table 5),[51] while shipments of certain other goods, such as linens, cottons, metals, metal manufactures, and coal progressed more and, in some cases, much more rapidly. The result was a steady and pronounced decline of the share of woollens in total exports (from 70% in 1700/1709 to 44% in 1760/1769)—though they remained by far their largest single component—and an increase in the share of the "other" goods, reflecting the broadening of the British economy and the widening range of its competitive manufactures.[52] The percentage contributions of these various commodities to the

[51] Deane, *First Industrial,* p. 53. N.B. The terms woolens (which include worsteds), cottons, cotton goods (or fabrics, or manufactures), linens, silks, apply only to cloth woven of those materials; we write of wool, cotton, or linen *products* when twist and yarn are added.

[52] Tables and comments in: Schumpeter, p. 12; Mathias, p. 466, Table 15; Minchinton, pp. 24–25; Eversley, p. 223, Table 1; Deane and Cole p. 30.

increase of total English exports between 1699/1701 and 1772/1774 can be calculated:[53]

Woollens and worsteds	21.1
Linens, silks, cottons, hats	20.6
Metals and metal manufactures	21.3
All other goods	37.0

From the 1780s, this "balanced growth" on a broad front was to give way to a different pattern. The method used to analyze this development will be to ascertain the contribution of each major group of exported commodities to the growth of British exports, by calculating the marginal changes in exports of these groups, i.e., the proportion of the net change in exports of each of them to the net change in total British exports.[54] The results of these calculations are given in Table 6, which is based on R. Davis's current values; as his first figures are for 1784/1786, we have used *official values* for calculating the percentage contributions of the major groups to the growth of total exports from 1780/1782 to 1790/1792:[55]

Woollens and worsteds	35.7
Cotton goods	16.3
Linens	4.8
Silks	1.1
Iron and ironwares	8.9
Nonferrous metals and manufactures	5.5
All other goods	27.8

During the 1780s, the exports of all the major commodities (except silks) increased at a fast pace (cf. Table 5), including those of woollens, which had been so sluggish earlier in the century. Of course, exports of cottons grew much more (10.7% per year in volume between 1783 and 1792) than those of other goods (except ironwares), but they started from

---

[53] From figures in Davis, "English Foreign Trade . . .," p. 302. The share of cottons was only 3.7%. Their ratio to total exports remained minute up to the 1780s.

[54] If X are total exports and X_c the exports of cottons, the contribution of cottons to the growth of total exports between the years t_0 and t_1 is: $C_c = (X_c t_1 - X_c t_0)/(X t_1 - X t_0) \times 100$. However, there is a difficulty for several periods, when some items are increasing and some others decreasing; in such cases, the percentages which have been calculated are those between the *net* increase in the exports of each growing item and the "*gross*" increase of total exports, i.e., the sum of those increasing items (which is equivalent to the *net* increase of total exports plus the amount needed to make good for the deficiency created by the decreasing items). This gives a more accurate idea of the contribution of each commodity to the growth of exports.

[55] As the changes in the price structure were not too serious during this period, this calculation is valid.

TABLE 6
Contributions of the Principal Products to the Increase of
Total British Exports (Current Values)[a]

Product	From 1784/86 to 1794/96 (%)	From 1794/96 to 1804/06 (%)	From 1804/06 to 1814/16 (%)	From 1784/86 to 1814/16 (%)	From 1814/16 to 1844/46[b] (%)
Woollen and worsted yarn and manufactures	18.1	6.0	22.8	14.0	10.8
Cotton yarn and manufactures	28.8	72.8	31.5	52.8	45.9
Other textiles[c]	10.4	3.3	8.6	6.9	9.8
Iron and Ironwares	9.6	3.6	—	—	16.9
Nonferrous metals and manufactures	10.0	3.8	12.3	7.9	16.6
All other goods	23.1	10.5	24.9	18.3	—

[a] The symbol — indicates that an actual decrease took place in the category between the years indicated.

[b] Pertains to exports from the United Kingdom (excluding exports to Ireland). Other columns pertain to Great Britain and include exports to Ireland.

[c] Linens (including linen yarn), silks, hats, haberdashery, garments.

Source. Percentages calculated from R. Davis, *The Industrial Revolution and British Overseas Trade* (Leicester, 1978), pp. 94–97, 100.

low levels (£ 336,000 O.V., in 1780/1782); thus, though their volume increased nearly fivefold in 10 years, their contribution to the growth of total exports (O.V.) from 1780/1782 to 1790/1792 was relatively modest (16%) and much inferior to that of woollens. For the slightly later period from 1784/1786 to 1794/1796 and in current values, their contribution is substantially larger (29%), but those of woollens, of the other textiles, and of "all other goods" remain very large, while that of iron wares is again under 10%.

It seems therefore that the leap forward of exports in the 1780s (and even the early 1790s) was not based mainly on the technological and organizational innovations in the cotton and iron industries and that the significance of those industries for the export trade at that time must not be overestimated.[56] Though the spectacular rise in cottons exports was a novel and crucial development, there was still a general advance on a broad front like that earlier in the century.

It was only during the 1790s and 1800s that the position changed rather drastically. The growth of the volume of cotton products exports accelerated and, from 1792 to 1802, reached the amazing and record rate of 17.3%

[56] Ashton, in Schumpeter, p. 14; Ashton, *Fluctuations*, pp. 62–63; Davis, "English Foreign Trade . . .," p. 298; Mathias, p. 98; Deane and Habakkuk, p. 78.

FRANÇOIS CROUZET

per year;[57] it was to go on during the next decade at a slower, but still impressive pace. As for woollens exports, they maintained from 1792 to 1802 the same relatively high rate of growth (4.9%) as from 1783 to 1792, but their volume (and its deviation from trend) reached a peak in 1801 and then fell markedly.[58] For the other types of goods, the rates of growth were much more modest after 1792 than from 1783 to 1792, and for silks and nonferrous metals, there was an actual fall in the volume of exports after 1796 and 1802, respectively.[59]

As a consequence of those differentials in the rates of growth after 1792, cotton goods (and yarns, which had started to be exported in growing quantities from 1794) were responsible for 72.8% of the great (72%) increase in British exports (C.V.) between 1794/1796 and 1804/1806, while the contribution of woollens was only 6%,[60] and that of metals and metal manufactures 7.4%.[61] These figures are consistent with the conclusions of M. M. Edwards, who puts in the 1790s and 1800s (later than his predecessors) the period of decisive progress for the cotton industry, and with Deane and Cole's view that the rise of the cotton industry at the end of the 18th century was partly compensated by a slowing down in the growth of the other textile industries.[62]

However, between 1804/1806 and 1814/1816, the contribution of cotton goods and yarn to the increase of total exports (which was itself modest: 16%) was much smaller than for the preceding decade, falling to 31.5%, the same as woollens and other textiles together, with a compensating larger share for nonferrous metals and manufactures and "other goods." These changes resulted both from a recovery of noncotton exports in 1814/1816 and from the fall in the prices of cottons.[63] Nonetheless, it seems that, from the resumption of war, up to 1812, cotton products were entirely responsible for the increase in total British exports, which, without them, would have actually declined.[64] And finally, if we compare the current values of exports in 1784/1786 and 1814/1816, we find that exports of cotton products had increased by 2283%, while those of woollens,

[57] There was an especially sharp rise in 1798 and 1799: Edwards, p. 73.

[58] Ashton, *Fluctuations*, p. 76; Wilson, p. 111: in the West Riding, the strong upward trend in activity since 1783 was broken down by a crisis in 1801 and 30 generally lean years followed.

[59] Between 1803 and 1815, the O.V. of iron goods exports never reached their peak of 1802 and their rate of growth is very slow.

[60] Owing to the fall of woollens exports after 1801.

[61] From 1794/96 to 1804/06, the C.V. of cotton products exports increased 330%; that of the other groups between 18% (woollens) and 31% (nonferrous metals).

[62] Edwards, pp. 8, 10, 12–14, 49–50, 73; Deane and Cole, pp. 54, 212–213.

[63] While the prices of non-cotton exports fell far less or not at all; Imlah, p. 106.

[64] If we compare the O.V. of exports in 1800/02 and 1810/12, exports of woollens, other textiles, metal goods, and "other goods" show a marked fall, while cotton goods and yarn progress by 236%; their increase is equivalent to 209% of the *net* increase in total exports and 100% of their *gross* increase.

other textiles, nonferrous metals, and "other goods" had increased three-
or fourfold only and iron goods exports had actually fallen, and that
cottonwares were responsible for over half (52.8%) of the increase in total
exports, against 14% for woollens, 7% for the other textiles, 8% for
nonferrous metals, and 18% for "other goods." Though the ascendancy
of the cotton industry is not overwhelming, the low level of its exports in
the 1780s must be remembered and, on the whole, the growth of British
exports during those crucial 30 years was very much "unbalanced."

The enormous increase in the overseas sales of cotton goods was due
mostly to their relative cheapness compared with other fabrics and to the
fact that they enjoyed an elastic demand; thanks to the opening of new
cotton lands in the United States and to technical innovations in Britain,
prices of cotton yarn and cloth fell, possibly as soon as the 1780s and
certainly from the 1790s, generating a disproportionate expansion in demand.[65] There was a substitution of British cottons for other fabrics—
linens, silks, mixtures of cotton and linen, possibly woollens—and for
non-British cotton goods, which previously had been either produced
locally or imported from Britain and other countries (for instance, East
India cotton goods); there was also the creation of a broader market,
through the overall expansion (in volume) of the demand for textiles
thanks to the falling prices of British cottons.[66]

The fast growth of cottonwares exports brought about a spectacular
change in the commodity structure of British exports, with the ratio of
cotton products to total exports rising dramatically; concomittantly the
shares of woollens and of linens, silks, and ironwares came down
sharply.[67] There was thus, for a time, a reversal of the trend toward a
broadening of the base of the British export trade which had prevailed in
the 18th century, and the dramatic expansion from the 1780s to the 1810s
was very narrowly based, becoming even more so.[68] On the contrary, the
decades after the end of the wars were marked by a renewed, though
rather slow, diversification of British exports.

Between 1814 and the 1840s, the export of cotton products increased so
rapidly in volume[69] that, despite the fall in their prices, their values
advanced at a higher rate than those of total exports (1.4% p.a. against
1.1%). Exports of wool products grew quite slowly in volume and hardly

[65] Edwards, pp. 31, 35, 239–241; Deane, *First Industrial*, pp. 63–64; Berrill, p. 358; Imlah,
p. 104.
[66] Edwards, pp. 8, 32–33. The fast increase in cotton yarn exports from 1794 corresponded also in part to a substitution by Continental weavers of British machine-spun yarn
to locally hand-spun yarn.
[67] Deane and Cole, p. 30; Imlah, p. 104, Table 9.
[68] This has been noted by Flinn, p. 59.
[69] Though more slowly than before 1814.

66   FRANÇOIS CROUZET

at all in value,[70] while exports of linens, metals, and metal goods displayed higher rates of growth than during the wars.[71] This period was thus still dominated by cotton; cotton yarn and goods were responsible for 46% of the increase in value of total British exports between 1814/1816 and 1844/1846.[72] The contribution of wool products was modest, that of other textiles—mostly linen products—far from negligible;[73] but, the novel and significant development was the important contribution made by metals and metal manufactures, which were responsible for about a third of the increase in total exports.[74]

However, Imlah has rightly pointed out that most of the increase in the value of textiles exports resulted from the progress of yarn and twist exports.[75] From 1814/1816 to 1844/1846, cotton yarn exports increased in volume over twice as much as cotton cloth; in value the former increased over threefold, while cloth rose only 13%; twist and yarn were thus responsible for 69% of the increase in cotton products exports. Woollen yarn exports were negligible in the 1810s, but exceeded £ 2 million in 1844/1846,[76] even though woollens and worsteds exports had fallen since 1814/1816. Likewise, exports of linen yarn were trifling before 1832, but they rose rapidly in the 1830s and were responsible for nearly one-half of the increase in linen products exports between 1816/1820 and 1838/1842.[77] In addition, exports of nonmanufactured iron rose also much faster than those of ironwares and accounted for 62% of the increase in iron products exports between 1814/1816 and 1844/1846. M. Lévy-Leboyer has stressed that these developments resulted from continental protectionism and from the progress in the production of finished goods in European countries; they were an example of international division of labor, with Britain expanding her sales to Europe of semifinished, capital intensive goods, in

[70] Though Davis' figures show a larger increase than the declared values—and also for linens exports (whence the differences in Table 8): *The Industrial Revolution* . . . ., pp. 97–100.

[71] Exports of iron and ironwares grew much faster than those of nonferrous metals and manufactures. But, before the 1850s, their value remained much lower than that of the latter.

[72] Imlah, p. 127, gives a higher figure (72%) for the contribution of cotton products to the increase of total exports from 1816/20 to 1838/42 because of his different periods of reference and because he has calculated his ratios to the *net* increase in total exports, while we have computed ours to the gross increase; if this last method is used for Imlah's periods of reference, the contribution of cotton products falls to 58%.

[73] The increased importance of linens exports results partly from the inclusion of exports by the Irish linen industry, which were excluded from previous figures of exports from Britain.

[74] The trend toward an increasing contribution by this group started in the late 1820s.

[75] Imlah, p. 127.

[76] Davis' figures (*The Industrial Revolution* . . . ., p. 100); Imlah, p. 212, gives a lower figure.

[77] Imlah, p. 127; also Lévy-Leboyer, p. 178; Clapham, I, p. 249; *Abstract*, pp. 195, 202.

BRITISH EXPORTS, 1783–1873   67

TABLE 7
Mean Rates of Growth, Principal Exports
(Percentage per Annum)[a]

Product	1814–1846	1846–1873	1814–1873
A. Declared values			
Cotton yarn and manufactures	1.4	4.8	2.8
Woollen and worsted yarn			
and manufactures	0.1	6.3	2.9
Linens	2.8	4.3	3.3
Metals and metal manufactures	3.2	5.7	5.1
Coal	8.3	8.7	9.2
Total exports	1.1	5.7	3.4
B. Volumes at 1880 prices			
Cotton manufactures	5.5	4.0	5.1
Woollens and worsteds	1.5	4.6	3.4
All other goods	3.4	5.7	5.1
Total exports	4.3	4.7	4.8

[a] Calculated by exponential adjustment.

Source. (A) B. R. Mitchell and P. Deane, *Abstract of British Historical Statistics* (Cambridge, 1962), pp. 302–304. (B) A. H. Imlah, *Economic Elements in the Pax Britannica* (Cambridge, Mass.: Harvard Univ. Press, 1958), pp. 94–97, 208–215, Tables 8, II, III, and IV.

which she had large comparative advantages, rather than those of labor-intensive goods.[78]

From 1846 to 1873, the position was quite different, but quite simple: exports of all the main categories of goods grew rapidly, both in volume and—still more—in value (see Table 7). But, this time, cotton products were rather the laggards, mostly because of the cotton famine during the American Civil War: their rates of growth per year were lower than those of total exports.[79] On the contrary, exports of woollen products,[80] of metals and metal manufactures,[81] of coal, and of "other goods" grew at a faster pace than total exports. Still, because cotton products accounted for a large share of total exports, their contribution to the increase of the latter's values between 1844/1846 and 1871/1873, remained considerable (27.4%), though far less than during the preceding 30 years. The relative contribution of metal goods also fell markedly, while that of woollen products increased, but the largest contribution to the advance of total exports came from "other goods" (33.3%). This was a period of diversification of exports and of general—and rapid—advance on a broad front.

As the absolute increase in the value of British exports from 1844/1846 to 1871/1873 was enormous (£ 186 million) and far superior to that of

[78] Lévy-Leboyer, pp. 177–178, 180–181; also Matthews, p. 129.
[79] Deviations from trend of the volume series are highly positive from 1849 to 1861, with their peak in 1860, but they fall sharply in 1861–1865.
[80] Deviations from trend reveal a strong acceleration of growth from 1848 to 1872.
[81] But their fastest growth took place in the early part of this period.

68   FRANÇOIS CROUZET

TABLE 8
Contributions of the Principal Products to the Increase of
Total United Kingdom Exports[a]

Product	From 1814/16 to 1844/46 (%)	From 1844/46 to 1871/73 (%)	From 1814/16 to 1871/73 (%)
A. Current values (Davis)			
Woollen and worsted yarn and manufactures	10.8		
Cotton yarn and manufactures	45.9		
Other textiles	9.8		
Iron and ironwares	16.9		
Nonferrous metals and manufactures	16.6		
All other goods	—		
B. Declared values			
Woollen and worsted yarn and manufactures	3.9	13.7	13.3
Cotton yarn and manufactures	46.4	27.4	29.3
Linen yarn and manufactures	13.7	3.1	4.0
Metals and metal manufactures	35.9	22.4	23.8
All other goods	—	33.3	29.7
C. Volumes at 1880 prices			
Woollen and worsted yarn and manufactures	9.9	13.3	12.6
Cotton yarn and manufactures	54.6	26.1	31.8
All other goods (including metals)	35.5	60.7	55.6

[a] The symbol — indicates that exports in the category decreased between the years indicated.

Source. (A) R. Davis, *The Industrial Revolution and British Overseas Trade.* pp. 97, 100; (B) See (A) in Table 7; (C) See (B) in Table 7.

1814/1816 to 1844/1846 (£ 12.5 million), the percentage contributions of the main products to the total growth of exports, from the end of the Napoleonic wars to the Great Depression (Table 8, column 3), are close to those of the later period and display therefore a pattern of "balanced growth."

During the combined period, 1814–1873, the changes in the commodity structure of British exports are now clear.[82] The share of cotton products in the value of total exports continued to increase, but much more slowly than during the French wars, to reach a peak (about 50%) in the 1830s, then to fall back gradually to 31% in 1871/1873. Woollen products continued their relative decline. The metal group, by contrast, experienced a

[82] Imlah, pp. 104, 107, Tables 9 and 10; Deane and Cole, p. 31, Table 9, p. 295; Mathias, p. 468, Table 17.

steady rise (at least up to the 1850s), reaching just over 20% of total exports values. The marked rise of the share of "other goods" completes this trend toward diversification, which was nonetheless limited by the supremacy of textiles (which remained over 50% of total exports in the 1870s). Even so, while the first upsurge in the value of British exports— from 1782 to 1802—had been the result, above all, of the dramatic rise of cotton goods exports, the second, in the 1850s and 1860s, was much more broadly based.

III. THE MARKETS FOR GROWTH

During the 18th century, up to the dispute with the colonies, there had been three major trends of change in the geographical pattern of English exports.[83] First, the share of total exports which went to Continental Europe had fallen markedly, from 82% in 1700/1701 to 40% in 1772/1773.[84] Second, exports to the British colonies in America—and especially to those of North America—had increased at a fast pace, so that the share of America in total exports had risen from 10% in 1700/1701 to 37% in 1772/1773. Third, a less important, but still significant development had been the progress of exports to other "captive markets," in Ireland, Africa, and the East Indies. If one compares exports from England and Wales (O.V.) in 1700/1701 and 1772/1773, the respective percentage contributions of the main areas to their increase appear as:

Europe	4.2
North America	41.8
West Indies	18.2
British Islands[85]	14.6
East Indies	13.5
Africa	7.8

The period from the 1780s to the end of the Napoleonic wars presents an intricate and shifting pattern of changes in the geographical distribution of British exports, largely as a consequence of the French wars, with their sudden closings or openings of markets, which forced British exporters to display a great deal of adaptability and ingenuity in switching their ship-

---

[83] *Abstract*, p. 312 (the percentages given in the text are calculated from tne figures in this table; they refer to official values and to exports from England); Davis, "English Foreign Trade," pp. 286–291, 302–303; Davis, *A Commercial Revolution* (The Historical Association, 1967), pp. 20–21; Davis, *The Rise of the Atlantic Economies* (London, 1973), pp. 306–307; Ashton, in Schumpeter, pp. 10–11; Minchinton, pp. 26–31; Flinn, pp. 58–59; Deane and Cole, p. 34; Deane, *First Industrial*, pp. 55–56; D. A. Fairnie, "The Commercial Empire of the Atlantic, 1607–1783," *Economic History Review*, N.S. **15**, No. 2 (1962), p. 314.

[84] Actually, exports to Europe had risen up to ca. 1760, but had fallen sharply afterward and were in 1772/73 hardly higher than in 1700/01.

[85] Ireland, Man, the Channel Islands.

FRANÇOIS CROUZET

TABLE 9
Percentage Contributions of the Major Geographical Areas to the
Increase in Total British Exports (Official Values)[a]

Area	From 1783/87 to 1788/92 (%)	From 1788/92 to 1793/97 (%)	From 1793/97 to 1798/1802 (%)	From 1798/1802 to 1803/07 (%)	From 1803/07 to 1808/12 (%)
Northern Europe[b]	16.5	—	30.5	24.2	—
Southern Europe[c]	6.0	—	8.4	7.7	46.8
Europe	22.5	—	38.9	31.9	(45.4)[f]
British North America	2.8	3.3	5.5	—	5.4
United States	25.7	48.9	22.6	27.1	—
British West Indies	16.8	16.3	12.6	—	⎫
Conquered West Indies		15.8	7.5	—	⎬ 44.3
Foreign territories in America[d]	0.4	0.2	0.5	19.6	⎭
America	45.6	84.4	48.7	—	(48.4)[f]
British Islands[e]	10.1	2.1	7.2	21.4	3.5
East Indies	18.9	13.7	—	—	—
Africa	2.9	—	5.1	—	—

[a] The symbol — indicates that exports to the area decreased between the quinquenniums considered.

[b] France and all countries to the north.

[c] Countries south of France, including the insular possessions of Spain and Portugal and Turkey.

[d] Foreign West Indies and Latin America.

[e] Ireland, Isle of Man, and Channel Islands.

[f] Calculated as percentages of subtotals to the sum of increases in subtotals.

Source. Calculated for the years 1783–1802 from Public Record Office. Customs 17·8 to 24; for the years 1802–1812 from F. Crouzet. *L'économie britannique et le Blocus Continental, 1806–1813* (Paris, 1958), Vol. II, p. 885, Table 3 (mainly based on Customs ledgers at the Public Record Office).

ments from one market to another.[86] These short-run kaleidoscopic changes cannot be considered in detail here,[87] but the most significant shifts in the destination of exports appear in Table 9, in which the contributions of the main geographical areas to the increase in Britain's total exports have been calculated from each quinquennial average of their official values[88] to the next, between 1783 and 1812.[89] It shows that the

[86] It seems that to them American markets were the dependent variable, as they pushed their exports to the New World when European markets closed or contracted.

[87] They have been studied for the period of the Continental Blockade in Crouzet, op. cit.

[88] Current values would be more satisfactory, but Davis' figures do not give the same complete coverage.

[89] The turning points which are mentioned below have been located through the calculation for each year of the percentage distribution of exports among the main areas.

advance of exports was achieved by a succession of shifts between the main trading areas in Europe and America,[90] one or two of them absorbing most of the additional exports for a few years, and also making good for the set-backs in other quarters, but giving way to different markets afterward.

In the mid-1780s, the recovery of exports from the depression of the American war was mainly due to rising European demand: but 67% of the increase in exports to Europe between 1783 and 1788 resulted from the sharp rise in exports to France, following the Eden Treaty of 1786. After 1788, the advance of exports to Europe slowed down markedly and it gave way to a sharp fall with the beginning of war against France in 1793. On the other hand, exports to the United States more than doubled within the 4 years after 1788 and they went on rising almost continuously up to 1801. They played a decisive part in the last phase of the leap forward of exports in the late 1780s and early 1790s: the export boom which culminated in 1792 was America-based and not Europe-based.[91] As, moreover, new markets were opened in the West Indies during the war, the New World was responsible for nearly the whole of the additional exports which were achieved between 1788 and 1798.[92] Then, for a few years up to 1802, there was a "return to Europe" and a partial reversal of the previous switch toward America, owing to a rapid recovery and increase of exports to Northern Europe, which played a vital part in the progress of exports during those years: the export boom of 1802, unlike that of 1792, was Europe-based. However, this movement was reversed as soon as war broke out again in 1803: exports to Europe declined, shipments to the United States rose rapidly again, and it was thanks to increased exports to the New World that total exports were maintained at an average high level between 1803 and 1807.[93] During the late years of the French wars, the Continental Blockade as well as Jefferson's and Madison's policies brought about sharp falls in average exports to Northern Europe and to the United States, while the invasion of Portugal and Spain by the French

[90] The East Indies were also important in the early years, but later on exports to them decreased.

[91] There is no reason to speak, as some writers do, of an "invasion of Europe" by British manufactures during the 1780s, thanks to their price advantage resulting from the recent technological breakthroughs, and to see this invasion as a decisive factor in the leap forward of exports from 1781 to 1792. If one is to find such an "invasion" of the Continent, it is during the few years from 1798 to 1802: but it was an invasion by cotton goods and cotton yarn: exports of cottons to Europe rose from £ 701,000 in 1797 (O.V.) to £ 4,773,000 in 1802 (cf. Edwards, pp. 14, 54, 63, 67, 243–244, Tables B/1 and 2).

[92] The "Americanization" of British trade, which had been set back by the conflict with the 13 colonies, had been resumed and intensified: in 1798, the share of America in total exports reached 61% (O.V.). Exports of cottons and woollens display the same trend.

[93] This shift was not as pronounced as the earlier ones and, because of the small increase in total exports between 1798/1802 and 1803/07, the figures for the contributions of the various areas in column 4 of Table 9 are not very significant.

and the Peninsular war opened widely to British exporters the markets of those countries and their American possessions; exports to Southern Europe[94] and to Latin America expanded enormously and more than made good the losses suffered in more northerly regions; these two areas were the outlets for the new exports of the years 1808/1812. Finally, the collapse of Napoleon's Empire brought about an ultimate shift to Northern Europe in 1813 and 1814.

However, if this 30-year period is considered as a whole, it is clear that the New World—and especially the United States, despite the vicissitudes in the last years of the wars—played a decisive part in the growth of British exports,[95] though the contributions from Europe, the East Indies, and Ireland were not unimportant, as is shown in the following calculation of the percentage shares of the cumulated *additional* exports to the main trading areas in the grand total of cumulated *additional* exports (O.V.) which were achieved between 1783 and 1812:[96]

Northern Europe	10.8	
Southern Europe	11.9	
Europe		22.7
British North America	2.6	
United States	32.3	
West Indies and		
Latin America	24.9	
America		59.8
British Islands	7.6	
East Indies	10.0	
Africa	nil.	

From the end of the Napoleonic wars to the 1840s, the growth of the value of British exports to Europe was quite slow, but only a shade slower

[94] Which were bolstered also by heavy smuggling from Malta to Mediterranean countries.

[95] The share of America in total British exports was 34% in 1783/87 and 49% in 1808/12.

[96] Additional exports are those over the 1783 level. Rather different results emerge from the comparison of Davis' current values for 1784/86 and 1814/16 (*The Industrial Revolution . . . .*, pp. 94, 97), as exports to Northern Europe had strongly recovered in the immediate postwar period; the percentage contributions to the increase of total exports between these two periods are as follows:

Northern Europe	29.9	
Southern Europe	16.3	
Europe		46.2
British North America	7.4	
United States	13.1	
West Indies	15.9	
Latin America	7.2	
America		43.4
British Islands	7.5	
Asia	2.8	

TABLE 10
Mean Rates of Growth, Exports from the United Kingdom to the
Major Geographical Areas (Percentage per Annum)[a]

	Current values		Volumes at 1880 prices	
	1814–1846	1846–1873	1814–1846	1846–1873
Northern Europe[b]	0.9	6.7	4.1	5.7
Southern Europe[c]	1.0	5.8	4.2	4.8
United States	−0.6	3.9	2.6	2.9
America except USA	0.2	4.4	3.4	3.4
Asia, Australasia, Africa	4.4	6.6	7.7	5.6
Total exports	1.1	5.7	4.3	4.7

[a] Rates of growth calculated by exponential adjustment.

[b] France and countries to the north, but includes Austria–Hungary for 1846–1873.

[c] Includes Turkey, the Middle East, and North Africa, as well as Austria–Hungary for 1814–1846.

Source. B.R. Mitchell and P. Deane, *Abstract of British Historical Statistics* (Cambridge, 1962), pp. 313–315, 318, 321, and 324 for the declared (current) values; volumes have been calculated by deflating the current values series by an index of export prices taken from A. H. Imlah, *Economic Elements in the Pax Britannica* (Cambridge, Mass.: Harvard Univ. Press, 1958), pp. 94–96.

than that of total exports (cf. Table 10).[97] Indeed, the value of exports to Europe shows a falling trend up to the early 1830s, while their volume stagnates up to the late 1820s. This recession was more pronounced than that in total exports and contemporaries had some grounds to think that the protectionist policies of most European countries were building up against British manufactures a "Second Continental Blockade," which may have stimulated exporters to divert their shipments to non-European markets.[98] Still, exports to Europe revived in the 1830s and their contribution to the increase of total exports values between 1814/1818 and 1842/1846 is not negligible (cf. Table 11), while their share of total exports, after a dip in the 1820s, returned to its previous level; but they made only a modest contribution to the cumulated additional total exports which were achieved from 1814 to 1846 (cf. Table 12).[99]

The course of exports to the United States in the same years was extremely peculiar.[100] Not only did they fluctuate wildly, but, after a fall in the postwar years, they rose to a peak in the boom of 1836, only to fall back in the 1840s to low levels (in 1842/1846, 23% under 1814/1818, C.V.),

[97] Our conclusions on this period are slightly different from those of Imlah, pp. 129–131.

[98] Clapham, I, pp. 479–481; Gayer, II, p. 647; Wilson, pp. 113, 116.

[99] Gayer, II, pp. 543–544 and Matthews, p. 70: Europe is not the dynamic factor of the export trade and has a minor influence only on the fluctuations of the British economy.

[100] The coefficient of correlation between exports to the USA and total exports (C.V.), for the period 1814–1846, is only +0.33, while it is much higher for the other regional series (+0.75 for Asia + Africa).

74   FRANÇOIS CROUZET

TABLE 11
Percentage Contributions of the Major Geographical Areas to the
Increase in Current Values of Total
United Kingdom Exports[a]

Area	From 1814/18 to 1842/46 (%)	From 1846/50 to 1869/73 (%)
Northern Europe	15.2	35.7
Southern Europe	13.9	12.5
Europe	29.1	48.2
United States	—	13.1
West Indies and Canada	—	4.6
Latin America	17.9	9.1
Africa	8.6	2.5
Asia and Australasia	44.4	22.3

[a] The sign — means that an actual decrease occurred in exports to an area. For sources and definitions see Table 10.

TABLE 12
Cumulated Additional Exports to the Major Geographical Areas as
Percentages of Total Cumulated Additional Exports from
United Kingdom (Current Values)[a]

Area	From 1814 to 1846[b] (%)	From 1847 to 1873[c] (%)
Northern Europe	8.2	26.3
Southern Europe	5.4	13.7
Europe	13.6	40.0
United States	4.5	17.2
West Indies and Canada	—	2.6
Latin America	28.8	9.5
America	9.9	29.3
Africa	8.7	2.7
Asia	44.3	17.5
Australasia		10.5

[a] For sources and definitions see Table 10.
[b] For 1814–1846 additional exports are calculated on the base of the average of the 3 years 1814/16, because the 1814 figures for some areas are abnormal.
[c] Additional exports are calculated from the base level of 1846.

so that the rate of growth of their values from 1814 to 1846 is negative and their share of total exports fell from 17.4% in 1814/1818 to 11.1% in 1842/1846.[101] Nonetheless, as R. C. O. Matthews has demonstrated, the proportional fluctuations of exports to the United States being of much greater amplitude than in exports generally, the state of the American market was—at least in the 1830s—the most important single factor in bringing prosperity or depression to British export industries.[102]

Most of the increase in the value of British exports resulted therefore from demand in markets outside Europe and the United States,[103] which were largely "new" markets for British manufactures: Asia (i.e., mostly India),[104] Africa and Latin America. Indeed, exports to Asia and Africa grew almost continuously and at a fast and accelerating pace (4.4% per year in values, 7.7% in volumes), and they were responsible for 44.4% of the increase in the value of total exports from 1814/1818 to 1842/1846 and for 53% of the total cumulated additional exports of this period; their share of total exports rose meanwhile from 7.9 to 21%. Exports to Latin America increased less significantly and more irregularly, with growth slowing down greatly after the boom of 1824/1825. Though an uncertain, expensive, and disappointing market,[105] Latin America still made a notable contribution to the growth of British exports, absorbing 29% of total cumulated additional exports down to 1846.

This shift of British exports toward some of the less developed countries in the trading world is remarkable.[106] The traditional explanation is that the hot climates and low standards of living prevailing in those areas—whose markets were moreover unprotected—made cheap cotton goods (which formed the bulk of their imports from Britain) especially acceptable and in growing demand there.[107] A more sophisticated interpretation is that exports to those areas were the dependent variable of imports from them by Great Britain and that they accelerated from 1820 onward owing to the growing demand for tropical produce in Britain and

[101] And their rate of growth in volume (2.6% per year) is quite modest.

[102] Matthews, pp. 43–45.

[103] And also outside the traditional markets in Britain's American colonies: exports to the West Indies and to Canada declined almost continuously, by 47% from 1814/18 to 1842/46 (C.V.). This is why, in Table 10, exports to America outside the USA have a very low rate of growth, despite the increase in exports to Latin America.

[104] At the end of the period, exports to Australia, which are included in the series "Asia," had become important.

[105] D. C. M. Platt, *Latin America and British Trade, 1806–1914* (London, 1972), pp. 3–4, 6–7, 9–11, 22, 29–31, 33–34, 36–37, 57–58, 65, on the factors which limited the expansion of British trade with this area; except during boom years such as 1824/25, this trade was not out of line with what it had been in the colonial period.

[106] The share of "advanced countries" (Northern Europe + USA) fell from 44% of total exports (C.V.) in 1814/18 to 27% in 1842/46.

[107] Clapham, I, p. 481; Imlah, p. 128.

other advanced countries, which resulted itself from their rapid growth in population and incomes.[108]

However, in volume, the contribution of Asia, Africa, and Latin America to the increase of total exports is markedly less than in value (46%, against 71%), while that of Europe is higher. The fall in export prices being most marked just after 1815 and slowing down later tends to minimize the growth of values to Europe, to which export volumes stagnated during the sharp fall in prices, while enhancing that to Asia and Africa, with their continuous progress in export volumes.

The period from 1846 to 1873 witnessed a growth of export values to all the main areas much more rapid than that between 1814 and 1846; the rate of growth of volume, though, did not increase markedly,[109] except to Northern Europe (cf. Table 10). Indeed, exports to Northern Europe showed the highest rate of growth (6.7% per year for values) and made the largest contribution to the increase of total exports between 1846/1850 and 1869/1873 (36%), though accounting for only 26% of cumulated additional total exports achieved from 1847 to 1873. Exports to Asia, Australia, and Africa grew slightly more slowly, but their contribution to the increase of total exports (25%) and their share of cumulated additional exports (31%) were smaller than during the period 1814–1846. This area and Northern Europe were responsible for 61% of the increase in total exports between 1846/1850 and 1869/1873, an interesting concentration upon the most advanced[110] and the least developed trading partners of Britain.[111] On the other hand, exports to Southern Europe grew at the same rate as total exports while those to America—especially to the United States[112]—increased much more slowly; nonetheless, those areas made a contribution to total growth which was not negligible. In geographical distribution, as in commodity structure, the fast growth of British exports in the 1850s and 1860s was broadly based, though Northern Europe, Asia, and Australia were particularly strategic.

In every period from the 1780s to the 1860s, a small number of markets was responsible for most of the growth of British exports; the Americas,

[108] Matthews, pp. 72, 77–78; Gayer, II, p. 544; J. R. Hanson II, "The Nineteenth-Century Exports of the Less Developed Countries," *Journal of Economic History*, 33 (1973), pp. 305–306.

[109] It did actually decline for the group Asia, Africa, Australasia, despite a fast growth of exports to Australia and New Zealand, which made a significant contribution to the increase in total exports.

[110] In Northern Europe, the Western countries (France, Belgium, Holland) had the fastest growth and contributed 17% to the increase in total exports.

[111] Hanson, pp. 305–306, on the acceleration in the growth of exports by the less developed countries after 1840.

[112] Clapham, II, pp. 229–230, on the relative decline of the U.S. market for Britain, following the Civil War.

though playing a vital role from the 1780s to the end of the French wars, were thereafter far less important.

IV. EXPORTS AND NATIONAL INCOME

"The growth in the importance of foreign trade can be illustrated by measuring its value against national income."[113] Unfortunately, for the 18th century, we have neither export values at current prices nor reliable national income estimates. Nonetheless, down to the 1770s official values of exports were unlikely to have been much different from their market values, while a few national income estimates, however tentative and uncertain, can give some rough orders of magnitude.[114] The available data are presented in Table 13 and, despite their conjectural character, might support some conclusions.

First, during most of the century up to the 1780s, the ratio of domestic exports to English national income (which we shall call the exports proportion) was quite modest[115] and remained generally under 10%. However, this ratio did not rise regularly and it underwent a fluctuation which fits rather well with the changes in the rate of growth of exports which have been analyzed earlier. It rose substantially between 1700 and 1759 (though the ratio given for the latter year must not be taken at its face value), as exports grew undoubtedly faster than national output which, according to Deane and Cole, progressed at a rate of only 0.3% per year from 1700 to 1745 and 0.9% from 1745 to 1760.[116] But most of this increase took place during the stage of relatively fast growth of exports from 1745 to 1760, while there had been only a small advance during the quasi-stagnation from 1714 to 1744.[117] Indeed, A. H. John has suggested that the rise in exports after 1748 was so fast that it had to be met partially by a transfer of output from the domestic to the foreign market.[118] On the other hand, the sharp fall in the exports proportion in Table 13 from 1759 to 1770 and 1783, which would have brought it back, at the end of the American war, to its level of the turn of the century, tallies perfectly with the negative growth of exports from 1760 to 1781.[119] Of course, this fall of the ratio

[113] Deane and Cole, p. 28; but they point out (p. 60) that we cannot make an adjustment for the changes in the proportion of output exported, which were due simply to a change in the terms of trade.

[114] Bairoch, p. 556; the GDP at current prices is the aggregate the most suitable to be compared to the exports values, while the figures available (in Deane and Cole) refer to gross national income or output at factor cost. But this does not matter much.

[115] Though we find for the early period a ratio of exports to income higher than other writers; see notes to Table 13, 1.

[116] Deane and Cole, pp. 310–311.

[117] Deane and Cole, p. 58, gives a different view on the years 1725–1745; also Cole, p. 338.

[118] Review of Deane and Cole, in *Kyklos*, 17, No. 2, 1964, p. 278; and in Jones, p. 186.

[119] Deane and Cole, p. 262, note 1, point out that their figure for national income in 1783 might be too high (but our majoration of the exports O.V. by 20% might also be excessive).

78   FRANÇOIS CROUZET

TABLE 13

Exports and National Income in the 18th Century[a]

	National income (£ Million) (A)	Exports (£ Million) (B)	Ratio of Exports to national income (%) (C)
1. ca. 1688	48	4	8.3
2. 1700	58.5 or 52	4.4	7.5 or 8.5
3. 1759	85	9.9	11.6
4. 1770	130	9.9	7.6
5. 1783	160	12.4	7.8
6. 1801	232	41.4	17.8

[a] N.B. Most figures in this table are highly tentative.

Notes. Figures are for England and Wales up to 1770, for Great Britain in 1783 and 1801. Export figures are triennial averages centered on the year specified, of official values, except in 1801, when declared values have been used; the O.V. of 1783 has been raised by 20% to take into account the price rise.

Sources. 1. Column A: Deane and Cole, p. 156. Column B: R. Davis, "English Foreign Trade, 1660–1770," in Minchinton, pp. 79, Table 1, 85, note 4, 93; Davis, *English Overseas Trade, 1500–1700* (London, 1973), p. 56; Deane and Cole, pp. 310, note 2, 319. We have assumed that the volume of exports in 1686/88 was the same as in 1699/1701, i.e., £ 4.4 million, that this figure corresponded more or less to current values in 1699/1701 and we have adjusted it to take into account the rise in prices from 1688 to 1701 (about 10%, according to *Abstract*, p. 468). The ratio in column C is higher than in Deane and Cole, pp. 228, 309 (5 to 6%), who have relied on King's trade figures which, according to Davis, underestimate the exports of 1688. 2. Column A: Bairoch, in *Annales,* **28**, pp. 556–557 (gross national product). Column B: Original official values for 1699/1701. 3. Column A: Estimations of Joseph Massie, adjusted by Deane and Cole, p. 279. 4. Column A: Deane and Cole, p. 156. 5. Column A: Deane and Cole, p. 262, Deane and Habakkuk, p. 75. 6. Column A: Deane and Cole, pp. 158–160, 161, Table 36. Column B: *Abstract*, p. 282: exports from the United Kingdom, somewhat inferior to those from Great Britain.

supports Eversley's view of a widening gap between export and home demand from 1750 (we would rather say 1760) to 1780, and his thesis that during this crucial period for the Industrial Revolution, foreign demand was not a major factor of expansion.[120]

Only in the last 20 years of the century did the exports proportion rise suddenly and rapidly, owing to the marked difference between the rate of growth of exports—4.6% per year from 1783 to 1800 in volume and even more in value—and that of total output which, according to Deane and

One can refer also to the figures for national income from 1751 to 1791 of J. E. Williams. "The British Standard of Living, 1750–1850," *Economic History Review, N.S.* **19**, No. 3. December 1966, pp. 584–585; A. J. Taylor, *The Standard of Living in Britain in the Industrial Revolution* (London, 1975), p. 38, has called them "something of a *jeu d'esprit.*" And, indeed, the ratios of exports to these national income figures are improbably high; still. their movement is interesting: 1751, 15.7%; 1761, 15.1%; 1771, 13.5%; 1781, 9.5%; 1791. 17.8%. The O.V. of exports for 1781 and 1791 have been raised by 20 and 30%, respectively. to take into account the price rise.

[120] Eversley, pp. 221, 229, 236, 247–249; also Flinn, p. 58.

TABLE 14
Exports as a Percentage of National Product, 1801–1871

Year	At current prices (A)	At constant prices (B)
1801	17.8	8.0
1811	13.6	6.8
1821	12.6	7.6
1831	11.0	8.0
1841	11.1	10.4
1851	14.3	15.2
1861	19.2	20.2
1871	24.7	23.6

Source. National product is taken from P. Deane and W. A. Cole, *British Economic Growth 1688–1959* (2nd ed.; Cambridge, 1967), p. 166, Table 37 (current prices), p. 282, Table 72 (constant prices). Exports (triennial averages centered on the quoted year) are from B. R. Mitchell and P. Deane, *Abstract of British Historical Statistics* (Cambridge, 1962), pp. 282–283 (declared values); and A. H. Imlah, *Economic Elements in the Pax Britannica* (Cambridge, 1958), pp. 94–97, Table 8 (volumes at 1880 prices). As Deane and Cole have calculated national product at constant prices with the Rousseaux index as deflator and as this index stands at 102 in 1880, the comparison with Imlah's volume series is valid.

Addendum. C. Feinstein has published, after the completion of this paper, a new series for Britain's Gross domestic product (decade averages, at 1851–60 prices); P. Mathias and M. M. Postan (Eds.), *The Cambridge Economic History of Europe*, Vol. VII, *The Industrial Economies*, Part I (Cambridge, 1978), p. 91, Table 28. The percentages of exports at constant prices (Imlah's volume series converted to 1851–60 prices through the Rousseaux index) are of the same order of magnitude as those in column B: 1801–10, 7.8%; 1811–20, 8.2%; 1821–30, 8.2%; 1831–40, 9.8%; 1841–50, 13.0%; 1851–60, 18.9%.

Cole, was only 1.5% in real terms (or 1.8%, with different base and weights).[121] From our calculations, the ratio of the current value of exports to national income reached about 18% circa 1801, having more than doubled since 1783.[122] Though Britain, around 1800, showed signs of becoming an "export economy," this development was not to proceed further for several decades.

This retrogression appears in Table 14, which is more valid than our guess-estimates for the 18th century, as it is based on Deane and Cole's series of national income figures at 10-year intervals (which, though still tentative in the early 19th century,[123] are not to be mistrusted too much) and on the current values of exports.[124] The exports proportion at current

[121] Deane and Cole, pp. 80, Table 20, 280, 311.
[122] This is a higher ratio than that (14 or 15%) given by Deane and Cole, pp. 28, 309, and Deane and Habakkuk, p. 68, note 2.
[123] Deane and Cole, pp. 164–165.
[124] Exports are from the U.K., national income figures for Great Britain. But this results only in a slight underestimation of the exports/product ratio in the first three decades of the 19th century.

prices fell steadily and markedly from its peak in 1801 to 11% in 1831, and did not rise again before midcentury.[125]

Deane and Cole have explained the fall of the ratio from 1801 to 1811 by two factors.[126] First, the war slowed down the growth of exports: in 1810/1812, their current values were not higher than in 1800/1802,[127] while national product at current prices had increased about 30%. Second, industrial prices, i.e., export prices, had fallen absolutely (5% according to Imlah's index) and still more relatively to agricultural prices, which had risen.

In the post-1811 period, export values fell after the war, then stagnated on trend up to the early 1830s and for the whole period from 1814 to 1846 grew at the very slow rate of 1.1% per year;[128] on the other hand, national income at current prices increased 13% from 1811 to 1831. The explanation of this contrast lies largely in the movement of prices: export values bore the brunt of the rapid fall in the prices of manufactures and especially of cotton products (which, moreover, were enlarging their share of Britain's exports), while the prices of many other goods and services did not come down as sharply; Imlah's index of export prices falls 58% from 1810/1812 to 1830/1832, while Gayer's index of domestic commodities falls 36% only between the same dates.[129]

However, as the volume of exports progressed much faster (4.3% per year from 1814 to 1846) than their value and as it has been found in other cases, such as the United States from the 1860s to 1913, that the removal of price changes can markedly alter the relationship between trade and output over time,[130] we have calculated the ratios between exports and national income at constant prices (Table 14, column B). They still show a decline in the exports proportion from 1801 to 1811, but there is a slight rise from 1811 to 1831, when the ratio is back to its 1801 level, and a marked advance from 1831 to 1841.[131]

In real terms, therefore, we need not think that from the early 1800s to the 1830s demand from the home market was expanding faster than demand from abroad[132] or that there was a serious diversion of resources from exports toward domestic investment and consumption.[133] Nonethe-

---

[125] Deane and Cole, pp. 29, 310; also P. Bairoch, *Révolution Industrielle et sous-développement* (Paris, 1963), pp. 259–260.

[126] Deane and Cole, pp. 161–162.

[127] 1800, 1801, and 1802 had been boom years for exports; 1810 was an excellent year, but 1811 a very bad one and 1812 medium.

[128] In 1830/32, they were 9% under their 1810/12 level.

[129] Imlah, pp. 94–95, Table 8; *Abstract*, p. 470.

[130] Saul, p. 5; J. D. Gould, *Economic Growth in History. Survey and Analysis* (London, 1972), pp. 225–226.

[131] This fits with Deane and Cole's growth rates (p. 311, Table 83).

[132] Deane and Cole's view, pp. 29, 310–311.

[133] Except during the Napoleonic war, when, despite the special circumstances of the

less, it is important that, during a period which saw the highest rate of growth of British industrial production during the 19th century,[134] and when Britain's industrial and commercial supremacy was almost unchallenged, there was little relative aggrandizement of the export sector in real terms and a definite setback at current prices.

However, after 1848, the growth of export values accelerated sharply with a yearly rate of 5.7% from 1846 to 1873, while there was also some acceleration in the growth of volume. On the other hand, there was some slowing down in the progress of industrial production and, possibly, of total national real product.[135] The exports proportion, both at current and at constant prices, increased sharply after 1841; it more than doubled in 30 years, to reach a peak at 24–25% on the eve of the Great Depression. The figures of Table 14 are corroborated by those which can be calculated from Miss Deane's more recent yearly figures from 1830 onward for the gross national product of the United Kingdom at factor cost:[136]

Ratios of the value of exports to GNP yearly averages (%)

1830/39	9.4
1840/49	10.6
1850/59	15.1
1860/69	17.2
1870/73	19.9

It is clear that it was only after 1850 that Britain really became "an export economy." Before this, there had not been any regular increase in the ratio of exports to national product, but rather some long swings, with peaks at current prices circa 1760 and 1801, and troughs circa 1781 and 1831.

As for the statistical relationship between exports and the growth of British national income, P. Bairoch has estimated that, between 1700/1710 and 1780/1790, foreign demand was responsible for 5 to 9% (his favorite percentage being 6.5%) of the *increase* in England's total product and the home market for 91 to 95% of this increment. He has also calculated that the home market absorbed 92 to 95% of the *total* output realized during

---

export trade around 1801 and 1811 (note 127), some diversion toward domestic investment in agriculture and toward defence is likely. See also infra, about the switch of some industries towards the home market.

[134] Deane and Cole, p. 170, Table 38.

[135] Deane and Cole, pp. 170, Table 38, 297, Table 77, 311, Table 83.

[136] P. Deane, "New Estimates of Gross National Product for the United Kingdom 1830–1914," *The Review of Income and Wealth*, Series 14, No. 2, June 1968, pp. 104–105, Table A. With triennial averages centered on the year specified, like in Table 14, the ratios are as follows: 1831, 8.6%; 1841, 10.4%; 1851, 13.5%; 1861, 15.9%; 1871, 19.8%. See also the "export proportion index" of W. Schlote, *British Overseas Trade from 1700 to the 1930's* (Oxford, 1952), pp. 75–76.

this period and exports 5 to 8% only.[137] These calculations, which allow to exports a marginal role only in British economic growth for most of the 18th century, are open to some criticisms on points of detail, but they appear roughly valid; indeed, if one calculates, from the figures in Table 13, the ratio of the additional exports to the increase in national income, between 1700 and 1783, it is 6.5 to 6.9% and so falls in the same range as Bairoch's.[138]

However, Bairoch has admitted that the situation was quite different after 1780 and he has suggested that from the 1780s to the 1860s foreign demand absorbed about 30% of the United Kingdom additional output and powerfully contributed to industrial expansion.[139] Borrowing his method, we have calculated in Table 15 the incremental ratios between the additional exports and the increase of national product for successive periods of the late 18th and 19th century.

It appears that the contribution from foreign demand to the increase of national product between 1783 and 1871 (28%) was of the order of magnitude proposed by Bairoch, but with significant fluctuations over time. During the decisive stage of the Industrial Revolution, in the 20 years which followed the peace of 1783, the incremental ratio of exports to national product seems to have been as high as 40%; but, from the early 1800s up to the 1830s and even circa 1841, it was quite low, not only at current, but also at constant prices; it rose sharply in the 1840s and from 1841 to 1871 it was about 37%. This movement fits fairly well with several of our preceding conclusions.[140]

A rough calculation, which is still more tentative, as long as yearly series of the current values of exports and of national product are not available,[141] seems to show that the aggregate additional exports were equivalent to one-half of the cumulated additional national output from 1783 to 1801; but, from 1802 to 1841, owing to the recession of exports values in the postwar period, the ratio would have been minute, while it rose to 33% for the period from 1842 to 1871. As for the percentage of total cumulated exports to total cumulated national product, it would have been about 13% for the periods from 1783 to 1801 and 1802 to 1841, but over 18% for 1842 to 1871.

[137]Bairoch, in *Annales*, pp. 557–558, 568.

[138] If the national income figure for 1759 is not too far off the mark, this ratio would have been much higher for the period 1700–1759: 17 to 21%; for 1759 to 1783, it would be only 3% (Bairoch, p. 558, gives 3 to 5%).

[139] Bairoch, p. 570.

[140] With the new series of GNP figures of Miss Deane, the results are somewhat different (at current prices; increases in exports being calculated between triennial averages centered on the year specified): 1831 to 1841, 24.7%; 1841 to 1851, 34.7%; 1851 to 1861, 21.5%; 1861 to 1871, 29.1%; 1841 to 1871, 26.8%.

[141] Yearly national income figures have been calculated by extrapolation between the years for which they are available in Deane and Cole; also exports values from 1783 to 1795.

BRITISH EXPORTS, 1783–1873   83

TABLE 15
Additional Exports as Percentages of Increases in
National Product[a]

Period	At current prices (%) (A)	At constant prices (%) (B)
From 1783 to 1801	40.3	
1801 to 1811	−0.6	1.7
1811 to 1821	[b]	10.2
1821 to 1831	1.2	8.9
1831 to 1841	11.4	19.5
1841 to 1851	34.5	34.2
1851 to 1861	37.1	54.5
1861 to 1871	39.4	33.5
1801 to 1841	3.9	11.7
1841 to 1871	37.9	37.0
1783 to 1871	28.3	
1801 to 1871	27.0	27.0

[a] The additional exports have been calculated between 3-year averages centered on the year specified.

[b] Both exports and national income were lower in 1821 than in 1811; the decrease in exports amounted to 44% of that of national income.

Source: see Tables 13 (for 1783) and 14.

For the later period, thanks to Miss Deane's yearly series for national product, one is on firmer ground; the ratios (in %) between aggregate additional exports and the cumulated additions to national product are as follows:

1830 to 1849   11.6

1850 to 1873   28.8

1830 to 1873   21.7

Over the same years, 1830–1873, total exports amounted to 14.8% of the sum of yearly GNP.

Without forgetting that exports are not income, there is a strong case for suggesting that they were a powerful engine of growth for the British economy from the end of the war of American Independence up to the first years of the 19th century, and again after the late 1840s; but in between their influence on long-term growth was very modest, though, of course, foreign demand was a crucial factor in short-term fluctuations.[142]

[142] Gayer, II, pp. 533, 545.

84   FRANÇOIS CROUZET

V. EXPORTS AND INDUSTRIAL PRODUCTION

As British exports were mostly—and increasingly—made of manufactured goods, the rise of overseas sales had a relatively greater impact on the demand for manufactures than on the growth of national income; moreover, the problem with which economic historians have been mainly concerned is the relationship between foreign trade and the *Industrial Revolution*. It would be most useful therefore to compare the evolutions of exports and of industrial production. Unfortunately, the data which are available for these two entities during the period under consideration are not comparable: industrial production's figures are for its "added value" or contribution to national income, which is net of the cost of raw materials,[143] while exports values are "final values" FOB, incorporating some transport and marketing costs. The ratios between exports and industrial production values are thus extremely high (44% in 1688, 76% in 1801, 65% in 1871) and can in no way be indicators of the actual share of industrial output which was exported (and of which we have no precise idea; if it is often admitted that it was as much as a third at the end of the 18th century,[144] this assumption has yet to be established).[145] Still, the changes in this ratio over time can be interesting.

It seems that this ratio increased significantly from circa 1700 to circa 1760 and then fell back between 1760 and 1780, but without a complete loss of its previous gains.[146] There was, of course, a rise of the ratio in the last 20 years of the 18th century, but it was not as large relatively as for the exports/national income proportion, as industrial production grew

[143] Except minerals, as these figures include generally manufacturing, mining and also building (which is another drawback).

[144] Deane and Cole, pp. 42, 312; Davis, *English Overseas Trade 1500–1700* (London, 1973), p. 8, estimates this share at over one fourth ca. 1700.

[145] John, in *Kyklos*, 17, No. 2, 1964, p. 279; see also Wilson p. 1. The present writer (*L'économie britannique*, p. 63) had estimated previously that, circa 1804, exports amounted to 35 or 40% of final industrial output; this was likely too much.

[146] This is corroborated by a comparison of the growth of exports volumes and of the index of industrial production (excluding building) of W. Hoffmann, *British Industry, 1700–1950* (Oxford, 1955), Table 54, part A. Though this index is not reliable, it is interesting that it grows very slowly up to 1760 and then accelerates—a movement quite different from that of exports. The mean rates of growth per year are:

	Exports volumes (%)	Industrial production (%)
1700 to 1760*	1.6	0.9
1760 to 1781	−1.5	1.2
1781 to 1800	5.1	3.6
1783 to 1792	6.0	5.5

(*From 1697 for exports.) Some figures of industrial output at current prices, which Dr. P. O'Brien has calculated and kindly allowed us to use, show a ratio of exports to output higher in 1780 than in 1701.

faster during those years than total output and, in the 1780s, not much slower than exports.

In the 19th century, the ratio of exports current values to industrial production's added values fluctuates with the exports/national income ratio: from a peak circa 1801, its falls to 1831. This fall is so sharp that it cannot be entirely explained by the much bigger share of cotton products, with their precipitous price fall, in exports than in total industrial output, and it might correspond to an actual decline in the proportion of output which was exported[147]—at least at current prices, for in volume exports rose faster than industrial production. The explanation might lie in the shift in exports toward lower quality goods, especially cheap cottons, and semifinished goods, not paralleled to the same degree in the structure of output for the home market. On the other hand, from 1841, there is a sharp upsurge of the exports/industrial production ratio, owing to both an increase in the rate of growth of exports and a decrease in that of industrial production, at least in volume.[148]

These hypotheses can be completed by looking at the exports/production ratio in some of the main industrial sectors, where data are somewhat more satisfactory. Such an analysis confirms the view that this ratio fluctuated over time and that there was a succession of shifts between the foreign and the home markets (cf. Table 16).

This will appear from the comparison of the respective growth rates of net imports of cotton wool in Britain (which give a rough index of production) and of the volume of cotton goods exports:[149]

	Net imports	Volume of exports
	(%/year)	(%/year)
1697-1749	2.6	0.1
1749-1772	2.3	10.9
1760-1783	5.3	2.9
1783-1792	14.1	10.7
1792-1802	10.1	17.3
1802-1814	1.4	8.4
1814-1846	6.6	5.5
1846-1873	2.3	4.0

[147] P. O'Brien's yearly series of the value of industrial output at current prices has a growth rate of 2.6% per year from 1814 to 1846, while exports current values grow at 1.1% only.

[148] Rates of growth per year:

	Hoffmann's index (excluding building) (%)	Volume of exports (%)
1814-1846	3.7	4.3
1846-1873	2.9	4.7

[149] Net imports of cotton wool into Great Britain up to 1814; consumption of cotton wool

86   FRANÇOIS CROUZET

TABLE 16
Exports and Production in Three Industries (Ratios of the Value of Exports
to the Value of the Industry's Final Product)[a]

	Wool (%)	Cotton (%)	Iron (%)
ca. 1695	ca. 40		
ca. 1760		ca. 33	
ca. 1772	ca. 45	ca. 22	
1781/83		16	
1787/89		23	
1795/97		37	
1799	ca. 55		
ca. 1805	31 or 37		18
1805/07		66	
1815/17		58	
ca. 1818			26
1819/21		54	
1820/24	23		18
1829/31		56	
1830/34	19		21
1839/41		52	
1840/44	19		30
1849/51		62	
1850/54	25		40
1859/61		64	
1860/64	30		40
1869/71		67	
1871/74	43		38

[a] N.B. Figures in this table for the 18th and the early 19th centuries are highly tentative.

Notes. The proportions in the table have been calculated from the following sources:

Wool. Estimates of the value of production and exports for 1695, 1772, 1799: Deane, ''The Output,'' pp. 209–210, 215, 220, Table 3, except the current value of exports for 1799, which is the figure of Davis for 1794/96, adjusted according to the increase in volume and the likely price rise. For 1805, Deane, ''The Output,'' p. 220, and Deane and Cole, p. 196, Table 47, have two different figures for the final value of output; we give therefore two alternative percentages, calculated from Davis' current values of exports for 1804/06 (*The Industrial Revolution . . . .*, p. 96). After 1805, the percentages are those of Deane and Cole, p. 196, Table 47, of the value of exports of woollen manufactures (yarn not included) to final product.

Cotton. Estimates of ''gross value cottons'' (Great Britain) up to 1815/17 and afterward ''value final product'' (U.K.), from Deane and Cole, pp. 185 and 187, Tables 42 and 43; exports at current prices up to 1815/17 from ibidem, Table 42, but they have been corrected for 1760 and 1772, as a majoration of the official values by a third, which Deane and Cole have applied, does not seem justified. For 1781/83, we have used Davis' current values for 1784/86 (*The Industrial Revolution . . . .*, p. 94), with an adjustment. From 1819/21, we have recalculated Deane and Cole's percentages of exports to product, from the exports figures in *Abstract*, pp. 302–304 (they include yarn), and the results are slightly different.

Iron. Estimated values of gross product, from Deane and Cole, p. 225, Table 56. The percentages are different, having been recalculated from the exports figures for iron, hardware, and machinery, in *Abstract*, pp. 302–304.

BRITISH EXPORTS, 1783–1873   **87**

During the first half of the 18th century, the "cotton" industry was
quite small, its exports were minute and the rather slow growth which it
enjoyed resulted almost entirely from increased home demand. But, from
1750 exactly, and up to the early 1760s, there was a "meteoric ascent" of
exports, which far outstripped the increase in inputs of cotton;[150] the
proportion of exports to total output reached between a third and a half
circa 1760. Then, after 1763, the growth of exports slowed down markedly, while that of production accelerated; exports' share of production
declined and seems to have been only about 16% in the early 1780s; all
this during the celebrated technological transformation of cotton spinning.[151] In the 1780s, both imports of cotton wool and exports of manufactures grew very rapidly, but inputs more so than export volumes, and it
was only in the 1790s that exports rose so decisively that the ratio of their
value to that of total output increased spectacularly to a peak of two-
thirds circa 1805.[152] This was also the period when cottons exports first
played a decisive part in the growth of total exports.[153] However, during
the postwar years, the share of exports (current values) in the final
product of the cotton industry declined to somewhat over 50% during the
1820s and 1830s; the home market seems thus to have increased its
share—in value, but likely also in volume—during this period of fast
growth of the cotton industry.[154] The postwar stagnation of cotton products
exports, the decline in their quality and the increasing proportion of yarn
and twist in their total contributed to this relative decline. After 1846, the
growth of both production and exports volumes slowed down,[155] but the
former much more than the latter, while export values increased sharply;
thus, exports' share of the value of the industry's production rose again
and reached 67% in 1869/1871.

For the woollen industry, the position in the 18th century is far from
clear, the available data and the glosses upon them being hypothetical and

in the U.K. afterward: *Abstract*, pp. 177–179. Volumes of exports are the official values up
to 1814; Imlah's series of volumes at 1880 prices (pp. 208–210, Table II) has been used
afterward, but it concerns only cotton *manufactures*; if yarn was included, the rate would be
slightly higher for 1814–46. See also Deane and Cole, pp. 51, 59, Tables 15 and 16.

[150] Deane and Cole, p. 59; John, in *Economica*, pp. 184–185; id., in Jones, p. 176.

[151] Eversley, pp. 224–225; Bairoch, in *Annales*, p. 565.

[152] From Deane and Cole, p. 185, Table 42. Edwards, pp. 25–26, gives some data which
show a lower exports/output ratio, while suggesting that it went on increasing up to the end
of the wars. But Davis' current values would point out to a very high exports/output ratio (in
values) ca. 1805 (*The Industrial Revolution . . .*, p. 96).

[153] See supra. For the period 1783–1814, the rates of growth per year are 5.5% for imports
of cotton, 12.3% for exports of cotton products.

[154] Deane and Cole, pp. 187–188. Matthews, p. 151, Table 25, gives data (from 1825 to
1842) which show a higher exports/output ratio, above 60% on average.

[155] The rates for 1846–1873 are influenced by the Cotton Famine and growth remained fast
up to 1860, but there is a deceleration in the consumption of cotton wool from 1845. The
exports values series has an inverse movement.

often contradictory.[156] Still, it seems that the exports/production ratio was already quite high (possibly 40%) at the end of the 17th century,[157] and that, despite slow growth during most of the century (0.9% per year from 1697 to 1772), exports volume advanced somewhat faster than production and slightly enlarged its share of total output: Hoffmann's index of the output of woollen and worsted cloth in the West Riding—which was the region with the fastest growth—progressed at only 0.8% per year from 1739 to 1772.[158] Though the ratio must have fallen during the depression of exports in the 1770s, it certainly rose a good deal in the 1780s and 1790s: the rate of growth of export volume is 4.9% per year from 1783 to 1802, much higher than that of the Hoffmann's West Riding index (1.7% from 1783 to 1792, 0.6% from 1792 to 1802); according to P. Deane, at the close of the century over two-thirds of the industry's output were exported[159]—a figure which seems too high and ought to be reduced to between 50 and 60%. But, as the volume of woollen exports fell markedly after 1801, and as their values declined and stagnated for a long time after the end of the wars, the ratio of exports to output fell sharply during the early 19th century to a level around 20%, where it remained up to the late 1840s. On the other hand, the fast rise of the value of woollen and worsted cloths and yarn exported after 1848 (6.3% per year from 1846 to 1873) brought about a sharp increase in the exports/output ratio, which exceeded 40% in the early 1870s.[160]

An overwhelming share of the output of the iron industry in the 18th century went to the home market.[161] Exports of iron goods nevertheless grew quite fast up to 1771 (with a yearly rate of 3.6% from 1697 to 1771), and W. E. Minchinton has rightly noticed that their weight grew faster than total English bar iron consumption, so that the ratio of export

---

[156] P. Deane, "The Output of the British Woolen Industry in the Eighteenth Century," *Journal of Economic History*, 17, No. 2 (1957), pp. 220, 222, and Deane and Cole, p. 52; criticized by Wilson, pp. 50–51.

[157] Deane, "The Output," pp. 209–210; Wilson, p. 42; Davis, *English Overseas Trade*, p. 8; but see also Ashton, *Fluctuations*, p. 75.

[158] Hoffmann, Table 54, part A. See, however, Deane, "The Output," p. 222. One must also stress the different experience of the various manufacturing districts: Wilson, pp. 41–44, 51.

[159] Deane, "The Output," p. 221.

[160] The ratio of exports to total output in the linen industry of *Great Britain*, which had been minute in the early 18th century, increased to about 25% ca. 1807. For the industry of the United Kingdom, the ratio declined from the beginning of the 19th century up to ca. 1830, and the rapid growth of output was largely absorbed by the home market. Later on, the ratio rose regularly, from 15% in 1830 to 54% in 1862, during the American civil war. From Deane and Cole, pp. 52–53, 60, 202–205. In the silk industry, the exports proportion seems to have had roughly the same movement; Deane and Cole, pp. 51, 53, 59, 207–208, 210.

[161] John, in *Economica*, pp. 183–184. There were practically no exports of unwrought iron (pig iron, bar iron) and all exports of iron goods were supplied by the secondary iron industry.

weights to supplies increased from 8% in 1715 to about 20% in 1770 and possibly more.[162] But exports fell sharply from 1771 to 1779/1781 and, though they grew rapidly in the 1780s (at a yearly rate of 9.6% from 1783 to 1792), this advance was not maintained, the growth rate falling to 3.1% from 1792 to 1802 and to 1.4% from 1802 to 1814. On the other hand, British production of pig iron seems to have more than doubled from circa 1760 to 1788, and to have increased fourfold between 1788 and 1806 (while the official value of exports of iron and steel goods increased only 65% between the last two dates); of course, the total supplies of raw materials to the secondary iron industry did not rise as much, as imports of bar iron grew quite slowly and eventually decreased from the late 1790s; moreover, a large part of the output of pig iron was used directly as castings.[163] We have attempted some rough calculations of the ratio between the pig iron equivalents of iron goods exported and the total consumption of pig iron in Britain (home production + equivalent of the bar iron imports); this would give ratios of 20% circa 1788, 22% circa 1796, and 20% circa 1805.[164] On the other hand, the current value of iron goods exported circa 1805 is 17.5% of the estimated value of the iron industry's gross product.[165] It seems therefore that the fast expansion and technological mutation of the iron industry—especially in its primary branch—in the late 18th and early 19th century were not accompanied by a rise of the exports/output ratio for iron goods,[166] and that the additional production was for the most part absorbed by the home market.[167]

Iron's export proportion seems to have risen during the immediate postwar years, when the industry suffered a severe depression, but it fell

[162] Minchinton, p. 42; confirmed by Deane and Cole, pp. 51, 55, 58–59; Bairoch, p. 561.

[163] Deane and Cole, pp. 51, Table 15, 221; Eversley, p. 236.

[164] From data in *Abstract*, pp. 131, 140, 145; Deane and Cole, pp. 55, note 3, 221–222. Figures for imports and exports are triennial averages centered on the year specified; wrought iron has been converted to a pig iron equivalent on the assumption that 1 ton of bar or wrought iron contained 33 CWT of pig. One can also calculate the ratio of the weight of iron and steel goods exported to the total supplies of bar iron (home produced and imported), as the chief raw material of the secondary iron industry. On the assumption that one-half of the pig iron produced in Britain was cast (Deane and Cole, p. 223, note 1), this would give ratios of 27% ca. 1788, 30% ca. 1796, 31% ca. 1805; these figures are comparable to the ratios given by Minchinton for the earlier period and might also fit with the data mentioned in note 167.

[165] Current values according to Davis, *The Industrial Revolution* . . . ., p. 96; product from Deane and Cole, p. 225, Table 56.

[166] Though it recovered in the 1780s from its low level of the 1770s.

[167] And also by the substitution of home produced bar iron to imports. However, there is a good deal of qualitative evidence about the strong dependence upon exports in the secondary iron trades of Birmingham and Sheffield, but it was given during the Parliamentary enquiry about the Orders in Council in 1812 and tended to stress the importance of exports, which were said to absorb in good years about half the output of these towns; Crouzet, p. 71, note 89.

to 15% in the late 1820s; exports thereafter picked up, with traditional sales of hardware increasingly complemented by growing shipments of semifinished products and machinery; though production also advanced substantially, the export ratio increased and approached 30% in the early 1840s; after 1850, it rose suddenly to around 40%.[168]

All the main British industries contributed to the rise in the ratio of exports to national income and industrial production in the 1780s; but, after 1792, the cotton industry and, to a lesser degree, the woollen industry were responsible for the whole of the further increase in the ratio which took place and created for a time an "export economy." After the early years of the 19th century, there was a setback and a shift of all industries—at least as far as values of exports and production are concerned—toward the home market. A new strong rise in the ratio of exports to industrial production did not take place before the mid-19th century, but this time it was very broadly based, on an increased exports proportion in all major industries.

Last, some conjectural examples of the incremental ratios between the additional value of exports by the main industries and the additional output they achieved can be suggested.

For the cotton industry, the ratios (in %) would be:[169]

From 1760 to 1784/86	13
From 1784/86 to 1805/07	87
From 1805/07 to 1839/41	42
From 1839/41 to 1869/71	79

As it could be expected, the contribution of exports to the growth of the cotton industry was small from 1760 to the mid-1780s, but it was over-whelming during the 20 years or so which followed;[170] it fell back during the four next decades to become again very large from circa 1840 to circa 1870. In the woollen industry, the ratio of additional exports to additional output might have been very high (83%) between 1772 and 1799, but it would be nil during the first four decades of the 19th century, before rising again to a high figure (about 40%) between 1850/1854 and 1870/1874.[171] As for the iron industry, if we use the same system of pig iron equivalents as earlier, the contribution of export demand to the increase in output (both

[168] Deane and Cole, p. 224.

[169] Calculated from the sources quoted in the notes to Table 16 and especially from Deane and Cole, pp. 185, 187, Tables 42 and 43.

[170] Bairoch, in *Annales*, pp. 565–566, gives estimates quite close to ours; he stresses (p. 567) that the high ratio around 1800 resulted from the exploitation of a privileged position following a technological breakthrough, in which the export trade had not been an important factor.

[171] Sources for these estimates in notes to Table 16.

in weight) would have been about one-fifth between circa 1788 and circa 1805. If the additional value of exports is compared with the additional value of the industry's gross product, the ratio would be 32% from circa 1805 to 1835/1839 and 43% from 1835/1839 to 1870/1874.[172] For British industry as a whole, it is likely that the incremental ratio of exports to output was modest before 1780,[173] but high from 1781 to 1802, after which it fell back to a low level from the 1800s to circa 1840 but was high again in the 1850s and 1860s.

With much that is conjectural and tentative, this paper has not been able to consider the whole gamut of problems relevant to its theme. The multiplier effects and the backward linkages of exports expansion, which Deane and Habakkuk have mentioned as important in the late 18th century,[174] have been neglected, with the question of the gains from trade and the influences of an enlarged market, thanks to growing foreign demand, upon the division of labor, technological innovation, and transfer of resources to high productivity sectors. Moreover, domestic exports have been considered per se and arbitrarily isolated from imports and from the related variable of the terms of trade. Indeed, there has deliberately been no attempt to tackle the problem of the sources of export expansion. Was foreign demand for British goods an exogenous, independently determined and random variable? Or should the explanation of its accelerations be sought "at home rather than abroad," i.e., in the increase of British demand for foreign products, resulting itself from rising population and incomes in Britain, as Deane and Cole have maintained for the 18th century?[176] Or did internal economic growth of itself lead to higher productivity in the export sector and thus to increased exports? This paper does not pretend to answer these questions and, if the impact of conditions on foreign markets has been stressed in several cases, this was as an explanation of relatively short-term movements of exports, especially during the French wars.

It seems that the pattern which emerges from this study is more intricate than is generally supposed, with a succession of shifts in the balance between foreign and home demand, in the role of the main industries in export expansion and in their various export markets. Finally, the most

[172] Sources in notes to Table 16: Deane and Cole, p. 255, Table 56; supra, note 164.

[173] However, from the sources used in Table 16, the increase in exports values, between 1695 and 1772, was equivalent to 50% of the increase in the output of the woollen industry.

[174] Deane and Habakkuk, p. 80.

[175] This is the view, for the mid-18th century, of John, in Jones, pp. 179–180, and in *Kyklos*, 17, No. 2 (1964), p. 279.

[176] Deane and Cole, pp. 83–89, 312; Cole, pp. 329–342. In some periods of the first half of the 19th century, foreign markets might have been a dumping ground for an over-production which the home market would not absorb, with manufacturers expanding their overseas sales in order to keep their factories going; cf. Imlah, p. 125; Edwards, p. 74; Wilson, pp. 123–125; Schlote, pp. 77–78.

interesting finding might be the contrast between several periods and their specificities. Particularly, in accordance with W. W. Rostow's intuitions, the 20 years from 1782 to 1802 have a marked originality, owing to their very high rate of growth of exports,[178] to the "leading sector" part which cottons played in export expansion, to the predominant role of American markets, and to the undoubtedly strong impact of foreign demand on Britain's economic growth (and though export expansion came after the technological breakthroughs, it certainly accelerated their diffusion). On the other hand, the later years of the French wars, after 1802, seem more akin to the postwar period, with its slower growth of exports, their diversion to underdeveloped countries, and their limited contribution to economic growth. Only in the mid-19th century did Britain become a full-fledged export economy.[179]

APPENDIX

Statistics and Their Sources

1. Exports from England and Wales, 1697–1800, official values (O.V.): Mitchell and Deane, *Abstract*, pp. 279–281; Schumpeter, Table II (for 1792–1800). For 1697–1708, this series uses the adjusted figures with revised estimates of the value of woollens of Deane and Cole, pp. 319, 322.

2. Exports from Great Britain, 1772–1814, O.V.: *Abstract*, p. 281; Crouzet, *L'économie britannique. . .*, p. 885, Table 3 (for 1805–1812).

3. Exports from the United Kingdom, 1801–1853, O.V.: *Abstract*, pp. 282–283.

4. Exports from the United Kingdom, 1796–1873, current (declared) values (C.V.): *Abstract*, pp. 282–283.

5. Exports of U.K. products, 1796–1873, volume at 1880 prices: Imlah, pp. 94–97, Table 8.

6. Exports from England and Wales, 1697–1791, and from Great Britain, 1792–1814, O.V., of cotton yarn and manufactures, linen yarn and manufactures (up to 1812), silk yarn and manufactures, iron and steel goods, nonferrous metals and manufactures: *Abstract*, pp. 293–295.

7. Exports from England and Wales of woollen and worsted yarn and manufactures (hats included), 1697–1808, Mrs. Schumpeter's values; from Great Britain, 1792–1814, hats not included; O.V.: *Abstract*, pp. 293–295.

8. Exports from the United Kingdom, 1814–1873 (in fact, from Great Britain excluding exports to Ireland, 1814–1829, but there is no difference

[177] Saul, p. 11.

[178] Flinn, p. 61, maintains that this was induced by fortuitous and ephemeral circumstances.

[179] F. Crouzet, *L'économie de la Grande-Bretagne victorienne* (Paris, 1978), pp. 110–117.

with U.K. exports, except for linens, for which an adjustment has been made), C.V., of cotton, wool, linen yarn and manufactures, metals and metal manufactures, coal: *Abstract*, pp. 302–304.

9. Exports from the United Kingdom, volume at 1880 prices, of cotton manufactures, woolen manufactures, goods other than cottons and woolens: Imlah, Appendix, Tables II, III, IV, pp. 210–215.

10. Exports from the United Kingdom to the main geographical areas, 1814–1873, C.V.: *Abstract*, pp. 313–315, 318, 321, 324.

11. Exports from the United Kingdom to the main geographical areas, 1814–1873, volume at 1880 prices: series 10 deflated by the exports prices index of Imlah, pp. 94-97.

[7]

The Industrial Revolution
and British overseas trade

The Industrial Revolution was the aggregate of the economic and social consequences that followed from the development of new productive techniques in
some British industries towards the end of the eighteenth century. It enormously
increased British industrial production, raised up a new class of wealthy industrial capitalists whose attitudes pervaded the governing classes, and created a
new form of relationship between employers and a workforce that was increasingly concentrated in factories built in great industrial towns.

Though a combination of changes made up the Industrial Revolution, the
principal driving forces came from the nature of the inventions in the textile
industries, which required factory organization; and the efficacy of those inventions, which lifted the market for their products, at home and abroad, to an
entirely new level. This first textile-based phase of the Industrial Revolution was
getting under way in the 1780s. By the 1850s a diversified, capital-intensive and
consciously triumphant industrial capitalism had stamped its imprint on Britain,
and was at last beginning to offer some of its fruits to the masses of the people. The
first tables of overseas trade in this book record the years 1784–6, when the
incipient Industrial Revolution had not materially influenced or been influenced
by overseas trade. The final ones record the years 1854–6, when a large part of the
produce of Britain's more advanced industries was being exported, and the
economy had become heavily dependent on the raw materials and foodstuffs that
were imported.

While the textile inventions provided the driving force for the Industrial
Revolution, little could have been achieved without the improvement of agriculture that took place during the same period. This was because the mid-eighteenth
century decades had seen a recrudescence of population growth in Britain at a
pace that had not been known for several generations. The relation between
population movement and economic growth in the eighteenth century has been
much discussed;[1] but the great underlying danger was that numbers would

1.   T. S. Ashton, *An Economic History of England; the Eighteenth Century* (1955), 59–62;
     J. D. Chambers, *Population Economy and Society in Pre-Industrial England* (1972); H.
     J. Habakkuk, *Population Growth and Economic Development since 1750* (1971) 25–50;
     D. Eversley, 'The home market and economic growth in England, 1750–1780', in
     E. L. Jones and G. Mingay (eds.), *Land, Labour and Population in the Industrial
     Revolution* (1967), 207–20; A. H. John, 'Agricultural productivity and economic
     growth in England, 1700–1760', *EcHR*, 25 (1965).

quickly outrun home food production and pose insoluble problems of food supply, as they had done in the past. It was avoided because the long slow process of agricultural improvement was sharply accelerated in the latter part of the century, and enabled home producers to supply domestic needs for bread and other basic foods right down to the 1830s, when population had trebled.[2] When a regular food deficit of substantial size appeared in the following decades, ample supplies were becoming available from America and Russia to meet the deficiency.

The improvement in agricultural efficiency had other important results. The vastly increased production from British soil was achieved without greatly enlarging the agricultural labour force. The rapid natural increase of the rural population was released from (or, according to point of view, driven off) the land, to augment the working force of the textile towns of Scotland and the north of England, the metal towns of the Midlands and North-East, the coalfields and the seaports. Down to 1815 the prosperity of landlords and farmers contributed strongly to the expansion of the home market for manufactures and imported goods. And, since agriculture was much the largest sector of the economy, employing even in 1851 almost as many people as the whole of manufacturing industry, its growing production accounted for a great part of the increase in national income.

The impact of increased agricultural production on overseas trade was a negative one, since it reduced the demand for imports of scarce commodities whose prices would have risen if demand had been much higher. Its success in this respect is illustrated in the history of controls on the trade in grain. In 1773, panic measures, that for the first time permitted almost unrestricted imports of grain, went through a Parliament that feared grain shortage. Forty years later the famous Corn Law of 1815 was passed, imposing severe restrictions on imports, to protect from foreign competition farmers whose production now seemed ample, though there were twice as many people to be fed. The Corn Laws of 1815, modified several times before their repeal in 1846, were thought by contemporaries to restrict British exports by preventing grain-producing countries from earning much by sales to Britain.[3] But it is unlikely that European surpluses would have been found, at any possible price, to supply the needs of such a fast-growing population in Britain. If British agriculture had not done so, the Industrial Revolution would have been stopped in its tracks by failure to feed its urban masses.

The role of overseas trade in Britain's economic development changed during this period. It was important to the modest industrial growth that was going on before the Industrial Revolution, but made little direct contribution to the advent of the Industrial Revolution itself and was not essential in the early stages of its development. Its importance reappeared in the further expansion of the matured industrial economy and the eventual rise towards a more widely spread prosperity.

Industrial growth in the first three-quarters of the eighteenth century largely took the form of diversification away from the old staple manufacture of woollen

2. The best discussion is D. C. Chambers and G. Mingay, *The Agricultural Revolution, 1750–1880* (1966).
3. J. B. Williams, *British Commercial Policy and Trade Expansion, 1750–1850* (1972), 198, 448, 455–6. Later history suggested that this view was mistaken.

64   *Chapter 5: The Industrial Revolution and British overseas trade*

cloth. It is true that after mid-century the woollen industry was shaking off a long stagnation as it concentrated in West Yorkshire, renewed its styles and cheapened its products, and so expanded in this area that it created labour shortage over much of the north of England. But industrial growth had begun earlier in the century, and continued more rapidly, in the many industries making small metal goods, in linen and silk manufacture, and in such smaller industries as pottery, shipbuilding, glass and cotton manufacture. The basis for this expansion was partly the home demand of a growing middle-income group of professional men, independent craftsmen, merchants and shopkeepers, small rentiers and farmers; and partly the demand of similar sections of society in the American colonies, growing explosively in population and wealth. and in Ireland, returning to some degree of prosperity after a century of war and repression. By the 1770s many of these industries were as dependent as woollens on export markets, sending between a quarter and half of their production overseas; though, unlike woollens, they looked not to Europe but to colonial and Irish markets where British merchants had special advantages.[4] Enlargement of scale made for greater specialization and intensified division of labour, so that costs were reduced despite the still primitive methods of production, and this expansion owed much to the growth of export trade.

Yet export trade had little to do, directly or indirectly, with the beginnings of the Industrial Revolution. The immense expansion of cotton manufacture from the 1770s and of other textile industries a little later, and of the bulk fabrication of metals at the end of the century, was associated not with small improvements but with a fundamental transformation in techniques and organization. The industries that had been in the van of progress in the 1770s in making buttons, locks, nails, firearms, cutlery, tools and the like changed little over the following 80 years. In the 1850s they still turned out their products in small forges with moulds and hand tools, and sold most of them at home; their overseas sales had lagged behind the growth in purchasing power of their markets, and were now trivial by comparison with the export trade of the reorganized textile industries. In the European market they had no advantages over similar industries in Saxony, northern and eastern France, and the Ruhr, and in America local products were squeezing them out. The Industrial Revolution passed them by, and they were not transformed before the latter part of the nineteenth century, and then often by imitating American or European examples.

It is true that some particular craftsmen's skills – those of instrument-makers, clock-makers and millwrights – were drawn upon for practical help by the pioneers of machinery. Important though such men were in the earliest days, they were soon replaced by a new breed of machine makers, entirely specialized to work on steam engines, textile machinery and machine tools.

Beyond this there was no important connection between the flourishing export industries of the mid-eighteenth century and the Industrial Revolution. There was no traceable movement of capital from them into the newer and more productive branches of industry; indeed, much capital was swallowed up in river navigations and canals to link the Birmingham area with its seaports. They absorbed growing amounts of labour, because the rate of growth of their total

4.   See R. Davis, 'English overseas trade, 1700–1774', *EcHR*, 15 (1962).

production outpaced improvement in their efficiency; the men of the Midland villages, with industry on their doorsteps, did not rot in poverty like the Dorset or Hampshire labourers, but they did not migrate in any numbers to the more advanced industries of the North.

The Industrial Revolution in fact involved a movement on to quite different paths of industrial development from those that were being successfully followed, a reversal of the relative decline of the textile industries that had been in progress for several decades, and the development of processes and products that found their first outlets in home rather than in export markets.

The authors of the best book on the early cotton industry, it is true, argue that overseas trade played an important part in stimulating the growth of the cotton industry into the factory era.[5] They point out that there was a surge of exports of British cottons for the African and West Indian trades in the 1750s and early 1760s, when political upheavals in India made supplies scarce. But these markets were lost when Indian supply became plentiful again in the mid-1760s; the trade had caused only a temporary acceleration of growth, which died away. The origins of its great leap forward were quite different.

A strong latent demand for calicoes and muslins had been revealed in the latter part of the seventeenth century, when Indian textiles had been allowed in freely. It alarmed the woollen interests, which secured legislation in a series of steps between 1700 and 1721 that stamped out the import. But the small British cotton industry was unable to produce yarn fine enough for fabrics of this kind; the demand remained unfilled (apart from some smuggling) and the British industry grew slowly as a producer of mixed cotton/linen and cotton/worsted fabrics. But it did grow, and this was important. For despite the obvious gains to be made by anyone who could spin ten or a hundred woollen threads simultaneously where one had been spun before, there were great technical difficulties in doing this with wool.[6] Consequently it was in the far smaller, but growing, cotton industry that the technical breakthrough was made by Hargreaves, Arkwright and Crompton. It was a breakthrough that not only made a British cotton yarn that was cheap by comparison with other textiles or Indian yarn; but also a yarn of a fineness rivalling the Indian, and therefore a basis for an essentially new industry making calicoes and muslins. This new factory industry was largely devoted, in its first 20 years, to catching up with the enormous home demand that now revealed itself.

Export trade had been important to the expansion of the metal industries of the mid-eighteenth century decades, but the cotton industry grew to a large scale, its total output pressing hard on the heels of the woollen and metal industries, before its export trade became very significant. All British exports were rising fast in the 1780s and 1790s; cotton goods accounted for less than a third of the increase in manufactured exports between 1784–6 and 1794–6. In the following decade, ending in 1804–6, however, cotton goods were going increasingly to export markets, and accounted for 84 per cent of the increase in manufactured exports.

The rapid rise of exports of cotton goods had hardly begun before the outbreak

---

5. A. P. Wadsworth and J. de L. Mann, *The Cotton Trade and Industrial Lancashire* (1931), 159.
6. As we saw above, they had still not been completely overcome in the 1820s (pp. 21–2, *supra*).

66   Chapter 5: The Industrial Revolution and British overseas trade

Table 34: Exports of cotton goods, as percentage of total production[1]

	Production (£000)	Exports (£000)	%
1760	.6	.3	50
1772–4	.9	.3	33
1784–6	5.4	.8	15
1794–6	10.0	3.4	34

1.   Production figures adapted from P. Deane and W. A. Cole, *British Economic Growth 1688–1959* (1967), 185.

of new wars in 1793 created a distortion of trade patterns that lasted for more than 20 years. The value of all exports rose very fast, for Britain controlled Europe's access to the outside world, and the wars lengthened the period in which it had a near monopoly of factory industry. Rapidly rising exports, and large and profitable re-exports, ensured a large current surplus in the balance of payments, which was used up in the financing of British armies overseas and in subsidies to allies. It was only after 1815 that Britain entered a period in which the mutual influences of industrialization and a great expansion of the volume of trade could work freely.

The 30-odd years following 1815 were in important respects years of stability in overseas trade. A tremendous growth of total trade had been achieved; now its value – though not its volume – stabilized at a high level. The share of textiles in the expanding export trade had rapidly increased until about 1810; then it levelled off, despite continuing technical improvements in the textile industries. The imports of industrial raw materials and foodstuffs paid for by these exports rose further in value and volume, but barely kept pace with the growth of population; in this respect, too, a stable position had been reached.

From the late 1840s export growth was vigorously renewed and balance of payments surpluses were greatly enlarged. In the decade 1847–56 the rate of growth in the value of exports was the highest ever recorded. The value of textile exports again rose steeply after a long interval (partly because their prices stopped falling) and a large new export of heavy ironwares, principally for railways, grew up. Imports of sugar, coffee, tea, etc., again outpacing population increase, were now joined by large regular grain imports for basic needs. This was the beginning of a new phase in Britain's commercial history, and I shall concentrate first on the period from 1815 to the late 1840s, before considering the fresh leap forward.

The textile industries, from the 1790s, and the heavy metal industries, from the 1840s, came to depend on export markets to dispose of a substantial part of their output. Two questions must be asked about this export trade. Did the enlarged scale of production that was made possible by exporting, and did the continuous (long-term) growth of production – two rather different things – make possible gains in efficiency? If these industries gained from scale and from continuous growth, then were the benefits, arising as they did partly from overseas sales, the same as those that would have been secured from an entirely domestic expansion?

I suggested earlier that export growth helped the metal and other industries of the mid-eighteenth century to become more efficient producers. Did overseas trade stimulate the technically advanced industries of the Industrial Revolution in similar ways?

If it did so, it was to a much more limited extent, and through external rather than internal economies. The cotton manufacture was quite unlike the eighteenth-century craftsman industries. These had been small industries divided into smaller sub-branches making and assembling parts of specialized products like guns and locks, nails and knives. In most processes a few hundred workers, and in many a few dozen, constituted the whole labour force, compared with the scores of thousands in cotton spinning or weaving. As these little industries became larger, a rationalization of their organization took place over long periods of time; but in cotton this was suddenly forced upon the industry by the need to follow the pioneers into the use of machinery and power, and once such rationalization had been achieved each single new productive unit, each single factory, though of optimum size for efficiency,[7] was only a small part of the whole industry. Home demand for the new cotton goods was quite sufficient to expand the industry to a size that embraced a large number of these factories and a considerable number of competing firms. By the 1790s, when further expansion of the industry was becoming heavily dependent on exports, it simply called for a larger number of similar mills. In the same way, once power weaving passed out of the pioneering stage in the 1820s, further expansion enlarged the number of broadly similar weaving sheds.

Beyond this were the economies of the industry as a whole; the external economies achieved by turning Lancashire and Yorkshire into great cotton and woollen concentrations centred respectively on Manchester and Leeds.[8] The specialized commodity markets and banking services, the networks of merchant houses and commission agencies, the machinery manufacturers and repairers cheek-by-jowl with the users of machinery, the labour force growing up to accept work in the mills as a natural destiny, the improved transport facilities and all the rest, contributed very substantially to the cheapening of textile production and Britain's long-continued lead in it. At this level, these industries did gain substantial advantages from large-scale and locational considerations.

In the manufacture of iron and heavy iron products, too, there were only limited direct gains in efficiency arising from the extra scale needed for export trade. The great new plants were built to provide for Britain's increasing internal needs. Above all, in the 1830s and 1840s they were to serve the demands of railway construction and maintenance, fluctuating violently on a steeply rising trend. It was the attempt to keep them fully employed in the downswing of British railway construction after 1847 that brought about the great surge of export trade in their products. This trade did not materially alter the size of the industry or the typical productive unit – though it helped to maintain a higher average level of use, and therefore, in the very long run, to keep down average costs.

A second type of gain came from the attraction of factors of production towards profitable and highly productive modern industries. The capital formation aspect will be discussed later. On the labour side, they attracted workers from less

7. This is, of course, an idealized view. But the irrationality of some decisions, creating plants of a size different from the optimum, does not affect the main argument here.
8. As the other industries had gains from their concentrations on Birmingham and Sheffield.

68   *Chapter 5: The Industrial Revolution and British overseas trade*

productive and less well-paid occupations and – probably on a much larger scale – gave first employment to an increasing proportion of the young workers coming on the labour market each year. So the average physical productivity of Britain's labour force was gradually raised.[9] On the other hand a major innovation such as the power loom threw great numbers of people into unemployment or underemployment during the early stages of its widespread adoption, a waste of resources as well as a social tragedy. But in the long-term this transfer towards more productive industries was of economic benefit to Britain.

Finally there were the advantages not of scale itself, but of constant rapid growth. Despite the cyclical ups and downs, the trend of physical production in the advanced industries was steadily upwards. Once the new types of machinery had been fully developed on the basis of pioneering innovations, there remained continued scope for small improvements. The water frame had represented so great a technical leap that it caused the scrapping of spinning wheels; regular improvements made newer machinery more efficient than older, but not to a degree that consigned the latter to the scrapheap. An industry that was regularly expanding always had a high proportion of relatively up-to-date machinery in its factories; and this was a further advantage of the cotton, woollen and heavy iron industries in Britain during most of the first half of the nineteenth century.

The expansion of production and the state of constant growth in the textile industries especially owed a great deal to export trade. In all these ways, as well as through the enormous direct savings made by the mechanical inventions themselves, these manufactures were cheapened, and the British user of cheap muslins or worsteds was the beneficiary. But who was the beneficiary if these goods were exported at competitive prices? This is the question of the terms of trade; the relationship (or group of relationships) of export and import prices. But it is necessary, before coming to this, to examine further the nature of the benefits from cheapness.

There is a conceptual difficulty in discussing the gains when a virtually new product comes into large-scale production, and thereafter is cheapened through technological improvement, reaping economies of scale and so on. The new kinds of cotton goods produced in the 1770s with factory-spun yarn were rapidly being cheapened from the time of their first introduction. The extent is graphically illustrated by Robert Owen's memories that he wrote down in his old age:[10]

> When I first went to Mr McGuffog [in 1781] there were no other muslins for sale, except those made in the East Indies, and known as East India Muslins, but while I was with him Mr Oldknow began to manufacture a fabric which he called, by way of distinction, British Mull Muslin. It was a new article in the market . . . which Mr McGuffog sold to his customers at half a guinea a yard. It was eagerly sought for, and bought up by the nobility at that price . . . The parties who were then so eager to buy this fabric at 10s 6d per yard would not

9. It is true that it was a movement towards industries whose product had a much larger content of imported raw materials than the older ones, which could have raised serious problems if there had not been a large export trade. But this does not affect the physical productivity of labour, measured in terms of value added per unit of labour input.
10. R. Owen, *The Life of Robert Owen, by Himself* (1857), 25.

now [1857] look at it; and a much better quality may be at this time purchased by the poor at two pence per yard.

The same point is made, if less vividly, by comparison of the official and real values of goods in overseas trade at the end of our period.[11]

Table 35: Official and real values in overseas trade, 1854–6
(£000)

	Official values	Real values
Cotton goods exports	144290	34908
Other manufactures exports	68346	48183
Other exports	20315	19410
Total exports	*232951*	*102501*
Re-exports	31570	21005
Imports	120777	151581.

The mechanization of cotton spinning and other processes in the textile industries bettered the consumers in Britain in a way that was related to the increased *quantity* of cotton fabric they could buy, rather than to the much less increased total *value* of those goods that appears in statistics of national income. An aged contemporary of Owen's who was able to buy 60 yards of muslin in 1857 for ten shillings was obviously better off to that extent than he had been in his youth when he could buy less than a yard for the same money; but in national income statistics, whether calculated from the sales or the supply side, consumption or production is included as ten shillings at both dates. Meanwhile, his ten shillings would have bought him less bread in his old age than in his youth.[12] The whole question of the material gains from the Industrial Revolution is befogged by this problem.[13]

Much of this cheapened production was exported; well over half of British

11. For reasons explained in the Appendix, this considerably underestimates the extent to which cottons had been cheapened since the first use of spinning machinery in the 1770s.
12. Something may be done by reducing national income to 'constant prices'; but when a single group of products of such great size as cotton goods falls enormously in price in relation to almost everything else, there is no unambiguously right answer to the index number problem.
13. Recent historical applications of the concept of 'social saving' offer hope that increased welfare arising from cheapened production may be taken into account in assessing such gains arising in particular industries. Social saving is the gain (in value terms) from producing a good, or providing a service, by the best available method rather than the second-best one that is available. It has been applied to particular services; to measure, for example, the nineteenth century from the development of railway systems. See G. Gunderson, 'The nature of social saving' *EcHR*, 23 (1970); C. M. White, 'The concept of social saving in theory and practice', *ibid.*, 29 (1976); R. W. Fogel, *Railroads and American Economic Growth* (Baltimore, 1964); P. D. McClelland, 'Railroads, economic growth and the new economic history', *JEcH, 28* (1968); G. R. Hawke, *Railways and Economic Growth in England and Wales, 1840–1870* (1970).

70   Chapter 5: The Industrial Revolution and British overseas trade

cotton manufactures were regularly exported after 1815, an important though smaller proportion of worsteds; well over a third of ironworks once the railway exports began in the later 1840s. Cotton manufactures, as we have seen, dominated all others, and were sold at rapidly falling prices. Looking at British trade statistics as a whole, there was a considerable worsening of the net barter terms of trade[14] (that is, in the physical quantity of imported goods that a given physical quantity of British goods would buy) from 1812 onward.[15]

It might be supposed that when the British economy was growing much faster than those of its customers and suppliers, a growing quantity of British exports could only be sold at falling prices, and growing imports would make demands on overseas producers that would lead to rising prices. But this formulation simply describes a tendency which always exerted some pressure but was normally overshadowed by other changes. Many markets were enjoying increased population with rising incomes per head, and entirely new markets were opening to British goods and being penetrated only by slow degrees. Europe's population was growing (though tariffs and prohibitions tampered capriciously with the rise of this market); the population and the wealth of the United States were growing very fast; Latin America, India and other parts of Asia were beginning to consume British goods on a large scale; Australia suddenly emerged after 1849 to buy lavishly with sacksful of newly-mined gold. The overall demand schedule for British manufactures was shifting outwards[16] and thus partially offsetting the adverse movement of the terms of trade.

There was a similar development on the side of imports. While the prices of foodstuffs and raw materials coming from Europe – largely corn, timber and wine – showed a tendency to rise, imports from beyond Europe of such things as sugar, tea, coffee and many raw materials fell quite steeply until mid-century. This was because new sources of supply were tapped, new lands opened to cultivation, and the fall in transport costs was beginning to be significant for goods brought over long distances (see table 36).

Despite new markets and new sources, the terms of trade did worsen, not merely from the very favourable levels of the war years, but even by comparison with the later eighteenth century. Today such changes cause alarm, for the cause is usually rising prices of imported primary products which cannot be countered by increasing export prices. But in the first half of the nineteenth century the import prices were tending to fall; the worsening of the terms of trade was due to the steep fall of export prices, which under competitive conditions reflected the declining real costs of producing the exported goods. A given combination of

14. 'Terms of trade' has many definitions (see W. W. Rostow, 'The terms of trade in theory and practice', *EcHR*, 3,4 (1951). The net barter terms of trade are those most commonly discussed, and are readily deducible from the statistics of this period. In principle the most useful concept is that of the double factorial terms of trade; that is, the relationship between changes in export and import prices, adjusted for changes in productivity on both sides. But these are not normally calculable; indeed, their calculation would be, in effect, the writing of the economic history of the countries of the world.

15. A. H. Imlah, *Economic Aspects of the Pax Brittanica* (Cambridge, Mass., 1958), 94–6.

16. On the other hand, European factory industry, which was insignificant in 1815, was competing seriously in European markets before mid-century.

Table 36: Movement of import prices $\left\{\dfrac{\text{real values}}{\text{official values}}\right\}$ 1784–1856

	Europe	Rest of world
1784–6	154.7	142.4
1824–6	179.1	131.7
1834–6	173.6	124.6
1844–6	142.4	93.4
1854–6	172.4	108.9

quantities of capital and labour employed in the cotton industry, added to imported raw cotton, produced a far greater quantity of cotton fabrics in 1845 than in 1815; but the produce was sold at a lower price because the raw cotton and other costs of production were less. The quantity of foreign goods received in return for the produce of this labour and capital was not necessarily smaller, and may have been much larger, in 1845 than in 1815.

Nevertheless, it is evident that some part of the gain from the increasing efficiency of British production was transferred to foreign buyers by the exchange of these cheap British manufactures for foodstuffs and raw materials produced abroad in old inefficient ways.[17] From this point of view, it may be asked whether turning resources to import substitution rather than to further expanding great industries by export sales might not have produced greater overall gains to Britain.[18] And these considerations underline once more the importance of the increase of agricultural production at home, which limited the need for imports of grain, and other foodstuffs, and so tended to keep down imports and prevent further depression of the terms of trade.

This leads on to the question of the gains of trade from the exploitation of comparative advantage, of differential factor endowments, in the sense first discussed by the classical economists,[19] and endlessly refined down to our own day.[20] It needs to be considered in terms of closely specified inputs rather than simple categories of labour and land, and rapidly becomes complex.[21] Two things

17. Not all were, of course; cotton was very much cheapened as American production became more efficient.
18. These questions were sometimes examined by contemporaries; the nineteenth-century view is summed up by John Stuart Mill, *Principles of Political Economy* (1848), Book 3, Chapter XVIII, section 5. Modern discussion includes J. R. Hicks, 'An inaugural lecture' (*Oxford Economic Papers*, V, 1953), especially 124–30, and B. Sodersten, *A Study of Economic Growth and International Trade* (Stockholm, 1964), 52–5.
19. R. Torrens, *An Essay on the External Corn Trade* (1815); D. Ricardo, *Principles of Political Economy and Taxation* (1821), 133–46.
20. On the later development of the theory, see J. Viner, *Studies in the Theory of International Trade* (1937). Modern expositions include I. F. Pearce, *International Trade* (1970); P. A. Samuelson, 'The gains from international trade once again', *Economic Journal*, 72 (1962); J. Bhagwati, 'The pure theory of international trade: a survey', in *Surveys of Economic Theory*, II (1965).
21. C. P. Kindleberger, *Economic Development* (New York, 1958), 239–45, examines some of the complications that in practice upset the simple workings of comparative advantage in international trade.

may be noted here, however. The first is that during most of the eighteenth century Britain's natural endowment with factors of the most obvious economic importance – particular kinds of equipment, qualities of labour, land for particular uses – was not markedly different from that of its nearer neighbours; many writers explain the favourable background to the British Industrial Revolution in terms of less tangible endowments, social and cultural factors such as a degree of religious toleration, a relatively open society, a government subject to some popular pressure, a freely working legal system, and so on. The Industrial Revolution itself involved the rapid creation of a unique set of material factor endowments in Britain – factories and machinery, labour specialized to serve them and entre-preneurs with skill in organizing them – a generation before other countries had them. This was the context in which Ricardo and his followers developed their theory, which indicated that a country should make full use of those factors with which it was best endowed, and enter international trade on this basis. It was a static theory, concerned with natural endowments, and not taking into account the changes that take place through the production of physical capital resources or new skills in labour. These requisites of modern exporting industry in Britain were fully employed, and indeed were only with some difficulty expanded rapidly enough to meet upsurges in demand.

Secondly, 'comparative advantage' has to be discussed in terms of foregoing the production of some things that could be produced with the available resources, in order to release resources for another commodity in which there are greater comparative advantages. But a great many of the goods that Britain imported could not possibly have been produced in Britain, or could have been produced only on preposterous terms. Some 80 per cent of imported goods can be classified in respect of their substitutability. Of these, only about one-sixth were reasonably capable of being substituted for by British goods in a similar price range in 1784–6, and after the wars, both in 1814–16 and in 1854–6, barely one-tenth were substitutable. The list of non-substitutable goods included sugar and the whole range of drinks except beer (which had ceased to be a general substitute for other drinks because of changing tastes and habits). The most essential raw material imports included many that Britain did not produce at all, such as cotton, hemp and jute, nearly all dyestuffs, palm oil and olive oil; and others for which some essential grades were only produced overseas, such as wool and timber. It included many goods for which demand was far outstripping possible home productive capacity, such as tallow, copper, flax and hides. And above all, by mid-century the resources of Britain's land, with the techniques available, had ceased to be sufficient to maintain the basic food supply.

By contrast, the list of goods that were reasonably substitutable, though quite a long one, was largely made up of minor products imported in tiny quantities. The important exceptions were manufactured textiles. Both silk and linen imports were heavily taxed or prohibited until well into the nineteenth century, and would otherwise have been imported in larger quantities. Nevertheless, silks were too expensive to have attracted a very great consumption, and linens were being driven out by the increasingly efficient British industry, which became an exporter after 1800. The prohibition of cotton goods had once been very impor-tant; but while their free import might have revolutionized British clothing habits in the eighteenth century, that possibility had disappeared before 1784 with the development of a powerful British industry. The import of iron had once been essential, providing half Britain's needs as late as the 1770s, but technical innovation made British production more economical during the next half-century. If the heavy taxation of timber imports after 1804 had an influence on demand, it was probably to turn it towards efficiently-produced British iron products rather than to expensive home-produced timber. Not until mid-century was there a serious beginning of imports of the products of modernized Continental textile industries. This marked the opening of a new phase of substitution, the exchange of manufactures for manufactures. In the seventeenth century this had been the typical trade between the countries of western and central Europe, as it is in the twentieth, when it has brought new relevance to the classical theory of international trade. But the trade of the early nineteenth century, carried on between Britain and less advanced neighbours, was of a totally different kind. The gains from trade through comparative advantage in the traditional sense were no doubt present, but they are difficult to conceptualize and even more to quantify.

Finally there is the question of the gains accruing to the economy through the maintenance of a regular surplus on the current balance of payments for goods and services.[22] This regular surplus was, in one of its manifestations, a building up of overseas investment, whether the surplus was retained in the form of balances owing from abroad (on a basis that from the national point of view was permanent, though made up of individual credits that were nominally for limited terms) or was turned to the deliberate buying of overseas properties or the stocks and bonds of overseas governments or forms. It had a similar long-term effect to home investment in raising national income.

Imlah has calculated the balance of payments surpluses on current account from 1816.[23] He suggests that there were large surpluses down to 1824 (continued for so long after the war because imports fell away faster than exports after 1815); then 20 years of modest surpluses, growing from 1844 and becoming very large after 1855. Though the actual figures must be treated with very great caution, their internal consistency suggests that the general pattern of change they suggest is a real one. Going back before 1815, contemporary figures and comments indicate a probability that the balance of payments surplus was already large during the long war period when the terms of trade were heavily favourable. This wartime surplus was dissipated in the costs of war overseas and subsidies to allies, but in so far as it led to increased exports of war materials it had some stimulating effect on national income.[24] The periods in which the balance of payments surpluses were growing to their highest levels ran from sometime in the 1790s to the breaking of the boom in 1824–5, and then from the mid-1840s through the rest of our period and far beyond.

The overseas investment of surpluses supplemented the working of domestic investment in pushing up aggregate national income. It may itself have contributed to the expansion of exports. But was it genuinely additional to, or was it to

22. On the theoretical questions involved, see F. Machlup, *International Trade and the National Income Multiplier* (Philadelphia, 1943); Kindleberger, *op. cit.*, Chapter XIV.
23. 'British balance of payments and export of capital, 1816–1913', *EcHR*, 5 (1952–3).
24. See J. L. Anderson, 'Aspects of the effect on the British economy of the wars against France, 1793–1815', *Australian Economic History Review*, 12 (1972).

74   Chapter 5: The Industrial Revolution and British overseas trade

some extent a displacement of, domestic investment?[25] Would a greater expansion of domestic investment have been a possible substitute for it? Would not domestic investment, above all in import substitution with its beneficial effect on the terms of trade, have created still greater overall gains? These questions assume that further domestic investment on a corresponding scale was possible, but it is difficult to see what would have attracted investors to it in the conditions of the time.

The eighteenth century was constantly trembling on the edge of depression because savings were being generated on a scale that could not readily find outlets. The evidence of abundance of capital is in the connected phenomena of the rising price of land and the fall in interest rates, and in the ease with which government borrowings in wartime were taken up without serious inflationary effect. Frequently recurring wars, in fact, relieved these pressures of surplus capital, and it was only in the great wars of 1793–1815 that government needs ran so far ahead of regular accumulation that price inflation did occur. When these wars were over, there was a return to a long period of capital surplus and low interest rates.

There is no clear information about capital formation during the Industrial Revolution. The absence of evidence that the rate of capital formation leaped from 5 per cent to 10 per cent during Rostow's take-off period, as his early model appeared to require,[26] has given rise to an unwarranted impression that it did not increase at all. There has never been any reason for this supposition, and the new figures that Dr Feinstein has in preparation should dispose of it. Nevertheless, the Industrial Revolution did not solve the problem of savings surplus at all easily, for the capital needs of the factory textile industries were modest, and largely met from the accumulation of profits within firms. From 1815 until the railway age was well under way, Britain was again an under-employed economy, with both savings and labour in excess supply. The mechanism for transforming savings into investment which could then provide employment worked very imperfectly in those years.

The great exporting industries were attractive to savings. The export of woollen and cotton goods, and later of heavy ironwares, resulted from the activities of many of the most able entrepreneurs of the time, the builders of the new industries. Much of the capital for expansion came from their accumulation of the profits they were making and through local banks, and they were easily able to attract any further capital they needed because these industries were identified with progress and British commercial leadership. They were able to continue expanding (particularly in physical volume of production) in the nineteenth century largely because export demand was strong, and they built up their capacity to serve these widening markets. The heavy metals industries, seeking outlets for their high productive capacity when home sales slackened, found them

25.   The situation may be contrasted with that of the years immediately before the First World War, when real national income rose only very slowly and the balance of payments surplus was at its all-time peak. However, the terms of trade had turned against Britain with rising import prices, and overseas investment was made to some extent at the expense of cutting back domestic investment from desirable levels.

26.   W. W. Rostow, *The Stages of Economic Growth* (1960), 39.

in railway building abroad. There was little scope for more rapid expansion of any of these industries in the home market. Without large export sales they would have grown little, or even declined, and the capital that was drawn into them would have had to find other outlets.

The second quarter of the nineteenth century shows evidence that Britain was building up a large aggregate surplus of labour, because of the rapid growth of population and the geographical and occupational immobility of most of the labour force. Though the numbers employed in export production in new industries were not very great, the total direct and indirect employment created was important. The long slow running down of agricultural labour was getting under way in the 1820s despite rapidly growing population; it left pockets of unemployment, near-starvation and desperately low wages over much of the country. The great age of Victorian domestic service was appearing, when even the poorest middle-class household could expect to keep its skivvy.

Shops were spreading rapidly, employing labour lavishly under appalling working conditions; the towns were full of hucksters, casual labourers and beggars; and a large emigration from Britain got under way. Despite the large export trade, and the import in return of goods that could not be produced in Britain, industrialization and its secondary influences were unable to expand fast enough to absorb the whole growth of population into employment.

Without a most unlikely restructuring of economy and society, it does not seem possible that any large part of the resources devoted to supplying the export trade and to overseas investment could have found alternative uses. No doubt a greater part of the population in some favoured areas could have stayed on the land, and more of the surplus could have gone into old-style low-productivity industry. Building and increasingly low-yielding transport improvements might have provided more outlets for capital, with no great benefit to the economy. But would the world outside have stood still? Would agriculture, even if it had had more investment and retained more labour, have been able to feed the whole British population for much longer? And would not the difficulty of finding outlets for accumulating capital have created a deflationary pressure that would have slowed down and ultimately strangled growth?

The advantages of a high level of exports, a high level of foreign trade in relation to national income, are certainly not so clear-cut as they seem at first sight. Once competitive conditions prevailed in overseas trade – that is, at least from 1815 – an important part of the gains was passed on to the foreign customers in low prices for British goods. Though it is impossible to quantify the overall effect, I have no doubt that Britain did have real gains, if only because the range of markets and import sources widened. Nevertheless, it was only by export trade that Britain was able to employ its resources of capital and labour as fully as it did before mid-century, and slowly increase national income per head at a time of rapidly increasing population. In principle, the powerful spring of saving could have been utilized to finance the domestic investment that would have been required to employ the growing labour force. But the eyes of the more progressive entrepreneurs were firmly fixed on the particular lines that had done so well, and that pushed so readily into overseas markets. The real range of expansion possibilities open to Britain was very limited, and prosperity without a large overseas trade does not seem to have been one of them. And finally, beyond all this, while a

76   *Chapter 5: The Industrial Revolution and British overseas trade*

diversion of resources might have made British agriculture sufficiently productive to feed everyone for another generation, it is difficult to see how it could have done so much longer. Great new overseas sources of food supply became available in the last third of the century; they were essential to British survival, but could be drawn upon only by the maintenance and further development of Britain's export capacity.

[8]

The Terms of Trade of the United Kingdom, 1798-1913

CONCEPTS of the terms of trade as a means of measuring a country's gain or loss from exchange of goods have been discussed by students of economic theory for a hundred years or more.[1] Until comparatively recently they have remained concepts only, without substantive application, but the tremendous disturbances in trading relationships and monetary standards in the last three decades have quickened interest in the subject. The various formulas devised for the measurement of relative movements of prices and quantities of exports and imports are now used with increasing frequency for the study of relatively current situations. They have not been applied much as yet to illuminate earlier trading history, largely because of the labor involved in deriving and organizing the limited data available. Apart from this difficulty there seems to be no very strong reason why they should not be as useful for economic history as for current analysis.

For no country is the value of systematic measurements of trade greater than for the United Kingdom through the nineteenth century. Here was a great and complex commercial community traversing a period of profound readjustment consequent on her industrial revolution and the Napoleonic Wars. Moreover, in the middle of the century she abandoned the old protectionist system for a free-trade policy more complete than has yet been embraced by any other great state. Index series on Britain's terms of trade can be constructed with a high degree of reliability through the second half of this century. For the earlier years, the nature of the data available imposes some limitations, but these are not serious enough to outweigh the advantage of having continuous series constructed with as much precision as possible and covering the whole of this important period in British trading history.[2] Such series should permit more exact and

---

[1] See Jacob Viner, *Studies in the Theory of International Trade* (New York: Harper and Brothers, 1937), Chaps. viii and ix. Specific applications and formulas are discussed, pp. 558–63.

[2] Two series already exist. F. W. Taussig's well-known index numbers on net and gross barter terms of trade cover the period from 1880 to 1913. F. W. Taussig, *International Trade* (New York: The Macmillan Co., 1929), pp. 411–19. Werner Schlote covered most of the nineteenth century with a series on the net barter terms of trade from 1814 to 1933, but he changed his components in 1854 so that the series is not strictly continuous and there are

Terms of Trade of the United Kingdom   171

revealing comparisons than have formerly been possible. They may also suggest further lines of investigation.

II

The basic data required for constructing indexes on the terms of trade are two sets of figures recording in different ways the values for exports, f.o.b., and for net imports, c.i.f. (cost, insurance, and freight, but without customs duties). One set gives the current market values for each year of the series. The other set gives "absolute" values computed for each year according to the prices prevailing in a base year. These values are used in two ways. Divide the current market values of exports and net imports by the corresponding absolute values for each year and the results constitute index numbers of export and net import prices respectively. The relative movements in these index numbers, that is to say, the ratio of net import to export prices, represent the net barter terms of trade. The absolute values serve another purpose also. Since they reduce the variety of weights and measures to a common base they provide a convenient indication of over-all quantity changes in the flow of exports and net imports. Divide the annual figures in the export and net import series by the corresponding figure for the base year and the results constitute volume indexes for exports and net imports by means of which the gross barter index numbers can be constructed, since by gross barter terms we mean the ratio of the physical quantity of net imports to the physical quantity of exports.

Yearly market values for exports are available in the series of values declared by exporters beginning in 1798. For imports and re-exports there are comparable values from 1854 on computed, at first, from price quotations and later from declared valuations. For the interval from 1798 to 1853 the estimates on import and re-export values presented in this JOURNAL two years ago can be used.[3]

Three series of absolute values are available. The old "official" values are essentially absolute values in terms of prices of 1694 and were recorded until 1869. Although they are by no means perfect

---

avoidable imprecisions which limit its usefulness. Werner Schlote, "Entwicklung und Strucktur-wandlungen des englischen Aussenhandels von 1700 bis zur Gegenwart," *Probleme der Weltwirtschaft* (Jena, 1938), Appendix, Table 15. See also below nn. 7 and 11.

[3] Albert H. Imlah, "Real Values in British Foreign Trade, 1798–1853," THE JOURNAL OF ECONOMIC HISTORY, VIII (November), 133–52.

for this purpose,[4] the figures for exports and gross imports can be used and I have done so up to 1864, reserving the remaining five years to join this series with the ensuing one. Unfortunately, absolute values for net imports are lacking for these years since the official values of re-exports, based on quite different prices for many commodities, cannot simply be deducted from gross imports to supply the net figures. Second, for the years from 1880 to 1899 there is a series on exports and gross imports, but not re-exports, prepared by the Board of Trade in terms of prices of 1900.[5] Third, from 1900 on, the Board provided a more detailed series, also based on the prices of 1900 and including re-exports.[6] With these series available it seemed worth while to fill in the gaps with as much precision as possible.

What remained to be done in order to establish a continuous series of absolute values from 1798 to 1913 was as follows: (1) Construction of a series of absolute values for exports and gross imports from 1865 to 1881. The extra years at each end of the series permit equating it with the old "official" values which closed in 1869 and with the Board of Trade's set of absolute values which began in 1880.[7] In computing these absolute values I prepared commodity price indexes from average import and export prices as reported annually in the

---

[4] There are two limitations. Somewhat different price tables were used for England, Scotland, and Ireland in recording these values so that variations in the flow of goods to or from these sections could distort results. Fortunately the fluctuations seem to have been comparatively small, however. Secondly, the base year is remote from the period under analysis. It would be better, tending to ensure more cognate conditions, if there were, say, three series of absolute values, each with its own price base in a mid-point year, to cover this period from 1798 to 1864. Two such series, joined by means of overlapping years, are used for the index numbers presented below for the years from 1865 to 1913. It would be possible to construct such series to use in place of the official values from 1798 on, but it would be necessary to use the official values in order to do so and it is questionable whether there would be sufficient improvement in precision to justify the very considerable amount of labor involved.

[5] *Parliamentary Papers*, 1909, [4954], CII, 53.

[6] *Ibid.*, 1914, [7432], LXXXIX, 30.

[7] Sir Robert Giffen prepared absolute values for exports and gross imports, in terms of prices of 1873 and of 1883, for various years from 1840 to 1883 and these could be used to bridge the gap, but Giffen's figures omit many years and do not form a continuous series. "Report to the Secretary of the Board of Trade," *Parliamentary Papers*, 1884–1885, [4456], LXXI, and "Third Report of the Royal Commission on the Depression on Trade and Industry," *ibid.*, 1886, [4797], XXIII, 329. Werner Schlote prepared tables of absolute values from 1801 on using six base-point periods for imports, seven for exports, and one for re-exports from 1801 to 1933. It is not quite clear whether he constructed these commodity by commodity or in lump, and whether he used Jevons' general price index or individual commodity indexes. His price movements strongly suggest that he relied on Jevons' general index, which would make the precision in using several base points rather more seeming than real.—Schlote, *Probleme der Weltwirtschaft*, Appendix, Tables 8–10 and 27.

Terms of Trade of the United Kingdom   173

Statistical Abstracts of the United Kingdom, using 1880 as the base
year simply because it was a fairly normal one. I then applied each
index to the declared value of that commodity exported or imported.
For major articles of trade on which average prices were not reported
I followed essentially the same practice used by the Board of Trade
for the series beginning in 1900 and used the price index of a closely
related commodity or group of commodities. In this manner series
of absolute values were constructed for 88 articles of export constituting, in the base year, 92 per cent of total value, and for 116
articles of imports, amounting to 90 per cent of the total value. The
absolute value of the articles not covered in this way, almost wholly
unenumerated ones, was calculated in a lump by means of a price
index derived from the totals on the enumerated articles. (2) Construction of a series of absolute values for re-exports for the years
from 1798 to 1899.[8] The method used was essentially the same employed
in constructing the absolute values of exports and imports described
above. Commodity price indexes were used with the market values
of each of the chief articles of re-export. Although only four articles
could be covered in this way in the first six years, eleven were separately calculated from 1804 to 1823, twelve from 1824 to 1864, and
fifteen from 1865 to 1899. The proportions these bore to the total
market value of re-exports varied a good deal, dropping as low as
44 per cent in 1835 and 40 per cent in 1898, and reaching such highs
as 85 per cent in 1809 and 83 per cent in 1866. The average was
in the neighborhood of 60 per cent. Other articles, though numerous,
were each generally very small in volume. The absolute values for
these were calculated in the aggregate by means of a modified gross
import index.[9]

Once the absolute values were completed the construction of the
indexes was a comparatively simple matter. These are given in some
detail in Table I in order to permit the fullest use of the results.

---

[8] One could, of course, follow the procedure used by F. W. Taussig for the years 1880
to 1899 and derive absolute values for net imports by applying a price index based on gross
imports to the market value of net imports. But some very large changes occurred in the
re-export trade through this longer period so that this easier method would produce rather
unreliable results here.

[9] The modification consisted in removing the commodities for which the absolute values
of re-exports were separately computed by means of their own price indexes. From 1880 to
1899 the import index was used without modification since the component data in the Board
of Trade series of absolute values for these years have not been published.

Only two component series are omitted. One is the absolute values of re-exports that are not used directly in constructing the indexes. The other is the index on the total volume of trade that is used for the series on the "total gain from trade." This index is constructed in the same way as the export and net import volume indexes except that here the total absolute value of exports and net imports for each year is divided by the total absolute value in the base year. The numbers vary only in decimal points from the average of the annual numbers given in the export and net import volume indexes. All index numbers used in constructing other series are carried to the first decimal point in the tables. It should not be inferred from this procedure that the index numbers are infallibly precise. In view of the limitations of data and methods they can better be regarded as close approximations.

The component elements and the methods of construction control the meaning of each index. These are indicated in Table I (pages 177–82), but some further comment may be useful. The export and import price indexes (Columns C and G) are derived by dividing the current market value for each year by the corresponding absolute value. They are presented here as basic elements for computing the terms of trade. If they are put to other uses or compared with other indexes the method of construction should be kept in mind. These indexes are, in a sense, weighted ones, but the weightings change annually and automatically with the changes in the volumes of the commodities traded.[10]

The four indexes on the terms of trade (Columns I to L) express the chief concepts capable, with existing data, of practical application. Each measures a different set of values with respect to "visible" trade, and "visible" trade alone. No one of them takes account of the many "invisible" elements—shipping and commercial services, capital movements, income from foreign investments, and so on—that entered into the balancing of the international accounts of the United Kingdom, though they may, with other data, cast some light on these matters.

The index showing net barter, or commodity, terms of trade (Column I) is a measure of the movements of the prices of exports and

---

[10] The differences in results from those of the usual type of index can be considerable, as Silverman has shown by comparing his export and import price indexes, constructed with monthly prices and fixed weightings, with those he prepared for Taussig by the method used here.—A. G. Silverman, "Monthly Index Numbers of British Export and Import Prices, 1880–1913," *The Review of Economic Statistics*, XII (1930), 139–48.

Terms of Trade of the United Kingdom 175

of net imports in relation to each other. It is constructed by dividing the index numbers in the export price series by the corresponding numbers in the net import price series.[11] Rising numbers, therefore, indicate "favorable" movement. Conversely, falling numbers, which predominate in this series until the mid-century, mean "unfavorable" movement; that is, the prices of the goods exported by Britain fell more rapidly or rose more slowly than the prices of the commodities imported.

The concept of gross barter terms of trade was introduced by Taussig twenty-five years ago.[12] It is simply and solely a measure of changes in the quantity relationships of exports and net imports. Again, as constructed here, falling numbers represent "unfavorable" movement and mean that a smaller quantity of imports are received in relation to the quantity of exports surrendered than in the base year. The index is a measure of relative, not total, quantities.[13]

Both these indexes deal with gain from a unit of trade. They do not take into account changes in the total volume of trade or, therefore, measure the total gain from trade in relation to the base year. To correct this limitation Jacob Viner has proposed another index which he calls, descriptively, "total gain from trade." [14] It ties the relative movements of export and net import prices (net barter terms) to an index of the total quantities of exports and net imports. Thus a rise in the total volume, whether the rise is of exports or imports or both, may be sufficient to convert an unfavorable movement in the net barter terms into a favorable movement in the total-gain index.

---

[11] This reverses Taussig's procedure by which a rise in the index numbers indicated "unfavorable" movement. The ratio used here is much less confusing, permits easier comparison with other indexes, and, as Jacob Viner has pointed out, does not involve any question of principle.—*Studies in the Theory of International Trade.* See note on p. 558. The complete formulas for the first three indexes (Columns I-K) are given by Viner with comment, *ibid.,* pp. 558–63.

Schlote constructed his index on net barter terms of trade by dividing a price index of exports of manufactured goods by the price index of *gross* imports for the years 1814–1853, and by the price index of imported raw materials from 1854 on. His index numbers show the general trends but are not very precise on short-term variations, and the series is not strictly continuous. Reduced to the same base, his index numbers for net barter terms of trade for 1814 is 136 to my 149; for 1815, 141 to my 153; for 1824, it is 144 to my 164; and for 1825, 129 to my 138. Schlote.—*Probleme der Weltwirtschaft,* Appendix, Table 17.

[12] F. W. Taussig, "The Change in Great Britain's Foreign Trade Terms after 1900," *The Economic Journal,* XXXV (1925), 1–10.

[13] For discussion of its limitations see Gottfried von Haberler, *The Theory of International Trade* (New York: The Macmillan Co., 1936), pp. 163–66; and Viner, *Theory of International Trade,* pp. 562–63.

[14] Viner, *Theory of International Trade,* pp. 563–64.

It allows for the fact which the first two indexes ignore, that an increase in the total amount of gain from trade is consistent with unfavorable movement in the net barter terms of trade when, as with Britain almost throughout this period, and especially after 1842, there is growth in the total volume of trade.

The fourth index was proposed very recently by G. S. Dorrance under the title "income terms of trade." The object is, like Viner's, to take changes in volume into account, but it aims at more precision by using the export volume index with the net barter terms. Thus it removes the element of doubt regarding whether the change in volume is for exports or imports. It would be more descriptive to call it "export gain from trade," however, since an index of "import gain from trade" is conceivable and might be relevant for a community with large invisible exports or other foreign credits acceptance of which in goods constituted a condition for national well-being. I have adopted the device but changed the name. Although suggested with the present-day export problems of Britain particularly in mind, it would seem to be a useful indicator of the well-being of a trading community, so far as this can be measured by export quantities and export-import price relationships.

The inclusion of so many series in the table that follows makes it a rather congested one. This disadvantage may be outweighed, however, by the convenience for comparing numbers for each year; and any one series can readily be followed in its column through the years. Taken together, the indexes supply a kind of bird's-eye view of a long and significant period of British trading history.

Among the more striking trends indicated by these indexes none stands out more clearly than the deterioration in the net barter terms of trade in the early years of the series. It was caused by more rapid fall in export than in net import prices, and much the greater part of the decline in the net barter terms occurred by the year 1839.[15] Indeed, the index number for this year stands less than ten points from the low mark (1860) of the entire period. In the middle years of the century export and import prices were somewhat steadier in

---

[15] The net barter terms moved a little less unfavorably in the postwar period, however, than could hitherto be supposed, because average prices of the goods actually imported dropped a little more than is shown in any of the wholesale price indexes on which we have formerly had to rely. From 1816–1818 to 1838–1840 the numbers in Silberling's unweighted index, the best available, fell 25 per cent, and in Jevons' 28 per cent. The net import index above, in effect a weighted one, shows a decline of 33 per cent for the same years.

Terms of Trade of the United Kingdom   177

TABLE I

THE TERMS OF TRADE OF THE UNITED KINGDOM, 1798–1913

Year	EXPORTS OF THE PRODUCE AND MANUFACTURES OF THE U. K.				NET IMPORTS				TERMS OF TRADE			
	A	B	C	D	E	F	G	H	I	J	K	L
	Current (Declared) Value	Absolute Value 1880 Prices	Export Price Index $\frac{A}{B}$	Export Volume Index $\frac{Bi}{Bo}$	Current Value	Absolute Value 1880 Prices	Import Price Index $\frac{E}{F}$	Import Volume Index $\frac{Fi}{Fo}$	Net Barter Terms of Trade $\frac{C}{G}$	Gross Barter Terms of Trade $\frac{H}{D}$	Total Gain from Trade Ix Trade Volume Index	Export Gain from Trade Dxl
	£ mill.	£ mill.	1880= 100	1880= 100	£ mill.	£ mill.	1880= 100	1880= 100	1880= 100	1880= 100	1880= 100	1880= 100
1798	32.2	7.5	430.4	3.4	45.1	23.3	193.6	6.7	222.3	197	12	8
1799	36.8	8.9	412.5	4.0	47.4	23.3	203.5	6.7	202.7	168	11	8
1800	37.7	9.1	414.1	4.1	51.7	25.6	202.0	7.4	205.0	180	13	8
1801	40.6	9.8	415.4	4.4	59.9	29.2	205.5	8.4	202.1	191	14	9
1802	45.9	10.1	456.5	4.5	40.6	24.7	164.4	7.1	277.7	158	18	12
1803	36.9	8.0	460.3	3.6	43.4	24.2	179.3	7.0	256.7	194	14	9
1804	38.2	8.9	429.2	4.0	47.5	25.0	190.0	7.2	225.9	180	13	9
1805	38.1	9.2	415.4	4.1	52.7	26.5	189.9	7.6	218.7	185	14	9
1806	40.9	10.1	403.2	4.5	44.8	24.5	182.9	7.0	220.4	156	13	10
1807	37.2	9.2	406.0	4.1	46.4	24.3	190.9	7.0	212.7	171	13	9
1808	37.3	9.7	386.3	4.3	45.9	25.7	178.6	7.4	216.3	172	14	9
1809	47.4	13.2	360.1	5.9	62.9	27.1	232.1	7.8	155.1	132	11	9
1810	48.4	13.4	362.6	6.0	77.3	37.0	208.9	10.6	173.6	177	15	10
1811	32.9	8.9	369.7	4.0	44.0	25.0	176.0	7.2	210.1	180	12	8
1812	41.7	11.6	360.6	5.2	47.0	22.4	209.8	6.4	171.9	123	10	9
1813	Records destroyed by fire											
1814	45.5	13.4	339.1	6.0	56.0	24.6	227.6	7.1	149.0	118	10	9
1815	51.6	16.5	312.9	7.4	53.2	26.4	201.5	7.6	155.3	103	12	11
1816	41.7	14.0	297.3	6.3	37.4	21.3	175.6	6.1	169.3	97	11	11
1817	41.8	15.7	265.5	7.0	49.6	27.9	177.8	8.0	149.3	114	11	10

Continued overleaf

TABLE I (Continued)

	EXPORTS OF THE PRODUCE AND MANUFACTURES OF THE U.K.				NET IMPORTS				TERMS OF TRADE			
	A	B	C	D	E	F	G	H	I	J	K	L
	Current (Declared) Value	Absolute Value 1880 Prices	Export Price Index $\frac{A}{B}$	Export Volume Index $\frac{B_1}{B_0}$	Current Value	Absolute Value 1880 Prices	Import Price Index $\frac{E}{F}$	Import Volume Index $\frac{F_i}{F_0}$	Net Barter Terms of Trade $\frac{C}{G}$	Gross Barter Terms of Trade $\frac{H}{D}$	Total Gain from Trade Ix Trade Volume Index	Export Gain from Trade DxI
Year	£ mill.	£ mill.	1880=100	1880=100	£ mill.	£ mill.	1880=100	1880=100	1880=100	1880=100	1880=100	Y 1880=100
1818	46.5	16.4	277.9	7.3	68.3	34.7	196.8	10.0	141.2	137	13	10
1819	35.2	13.1	267.7	5.9	45.8	28.0	163.6	8.0	163.6	136	12	10
1820	36.4	15.0	242.0	6.7	43.8	29.1	150.5	8.4	160.8	125	12	11
1821	36.7	16.0	229.0	7.2	36.1	27.5	131.3	7.9	174.4	110	13	13
1822	37.0	17.4	213.2	7.8	36.8	28.3	130.0	8.1	164.0	104	13	13
1823	35.4	17.2	206.3	7.7	44.8	34.5	129.9	9.9	158.8	129	14	12
1824	38.4	19.1	200.9	8.6	43.7	35.6	122.8	10.2	163.6	119	16	14
1825	38.9	18.5	210.1	8.3	66.5	43.8	151.8	12.6	138.4	152	15	11
1826	31.5	16.0	196.3	7.2	43.1	35.6	121.1	10.2	162.1	142	15	12
1827	37.2	20.5	181.6	9.2	52.0	44.2	117.6	12.7	154.4	138	17	14
1828	36.8	20.7	177.7	9.3	50.8	44.3	114.7	12.7	154.9	137	18	14
1829	35.8	22.0	162.7	9.9	47.5	42.7	111.2	12.3	146.3	124	17	14
1830	38.3	24.0	159.6	10.8	50.3	45.9	109.6	13.2	145.6	122	18	16
1831	37.2	23.8	156.1	10.7	55.3	49.0	112.9	14.1	138.3	132	18	15
1832	36.5	23.9	153.0	10.7	45.2	42.6	106.1	12.3	144.2	115	17	15
1833	39.7	27.5	144.6	12.3	52.0	45.0	115.6	12.9	125.1	105	16	15
1834	41.6	28.9	143.8	12.9	57.6	47.9	120.3	13.8	119.5	107	16	15
1835	47.4	30.8	154.0	13.8	59.5	46.2	128.8	13.3	119.6	96	16	15
1836	53.3	33.4	159.6	15.0	75.6	56.8	133.1	16.3	119.9	109	19	17
1837	42.1	24.5	147.9	11.0	61.1	53.3	114.6	15.3	129.1	139	18	18
1838	50.1	35.6	140.8	16.0	70.9	60.7	116.8	17.4	120.5	109	20	19
1839	52.2	37.4	139.5	16.8	81.6	61.4	132.9	17.7	105.0	105	18	18

Terms of Trade of the United Kingdom 179

TABLE I (Continued)

	EXPORTS OF THE PRODUCE AND MANUFACTURES OF THE U.K.				NET IMPORTS				TERMS OF TRADE			
	A	B	C	D	E	F	G	H	I	J	K	L
Year	Current (Declared) Value	Absolute Value 1880 Prices	Export Price Index $\frac{A}{B}$	Export Volume Index $\frac{Bi}{Bo}$	Current Value	Absolute Value 1880 Prices	Import Price Index $\frac{E}{F}$	Import Volume Index $\frac{Fi}{Fo}$	Net Barter Terms of Trade $\frac{C}{G}$	Gross Barter Terms of Trade $\frac{H}{D}$	Total Gain from Trade Ix Trade Volume Index	Export Gain from Trade DxI
	£ mill.	£ mill.	1880=100	1880=100	£ mill.	£ mill.	1880=100	1880=100	1880=100	1880=100	1880=100	Y 1880=100
			100	100			100	100	100	100	100	100
1840	51.4	40.2	127.8	18.0	81.2	67.4	120.5	19.4	106.1	108	20	19
1841	51.6	40.4	127.8	18.1	74.0	63.6	116.4	18.3	109.8	101	20	20
1842	47.4	39.3	120.6	17.6	68.0	65.1	104.5	18.7	115.4	106	21	20
1843	52.3	46.3	113.0	20.8	63.2	70.6	89.5	20.3	126.3	98	26	26
1844	58.6	51.6	113.5	23.1	70.8	77.3	91.6	22.2	123.9	96	28	26
1845	60.1	49.7	120.9	22.3	79.1	85.8	92.2	24.7	131.1	111	31	29
1846	57.8	51.9	111.4	23.3	78.1	75.6	103.3	21.7	107.8	93	24	29
1847	58.8	49.4	119.1	22.1	100.4	90.3	111.2	26.0	107.1	118	26	25
1848	52.8	52.0	101.5	23.3	79.8	94.6	84.4	27.2	120.3	117	31	24
1849	63.6	64.4	98.7	28.9	89.3	104.0	85.9	29.9	114.9	103	34	28
1850	71.4	69.9	102.2	31.3	91.0	100.0	91.0	28.7	112.3	92	33	33
1851	74.4	74.8	99.4	33.5	97.0	110.1	88.0	31.6	113.0	94	37	35
1852	78.1	76.9	101.5	34.5	97.0	108.6	89.3	31.2	113.7	90	37	38
1853	98.9	84.0	117.8	37.7	131.7	121.8	108.1	35.0	109.0	93	39	39
1854	97.2	82.5	117.8	37.0	133.8	120.7	110.9	34.7	106.2	94	38	39
1855	95.7	88.9	107.6	39.8	122.5	127.7	95.9	31.9	112.2	80	34	39
1856	115.8	101.4	114.2	45.5	149.1	127.7	116.8	36.7	97.8	81	39	44
1857	122.1	100.2	121.9	44.9	163.7	133.5	122.6	38.4	99.4	86	41	45
1858	116.6	106.6	109.4	47.8	141.4	133.7	105.8	38.5	103.4	81	43	49
1859	130.4	116.5	111.9	52.2	153.9	140.6	109.5	40.4	102.2	77	46	53
1860	135.9	124.0	109.6	55.6	181.9	159.2	114.3	45.8	95.6	82	47	53
1861	125.1	113.6	110.1	50.9	183.0	161.8	113.1	46.5	97.3	91	47	50

Continued overleaf

TABLE I (Continued)

Year	Exports of the Produce and Manufactures of the U.K.				Net Imports				Terms of Trade			
	A Current (Declared) Value £ mill.	B Absolute Value 1880 Prices £ mill.	C Export Price Index A/B 1880=100	D Export Volume Index Bi/Bo 1880=100	E Current Value mill. £	F Absolute Value 1880 Prices mill. £	G Import Price Index E/F 100 1880=	H Import Volume Index Fi/Fo 100 1880=	I Net Barter Terms of Trade C/G 100 1880=	J Gross Barter Terms of Trade H/D 100 1880=	K Total Gain from Trade Ix Trade Volume Index 100 1880=	L Export Gain from Trade DxI 100 1880=Y
1862	124.0	98.4	131.1	44.1	183.5	150.5	121.9	43.3	107.5	98	47	47
1863	146.6	101.2	144.8	45.4	198.6	159.2	124.8	45.8	116.0	101	53	53
1864	160.4	104.7	153.2	46.9	222.8	161.0	138.4	46.3	110.7	99	51	52
1865	165.8	122.5	135.3	54.9	218.1	170.5	127.9	49.0	105.8	89	54	58
1866	188.9	135.0	139.9	60.5	245.3	192.0	127.8	55.2	109.5	91	63	66
1867	181.0	137.8	131.3	61.8	230.7	189.1	122.0	54.4	107.6	88	62	66
1868	179.7	146.6	122.6	65.7	246.6	203.0	121.5	58.4	100.9	89	62	66
1869	190.0	156.0	121.8	69.9	248.4	210.7	117.9	60.6	103.3	87	66	72
1870	199.6	168.1	118.7	75.3	258.8	224.0	115.5	64.4	102.8	86	71	77
1871	223.1	188.6	118.3	84.5	270.5	249.6	108.4	71.7	109.1	85	84	92
1872	256.3	196.2	130.6	87.9	296.4	255.3	115.8	72.4	112.8	82	89	99
1873	255.2	189.0	135.0	84.7	315.5	272.6	115.7	78.4	116.7	93	94	99
1874	239.6	187.6	127.7	84.1	311.0	275.2	113.0	79.1	113.0	94	92	95
1875	233.5	186.4	119.9	83.5	315.8	294.8	107.1	84.7	112.0	101	94	94
1876	200.6	181.9	110.3	81.5	319.0	304.7	104.7	87.6	105.3	107	90	86
1877	198.9	187.4	106.1	84.0	341.0	318.4	107.1	91.5	99.1	109	88	83
1878	192.8	188.4	102.3	84.4	316.1	318.0	99.4	91.4	102.9	108	91	87
1879	191.5	198.4	96.5	88.9	305.7	322.2	94.9	92.6	101.7	104	93	90
1880	223.1	223.1	100.0	100.0	347.9	347.9	100.0	100.0	100.0	100	100	100
1881	234.0	244.1	95.9	109.4	334.0	336.6	99.2	96.8	96.7	88	98	106
1882	241.5	254.9	94.7	114.3	347.8	352.9	98.6	101.4	96.0	89	102	110
1883	239.8	261.5	91.7	117.2	361.2	380.6	94.9	109.4	96.6	93	109	113

Terms of Trade of the United Kingdom 181

TABLE I (Continued)

	EXPORTS OF THE PRODUCE AND MANUFACTURES OF THE U.K.				NET IMPORTS				TERMS OF TRADE			
	A	B	C	D	E	F	G	H	I	J	K	L
	Current (Declared) Value	Absolute Value 1880 Prices	Export Price Index $\frac{A}{B}$	Export Volume Index $\frac{Bi}{Bo}$	Current Value	Absolute Value 1880 Prices	Import Price Index $\frac{E}{F}$	Import Volume Index $\frac{Fi}{Fo}$	Net Barter Terms of Trade $\frac{C}{G}$	Gross Barter Terms of Trade $\frac{H}{D}$	Total Gain from Trade Ix Trade Volume Index	Export Gain from Trade DxI
YEAR	£ mill.	£ mill.	1880=100	1880=100	£ mill.	£ mill.	1880=100	1880=100	1880=100	1880=100	1880=100	Y 1880=100
1884	233.0	264.7	88.0	118.6	327.1	369.3	88.6	106.1	99.3	89	110	118
1885	213.1	253.8	84.0	113.8	312.6	373.2	83.8	107.2	100.2	94	110	114
1886	212.7	268.0	79.4	120.1	293.6	373.2	78.7	107.2	100.9	89	113	121
1887	221.9	281.2	78.9	126.0	302.9	389.4	77.8	111.9	101.4	89	119	128
1888	234.5	294.3	79.7	131.9	323.6	405.4	79.8	116.5	99.9	88	122	132
1889	248.9	305.2	81.6	136.8	361.0	447.8	80.6	128.7	101.2	94	133	138
1890	263.5	304.1	86.6	136.3	356.0	450.1	79.1	129.4	109.5	95	145	149
1891	247.2	287.7	85.9	129.0	373.6	470.9	79.3	135.3	108.3	105	144	140
1892	227.1	277.9	81.7	124.6	359.2	469.4	76.5	134.9	106.8	108	140	133
1893	218.1	271.3	80.4	121.5	345.6	462.5	74.7	132.9	107.6	109	138	131
1894	215.8	281.2	76.7	126.0	350.4	505.8	69.3	145.4	110.7	115	153	139
1895	225.9	304.1	74.3	136.3	356.8	536.2	66.5	154.1	111.7	113	164	152
1896	240.2	319.4	75.2	143.2	385.6	574.1	67.2	165.1	111.9	115	175	160
1897	234.2	315.1	74.3	141.2	391.1	573.3	66.6	168.9	111.6	120	174	158
1898	233.4*	315.1*	74.1	141.2	409.9	614.3	66.7	176.6	111.1	125	181	157
1899	264.5†	330.4†	80.1	143.9	420.0	624.1	67.3	179.4	119.0	125	197	171
1900	291.2	318.6	91.4	138.8	459.9	634.2	72.5	182.3	126.1	131	208	175
1901	280.0	321.6	87.1	140.1	454.2	647.6	70.1	186.1	124.3	133	209	174
1902	283.4	341.6	83.0	148.8	462.6	667.6	69.3	191.9	119.8	129	209	178

* Ships not included prior to 1899 } Adjustments made for indexes.
† Ships included after 1898

Continued overleaf

182   *Albert H. Imlah*

TABLE I (Continued)

	EXPORTS OF THE PRODUCE AND MANUFACTURES OF THE U. K.				NET IMPORTS				TERMS OF TRADE			
	A	B	C	D	B	P	G	H	I	J	K	L
YEAR	Current (Declared) Value	Absolute Value 1880 Prices	Export Price Index $\frac{A}{B}$	Export Volume Index $\frac{Bi}{Bo}$	Current Value	Absolute Value 1880 Prices	Import Price Index $\frac{E}{F}$	Import Volume Index $\frac{Fi}{Fo}$	Net Barter Terms of Trade $\frac{C}{G}$	Gross Barter Terms of Trade $\frac{H}{D}$	Total Gains from Trade Ix Trade Volume Index	Export Gains from Trade Dxl
	£ mill.	£ mill.	1880= 100	1880= 100	£ mill.	£ mill.	1880= 100	1880= 100	1880= 100	1880= 100	1880= 100	Y 1880= 100
1903......	290.8	350.6	82.9	152.7	473.0	673.5	70.2	193.6	118.1	127	209	180
1904......	300.7	358.2	83.9	156.0	480.7	681.2	70.6	195.8	118.8	126	214	185
1905......	329.9	393.7	83.8	171.5	487.2	687.7	70.8	197.7	118.4	115	222	203
1906......	375.6	433.3	88.7	184.4	522.8	708.0	73.8	203.5	120.2	110	235	222
1907......	426.0	457.6	93.1	199.3	553.9	717.4	77.2	206.2	120.6	103	245	240
1908......	377.1	421.1	89.6	183.4	513.3	690.6	74.3	198.5	120.6	108	232	221
1909......	378.2	438.9	86.2	191.2	533.4	709.9	75.1	204.1	114.8	107	228	219
1910......	430.4	478.6	89.9	208.4	574.5	723.7	79.4	208.0	113.2	100	236	236
1911......	454.1	496.1	91.5	216.1	577.4	745.8	77.4	214.4	118.2	99	254	255
1912......	487.2	533.3	93.1	227.9	632.9	803.1	78.8	230.8	118.1	101	271	269
1913......	525.5	542.9	96.8	236.5	659.2	831.8	79.2	239.1	122.2	101	291	289

Terms of Trade of the United Kingdom   183

relation to each other, and both recovered a good deal from the low points reached in 1848–1849. The rate of decline in the net barter terms of trade was checked, but there was no very clear trend until the great depression which began in 1874. Then, in contrast to the beginning years of earlier depressions, export prices fell off more sharply than net import prices and the net barter terms moved unfavorably until 1882. Thereafter, to 1913, net import prices declined more and then recovered less than did export prices. The net barter movement was generally favorable.

The indexes of "total gain from trade" and "export gain from trade," both taking quantity changes as well as price ratios into account, moved steadily upward and in fairly close unison except during the last years of the Napoleonic Wars. From 1806 to 1814 the deterioration in the net barter terms of trade more than offset the growth in the physical volume of total trade (10 per cent) and even the considerable rise in the quantity of exports (33 per cent). From 1815 to 1842 both indexes of gain from trade show fairly steady improvement, but the numbers were held in check by the fall in the net barter index. The year 1843 marks a definite turning point with a huge jump in the numbers in both indexes (25 and 30 per cent). Not only did the physical volume of exports and net imports grow much more rapidly thereafter but the price ratios also ceased to repress the index results. After 1843 the numbers doubled, redoubled, redoubled again, and came close to completing still a fourth cycle by 1913.

III

The tremendous decline in British export prices in the years after 1815 needs further examination. It is usually attributed to the rapid application of cost-reducing machine methods of manufacture in major export industries. If this theory is correct, the falling off in the net barter terms of trade does not signify deterioration in Britain's economic position in the world, and domestic discontents can be laid to the problems of social readjustment to postwar conditions and to the machine age. Certain circumstances lend plausibility to this explanation. In no export industry did prices fall with more rapidity after the war than in cottons where the new techniques were most extensively applied. From 1816–1818 to 1849–1851 export prices fell 72 per cent. In the woolen industry mechanization was only a degree or two less thorough. Export prices fell 63 per cent in the same period. In these years cottons and woolens together made up more than

184   *Albert H. Imlah*

half of the British export trade [16] and exerted a corresponding influence on the average of British export prices. Other exports were mainly manufactured goods, but their industries were much less mechanized at that time. Prices fell only 45 per cent.

There are certain inadequacies in this explanation, however. It over-simplifies the matter and obscures the importance of other contributing factors whose presence significantly modifies appraisal of the situation as a whole. It leaves us, too, with the rather troublesome task of explaining adequately the change in price trends in the third quarter of the century when cost-reducing processes of manufacture continued to be applied, especially in other industries.

One other important factor was the decline in the prices of imported raw materials, especially in the two export industries most largely mechanized, cotton and wool. There is a remarkably close correlation here between the price movements of the raw material and those of the finished products exported over these years. In spite of enormous increases in consumption, foreign and colonial production kept pace, stimulated, somewhat sporadically, by British investments, particularly in auxiliary services, and perhaps by the very low tariff rates on cotton and wool. [17] Import prices of raw cotton fell about as rapidly as export prices of the finished fabrics, and import prices of wool fell more rapidly. [18] The interrelationships of import and export prices,

---

[16] Cottons constituted 40 per cent of the total value of exports in 1816, and in spite of the phenomenal fall in prices, the same in 1850. By 1880 they had fallen off to 34 per cent. Woolens were 22 per cent in 1816, 15 per cent in 1850, and 9 per cent in 1880.

[17] Since the tariffs on cotton and wool were specific duties, the relation to value varied with price movements but, unlike the duties on most other goods, they were reduced to very moderate proportions and finally repealed in this period. The duty on foreign cotton, for example, figures at about 7 per cent ad valorem in 1826 and, though the levies were cut in half in 1833–1834, at about 6.2 per cent in 1844 on the eve of complete repeal. East Indian cotton was admitted at lower duties. In the case of wool, the growing needs of the industry were placed ahead of domestic sheep raising. The duties on foreign wool were reduced substantially in 1824–1825 and, though the ad valorem effect also fluctuated with price changes, the average rate could not exceed 8 per cent and rarely exceeded half that figure on the better grades until repeal in 1844. Wool from British colonies was admitted free after 1825 and Australia soon became a major source of supply.

These light duties stand in contrast to an average rate of 43 per cent on the value of other net imports in 1844.

[18] The import values, and therefore the import price movements, cited throughout this paper are measured before tariff duties were collected. Duties do not enter into the international accounts directly affecting the terms of trade. They are elements in the manufacturer's costs, of course, and as such have some bearing on export prices. The fact that the duties on cotton and wool were reduced and finally repealed in this period means that the cost of the imported raw material to the British manufacturer fell still more rapidly than is indicated by the index numbers in Table II or by the percentages stated below.

Terms of Trade of the United Kingdom   185

markets, foreign investments, tariff rates, and other factors affecting the British trading position in these years need closer examination. All that is intended here, however, is to supply a little more systematic data on the net import price movements of cotton and wool and to comment on the significance of a few points in relation to the effects of machine processes and of tariff reform.

Index series for the price movements of cottons, woolens, and other goods are given in Table II (pages 186–88) for the years 1814 to 1880. The indexes for exports, and for net imports omitting cotton and wool, are constructed in exactly the same manner as those given in Table I.[19] The net import indexes for cotton and wool required a different procedure, since certain peculiarities in the price lists for the official values make them unsuitable for separate use with these commodities. The net import index for cotton is based on price series for East Indian and American cotton and takes into account the changing proportions of the East Indian and American supplies taken. For wool, only one adequate price series was available from 1814 to 1821, and the numbers are given in parentheses since they are not very dependable as a measure of net import prices for these years. From 1822 on, Spanish Leonesa and Saxon price series were used, and from 1834, when this became important, Australian also. From 1854 on, net import values for cotton and for wool were used with net import quantities which should produce very accurate results. The ratios of import and export prices supply a kind of net barter index for each group [20] and I have called them that for lack of a better brief descriptive title.

---

[19] This method, by averaging all kinds of cotton exports together, could minimize price decline for articles which, requiring much fabrication, should show the results of improved machine processes more markedly, and exaggerate that in yarn which requires little processing, when, as was the case until the mid-century, the proportions of the yarn exported increased considerably. Actually the difference in the rates of price decline from 1816–1818 to 1849–1851 is almost negligible, however. Prices of cotton-yarn exports fell 71.4 per cent, while those of other cotton exports fell 72.4 per cent. That the decline in the price of yarn should have so closely matched that in articles more strongly affected by labor-saving machinery was undoubtedly due largely to the corresponding decline in the price of the raw material.

[20] To reconcile these numbers with those given for the terms of trade in Table I it is necessary to take three factors into account: the more precise method used for calculating net import prices of cotton and wool, and not only the proportions of cotton and woolen exports to the total (see above, note 16), but also the proportions of the imports of each to the total figure. Net imports of raw cotton constituted 13.8 per cent of the total value of British imports in 1816, 18.2 per cent in 1850, and 10.7 per cent in 1880. Net imports of wool rose from just under 3 per cent in 1816 to slightly more than 3 per cent in 1880. Their price movements consequently exerted much less influence on average import prices than did those of cotton and woolen exports on average export prices.

TABLE II

Price Movements of Cottons, Woolens, and Other Exports and Net Imports, 1814–1880

1880=100

Year	Cotton					Wool					Omitting Cotton and Wool				
	Exports of Yarn and Mfr.		Net Imports of Raw Cotton		Net Barter Terms of Trade	Exports of Yarn and Mfr.		Net Imports of Raw Wool		Net Barter Terms of Trade	Exports		Net Imports		Net Barter Terms of Trade
	Price Index	Volume Index	Price Index	Volume Index		Price Index	Volume Index	Price Index	Volume Index		Price Index	Volume Index	Price Index	Volume Index	
	A	B	C	D	E	F	G	H	I	J	K	L	M	N	O
1814	550	5	414	4	133	336	11	(520)	7	(65)	213	6	218	7	98
1815	452	7	312	7	145	341	14	(459)	6	(74)	210	7	190	7	111
1816	428	5	292	6	147	358	11	(418)	3	(86)	192	7	166	6	120
1817	371	6	303	8	122	360	11	(415)	6	(87)	186	7	162	8	115
1818	406	7	289	12	140	321	12	(396)	11	(81)	187	8	184	9	102
1819	391	5	196	10	199	326	9	(370)	7	(88)	179	6	159	8	113
1820	352	7	168	10	210	320	8	(280)	4	(114)	164	6	144	8	114
1821	327	7	145	8	226	294	11	(251)	7	(117)	159	7	124	8	128
1822	305	8	135	9	219	273	12	246	9	111	155	6	127	8	122
1823	294	8	131	13	224	254	11	250	8	102	152	7	128	9	119
1824	291	9	129	10	226	246	12	252	10	98	150	7	120	10	125
1825	296	9	193	15	153	261	11	250	19	104	165	7	144	12	115
1826	267	7	114	11	234	247	10	195	7	127	156	6	122	10	128
1827	251	10	102	18	246	231	11	201	12	115	146	7	121	12	121
1828	244	10	94	15	260	224	11	206	13	109	144	8	117	12	133
1829	236	11	96	14	246	217	10	192	9	113	137	8	113	12	121
1830	223	12	102	18	219	218	11	213	14	102	130	8	110	12	118
1831	207	11	100	19	207	218	12	195	13	112	129	9	115	13	112
1832	186	12	105	19	177	206	13	168	12	123	125	9	107	11	117
1833	187	13	133	20	141	207	15	167	16	124	124	9	112	12	111
1834	188	14	139	22	135	226	13	180	20	126	125	10	117	12	107
1835	198	15	159	24	125	238	15	176	17	135	130	11	122	12	107
1836	197	17	155	26	127	260	15	167	28	156	146	11	131	14	111

Terms of Trade of the United Kingdom 187

TABLE II (Continued)

Year	COTTON					WOOL					OMITTING COTTON AND WOOL				
	Exports of Yarns and Mfs.		Net Imports of Raw Cotton		Net Barter Terms of Trade	Exports of Yarns and Mfs.		Net Imports of Raw Wool		Net Barter Terms of Trade	Exports		Net Imports		Net Barter Terms of Trade
	Price Index	Volume Index	Price Index	Volume Index		Price Index	Volume Index	Price Index	Volume Index		Price Index	Volume Index	Price Index	Volume Index	
	A	B	C	D	E	F	G	H	I	J	K	L	M	N	O
1837......	189	14	113	26	167	259	9	140	20	185	132	10	116	13	114
1838......	174	18	111	34	157	234	13	146	22	160	125	12	116	15	108
1839......	169	19	123	25	137	255	13	139	25	183	122	14	134	16	91
1840......	158	21	100	40	158	245	11	145	21	169	117	14	126	17	93
1841......	158	20	99	32	160	238	13	135	24	176	113	15	124	16	91
1842......	148	19	83	35	178	219	13	125	19	175	106	15	109	16	97
1843......	133	23	74	46	180	213	17	113	20	188	106	16	95	17	112
1844......	133	26	78	43	171	198	22	118	28	168	108	17	96	19	113
1845......	131	27	66	49	198	189	22	123	33	154	105	17	99	21	106
1846......	128	27	77	29	166	182	19	110	27	165	116	17	109	20	106
1847......	132	23	96	29	138	161	24	98	25	164	116	19	115	25	101
1848......	114	26	65	46	175	162	19	86	28	188	107	17	89	24	120
1849......	111	32	81	48	137	135	30	92	28	147	104	23	87	27	120
1850......	116	32	111	41	105	128	38	101	26	127	105	25	88	27	119
1851......	112	36	87	47	129	121	39	100	30	121	102	26	88	30	116
1852......	112	35	84	59	133	113	43	113	36	100	104	29	90	27	116
1853......	116	37	92	54	126	130	43	114	47	114	121	36	113	32	107
1854......	110	39	85	56	129	131	39	111	36	118	127	34	117	32	109
1855......	106	44	87	56	122	122	39	125	31	98	128	31	116	29	110
1856......	109	46	95	64	115	135	44	136	39	99	121	42	121	33	100
1857......	115	45	113	60	102	133	50	134	41	99	131	42	124	35	106
1858......	110	52	107	64	103	140	44	127	44	110	121	38	104	35	116
1859......	115	56	109	76	106	142	51	129	46	110	120	44	109	36	110
1860......	115	60	96	83	120	148	52	129	51	115	119	45	127	40	94
1861......	113	55	114	71	99	160	44	122	41	131	118	42	112	43	105

Continued overleaf

TABLE II (Continued)

	COTTON					WOOL					OMITTING COTTON AND WOOL				
	Exports of Yarn and Mfs.		Net Imports of Raw Cotton		Net Barter Terms of Trade	Exports of Yarn and Mfs.		Net Imports of Raw Wool		Net Barter Terms of Trade	Exports		Net Imports		Net Barter Terms of Trade
Year	Price Index	Volume Index	Price Index	Volume Index		Price Index	Volume Index	Price Index	Volume Index		Price Index	Volume Index	Price Index	Volume Index	
	A	B	C	D	E	F	G	H	I	J	K	L	M	N	O
1862	129	38	218	24	59	161	51	118	54	136	116	48	116	45	100
1863	168	37	323	32	52	145	69	130	49	112	116	53	108	48	107
1864	190	38	340	48	56	147	79	148	66	99	119	54	113	46	105
1865	173	44	263	50	66	137	90	128	57	107	118	56	111	49	106
1866	175	56	219	70	80	139	92	130	76	107	120	58	112	52	107
1867	149	63	161	65	93	139	90	126	63	110	117	57	115	53	102
1868	136	66	159	72	86	131	95	108	65	121	111	61	115	56	97
1869	138	64	179	68	77	135	101	103	62	131	111	68	110	60	99
1870	131	72	155	78	85	129	100	110	75	117	109	73	109	62	100
1871	126	76	116	101	109	132	122	101	82	131	111	83	108	67	103
1872	132	82	147	81	90	141	132	102	74	138	127	85	112	72	113
1873	128	81	139	93	92	128	116	111	85	115	141	82	113	76	125
1874	120	82	125	93	96	125	110	98	88	128	133	81	112	77	119
1875	117	81	121	88	97	120	108	110	85	109	121	81	105	84	115
1876	107	84	104	92	103	112	99	105	95	107	112	77	105	87	107
1877	105	87	100	85	105	107	95	107	97	100	107	80	108	92	99
1878	102	86	95	85	107	103	97	97	88	106	102	82	100	92	102
1879	98	87	94	91	104	96	99	105	76	91	96	89	95	94	101
1880	100	100	100	100	100	100	100	100	100	100	100	100	100	100	100

Terms of Trade of the United Kingdom   189

The role played by machine techniques in reducing British export prices after 1815 is rendered less predominant by these indexes. That of raw materials, presumably from their part in manufacturing costs and perhaps also from the effect of price decline on foreign purchasing power, is brought into clearer prominence. In the first period every decline in export prices was preceded or accompanied by a sharp drop in net import prices. The brief upward movements in net import prices were accompanied by a momentary slowing or reversal of the downward trend in export prices. The short-term rates of movement varied, export prices moving generally a little more slowly than import, though British exports were still predominantly consumers' goods, more sensitive to market conditions than capital goods which did not assume importance until the mid-century. But the correlation in the movements over the three decades as a whole is suggestively close. From 1816–1818 to 1849–1851, net import prices of raw cotton fell 68 per cent as compared to 72 per cent for exports of British manufactured cottons. The woolen industry, with the high reputation of its products and with its clientele in the better income classes, was perhaps under less pressure to cut prices quickly in times of depression. It was also slightly less mechanized and still drew the greater part of its supplies from home production. With 1822–1824 as the beginning date, when the net import price index for wool is more secure, net import prices fell 61 per cent while export prices of woolen goods fell only 50 per cent. In the group of other goods, net import prices dropped 48 per cent from 1816–1818 levels while export prices declined 45 per cent.

A little closer examination of these price movements indicates definite precedence for the decline in raw-material prices and suggests an effect of tariff reform. Comparing net import prices of cotton and wool in 1842–1844, just before the moderate duties on these were repealed, with the same initial years in each case, we find that the net import prices of raw cotton, before customs charges of course, fell 73 per cent, while export prices of British cottons fell 66 per cent. Net import prices of wool dropped 52 per cent while export prices went down only 19 per cent. On the other hand, in the catch-all category of other goods where machine methods of production were generally less important and tariff rates were high, export prices dropped slightly more (43 per cent) than did net import prices (41 per cent) in this shorter period. With respect to tariff reform, it is significant that the price series for East Indian, Demerara, and

American cotton all reached their lows by 1845, the year of repeal. They did not break through in 1848 when many other raw materials went lower. In other words, some of the benefits of tariff reduction accrued to foreign producers.[21]

From the mid-century on, the trends marked by the indexes are appreciably different. The rate of decline in all three classes of export goods was much less rapid and, indeed, all three showed tendencies to improvement in the first two decades in some correspondence with higher import prices. Improving machine techniques continued to exert their influence in varying degrees, but the probability seems very strong that higher import prices contributed to the distinctly slower tempo in the decline of export prices. Net import prices of raw cotton were 4 per cent higher in 1878–1880 than in 1849–1851, wool 3 per cent higher. Other commodities were up 12 per cent but, thanks to tariff reductions, without raising the costs to British consumers commensurately. Export prices of cotton goods had fallen only 12 per cent from the 1849–1851 average. Woolen goods, which had lagged behind the decline in wool prices at the mid-century, had made up the distance, falling 22 per cent. Other goods fell only 4 per cent.

IV

It was to be expected that the trading history of Britain should show some marked differences between the first postwar years and the rest of this century of relative peace. In the first place, the former was inevitably a period of price recession. Some degree of subsidence from the inflated levels of the war period was to be expected whether or not machine techniques were applied and new areas of production developed. In the second place, it was a period of very high British tariffs. Revenue needs during the war period had sharply reversed Pitt's reforms of the 1780's. Moreover, wartime changes in the economy, as well as the habits developed under the high rates, generated a very active demand for retention of the stiff duties. At first, manu-

---

[21] The net import index for cotton fell one point below the number for 1845 only because a higher proportion of cheaper East Indian cotton was taken in 1848.

The case of wool is not so clear cut. The price series used for Australian wool, which was duty free, reached its low point in 1843, but improvements in quality and grading confuse the matter, and Australian wool continued to offer strong competition to the higher priced wools hitherto taken from other sources. A major factor in the decline of the net import index from the mid-thirties on was the increasing proportions of the cheaper wools taken. This accounts also for the greater part of the sharp drop in the net import price index in 1847–1849.

Terms of Trade of the United Kingdom   191

facturers were not far behind the agricultural and shipping interests in defending protection for their own products. However, as they accumulated experience they concluded, by the 1840's, that the tariff system was a root cause of many of their difficulties.[22]

In certain respects the indexes presented here supply evidence that tends to confirm their judgment. They show frequent and large fluctuations in prices disturbing the postwar years, and high protectionism almost certainly aggravated their violence. If this is true, then it is reasonable to assume that the free-trade program contributed to the more satisfactory price history after the mid-century.[23] Theoretically, tariff reductions should have promoted deterioration in the British terms of trade. Lower duties should either have reduced costs to British manufacturers leaving them more margin for trimming export prices, or have raised import prices, or have combined the two. In cottons and woolens the duties cancelled in 1845 were too light to offset other factors though cotton-price movements were consistent with theory. That import prices of wool dropped more than export prices in 1846, improving the net barter terms, can be attributed to the pressure untaxed colonial and domestic wool exerted on prices. But for the wide variety of other goods exported and imported there is a distinct and fairly durable upturn in the net barter index from the trough of 1849–1851, though for most of these goods gradual yet substantial tariff cuts were made in the twenty years following Peel's first free-trade budget in 1842. It was the improvement in the terms of trade for these other goods that largely offset the continued decline in the textiles and steadied the net barter movement for British trade as a whole. Undoubtedly many factors entered into the making of this curious phenomenon, but among them must be included improvement in foreign and domestic purchasing power for British manufactures and the development of wider and safer markets for British capital abroad which the free-trade movement encouraged.[24]

[22] See Albert H. Imlah, "The Fall of Protection in Britain," *Essays in Honor of George Hubbard Blakeslee* (Worcester: Clark University, 1949), pp. 306–20.

[23] This change in price trends is usually attributed to three main factors coming into operation in the fifties and sixties: the Crimean, American, and Prussian Wars; new and large supplies of gold; and export of capital goods. These are conveniently reviewed in W. W. Rostov, *British Economy of the Nineteenth Century* (New York: Oxford University Press, 1948), pp. 20–24.

[24] In weighing the effects of British protective duties on world prices it should be kept in mind that British exports and imports constituted an enormous share of all international trade throughout this period. Together they were over 30 per cent of the estimated world total in 1800, and they were still approximately 25 per cent in 1850. Furthermore, British

The net barter index in Table I brings out rather clearly the frequency and violence of price fluctuations in the postwar protectionist decades. Eight times between 1815 and 1850 the numbers rise or fall by more than 10 per cent from one year to the next (1817, 1819, 1825, 1826, 1833, 1839, 1846, and 1848), and most of these are "favorable" movements caused by collapse of import prices preceding that of exports in depression years.[25] In the sixty-three years after 1850 the relative movements of export and import prices are much more moderate and gradual. Only once does the change in the net barter numbers from one year to another reach 10 per cent, and that is for 1862 during the cotton famine that accompanied the American Civil War.

The occasions on which British export prices reversed their downward trend have some revealing features. This occurred five times in the period from 1815 to 1850—in 1818, 1825, 1835–1836, 1845, and 1847. All but one (1845) of these upturns in export prices were preceded or accompanied by a larger improvement in import prices. In addition, all but one boom (1835–1836) were similarly preceded or accompanied by a considerable rise in the gross barter index, that is to say, the volume of imports rose more than that of exports. In every case there was a considerable improvement in foreign purchasing power for British goods.[26] Finally, these were years of unusually heavy British investment abroad, on two occasions mainly to the Americas. The rise in import prices in each of these years is

---

net imports were regularly substantially larger than exports (see "Current Values" in Table I). The British market was paramount and exerted a profound influence on world prices of the staples imported. British tariffs on these goods could aggravate price fluctuation by depressing world prices in years of ample supply in relation to British demand, though in years of short supply the burden was probably borne by British consumers.

The gradual reduction in the direct toll taken by British customs duties is indicated by the following figures. In 1841 when virtually every article of import was subject to tax, net customs collections constituted 31.8 per cent of the current value of net imports. In 1847, with the suspension of the Corn Laws, the average rate dipped to 21.6 per cent. Ten years later it had fallen to 14.1 per cent, and by 1867 it was down to 9.7 per cent with spirits, wine, and tobacco contributing half the revenue, sugar and tea, more than a third.

[25] The estimates of market values of imports may tend to be a little high in years of rapidly rising prices—See Imlah, "Real Values," p. 145. The import price index numbers may, therefore, be a little too high, and the net barter numbers a little too low, in such years as 1818 and 1825. Allowance for this does not alter the fact of sharp fluctuations though it may moderate the degree in some cases.

[26] In the one case (1835–1836) where the volume of imports did not rise appreciably more than that of exports, the improvement in prices, and large investments abroad, strengthened foreign purchasing power for British goods while very good harvests reduced domestic costs of foodstuffs and, with good conditions of employment, left a larger margin for purchase of manufactured goods in Britain itself.

Terms of Trade of the United Kingdom   193

partly attributable to their influence,[27] just as the ensuing collapse may be laid in part to sudden cessation of lending. These bursts of foreign lending were part of the boom psychology. They may have been as important in boosting import prices as the larger British acceptance of imports, which was also related to boom-time speculation.

Another contrast, shown by the gross barter index, is that Britain in the first period was more heavily an importing country in terms of quantity relationships than later in the century.[28] One group of years is particularly interesting in this respect. The numbers in the gross barter index for 1825–1829 are not exceeded by any other quinquennium from 1815 to 1913,[29] and the average rate of the customs duties, 38 per cent measured ad valorem, was the highest of any five-year period from 1798 on. One reason for this pre-eminence, the poor harvests which compelled "sudden and extraordinary" importations of foodstuffs, supplies a clue to the forces at work. Thanks to the heavy duties of the Corn Laws, the credits earned in the producing countries were substantially less than English consumers paid. Moreover, as Jenks has pointed out,[30] since the grain came in large part from regions that did not have the habit of trading much with Britain, the credits were not used for the purchase of British goods. In this case British imports did little to promote better markets for British exports. Simultaneously, British loans to areas of established trade almost ceased after the bursting of the bubble of 1825. Import prices slumped. Cotton dropped in three years to less than half the inflated price of 1825, 30 per cent under the previous low.

---

[27] The tendency of foreign loans to raise export prices in the borrowing country is very clearly illustrated in 1835–1836 when British loans were largely channelled to the United States. British imports from America rose in price while those from other areas were relatively little affected and even went down. Indian cotton prices did not rise with American, for example.

[28] This circumstance is quite consistent with the price trends. It is interesting that in terms of values also, Britain was somewhat more heavily an importing than an exporting country at the beginning and in the middle than at the end of the series, though the growing magnitude of her adverse balance of visible trade tends to obscure this fact. In 1798–1800 the adverse balance constituted 14.9 per cent of the total value of Britain's visible exports and net imports; in 1816–1818, 8.9 per cent; in 1849–1851, 14.0 per cent; and in 1911–1913, 12.1 per cent. Thus Britain's "invisible" credits, whether from foreign investments, shipping, or other sources, were not less important in the beginning and middle than at the end of the period. Possibly they were as important in 1816–1817 also, but were left to accumulate for such a burst of imports and foreign loans as occurred in that boom year 1818.

[29] The average of the gross barter index for these years was 138.5. In the years 1900–1904 another peak was reached at 129.1.

[30] Leland Hamilton Jenks, *The Export of British Capital to 1875* (New York: Alfred A. Knopf, 1938), p. 61.

These various circumstances, whose effects are made more measurable by the indexes, indicate some of the problems of industrial expansion for a trading and capital exporting country under a system of high protection. Free trade could supply some remedy to moderate the spasmodic impulses and disturbing fluctuations both in capital and in commercial relations. The opening of British markets freely to staple commodities from all over the world promoted steadier development of regular sources of supply of the wide variety of goods increasingly needed as well as wider habits of exchange of goods. It tended also to mean broader and sounder investment opportunities because free trade afforded better prospect that borrowers' commitments could be met. Debtor countries were less dependent on one or two lightly taxed commodities, such as cotton, to earn credits with which to meet obligations in Britain. Not only was British foreign investment thereafter less a thing of fits and starts, but it, too, was rather more diversified. Loans were channelled a little less exclusively to special areas, as to the Americas and particularly to the United States in 1825 and 1835–1836. Thus Britain found in free trade a commercial policy in better harmony with her interests as an industrial, trading, and investing nation. Further extension of machine methods of production could proceed with much less distressing disturbance in price relationships, and with fewer panics and lighter losses for her foreign investors. That a large effect on world prices should have been exerted is not surprising when it is remembered that through British ports in the mid-century flowed goods constituting nearly a quarter of the value of all international trade.

Tufts College and the Fletcher School   ALBERT H. IMLAH

[9]

THE LONDON SUGAR MARKET, 1740–1769

By RICHARD PARES

I

THE papers of Messrs Wilkinson and Gaviller contain much information about the London sugar market.[1] They do not furnish a continuous series of prices current, from which statistical tables or graphs could usefully be constructed; but the letters, and the prices which are incidentally mentioned, make it possible to give a connected account of the development of the market during these years. In this article I propose first to offer some general remarks, and to illustrate them by a chronological account of the state of the market from 1740 to 1769.

In this period the total supply of sugar at the London market almost doubled. In the first three years, the average output (which means, in practice, the average exportation to England) of the six British sugar colonies was 38,725 tons. In the last three years there were ten sugar colonies, to all intents and purposes, and their average total output was 70,320 tons.

Most of this sugar came to London, and it was the London market which ruled the price. In some years, such as 1740 and 1751, the prices at the outports —chiefly Bristol and Liverpool—were as much as 3s. higher than at London; in other years such as 1741 and 1757, the boot was on the other leg. When the differences of prices rose as high as this, sugar was sent round, one way or another, from port to port, and the prices were gradually equalized. What the consumption of Bristol may have been, I do not know; that of Liverpool was small, and would have been still smaller if slave-traders seeking to remit the proceeds of their sales from the islands to England had not sometimes chosen cargoes of sugar as the best method of doing so; in this way, the Liverpool price probably depended, in part, upon the state of the slave trade.

Nearly all the sugars which the House[2] handled were the property of the planters. They could, if they chose, sell their crops in the islands; and they frequently did this, whenever they had any reason, good or bad, to think that it would pay them better than consigning their sugars to England. The House showed no resentment when they did so; indeed, when the prices in the islands were good, it congratulated them, and condoled, at the same time, with such of its correspondents as were merchants, upon their misfortune in having bought at such an unpropitious season. Occasionally, however, it scolded the planters for their short-sightedness: if they had to remit to England in order to pay their debts or to buy their stores, they might find that sugars would have been a better remittance than bills of exchange—the premium of exchange might be too high, or the drawers men of doubtful character. These were just the circumstances in which the merchants in the islands would buy sugars rather than

---

[1] In *Essays presented to Sir Lewis Namier* (London, 1956), pp. 75–107, I have given a general description of the work of this House, and have explained why I have only dealt with the papers down to 1769.

[2] The firm of the House from March 1740 was 'H. Lascelles and Son'; from September 1743 it was 'Lascelles and Maxwell'; from March 1763 it was 'Lascelles, Clarke, and Daling'; from April 1765 to the end of the period discussed, it was 'Lascelles and Daling'. I shall not make these distinctions in this article, but shall refer to it continually as 'the House'.

bills. Many merchants, especially slave merchants, had to remit, and others bought sugars to send them to Europe as a speculation. These men had to choose between buying sugars and buying bills, just as the planters chose between selling sugars and selling bills. The House, more often than not, condemned these merchant correspondents for buying—not only because bills would have been a better remittance, but because the buyers of sugar in the islands did not always know what they were doing. Very little difference in price was made between good sugars and bad, whereas in London the difference between good and bad would have been much greater; presumably this may have been, in part, a relic of the earlier conditions, when sugar was currency in the islands, and bad sugar fetched nearly as much as good sugar there. The House pointed this out more than once; but it is fair to add that there were a few occasions when low sugars could be remitted even more profitably than fine ones.

Whether the sugars were the property of planters or of local merchants, they were sold on the same terms in London. That is to say, the House acted as sugar-factors, selling for a commission, normally of $2\frac{1}{2}$ per cent.

There were four classes of buyers: the grocers, the refiners, the exporters and the speculators, of whom the first two accounted, in all probability, for more than nine-tenths of the trade. Sugar was only in demand for export on rare occasions after 1733. In the seven years immediately after the Peace of Utrecht, our exports of raw sugar were hardly ever less than a quarter of our imports, and sometimes more than a third. In the ten years after 1734 they only once rose above 10 per cent. To put the matter another way, before 1733 it was very unusual for the total quantities re-exported to fall below 100,000 lb. In the years after 1733, re-exports only reached that level six times. The chief and regular market for these re-exported sugars was Ireland; but upon certain occasions there was a demand for re-export to Germany and Holland. This happened in 1743, 1748, 1749, 1756 and 1759.[1] In all these years, except 1743, the explanation is the same: the blockade of France and of the French sugar colonies, by withholding French sugars from Europe created an accidental demand for the re-export of English sugars.

The two great influences in the London sugar market were those of the grocers and the refiners. They did not demand exactly the same kinds of sugar; the grocers were attracted by colour, the refiners by a strong grain.

The sugars for the pans [the House wrote to John Harvie, on 27 November 1752] do always sell for more, colour for colour, than those fit only for the Scale, And for the former, they ought to be of a grey Colour and a rough grain which you will feel between your finger and thumb, and the better they have been cleaned the brighter they will appear to be, and sell the better. Some Sugars, and especially from Liguinea,[2] are very bright, but they have a yellow Cast, or more a Straw Colour, which are therefore not those chosen by the Sugar Bakers but are best for the Grocers who also buy, and use for the Scale all lower Sugars that are soft, and of a weak grain.[3]

The House often spoke as though the colour-scale had some absolute validity: thus, they once mentioned with surprise the fact that certain sugars 'ten

---

[1] These figures are drawn from the Public Record Office, T. 64/274.

[2] Liguanea, the district immediately north of Kingston, Jamaica.

[3] I do not intend to give continual references to the documents, which were destroyed in the war and now only survive, so far as I know, in my transcript; but where a convenient opportunity offers, I will indicate in the text the date of the letter quoted, in order that, when I shall have deposited my transcripts in some public place, the references may be verified.

shillings better in colour' than others only fetched, in fact, three shillings more at market. This illusion made them rejoice at the fact that the refiners would give more than the grocers for a sugar of a certain colour. They spoke as though they were getting something for nothing; but this was mere confusion of mind.

In the early correspondence of the House the grocers are spoken of as if they dominated the market: it is their manœuvres, their exploitation of the rumours of good crops, or of large fleets arriving, which appears to have regulated the market. They must have included some wholesalers, for, at the time of the Jacobite rising of 1745, the House explained why the grocers only bought from hand to mouth by saying that communications with the north were uncertain, so that only the London market needed to be supplied. From 1750, or thereabouts, the refiners appear to have had more influence. This is explained partly by the great increase in the number of sugar refining houses. 'The number of Sugar Houses has increased greatly in this place the last three years', the House told Jonathan Blenman on 14 March 1753, 'and also in the OutPorts and the luxury of the people has also increased, for the meanest now use hardly any other but improved Sugar, and it is Computed, that at least, ⅓rd is wasted or lessened in improving'.

Probably the change of taste which the House described in this letter accounted, in part, for the much greater consumption of raw sugars in England after 1750—though somewhat less than a pound of refined sugar may have been used in place of every pound of sugar which would have been consumed unrefined. Indeed, the increase of raw sugar production in the colonies was not keeping pace with the increased demand, mainly of the refiners. As a result, the refiners began to find that the price of their raw material rose upon them, and the increased expense led to financial loss. 'As Sugars bore high Prices, last Year', the House continued in the letter to Blenman which I have already quoted, 'many of the Sugar Bakers suffered Considerably and some of them as well as some of the Grocers are now applying to Parliament for the introduction of foreign Sugars'. They did so indeed, and without success; but, about this time, Parliament tried to bring about the required increase in raw sugar production by other means, namely by promoting the settlement of the uncultivated lands in Jamaica.

Unlike the grocers, who could, by purchasing at any season of the year, take full advantage of the state of the market, the refiners were not entirely their own masters. They had to keep working in the winter because, if they had let their sugar-houses go cold, the stocks of ready-made sugar would have mouldered. In the summer, however, they were under no such necessity, therefore they went out of the market in the spring, or only bought if the price suited them.

A last, and only occasional influence in the sugar market was that of the speculators. They do not appear very distinctly as a class in the correspondence of the House. Their existence is probably hinted at in numerous phrases about the quantity of sugar at market 'in the first hands'. Twice, however, the House described them rather more distinctly. In April 1752 they said that 'the great rise in the Market some time ago was owing to some People buying on speculation and not from any great want to Supply it'. Again, on 25 August 1752 they wrote to Gedney Clarke, 'We are glad to see some of the great dealers buying upon speculation of its advancing as it will be their Interest to hold up the market'. If mentions of speculators are infrequent, this is probably explained by the deliberate policy of the refiners. Mr Walter M. Stern has explained in his article on 'The London Sugar Refiners around 1800' (*Guildhall Miscellany*, February 1954), that the Sugar Refiners' Committee set its face against dealings in jobbed or second-hand sugars: in 1773 they branded everybody who did not comply as a person of 'very mean, base and infamous character, and ought to be despised, shunned, detested, and excluded from all bodies and societies of men whatsoever'.

The sugars passed from seller to buyer through the hands of the factors and the brokers. Only rarely were sugars sold at public sale in London; the chief exception consisted of the King's sugars—that is, those which had been received in kind, in payment of the 4½ per cent export duty at Barbados and the Leeward Islands. I do not remember an instance in which the House itself put up sugars for sale in this manner. It is not quite clear whether the services of the broker were used always. We read of a 'sugar buyer' who frequented Henry Lascelles's house, apparently in his professional capacity. On many occasions the House described itself as having 'higgled' the sugars all about the town, or 'shown them to the grocers' or 'applied to all the sugar bakers in town'. But it would not be safe to conclude that the services of the brokers were dispensed with on these occasions: the phrases quoted may only mean that the factor took the decision whether to sell, and at what price, and used the broker as a mere instrument. This, we know, was their normal relation. Sometimes the broker is explicitly mentioned as having carried a sample of certain sugars in his pocket. More often, the samples appear to have been arranged on a 'board'. On 24 September 1745 the House wrote thus to Samuel Husbands:

> As to the Sorts of those Sugars, it signifies nothing in respect to the denomination given them abroad, the Rule being to sell them according to their appearance here, and it often happens there's several Shillings difference a hundred between some people's first Whites and others, and between one part and another of a parcel of Casks shipped by the same person, the least shade of whiteness by which one Cask of Sugar exceeds another makes a difference in value, and yet it would not be perceived otherwise than by a Comparison of the Samples, shown together on one board; and the more Shades or degrees that appear between the samples of some and others make Still greater the difference in Value.

The samples could not always be exactly representative, for different parts of the same cask might be of different qualities, especially when the sugars had been cured in cask, a practice common in the Leeward Islands (but uncommon in Barbados, where the sugars were cured in pots and blended together afterwards in the cask). In cases of this sort, the buyer was entitled to expect an allowance on the price if the sugar did not answer the sample. There were some references to sugars 'sold with all faults'—here, no allowance would be made, but the practice was unusual.

If the buyer did not pay and the sugars had to be put up for sale again, he must—at least, so the House thought—pay any difference between the price he had offered and the price they ultimately fetched.

The sugar factor's art consisted mainly in the power to take two decisions—when to sell, and in what lots.

It was always his interest and his inclination to sell rather than keep: before he could land the sugars he had to advance the duties and the freight out of his own pocket, sometimes to the tune of several thousand pounds if a large fleet came in together. Of course he wanted to get this back as soon as possible. Moreover, most planters, when they shipped their sugars for England, drew bills of exchange on the factors for a part, at least, of their supposed value. Since the purchasers of sugar only paid in two months, and this term was sometimes extended by another month or two, the factor could not be in cash for the sugars in time to answer the bills of exchange unless he sold as soon as possible. More than once the House acknowledged, not without some shame, that it had made forced sales in order to meet the bills drawn upon it—naturally, in such cases, it would sell first the sugars of the same planters who had drawn the bills, but it did not always stop there. When the House kept sugars long, it wrote as though it had conferred a service upon its correspondents for the sake of a better market. 'We can truly assure you', they told Philip Gibbes on 23 August 1751, 'that it is against our inclination to keep Sugars any considerable time upon hand, and we never do so but with the sole view of service to our Imployers being manifestly against our own Interest to be long in advance for freights and duties whereon we do never charge any Interest'.

There seems to have been no general rule about the way to put up sugars together into lots. Sometimes more money could be made by selling the high and the low sugars separately, but more often the House found it better to sell large mixed lots—perhaps as many as sixty hogsheads—together at an average price. This must certainly have saved them trouble, but when they did it they represented it as having been an advantage to the planter, on the whole. Most planters objected to having their sugars sold along with those of other planters; indeed, it stands to reason that when this was done, an injustice was probably inflicted upon somebody or other. The House did not often admit to having done it at all, but once or twice they defended it as harmless.

We note your desire [they wrote to William Bryant on 30 July 1746], to have your Sugars always sold Separate from any others, which we shall strictly observe; but we do declare it as a matter of fact, that we never, in selling sundry parcels together, made use of the good to pass off those that were worse, but have always rated every mark and the different Sorts of every mark according to their goodness, and to the best of our Judgement, and if any particular mark has been disliked we have thrown it off, as otherwise it would not be doing justice to the good.

Different classes of sugar naturally had their particular reputations and their particular fortunes, but it is hard to say anything definite about this. The House itself often risked generalizations on this subject, but they were mostly untrustworthy, like all merchants' generalizations of the period: a few years, or even a few months, in which the market remained subject to the same laws, could usually give the House an illusion of fixity which any extended research into its papers will show to have been unwarranted.

Much was said of the difference between the sugars of the several islands, or even parts of the same island; not all these general remarks were untrue, but there were numerous exceptions. The brown sugar of Barbados, the island with which the House did most of its business, was probably, as a whole, somewhat finer than the average of all the islands, though its weak grain rendered it suitable for the grocers only. In Barbados itself, the produce of the windward part of the island was generally deemed the best, but a local spell of dry weather, or some other misfortune, might cause it to forfeit its reputation. The sugars of St Kitts were mostly fine: the island had a rich soil, and much of it had been settled after 1713 and was therefore less exhausted than that of Barbados. Antigua sugar was mostly inferior to that of Barbados and St Kitts, but there were some very fine Antigua sugars and, towards the end of the period I am discussing, the House often wrote as though Barbados could not well compete with the Leeward Islands in muscovado sugars. Jamaica was still, in some respects, a frontier settlement, and its production was often very slovenly. In the early part of the period the House spoke as though it consisted almost entirely of low brown sugars. But Jamaica improved both in quantity and quality, and there were very fine Jamaica sugars, of a beautiful straw colour, before the end of the Seven Years' War, even though Jamaica sugars were still not equal, as a class, to most others:

The Jamaica Sugars [the House wrote on 4 September 1756 to J. and A. Harvie], are in general very low and weak in quality, and not esteemed here nor abroad, which is chiefly owing to a want of care, and a slovenliness in the making of them. The Planters in the Leward Islands are careful and industrious, and their Sugars are in request, and we can sell them as fast as they are landed. Indeed the Sugar Bakers seldom work Jamaica Sugars without mixing them in the pans with those of the Leward Islands.

Not only particular islands or districts but even, on occasion, particular plantations might have their own reputation, good or bad, and the House often warned a correspondent that his mark would lose its esteem unless he amended his methods. Once or twice they reported that a sugar-refiner had vowed never to buy any more sugars of a certain mark. But it was not easy for the planter to standardize his production. 'You know', the House wrote to Samuel Husbands on 24 September 1745, 'that no plantation makes Sugar every day of equal goodness, but Some days better and others worse, and the canes of part yeild a better Sugar than those of another, so that unless you was to mix all the denomination of one Crop together in one Mass before it was casked, there will be a variety upon Comparison between the samples of some Casks and others.' To make matters worse, the planter did not always know the final result of what was being done under his own eye, for, as the House pointed out more than once, some sugars improved on the passage to England, while others did not, and nobody seems to have been able to foresee which was which. This probably accounts for a great deal of the indignation which the correspondents of the House appear to have expressed when they learned how their products had sold.

More important, and more useful, than the distinction between one island and another, or one plantation and another, is the contrast between the fate of fine and coarse sugars, above all between those of clayed and muscovadoes. Certain qualities of sugar were permanently in demand for particular purposes —thus, Barbados sugars, especially the clayed, were bought for making preserves, while dark brown sugars were wanted for home made wines, especially elder wine. Brown sugars were most wanted for exportation, when there was any demand of that sort, but if they were very dark the refiners did not like them for they were liable to waste most in refining. Besides these permanent properties attributed to certain classes, their fortunes were sometimes affected in different ways by more temporary influences. For example, when the price of sugar was high so that the poor could only just afford it, the coarser kinds were in more demand, and fell less in price, than the finer. The same thing might even be true when it was corn, rather than sugar itself, that was dear.

The House wrote much and often on the contrast between clayed and muscovado sugars. Claying seems to have originated in Barbados. It is described by Mr Deerr[1] as 'the process of covering the upper surface of the impure magma of crystals and molasses, contained in an earthenware cone, with a layer of wet clay, whence the water percolated slowly through the material, displacing the molasses'. It required more capital and more care than making muscovado sugars. To Florentius Vassall, a Jamaica planter who thought of taking up claying, the House wrote on 10 December 1750,

unless you can get into the method of making the finest sort it is impossible that your claying of Sugars can answer...we do not pretend to be Planters or to understand thoroughly the Business of the Boyling House but we know in Bdos. the liquor is strained from the Clarifying Copper through one Woollen straining Cloth and afterwards to the next Copper through two Straining Cloths and unless the liquor is properly cleansed and strained, it is impossible that the sugar made from it, will strike well under Clay.

Many planters, however, in Barbados thought the additional price was worth the trouble, the more so because the process, especially if repeated (this was known as 'double claying'), yielded more molasses than the production of muscovado, and therefore made the island's considerable output of rum possible. The result was a sugar which could compete, though not always with success, against sugar refined in Europe: if the process was properly carried out, no trace of the clay remained visible, but the taste and smell of the sugar were, at best, somewhat affected. The second and third qualities of clayed sugars were scarcely distinct from muscovado—the Customs Officers often confused them, perhaps deliberately, and the prices were comparable: thirds commonly fetched no more than a good muscovado, if as much; low seconds began in price where muscovado left off, whereas first whites were, at best, 50 per cent or more above the price of the best muscovado. How many planters went in for claying, and what proportion of the island's total crop was clayed, are questions which cannot be answered from the Customs statistics or any other source; the planters clayed more in some years than in others, according to their expectations of the market; and this variation in supply, which seems to have been considerable, partly accounts for the ups and downs of price. As a rule, claying seems to have been general in Barbados, from the many references to clayed sugars in the correspondence of the House.[2] This would explain the fact that, unlike that of many other islands, the total crop of Barbados, measured in tons, was considerably lower in the fifty years after 1733 than in the fifty years before, and yet the island enjoyed considerable prosperity in this period, doubtless because the smaller tonnage was more than compensated by the higher value per ton. In some years clayed sugars did better than muscovadoes, in other years vice versa. Since clayed sugar was particularly used for preserving, its price depended in part upon the English fruit crops. The presumption was that the clayeds were usually bought by the grocers, in competition with London-made refined sugars (especially, it seems, the kind known as ground lump sugar) which usually governed the price. But there were times when the refiners bought the clayed, even the finest, because, at their price, they were the cheapest sugars to refine. This was particularly likely to happen when the price of brown sugars was, for some reason, disproportionately high,—for

[1] *The History of Sugar* (London, 1950), i, 109.
[2] In the prices current quoted by the House in its letters during this period, there seem to be fifty-four references to the price of Barbados muscovado sugar, and fifty-five to that of clayed sugar, which was almost exclusively a Barbadian product.

LONDON SUGAR MARKET

example, when the crops had failed in Jamaica, the chief producer of brown sugar, so that the total supply of muscovado was reduced, or when (as I have already said) the high price of sugar as a whole or the high cost of living in general caused the consumption to confine itself largely to muscovado.

The history of the sugar market in these years is, of course, one of seasonal and accidental fluctuations. A certain rhythm of the seasons can be discerned, though most generalizations that were made about it were too precise. One of the House's correspondents, Thomas Stevenson of Barbados, seems to have had a theory on this subject.

We accept [they wrote to him on 6 August 1762] of the proposal you make of consigning us your whole Crop, and to keep your Sugars till between the 15th of April and the end of May in every year, War or Peace, charging interest on our advance for freight and Duties from a reasonable time after we received the Sugars and charging the same in the Accot. of Sales with the other charges. We do not think your Scheme will always answer, having found in some years that Sugars have sold better before Christmass than in the Spring.

In general, although some refiners with full stores of ready-made sugar stopped working when the warmer weather diminished the danger of mouldering, there was a brisk demand for sugar in the spring when the first consignments came home to a market which had been starved during the winter; at these times, especially in war when a large fleet came together, the first prices were very much the best, and those who were only two or three days late in getting their hogsheads out of the hold might lose as much as 2s. or 3s. per cwt. for their tardiness. The market then flagged until October, when much business was done. By Christmas it was usually dull again, because frost and bad weather would prevent the buyers from taking delivery for distribution in the provinces. But these were only rough tendencies to which there were many exceptions—e.g. in 1753 the spring market was low, but prices were higher in October and higher still at Christmas.

About the casual fluctuations of the market the historian is hardly better able to generalize than the House itself. Variations in supply and variations in demand succeeded and traversed each other in a series of bewildering movements, most of them small. War caused many variations in supply, so that the mere rumour of it was enough to send the price of sugar up and the mere rumour of peace enough to send it down. The risk of capture by enemy privateers and men-of-war was very high—a fact which can be seen in the insurance premiums which sometimes rose to 30 per cent. Though enemy action might reduce the immediate supply of sugar, the ultimate effects of war might increase it in the long run: if an enemy sugar island was conquered and its produce was admitted to the British market, it would bear down the price of British sugars: thus, in 1760, the House had to lament the unfortunate acquisition of Guadeloupe which was preventing a rise in the London price. Moreover, if the enemy sugar island was permanently annexed, as many were in 1763, the total supply of sugar in London would be permanently increased.

Besides war, the weather caused frequent and sudden variations in supply. Some islands were more subject to drought than others—above all Antigua, whose total output fluctuated widely: in 1753 it was 12,459 tons, in 1754 only 3,158, but in 1755 it rose again to 10,645. The other islands were not quite so mercurial unless they were struck by a hurricane; this happened to one or other of them every three or four years, upon an average, and the effects, exaggerated in advance by rumour, often had a great effect upon the London price—the House often used the threat of such a reduction of the supply as a point in its eternal argument with the buyers.

There were also variations in demand. Some of these, too, were attributed to war: for example, the increased taxes upon sugar itself which were levied in 1747 and 1759, as well as high war taxes in general. These were believed to reduce the purchasing power of the English consumer and disincline him to spend money on sugar. Other causes had the same effect—for instance, the bad harvest of 1740, which raised the price of corn, was believed to keep that of sugar lower than it would otherwise have been. When, however, corn was so scarce that the government forbade its use in the distilleries (this happened in the war years 1758–9 and in 1766 in peacetime), then the price of sugar was sure to go up, for the distillers used the molasses which the London sugar refiners turned out as a by-product, and the steep rise in the price of molasses enabled the refiners to pay more for their raw sugars. Once or twice the distillers even used sugar itself, but this does not seem to have answered very well.

Besides these influences of war and the weather, variations in demand also resulted from economic causes which the House could only discern or describe dimly. More than once they complained of the 'scarcity of money' which not only forced buyers to pay slowly but reduced the consumption altogether: when money was tight, the refiners could not dispose of their product, their stores were over-stocked, and they could not buy or work fresh raw sugars.

By its own account, the House did not make a very good hand of foreseeing these fluctuations. In 1744 the outbreak of war with France appears to have taken them by surprise: they sold sugars just before it took place, and held on to sugars too long at the peace in 1748. 1756 was a repetition of 1744. In 1758 they sold sugar because they wrongly believed that a peace would be negotiated; by the end of 1761 and the beginning of 1762 they were expecting a peace negotiation which would lower the price of sugar and got, instead, a war with Spain which raised it. On all these occasions but the last, they knew that a development such as ultimately took place was on the cards, but they miscalculated the exact time at which it would take place, and they lost the benefit of 2s. or 3s. movement in price. To do them justice, their record was probably better than one would think from reading their correspondence: where they had miscalculated they had to apologize, but where they had guessed right they did not always feel called upon to boast, therefore we know less about the successes than about the mistakes.

After a few months in London George Maxwell discussed, in a letter to a friend, his recent education in the art of selling sugars. 'I find', he wrote on 16 November 1743, 'there is still more to be learned, and that is, to form a right judgement of the times and Seasons, when to sell and when to keep, but the times since my arrival have been so changeable as to puzzle the Judgement of the oldest Sugar Sellers of Them all in regard to Muscovadoes and the browner claids and the reson is because ne'er a man of them is a Conjurer.' Two years later it was the same story. 'Nothing can be more fluctuating than the Market for Sugar, the Continuance of an easterly wind for a few weeks shall raise it, and a westerly wind with the bare expectation of the arrival of Ships shall lower it again.'

The history of these fluctuations cannot be effectively presented in general terms: the purpose of the second part of this essay is to exhibit them in detail by a brief chronological account.

II

The oldest letter-book of the House opens in March 1740. The price of brown sugar appears to have been satisfactory: Barbados muscovadoes, not of very good quality, were selling at 30s. to 32s. The ships seem to have gone out late to the West Indies, probably because of the Spanish war which had begun the previous year, and they were not expected back for some months. This circumstance was enough to counteract some unfavourable influences, such as that of the long frost which caused an entire cessation of business, and the late, cold spring, with a prospect of a short crop of soft fruit which needed clayed sugars to preserve them. The market continued dull until the end of May, when brown sugars began to be in demand. Even clayed sugars were bought by the refiners, since there was so little brown sugar at market; but the finest of all were not wanted. As often happened when the prices of all sugars were relatively high, brown sugars kept up better than white, and those white clayed sugars which were most akin to the browns did better than the finest qualities. Not until the end of July did the fleets come home from the West Indies; even then the prices fell by no more than 2s., for some of the islands had made short crops. The grocers did their best to resist a rise of price, buying 'from hand to mouth' throughout the year; but the news of a hurricane and of some other disaster which befell the Leeward Islands ships caused the price to start by 2s. or 3s. in November, and on the 24th of that month middling Jamaica muscovadoes were selling at 35s. the cwt. Brown sugars still did better than clayed at the end of the year. On 6 December the House complained that, while muscovadoes sold at 33s. and 34s., clayed sugars, ' 10s. a hundred better in colour' would only fetch 36s. to 37s.; but fine clayeds, about the same time, were fetching 41s. to 47s.: the grocers might boycott them, but the refiners were buying them 'as being by much at present the Cheapest Sugar in Proportion at Market'.

The market remained dull until the middle of 1741, and muscovadoes remained within the range from 30s. to 36s. per cwt. The crops in most of the islands were good, especially for brown sugar, and this explains the fact that clayed sugars, which were produced by hardly any other island except Barbados, now did much better than muscovadoes. The corn harvest of 1741 in Great Britain was much better than that of the previous year; and, when wheat began to come down from famine prices, the average consumer could probably afford a better class of sugar.

There is a gap in the records from February 1742 to September 1743. When the correspondence reopens, muscovadoes were low, because the Leeward Islands and Jamaica fleets were expected shortly: the Jamaica sugars were selling at 27s. to 34s., and they would have been really low but for re-export, which was 'owing to less being made this year than formerly at some of the foreign plantations'. (Great Britain, at this time, was only at war with Spain, which produced little or no sugar for the European market; it was a war with France which might create a demand for the re-export of British sugars by withholding French sugars from Europe.) The House was expecting Jamaica sugars to arrive at any moment, and therefore sold Barbados muscovadoes; but in the middle of September came the news that a large fleet from Jamaica had met with a terrible storm, so the prices went up—not for clayed sugars, which were doing well already, and could not be affected by anything that happened to a Jamaica fleet. The disaster turned out to be less serious than it

THE ECONOMIC HISTORY REVIEW

had been thought to be: the fleet reassembled and sailed again, but it met another storm, and some of the ships had to get into the outports, so that the London prices kept up well. Trade, however, was dull, as usual, in the depths of winter. The suspense was heightened by a political event. In February 1744, a bill was brought in for increasing the duty on sugar; the Ministry argued that this duty would be paid by the consumer. The House did not agree with them, 'yet being desirous to do the utmost in our power for the interest of our employers we chose to see the issue of this bill and its effect upon the market, before we would expose those to Sale that are come to hand—it may be that such an imaginary notion may give a greater Start to Sugars, though we do not see any reason for it'. The bill was defeated, for the time being;[1] but into the midst of the suspense which it created came a declaration of war by France. The House was taken by surprise: 'That was an event by no means expected, but it was rather believed our King would have declared first. It was unlucky as we had kept so long, and that same day we sold a great many others, however we acted according to the best of our Judgement and we were affraid of the arrival of some Ships with new Sugars from St. Kitts.'

This war, of course, raised the price of sugars higher than they had been for many years: in July 1744 Jamaica muscovadoes were selling from 34*s.* to 41*s.* But about that time, a vast fleet arrived from the Leeward Islands, which lowered the market for all but the finest muscovadoes. The crops in the islands were no more than average, but were magnified by rumour, and their effect on the market was exaggerated by the fact that, as always in a war with France, the entire produce of the West Indies arrived at once in one or two very large fleets. But this also meant that, in between the fleets, very little new sugar arrived and the market had time to recover, which it seems to have done at the end of 1744: in February 1745 muscovadoes were selling from 32*s.* to 40*s.*, clayeds from 38*s.* to 53*s.*

1745 was a year of great animation, for one reason or another. At the beginning of March came the much-delayed news of a dreadful hurricane at Jamaica. Once more the House had been caught on the wrong foot: they had been afraid of a few ships dropping in from the Leeward Islands to damp the market, and had sold off all the sugars they had. In June they were expecting the arrival of a large convoy from Jamaica so, once more, they sold everything they had. The convoy did indeed arrive, but only nine ships strong: it had been scattered, and eighteen ships had been taken. Prices bounded on this news; but many other ships of the convoy got safe to Ireland, and on 24 September the House reported, 'such Sugars as sold three weeks ago at 44*s.* per cwt. are now reduced to 40*s.*, only 39*s.* offered for them'. Evidently, the partners in the House were tearing their hair: they did not know what to do. Something worse still was in store for them. The Young Pretender landed in Scotland, and the great political crisis which followed this news completely upset the market.

'We were several Days [the House wrote on 9 October 1745] in Selling your Sugars and they were Shown to Several Grocers, many of which Seem quite unwilling to trade in these times of diffidence. Money is not to be borrowed now upon the best Security at the legal interest. Trade is quite at a Stand, because people do not know whom to trust. Yours are sold to people of Substance and we thought it better to sell them than to keep, as things grow daily worse

[1] See my book, *War and Trade in the West Indies* (Oxford, 1936), pp. 503–4.

LONDON SUGAR MARKET   265

and worse...the Rebellion has, we may reasonably Compute, prejudiced you in the Sales of the above Sugars one hundred pounds, and how much more on those that are to come God knows.

About the same time they wrote that sugars had fallen 10s. or 12s. per cwt. in the last six weeks, only a false rumour that the Dutch intended to declare war on France, which created a 'smart demand for the exportation of brown Sugars', keeping the market up at all. But in January, after some weeks of buying from hand to mouth, it became clear that the rebellion was likely to be suppressed. Muscovadoes sold from 43s. to 49s. per cwt. in February 1746, because so many ships were taken by the French. In March, sugars sold 'vastly high'; in April the market was dull, for the grocers and refiners bought sparingly in expectation of the arrival of fleets: 'three or four of them', the House wrote in June, 'buy ten hhds. only in Company to divide in several shares'. The suspense was relieved at the end of July by the arrival of a large fleet from the Leeward Islands and the expectation of another from Jamaica. Muscovadoes were now down to 38s. to 46s. per cwt.; even clayeds suffered since, when muscovadoes were cheap, the grocers supplied themselves with 'a coarse kind of refined Sugars called bastards which answer well enough in the room of Claids'.

The fleets from Barbados and the Leeward Islands arrived at the beginning of August: the Jamaica fleet was expected soon after, so the House sold as many sugars as they could, and they were right to do so, for the prices fell by 4s. for whites. The Jamaica fleet then turned out to be small but the prices did not rise, since single ships dropped in throughout the summer and the second fleet from the Leeward Islands was expected. This fleet reached Portsmouth in November, but easterly winds prevented it from getting round to London, so that the market grew better for a time. The House complained of heavy sales throughout the year.

A false rumour of peace lowered prices a little at the beginning of 1747: muscovadoes sold from 35s. to 45s. When it became clear that the war would continue, a great rise began. It was known that the crops had failed all over the British West Indies, although there were still some sugars of the previous crop to come home from Jamaica, and the English market was well supplied for several months. A long tug-of-war ensued between the buyers and sellers: the buyers were in no hurry for an immediate supply, and the consumers' demand was sluggish: 'the Scarcity of Money', the House wrote on 20 May 1747, 'is a general complaint. We find the consumption of Sugar decreases daily: for, as taxes increase people must learn to live with frugality, and nothing is more true than that the high price of Sugar lessens the consumption'. A few months later they stated more specifically that 'the midling sort of People in the Country, we are well informed, use Mellasses now that formerly used brown Sugar'. In these circumstances the grocers and refiners both bought from hand to mouth, in the hope that the failure of the crops in the islands would prove to have been exaggerated, but the prospects of the 1748 crop were blasted by the news of a hurricane in the Leeward Islands. In December, Barbados muscovadoes were selling at 40s. to 43s. and first whites had got up to 57s. to 63s., the highest price for many years. The hurricane seems to have been exaggerated, and good crops were expected from Jamaica.

In May 1748 it became clear that peace would be made: the refiners stopped work and the grocers sold off their stock on hand, in the hope that prices would

18

fall. Only the talk of foreign demand kept them up at all. On 1 July the House reported that some Jamaica muscovadoes had sold at 26s. per cwt. which would have fetched 45s. before the news of the peace. The demand for exportation amounted to very little. The French and Dutch markets were bare of sugar because of the war, but this was only a temporary scarcity, and the House foresaw a dismal future. 'The suddenness of the peace,' they wrote on 1 July 1748, 'will greatly affect people abroad by Reducing greatly the Value of Sugars, and the Factors here don't chuse to be in advance and there is too much Reason to believe that Many Bills this Year will be protested. Sugars will lye a dead-Weight on the hands of the Factors, or Sell for a triffle, and Commission business will be very bad.' We have no means of knowing whether their fears were realized, for there is a gap in the records from August 1748 to August 1750.

On 20 August 1750 Jamaica sugars were sold at 24s. to 34s. per cwt.—worse prices than any during the war from 1739 to 1748. The market was dull, since there was a great stock of sugars in the first hands, and the price of London refined sugar was low. At the end of the year rumours of dry weather in Jamaica and short crops in some other islands encouraged some sales but the House reckoned that there were 15,000 hogsheads of sugar at market, and believed that any improvement would be only temporary. They seem to have been right: very little change in the market was noticed before the end of 1751: although the crop of that year was small in Jamaica, a great deal of the 1750 crop had remained in the islands for want of shipping, and came home in August 1751.

At the end of November 1751 came the news of a hurricane at the Leeward Islands and Jamaica. The price of brown sugars started upwards by 4s. per cwt. in a few days, and the total movement amounted to more than 10s. Clayed sugars were less affected, since they came only from Barbados. The House considered this rise of price to be merely speculative: there was no scarcity of sugars for present consumption, and the effect of the hurricane upon the size of the crops was still a matter for guessing. For some time, it looked as though the House was right: the price of Jamaica muscovadoes fell 5s. between 26 February and 10 April 1752 at which date it stood at 32s. to 40s. per cwt. But the speculators proved right in the long run: some of the ships from the Leeward Islands came home not half loaded so that the London refiners had to start using Barbados clayed sugars in August. At the beginning of December Barbados muscovadoes were selling at 36s. to 43s. Clayed sugars did not fully share in the general advance: they stood at various prices from 42s. to 56s., and if, at the beginning of 1753, they rose somewhat higher, it was only because the refiners found brown sugars so scarce and dear that they were forced to work the clayed. There were several causes for this disproportion. There was still no shortage of London refined sugar, by whose price that of all clayed sugars was principally governed. Moreover, when all sugars were high, it was, as before, the cheaper kinds which sold best, since the consumers bought a lower class than was customary. Thus it was the refiners who suffered most in this year of high prices, for their raw material was dearer than they could afford and they could not recover their cost in the price of their own article. This, no doubt, is the reason why they took part, in March 1753, in the agitation for the introduction of foreign sugars.

Meanwhile, the price of brown sugars began to fall: on 14 March it was 5s. lower than it had been on 24 January. Prospects of the crops were good in all the islands, and a long period of plenty set in. Almost every year from

1753 to 1762, the House complained that unprecedented quantities had been imported. This was, indeed, a decade of unexampled progress in Jamaica[1] and the House began to fear that, in the long run, the supply would permanently exceed the demand.

When the crops began to come home, the prices fell further: good muscovadoes dropped from 38*s*. to 34*s*. During the course of July, and in September, Barbados muscovadoes generally ranged from 26*s*. to 34*s*. All this summer, the refiners held off the market, so far as they could, in order to lower the price; the factors would have liked to lock up their sugars too in hopes of something better and, indeed, some of them did so—not so the House, which had to sell in order to answer bills of exchange drawn upon it. Clayed sugars held up better, as they were not affected by the production of Jamaica, but even they began to come down in November, since the refiners (who had plenty of made sugars in their stores) had been able to supply themselves cheaply with raw material and brought down the price of their own goods: at the end of the year, first clayeds stood at 39*s*. to 53*s*. per cwt. The House reported on 8 December 1753 that the market had 'drooped again, of late, and very flat at present, and no wonder, as there is Computed to be 20,000 Casks[2] of brown Sugars in the first hands besides some to come from Jamaica and the Leeward Islands, which will be more than the Consumption will take off for a long time, and the importation from last Crop will greatly exceed the annual home Consumption'.

In a letter of 12 January 1754 to Thomas Stevenson they gave more precise figures: the importation was 'computed at the quantity of at least 90 thousand hhds., and reckoning them at 14 cwt. each....Into this Port have come 75 thousand of the number, which exceeds the consumption above 20 thousand, and it is wonderful how our market has kept up, so well as it has done and contrary to our expectation'. The state of the market was not due only to a plentiful importation: money was said to be 'scarcer here, at present, than ever was known, and the Sugar Buyers took about double the time, and some more in paying than they did formerly'.

The effect of the large importation of 1753 was long felt. The crop of 1754 was a little smaller than that of 1753, chiefly because Antigua, which had made a phenomenal crop in the previous year, was now afflicted by drought, and Barbados was also below the average. The market improved somewhat in the summer—Barbados muscovadoes stood on 7 July 1754 at 35*s*. to 43*s*. But Jamaica had done well, and in any case, the refiners had large stocks of manufactured sugar on hand, the produce of the previous year's importation. Towards the end of the year prices fell again: on 10 December sugars were sold for 39*s*. per cwt. which would have yielded 43*s*. in September; and by the beginning of January they were 2*s*. lower still.

Now, however, the diplomatic tension between England and France began to blow up into the Seven Years' War. The crisis deepened very slowly, with many fluctuations, which caused the prices of sugar to go up and down by 1*s*. or 2*s*. at a time. Another large importation was on the way from Jamaica, and even the danger of war could not keep the price up: on 30 July 1755 Jamaica sugars were quoted at 26*s*. to 36*s*. Once more the importation was

---

[1] For the figures, see Deerr, *op. cit.* 1, 198.

[2] The House never explained just what they meant by 'Casks'. Most casks were hogsheads of 14–18 cwt. apiece, but there were also some tierces, each of which could be reckoned as two-thirds of a hogshead, as well as a number of barrels which contained, on an average, one-sixth of a hogshead.

said to exceed the consumption: 80,000 casks were said to have come into the port of London, which was, in the opinion of the House, 20,000 casks more than could be consumed on the spot. But at the beginning of 1756 there arose, from two quarters, a demand for exportation: the British navy had seized many homeward bound ships from the French West Indies (without any declaration of war) and 12,000 casks of sugar were said to have been lost in the earthquake at Lisbon. Since Ireland was largely supplied from Lisbon and Hamburg from the French Atlantic ports, a brisk demand sprang up and, according to the House 11,000 casks were re-exported from London between 1 November and 30 January.[1]

The 1756 crops were large again, and much of the previous importation was still on hand in London in April 1756. The House wrote on 13 May 1756 that even if war was declared against France (an event which happened, greatly to their surprise, five days afterwards), 'we do not see room to expect a rise in the value of raw Sugars, as the Sugar Bakers have large Stocks of improved Sugars on hand, and the prices of them considerably fallen'. They were wrong: although the war had no immediate effect (indeed, sugars fell 5s. or 6s. by the beginning of August) yet, when the French began to take our sugar ships, the price began to rise in the home market and, at the same time, the seizure of more French ships by the Royal Navy stimulated the demand for re-exportation. Thus, even a large crop in Jamaica was not enough to prevent the price from going up at the end of the year. Jamaica muscovadoes were quoted at 30s. to 40s. per cwt. on 8 January 1757, and they went still further, for the great scarcity of corn induced parliament to forbid the distillation of wheat. This advanced the price of molasses from 11s. to 22s. per cwt., and the distillers even made an attempt at using brown sugars, though without success. Once more, the House had allowed itself to be taken by surprise: 'it had been lucky', it wrote on 9 February 1757, 'if we could have kept our Jamaica Sugars to the present time, but that was not to be done as our Employers drew upon us too fast, and above the value of the Effects consigned us'. Clayed sugars alone experienced little of this rise, for the town was still full of refined sugars, which had been manufactured from the importation of the previous crop.

It is difficult to say what were the prices in 1757: large fleets came home from almost every island except Barbados and made a great impression, for the time being, on the sugar market, already lowered by the great supplies of refined sugar on hand from the previous year. 'It happens also', the House wrote on 3 September 1757, to Gedney Clarke, 'that the country people are poor, and have not been able to afford to buy Sugar, on account of the dearness of Grain, and they have hardly been able to purchase Bread for the support of their Families. These Circumstances have greatly reduced the value of Sugars, and the Buyers have bought most sparingly.' Only the demand from the distillers seems to have kept up the price.

Mellasses once rose as high as 37s. per cwt. [the House wrote on 24 February 1758 to Thomas Stevenson], and is now down to 28s. per cwt. and in little demand. The high prices for mellasses induced the Sugar Bakers to work briskly for a time, and now their Houses are all full, and a slow vent for their goods, which makes them stand still. There would seem already too much Sugar made for the consumption. At least, I think, for certain, it must be the case in a few

---

[1] It is interesting to compare the information given by the House with the official statistics in Public Record Office, T. 64/274. In 1755, 15,525 cwt. of sugar were re-exported to Germany, 16,840 cwt. to Holland, and 64,985 cwt. to Ireland; in 1756, the respective figures were 53,511 cwt., 26,733 cwt., and 87,064 cwt. All these figures are very much in excess of the averages.

years, as the Plantations are increasing in Jamaica. The Distillation has been a great aid in the consumption of Sugars, which must otherwise have been miserably low at this time, but that may not be the case next year, there being a prospect for a good harvest.

Once again the Royal Navy came to the rescue: in the summer of 1758 great numbers of Dutch ships were seized carrying French sugars home from the West Indies and, during the resultant lawsuits in the prize courts, all these sugars were locked up, so that the Dutch and German markets were very bare. Great quantities were therefore demanded for re-exportation from England. This happy circumstance kept up the price until the middle of 1759. Instead of complaining, as it had done for so many years past, of large importations and stocks hanging over from one year to another, the House exulted, on 31 July 1759, over the fact that 'our market is almost quite bare of Sugar and the prices advanced far above they have been at any time since the war'. On the same day they reported that Barbados muscovadoes had sold at 50s. to 56s. per cwt. A few months later even these prices were made to look insignificant, and the House had to apologize for them. 'At the time we sold these Sugars', they wrote on 20 November 1759 to J. and A. Harvie, 'we consulted your Interest and we thought we did well, as there were great crops expected home from Jamaica. We find since, that the Crop will fall short of the quantity that was expected by 12 to 15,000 hhds. The market has since advanced.' According to the figures given by Mr Deerr, the House must have been wrong, for the Jamaica crop was, in fact, half as large again in 1759 as in 1758; and this, perhaps, is the reason why the prices fell in the first months of the next year. Moreover, a series of better corn harvests in England enabled parliament to permit distillation of wheat once more; the price of molasses fell from 30s. to 13s. per cwt., and this must have had an effect upon that of raw sugars. At the same time, vast quantities of sugar flooded in from conquered Guadeloupe. Even the demand for re-export fell off, since the suits against the Dutch ships in the prize courts had been determined one way or the other. Great was the fall in the prices: on 18 July 1760 the House reported that clayed sugars which would have sold as high as 84s. per cwt. that time last year, had now gone for 52s. 9d. and muscovadoes had likewise been reduced from 45s. to 30s.

At the beginning of 1761 prices were held up by many captures of ships bound homeward from the West Indies, but lowered by the peace negotiations which ultimately proved abortive. The House was complaining once more of vast fleets and importations exceeding the possible consumption. 'Should there come a peace', they wrote on 5 September 1761, 'an event which is expected, as there are Negociations between our Court and that of France, the market would fall perhaps as low as at any period that ever was known.' However, things were not quite as bad as that: instead of the peace with France there was a war with Spain, which gave 'an immediate Start to Sugars'. Prices advanced more than 6s. in January 1762, but began to fall again in the summer when it became clear that this time peace would really be made. 'On the certain prospect of a Peace', the House wrote on 31 August 1762 to Alexander Harvie, 'the Stock of 4 per Cent Annuities have lately risen above 20 per Cent. Sugars are in no request and we have many hundreds of Casks from Barbados and cannot sell a Cask unless we would abate 6 or 7 Shillings a cwt. of the prices at which they were sold at the beginning of this month.' On 11 November, muscovadoes were selling from 33s. to 42s. per cwt. The market fell again in March (by 3s.) upon the ratification of the definitive treaty of peace. The

House foresaw a dismal period, as after the previous war. 'We are sorry to add', they wrote on 14 May 1763, 'that we have in that Respect but a Melancholy prospect before us for a twelvemonth at least.'

Unfortunately the records of the House do not show us whether these fears were realized, since there is another break from June 1763 to April 1765. The next letter-book opens cheerfully: there had been a very short crop in Antigua, and Jamaica had made relatively little (though more than it would have made in a good year before the war). Prices therefore were at least 10s. better than the House would have expected in peacetime. In May, Jamaica sugars sold at 30s. to 40s. per cwt., and in August for 34s. to 40s. per cwt. Barbados, which had made a good crop, profited by the misfortunes of others. At the end of October Barbados muscovadoes were selling from 39s. to 45s. per cwt., and first whites from 52s. to 57s. (Once more clayed sugars benefited disproportionately from the failure of crops in Jamaica.) But the House warned its customers that these good times would not last. 'In a plentiful year for Sugars', it wrote to Gedney Clarke on 14 November 1765, 'yours would not fetch what they have now by 8 or 10s. or more per cwt.' Indeed, sugars fell by 6s. per cwt. from January to March, and another 6s. in April, for a good crop was expected, especially from Antigua, in 1766. However, once more sugar producers had struck it lucky, in spite of the vast importation: for the Government once more prohibited the use of wheat in the distillery, and the price of molasses rose. This time, however, sugar benefited less from this circumstance than it had done in the previous decade: the distillers seem to have wanted to avoid using molasses, and they partly succeeded in doing so. The price of muscovadoes remained pretty constant, from 31s. to 40s. per cwt., until the end of August, when it rose to 35s. to 43s. per cwt.: the crops were fair in most of the islands, but there was still a prospect that sugar would have to be used in the distillery. In 1768 the prices began to fall again, for there was another large importation from the islands: by 15 November Barbados muscovadoes were selling from 30s. to 37s. per cwt. 'Had not Jamaica, Antigua etc. somewhat failed in their Crops this year (altho' we have had about as many as came last year quite up to March) Sugars would have been almost a drug, altho' the year has been favourable for fruit.' Thus the House wrote to a Barbados planter on 10 November 1768.

At this point the correspondence of the House, so far as I have preserved it in my transcripts, comes to an end. Perhaps one should not attend too much to its somewhat apologetic tone. The House was always complaining of excessive importations, and indeed, as I have said at the beginning of this article, the production of the British West Indies had risen by something like 80 per cent between 1740 and 1769. But the prices had never relapsed to the level of the 1730's. A temporary glut may have taken place for a year or two after each of the wars, but the letters of 1765 to 1769, and the prices quoted in them, show that, for one reason or another, sugar producers could do very nicely even in peacetime. The House sometimes wrote as if the higher prices were explained by the additional taxes which were laid upon sugar in this period; but these only amounted to 3s. per cwt. (1s. 6d. in 1747 and 1s. 6d. in 1759). It is more likely that, in spite of the House's jeremiads about the excess of the production over consumption, the demand for sugar in England, for use in coffee and tea above all, was keeping pace; in the next generation, we know that it was to exceed the consumption, and to create a lively agitation for free importation of foreign sugars.

All Souls College, Oxford

[10]

THE
ECONOMIC HISTORY
REVIEW

SECOND SERIES, VOLUME XXIX, No. 1 1976

The Colonial Trades and Industrial
Investment in Scotland, c. 1700–1815

By T. M. DEVINE

I

THE economic history of Scotland in the eighteenth century is dominated by the dramatic rise of the colonial trades. By far the most important of these was the importation of tobacco from Virginia, Maryland, and North Carolina and its later sale in continental European markets, although in the last two decades of the century, the trade in sugar, cotton, and rum, from the West Indies, also assumed significance.[1] In the middle decades of the eighteenth century tobacco formed just under half of all Scottish imports, by value, from outside the United Kingdom, in 1772 accounted for 80 per cent of all imports from North America and the West Indies combined, and in 1762 contributed 52 per cent of all Scottish exports.[2] In the perspective of Britain as a whole the achievement of the Scots traders was, in a sense, even more remarkable. In one year in the 1750's, Scottish imports of tobacco exceeded those of both London and the English outports combined. For most of the rest of the period up to the American War, the merchants of the north struggled with those of the capital for predominance. Especially during the "golden age" after about 1750, Scottish-American commerce was almost entirely controlled by the great trading houses of Glasgow. In the ten years 1766–76, for instance, only a mere 2 per cent of

---

[1] For the rise of the American and West India trades see T. C. Smout, 'The Development and Enterprise of Glasgow, 1556–1707', *Scottish Journal of Political Economy*, VII (1960); Jacob M. Price, 'The Rise of Glasgow in the Chesapeake Tobacco Trade, 1707–75', reprinted in P. L. Payne, ed. *Studies in Scottish Business History* (1967), pp. 299–318; Jacob M. Price, *France and the Chesapeake* (Ann Arbor, Michigan, 1973); J. H. Soltow, 'Scottish Traders in Virginia, 1750–75', *Economic History Review*, 2nd ser. XII (1959); T. C. Barker, 'Smuggling in the Eighteenth Century: the Evidence of the Scottish Tobacco Trade', *The Virginia Magazine of History and Biography* (1954); T. M. Devine, 'Sources of Capital for the Glasgow Tobacco Trade, c. 1740–80', *Business History*, XVI (1974); T. M. Devine, *The Tobacco Lords* (Edinburgh, 1975). I am grateful to my colleagues, Prof. S. G. E. Lythe and Dr John Butt, for their comments on earlier drafts of this article.

[2] Price, loc. cit. 299–301.

tobacco imports was landed outside the twin satellite ports of Greenock and Port Glasgow.

The success of the Clyde ports in Atlantic commerce has not failed to attract the attention of historians. But, by and large, there has been little examination of the possible links between this trading activity and the expansion of the Scottish domestic economy. Indeed, until fairly recently it was simply assumed that the growth of the tobacco trade must have had a major impact on the more primitive indigenous economy through the effect of demand pressures and the impact of capital flows. It was once acceptable, for example, to explain the late eighteenth-century development of the cotton industry as the fruit of a transfer of resources from the tobacco trade (which, according to this interpretation, had collapsed during the American War of Independence) to manufacturing.[1] Few economic historians would now accept these *simpliste* arguments. Several writers in the last two decades have emphasized how Atlantic commerce was essentially an entrepôt trade, the multiplier effects from which were likely to have been slight. The lack of evidence for any important examples of links between "trade" and "industry" has also been stressed and it has been fairly shown that it is not possible to develop a reasonable argument on the basis of a few instances culled in the main from secondary sources.[2]

Nevertheless, some doubt still surrounds this whole issue, if only because the problem has not yet been assessed in a systematic manner through the study of relevant original material. Here it is the intension to examine one facet of the question, namely the extent of capital movement between "trade" and "industry", through the examination of several extant sources which all contain information on the investments of eighteenth-century Glasgow colonial merchants. This material can be grouped in six categories: (1) business records: the private accounts of several traders are available;[3] (2) local and national registers of deeds: these contain contracts of copartnership and other legal documentation of mercantile financial interests;[4] (3) legal processes in Court of Session records;[5]

[1] H. Hamilton, *The Industrial Revolution in Scotland* (1932), p. 121; L. J. Saunders, *Scottish Democracy, 1815–40: The Social and Intellectual Background* (Edinburgh, 1950), p. 98; J. Cunnison and J. B. S. Gilfillan, eds. *The Third Statistical Account of Scotland: Glasgow Region* (Glasgow, 1958), p. 103.

[2] M. L. Robertson, 'Scottish Commerce and the American War of Independence', *Econ. Hist. Rev.* 2nd ser. IX (1956), 130; H. Hamilton, *An Economic History of Scotland in the Eighteenth Century* (1963), pp. 142, 168; R. H. Campbell, 'An Economic History of Scotland in the Eighteenth Century', *Scottish Journal of Political Economy*, XI (1964), 19; R. H. Campbell, 'The Anglo-Scottish Union of 1707: II The Economic Consequences', *Econ. Hist. Rev.* 2nd ser. XVI (1964), 472; R. H. Campbell, *Scotland since 1707* (1965), p. 40; R. H. Campbell, 'The Industrial Revolution in Scotland: A Revision Article', *Scottish Historical Review*, XLVI (1967), 47; R. H. Campbell, 'The Union and Economic Growth', in T. I. Rae, ed. *The Union of 1707: Its Impact on Scotland* (1974), pp. 63–4; T. C. Smout, *History of the Scottish People, 1560–1830* (1969).

[3] Glasgow City Archives (G.C.A.): Smith of Jordanhill Papers; Dunlop Legal Papers; Oswald Account Book; Sederunt Book of the Trust of George Oswald; Sederunt Book of James Somervell, 1791–7; Journal of John Leitch, 1798–1806; Speirs Papers (Xerox copies, originals in the possession of Major Crichton-Maitland, Houston House, Houston, Renfrewshire). James Finlay & Co., Glasgow: Finlay MSS. Mitchell Library, Glasgow (M.L.): Bogle MSS; Campbell of Hallyards Papers. Baillie's Institution Library, Glasgow: Sederunt Book of Archibald Ingram. Scottish Record Office, Edinburgh (S.R.O.): McDowall of Garthland Papers; Papers of William Cunninghame; Papers of the Buchanans of Auchintorlie.

[4] G.C.A. B.10/15, Burgh Court Register of Deeds; B.10/12, Burgh Court Register of Probative Writs. S.R.O. Register of Deeds.

[5] S.R.O. Unextracted Processes; Bill Chamber Processes; RH 15 series of business records extracted from Court of Session records; Signet Library, Edinburgh (S.L.), printed session papers.

COLONIAL TRADES 3

(4) Register of Sasines: this incorporates all deeds of land transfer in Scotland and sometimes includes details of industrial partnerships involved in land negotiations;[1] (5) wills and testaments;[2] (6) newspapers and contemporary journals: these often contain details on the establishment or ending of parternship agreements.[3]

II

The first conclusion that can be drawn from these data is that it was fairly common for merchants to hold industrial investments. According to my calculations,[4] there were 163 Glasgow merchants of partnership status involved in the American trades between about 1740 and 1790. Eighty-five of this number had a share in at least one copartnery engaged in manufacturing and extractive industry. Several, however, especially among the élite of the merchant group, had multiple interests in a variety of concerns. Between about 1770 and 1815, 21 traders held capital in one industrial firm, 19 in two, 11 in three and nine in four. Of the remainder, three merchants had money in six units, one in seven, three in eight, one in nine and two in ten. The peerless James Dunlop, mainly because of his extensive coal-mining investments, held sums of varying amounts in no less than 17 different partnerships.[5]

Again, if the sources examined do give a reasonable indication of trends, it is possible to suggest a broad correlation between the expansion of such industrial interests, commercial success in the tobacco trade and the changing condition of the domestic economy. The period between 1660 and 1730 witnessed in effect the infancy of Scottish transatlantic commerce. Before 1707, illicit trade with England's colonies inevitably operated within narrow limits. After the Treaty of Union, an early phase of rapid advance was followed by an era of stagnation as temporary depression in tobacco markets and more rigorous customs administration combined to keep the rate of development at a stubbornly low level.[6] These years up to about 1730 were apparently reflected in marginal merchant commitment to industry, only nine manufactories being established by colonial traders between 1660 and 1730. In the following period, however, the accumulation of surpluses as a result of major trade expansion and, perhaps also, parallel advances in the domestic economy, encouraged a greater degree of merchant participation in industry. In the decade 1730–40, seven industrial partnerships involving tobacco merchants were established, between 1740 and 1750 an additional 11, and in the following decade, a further seven.

Merchant interests covered a wide range of industrial activities but seem by

---

[1] G.C.A. Burgh Register of Sasines. S.R.O. General Register of Sasines; Particular Register of Sasines.
[2] S.R.O. Commissariat of Glasgow Wills and Testaments.
[3] *Glasgow Mercury; Glasgow Courier; Glasgow Herald and Advertiser; Glasgow Advertiser and Evening Intelligencer; Glasgow Journal; Glasgow Weekly Magazine; Glasgow Magazine and Review; Caledonian Mercury; Edinburgh Evening Courant; Edinburgh Advertiser; Scots Magazine.*
[4] For the basis of these calculations see Devine, op. cit. app. 1.
[5] Bell's Tannery, Ropework Manufactory of Glasgow, Glasgow Bottlework Co., Dumbarton Glasswork Co., Duntocher Cotton Co., Govan Coal Co., Knightswood Coal Co., Elderslie Coal Co., Fullarton Coal Co., Banknoch Coal Co., Hamilton Farm Coal Co., Sandyhills Coal Co., Rutherglen Muir Coal Co., Camlachie Coal Co., Skaetrig Coal Co., McBrayne, Stenhouse & Co., linen printers and manufacturers, Dumbarton Brewery Co.
[6] Smout, loc. cit. Price, op. cit.

4   T. M. DEVINE

and large to have been regionally concentrated in west-central Scotland, and,
in particular in the town of Glasgow itself. (See Table 1.)

Table 1. *Gross Total of Industrial Units with some Element of
Glasgow Colonial Merchant Capital in Stock, c. 1700–1815*

Manufacture	Total no. units	No. outside Glasgow	No. outside West-Central Scotland
Textiles (silk, linen, wool)	23	2	–
Textiles (cotton-spinning)	12	10	1
Textiles (finishing processes)	9	4	1
Iron (malleable)	4	–	–
Iron (pig)	3	3	–
Mining (coal)	14	8	1
Mining (other minerals)	2	–	2
Sugarhouses	7	2	–
Rope and sailcloth manufactories	3	2	–
Leather manufactories	4	–	–
Glassworks	3	2	–
Breweries	2	2	–
Soapworks	2	–	–
Tobacco-spinners	1	–	–
Potteries and delftworks	1	–	–
	90	35	5

In this area, which was the major focus of rapid economic growth in eighteenth-
century Scotland, entire industries were dominated by the capital of "tobacco
lords" and West India merchant princes. Each of the three Glasgow companies
concerned with the tanning of leather and boot and shoe manufacture were
under their control in the 1770's and 1780's (see Table 2).

Table 2. *Glasgow Tobacco Merchants and the West of Scotland Leather Industry*

Tannery	Merchant partners	Capital	Merchant share
Bell's Tannery (1770)	John Coats Campbell, John Bowman, James Dunlop, Lawrence Dinwiddie, Alexander Speirs	?	75 per cent
Glasgow Tanwork Co. (1777)	John Bowman, Alex. Speirs, Robert Bogle, Walter Monteath	?	90 per cent
Francis Hamilton and Co. (1764)	Hugh Wylie, Francis Hamilton	£2,400	50 per cent

Sources: S.R.O. Register of Deeds, 232/817 MACK; G.C.A. Register of Sasines
10/30–1, 14 March, 1777, 10/198–202, 6 Dec. 1793; G.C.A. Register of Deeds,
B.10/15/7651.

Furthermore, as befitted their position in the Atlantic trades, the Clyde ports
developed as the centres of a vigorous sugar-processing industry in the later
eighteenth century. Between 1750 and 1810 there were four major sugar houses
in Glasgow itself and, in addition, two in Port Glasgow and two in Greenock.
All these ventures attracted the capital of colonial merchants (see Table 3).

A similar pattern of merchant dominance is reflected in the rope and sailcloth
industries of the Clyde region. In the 1770's, James Corbett and Co., "the Rope

COLONIAL TRADES 5

Table 3. *Glasgow Colonial Merchants and the West of Scotland Sugar Industry,
c. 1740–1817*

Sugar House	Merchant partners	Capital	Merchant share
South Sugar House (1740's–96)	Alex. Houston, William McDowall, George Alexander, and James Oswald	£8,000	5/6
King St Sugar House (1780's–90's)	James Buchanan, Andrew Buchanan, Thomas Wallace	£6,000	90 per cent
Easter Sugar House	George Bogle	?	?
Wester Sugar House (1773)	Alexander Speirs	?	?
Greenock Sugar House (1765)	James Hopkirk, Arthur Connell	?	?
Greenock Sugar-House (1788)	John Campbell sen., James Gordon, Henry Riddell	?	80 per cent
Port Glasgow Sugar House	George and William Crawford, Andrew Buchanan, William Cunninghame, Robert Dunmore	?	?
Sugar House Co. of Port Glasgow (1770'2)	John Leitch, Richard Dennistoun John Gordon, David Russell	?	50 per cent
Newark Sugar Refinery (1809–17)	Robert Dennistoun, Alexander Campbell, James Campbell	?	?

Sources: S.R.O. Unextracted Process, Innes Durie B7/1; S.R.O. GD237/139, Minute of Meeting of Partners of South Sugar House; S.R.O. GD237/143/4; M. L. Bogle MSS, Bundle 54; G.C.A. Speirs Papers, TD131/4–5; S.R.O., Particular Register of Sasines (Renfrew), 25/50, 41/89; M.L., Campbell of Hallyards Papers, Trustees of R. Dennistoun to trustees of A. Campbell, 15 Dec. 1823; *Glasgow Mercury,* 29 Dec. 1789; *Glasgow Courier,* 29 Nov. 1798.

Manufactory of Glasgow", had fifteen partners. Ten of them were involved in the Atlantic trades.[1] George Buchanan Jr, James Somervell, James Dennistoun, and James McDowall, four well-known "tobacco lords", were the principal figures in the 1780's, in a separate firm, the Glasgow Ropework Co.[2] At Greenock, the two Ritchie brothers, James and Henry, owned 75 per cent of the shares in the town's rope manufactory while the Port Glasgow Ropework Co. had Alexander Speirs and Thomas Hopkirk among its partners.[3]

In the last 30 years of the eighteenth century a tight-knit and exclusive group of tobacco importers acquired control of almost the entire west of Scotland glass industry. Through a complicated series of mergers and the creation of some new foundations a giant industrial complex had evolved by about 1795. In 1786, the total capital of the original partnership group, which included Peter Murdoch, James Gordon, James Hopkirk, Thomas Donald, and Andrew Houston, amounted to £12,000 divided between two glass-making concerns.[4] By 1813, this

[1] G.C.A. Register of Sasines, 23 Oct. 1789; S.R.O. GD532/1, Disposition and Assignation, the partners of the Glasgow Ropeworks to John Hay and others (1786).
[2] *Glasgow Mercury,* 8 Dec. 1785.
[3] S.R.O. Register of Deeds, 246/1/580 DAL; S.R.O. CC9/7/80/514, Testament of Thomas Hopkirk; G.C.A. Speirs Papers, TD1/131/5, Ledger C.
[4] G.C.A. Register of Sasines, registered 11 Nov. 1793; S.R.O. Register of Deeds, 216/802 DAL; S.R.O. Unextracted Process, Currie Nack, D/5/14, Memorial for the partners of the Dumbarton Glasswork Co.; S.L. Court of Session Process 422/53.

6   T. M. DEVINE

figure had risen to £84,000 and the operations of the company had been expanded to involve the Dumbarton Glasswork Co. (the title of the partnership by
1813), the flint glass manufactory at Verreville, the Greenock Bottlework Co.,
the Glasswork Co., and two brewery firms.[1]

III

The two critical industrial developments in eighteenth-century Scotland were
the advance of the "heavy" industries of coal and iron and the even more crucial
expansion of textile manufacture, notably in linen and cotton. The evidence
suggests, at least in the important west-central region, that tobacco traders were
one of the investing groups involved in these changes and that their role was
particularly significant in the mining and metallurgical industries.

Two of the three malleable ironworks in Scotland at this time were situated in
the Glasgow area. Both of these—the Smithfield and Dalnottar companies—
were financed by colonial merchants. The former was founded in 1734 when a
number of traders erected a slitting mill on the banks of the River Kelvin to
manufacture nails for sale in North America;[2] the latter was set up 35 years later
by the Murdochs and William Cunninghame, "for the manufacturing of hoes,
bills, axes, spades, raills, hinges, anchors, belts and every kind or species of
ironware also of making of Barr plate and red iron barr steel of the different kinds
and all manner of steelwork". The initial capital stock of £6,000 was increased to
£12,000 in 1787.[3]

In the later eighteenth and early nineteenth century, the expansion of the
English pig-iron industry was reflected, albeit on a much smaller scale, in development of Scottish pig-iron production. Between 1779 and 1815, nine separate
units were formed with a total furnace capacity which rose from 4,000 tons in
1780 to 32,000 in 1813.[4] In one of these, Muirkirk Iron Co. (established in 1787),
colonial traders held over 75 per cent of the share capital, and they also had
interests in two others, Shotts (established in 1801) and Clyde (established in
1784).[5]

Most tobacco merchants owned estates and the majority of their properties
lay across the rich seams of the central coalfield.[6] Some were content simply to
lease their land to persons experienced in the extraction industries—an option
guaranteed to cut the risks inherent in any eighteenth-century mining activity.[7]

[1] S.R.O. Unextracted Process, Currie Mack D/5/14; Register of Deeds, 246/1/580 DAL; Adams Mack
Misc. 22, Day Book of Dumbarton Glasswork Co., Balance Book of Dumbarton Glasswork Co. See also
John C. Logan, 'The Dumbarton Glasswork Company: A Study in Entrepreneurship', *Bus. Hist.* xiv
(1972), 61–81.
[2] S.R.O. GD237/151/3; *Glasgow Mercury*, 1 July 1784, 1 Dec. 1785, 8 June 1786.
[3] G.C.A. Register of Deeds, B.10/15/7460; S.R.O. Register of Deeds, 249/829 DUR; S.L. Court of
Session Processes 180/8, 409/22.
[4] John Butt, 'The Scottish Iron Industry before the Hot Blast', *Journal of the West of Scotland Iron and Steel
Institute*, xxiii (1965–6).
[5] S.R.O. GD237/151/3, Contract of Copartnery of Muirkirk Iron Co.; Register of Deeds 260/358 DUR;
Currie Dal, C/11/9, Clyde Ironworks versus Collin Dunlop; Bill Chamber Process, ii, 39,288 (1816).
[6] T. M. Devine, 'Glasgow Colonial Merchants and Land, c. 1770–1815' in J. T. Ward and R. G.
Wilson, eds. *Land and Industry* (Newton Abbot, 1971).
[7] B. F. Duckham, *History of the Scottish Coal Industry* (Newton Abbot, 1970), ch. vi. For one such case see
S.L. Court of Session Process, 374/5, Petition of Andrew Houston esq. of Jordanhill and others . . . 2.

Others, however, preferred to engage directly in the process and shouldered all the burdens of capital expenditure. Thus, Thomas Hopkirk financed the working of coal on his lands of Dalbeth.[1] Archibald Smellie "wrought extensively the coal" on his estate of Easterhill.[2] As the majority share-holder in the Monkland Canal, completed in 1793, and as the owner of property which lay across the extraordinarily rich Monklands coalfield, Andrew Stirling, scion of a famous family of Virginia merchants, had the motivation to exploit his mineral resources on a considerable scale. He went on to form "the Monkland Coal Co." with an initial capital of £3,500, of which he held four-sevenths.[3]

In the later eighteenth century there was a proliferation of coal companies such as these in the western Lowlands and "tobacco lords" were involved in several of them. William French owned half the capital in the Easter Barrachney "coal-work" which operated mines about three miles from Glasgow.[4] From 1793 the Sandyhills and Camlachie Coal Works in Lanarkshire were carried on by a syndicate which included the Dennistoun family. They were also interested in the Dunmore Coal Co. in Fife.[5] The most striking example of merchant activity in mining, however, was the role of the two great dynasties, the Dunlops and the Houstons, in the coal-bearing area around Glasgow. In June 1768 a coal tack was granted by the Town Council of Glasgow to Colin Dunlop, Alexander Houston, Gabriel Gray, and James McNair, to work lands in Gorbals and Govan.[6] Houston and Dunlop were involved in both the American and Caribbean trades. The latter two were "experts" in mining. This venture was only the initial phase in a project which was eventually to include mines in three counties and which was to end in the partners being accused of trying to organize a monopoly of the west of Scotland coal trade. Between 1768 and 1773, a series of coal-tacks was awarded the company in Dumbartonshire, in Knightswood, and in Jordanhill.[7] In 1773, Colin Dunlop's son, James, joined the firm and by that date the Little Govan Coalworks and the Knightswood Coal Co. were their "principal objects". In 1800 the first of these was valued at £20,000.[8] The deaths of the two original partners did not interrupt the momentum of expansion. James Dunlop and Andrew Houston carried on the policies of their fathers in buying up mineral rights in the barony of Glasgow and in Lanarkshire. Dunlop in these years probably became the most powerful coalmaster in the west of Scotland. In 1793, it was reckoned the value of "utensils", machinery, and waggonways alone at his various collieries was in the region of £30,000. He "engaged . . . in merchandise, in shipping, in the coal trade to a great extent and embarked in almost every mercantile undertaking". His largest mine within his own lands lay at Fullarton in Lanarkshire. Within a 16-year period from 1777 to 1793, Dunlop expended £10,000 on this single venture. He also had a three-eighths share in the Elderslie

[1] G.C.A. Dunlop Legal Papers, Disposition of John Dunlop in favour of Thos. Edington (1795).

[2] Anon. *Old Country Houses of the Old Glasgow Gentry* (Glasgow, 1870), xxxvii.

[3] G.C.A. Register of Deeds, B.10/15/9695, Contract of Copartnership among Andrew Stirling and others.

[4] *Glasgow Mercury*, 10 Oct. 1787.

[5] Ibid. 15 Oct. 1793; *Glasgow Herald and Advertiser*, 25 July, 1808.

[6] S.R.O. Register of Deeds, 259/809 DUR; S.R.O. Bill Chamber Process, I, 29,063.

[7] Ibid. 259/869 DUR; 292/758 DUR.

[8] S.R.O. GD237/139. For the subsequent history of these works see P. L. Payne, 'The Govan Collieries, 1804-5', *Bus. Hist.* III (1961).

8   T. M. DEVINE

Coal Co., which worked mines in Renfrewshire, a 50 per cent interest in Rutherglen Muir Coal Co. and owned a quarter of the capital in the Sandyhill Coal
Work. In addition, he was involved in the Banknock, Camlachie, and Hamilton
Farm coal companies and had a majority share in the New Smithills Coalwork,
near Paisley.[1]

Until well into the nineteenth century textile manufacture was the single
biggest industrial sector in Scotland. Tobacco merchants invested in a wide range
of linen manufacturing and bleaching concerns in and around Glasgow (see
Table 4):

Table 4. *Tobacco Merchants and the Linen Industry in
West-central Scotland, c. 1700–1800*

Firm	First-known decade of merchant involvement
Haarlem Linen and Dye Manufactory	1730–9
Glasgow Inkle Factory Co	
Shuttlefield Factory Co.	
Cumberland Factory Co.	
Pollockshaws Printfield Co.	1740–9
Milngavie Factory Co.	
Silvercraigs Weaving Factory Co.	
Holland Manufactory Co.	
Brown, Carrick & Co.	
And. Buchanan & Co.	1760–9
Cudbear Works Co.	
Graham, Liddell & Co.	
James McGregor & Co.	1770–9
Joshua Johnston & Co.	
McBrayne, Stenhouse & Co.	
Coats, Campbell	1780–9
A. and J. Newbigging & Co.	
Milton Printworks	
Endrick Printfield Co.	
John Renfrew & Co.	1790–9
Spreul, Somervell & Co.	
Kilbarchan Bleachfield Co.	

Sources: G.C.A., Burgh Court Register of Deeds; S.R.O.,
Register of Deeds; Glasgow newspapers; S.L. Court of Session
Processes.

Some of these firms were pioneers of their type. The manufacture of inkles began
in Scotland in 1741 when Alexander Harvie brought back knowledge of the
process from Haarlem in Holland.[2] From that date until the 1780's, the "Inkle
Factory" was financed by a succession of colonial traders.[3] The most successful
printing and bleaching concern in the west of Scotland was William Stirling &
Sons but the fortune of the family had originally been made in the Virginia
trades.[4] Another outstanding figure in the development of bleaching technology

[1] *Glasgow Courier*, 15 May 1794, 17 Dec. 1791; *Glasgow Journal*, 7 Jan. 1794; S.R.O. Unextracted Process, 1 Adams Mack S/15/106; Register of Deeds, 292/158 DUR; Particular Register of Sasines (barony
of Glasgow), 26/215; G.C.A. Dunlop Legal Papers, State of the Funds of James Dunlop, 23 March,
1793; S.L. Court of Session Process 406/21.
[2] "Inkle" was a kind of linen tape.
[3] G.C.A. Register of Deeds, B.10/15/5664, 6849; Speirs Papers, TD131/4.
[4] John McCure, *A View of the City of Glasgow* (1736), p. 170.

was James McGregor. His firm was the first to use chlorine as a bleaching agent in Scotland and he was backed financially in his activities by such "tobacco lords" as James and Henry Glassford and John McCall.[1] The Glassford family also had interests in two other famous manufactories of the period, the Glasgow Cudbear Works and the Prestonpans Vitriol Co. The foundation of the latter in 1749 has been described by Prof. Henry Hamilton as "an epoch-making step in the history of bleaching".[2] In 1779, the first of these was managed by George Mackintosh and by Adam Grant, "dyer in Glasgow". The bulk of the capital, however, was supplied by John Glassford, James Gordon, George Bogle, and John Robertson, who were all extensively committed to the colonial trades.[3] Over a decade earlier, Glassford had become a member of the Prestonpans Vitriol Co. By the 1790's, his son held all the shares in the business.[4]

The relationship between colonial merchant capital and the new cotton industry particularly invites examination. In the period selected for special study this alone experienced the rapid expansion, massive productivity gains, and novel technological innovation characteristic of an "Industrial Revolution". Moreover, as has been already observed, an earlier generation of writers thought that the industry's speedy rise from the 1770's could be explained in terms of a transfer of capital from foreign trade to domestic manufacturing as colonial merchants desperately sought new investments to replace the "lost" tobacco trade during the American War. Recently material has become available in this *Review* which allows this theory to be tested.[5] Dr S. D. Chapman in 1970 published a list of Scottish cotton-spinning companies functioning in the year 1795. Clearly there are some dangers in using these data as the basis of a measurement of the significance of mercantile capital in the industry. Chapman's enumeration includes only those firms which held insurance policies with the Sun Fire Office in London. Inevitably, therefore, his list is incomplete. In addition, the difficulties in using insurance valuations as criteria for measuring patterns in fixed capital formation are now well known.[6] Again, in this particular case, it might be argued that consideration only of the year 1795 might underestimate the role of the colonial merchants because it antedated their investment in such major ventures as the New Lanark Co. and James Finlay & Co. By the early nineteenth century these were among the most important units in Scottish cotton manufacturing.[7]

[1] *Glasgow Mercury*, 19 Jan. 1790.   [2] Hamilton, *Economic History of Scotland*, p. 140.
[3] S.R.O. Register of Deeds, 295/143 DAL; Particular Register of Sasines (Glasgow), 26/97; G.C.A. Register of Deeds, B.10/15/8132, 9009.
[4] S.R.O. Bill Chamber Process, II, 38,634; Register of Deeds, 279/387 DUR, 275/286 MACK; S.L. Court of Session Process 438/18.
[5] S. D. Chapman, 'Fixed Capital Formation in the British Cotton Industry, 1770–1815', *Econ. Hist. Rev.*, 2nd ser. XXIII (1970).
[6] S. Pollard and J. P. P. Higgins, eds. *Aspects of Capital Investment in Great Britain, 1750–1850* (1971), pp. 108-13.
[7] From 1810 three West India merchants, Robert Dennistoun, Alexander Campbell and Colin Campbell provided £80,000 (or just slightly less than half the total) to the capital stock of the New Lanark Co.—S.R.O. GD64/1/247, Contract of Copartnery of New Lanark Co. 5 Oct. 1810. From the mid-1790's, Leitch, Smith & Co. and Somervell, Gordon & Co., traders to America and the West Indies, held one-third of the stock of £75,000 in James Finlay & Co. who by the early nineteenth century owned three of the biggest water-powered mills in Scotland.—James Finlay and Co., Glasgow, Finlay MSS, Balance Book, 1789-1800.

Yet these are not insurmountable obstacles. The intention here is merely to discern in *approximate* terms the role of Glasgow colonial traders in cotton spinning. Examination of a later period would probably have diminished their significance. Formation of new cotton ventures continued unabated in the later 1790's and early 1800's and yet, according to the sources consulted, this was not paralleled by similar increases in merchant investment. Moreover, as far as this analysis is concerned, where only the relationship between the sizes of various units is relevant, Chapman's data are likely to be of value since they do contain most firms in which colonial merchants had interests in 1795.

Dr Chapman suggested that the policy valuations of Scottish cotton mills approached £292,180 in that year. The valuation of companies financed wholly or partly by colonial traders was calculated at £50,100 or about 17 per cent of the total figure (see Table 5):

Table 5. *Scottish Cotton Firms and Colonial Merchant Investment, c. 1795*

Firm	Location of mill	Policy valuation (with position on list)	Colonial merchant partners	Merchant share of capital	Source
Ballindalloch Mill Co.	Balfron, Stirling	£10,300 (3)	Robert Dunmore	⅓	S.L. Court of Session Process 368/21
George Houston & Co.	Johnstone, Renfrew	£7,800 (12)	William McDowall	⅓	S.R.O. GD237/134
Linwood Mill Co.	Paisley, Renfrew	£7,000 (16)	James and Alex. Oswald	⅓	S.R.O. Particular Register of Sasines (Renfrew) 48/229
Deanston Cotton Mill Co.	Deanston, Perthshire	£7,700 (14)	Messrs. Leitch and Smith; Somervell, Gordon & Co.	½	James Finlay & Co., Glasgow. Finlay MSS, Balance Book, 1789–1800
Houston, Burns & Co.	Lochwinnoch, Renfrew	£6,900 (15)	William McDowall	⅓	S.R.O. GD 237/134
Reynolds, Monteach & Co.	Glasgow	£2,800 (35)	James Dennistoun, James Dennistoun Jr	⅓	S.R.O. Particular Register of Sasines (Renfrew) 42/217
James Monteath & Co.	Anderston	£8,300 (9)	James Dennistoun, James Dennistoun Jr	⅓	S.R.O. Particular Register of Sasines (Renfrew) 42/217

Notes:

1. Firms and policy valuations are extracted from Chapman, loc. cit. 262–3.

2. One other firm operating at this time for which no policy is listed was the Culcreuch Cotton Spinning Co., established 1792. The Speirs and Murdoch families, colonial merchants, held half of the £6,000 share capital.—S.R.O. Cunninghame Graham Muniments, GD22/1/219, Contract of Copartnery of Culcreuch Cotton Spinning Co. 26 July 1792.

3. Six tobacco merchants (Andrew, James, and William Robertson, Robert Dunmore, Robert Bogle, and Robert Mackay) had earlier helped to finance an unsuccessful jenny factory on George Dempster's estate of Skibo on the Dornoch Firth. They provided £500 of the £2,300 capital.—Sinclair Calder, 'The Industrial Archaeology of Sutherland' (unpublished M.Litt. thesis, University of Strathclyde, 1974), p. 118.

Evidently, therefore, the colonial merchants represented a minority financial interest in the industry and even in those firms in which they had a share they never supplied more than half of the total capital. In addition, such investments as did occur were not conditioned by a desire to transfer assets from the tobacco trade. Rather they were related to a continuing process, which as we have seen long antedated the American War, of diversification coupled with retention of major interests in overseas commerce. After 1783, the great Glasgow tobacco houses managed to re-establish links once again with their planter customers in the United States, though the bulk of the American produce they now acquired was shipped directly to Europe without paying duty at U.K. entrepôts. There was thus no need to redeploy investments elsewhere.[1] On the contrary, merchant correspondence indicates that commercial difficulties in the 1780's meant that resources had to be concentrated on the American sector.[2] This may explain why no less than 17 of the 25 merchants who did join cotton partnerships were primarily involved in Caribbean rather than in North American trade. It was they who were importing the "sea-island" cotton on which, until the last few years of the century, the new industry flourished. There were obvious possibilities for integration.

IV

No single explanation can satisfactorily account for all the instances of industrial investment described in this article. In some cases they developed through a straightforward process of vertical integration. The Clyde tobacco trade required access to a variety of industrial producers because, put simply, the system operated by the Scottish merchants involved the exchange of consumer goods for the primary produce of Virginia and Maryland. This entrepôt trade, however, developed from an economy with only a primitive industrial structure. In the west of Scotland there were few manufactories in the early eighteenth century of the scale needed to cater for the bulk and quality requirements of the merchant houses. The Rev. Alexander Carlyle, who had been a student at Glasgow in the 1740's, wrote that, "There were not manufacturers sufficient either there or at Paisley to supply an outward-bound cargo for Virginia. For this purpose they were obliged to have recourse to Manchester. Manufacturers were in their infancy."[3] One alternative, as Carlyle indicated, was to look outside Scotland for suppliers; another was for "tobacco lords" to found their own ventures when their financial position allowed.

The search for additional returns was also likely as merchants sought to employ spare funds, spread risk, and divert at least some of their capital away from the profitable, though notoriously hazardous, Atlantic trades. Accruals were used to extend commercial operations but since the benefits of size were limited and fixed capital requirements few, there was an incentive also to diversify. Because dividends from shares in tobacco firms were rigorously controlled,

---

[1] Devine, op. cit. ch. 11; Price, op. cit. 728–31; W. A. Low, 'Merchant and Planter Relations in Post-Revolutionary Virginia, 1783–89', *Virginia Magazine of History and Biography*, LXI (1953), 308–17.

[2] Library of Congress, Washington, James Dunlop Family Papers.

[3] J. H. Burton, ed. *Autobiography of the Rev. Dr. Alexander Carlyle containing Memorials of the Men and Events of his time* (Edinburgh, 1860), p. 73. This point is substantiated in M. L. Bogle MSS, George Bogle's letterbook, 1725–31.

12   T. M. DEVINE

persons who wished to maximize income sought alternatives.[1] This process may
have been facilitated because, at least in the first half of the eighteenth century,
Scotland seems to have suffered from a deficiency of capital in relation to investment opportunities. Entrepreneurs, managers, and technical experts with trade
contacts and relevant skills, but in need of finance, commonly combined with
wealthy overseas traders. The typical pattern was for the merchants to act as
sleeping partners in the manufactory, in many cases providing the bulk of the
capital stock and normally relying on skilled personnel to superintend the daily
routine of production and management. The expansion of structure of this kind
was possible because in Scots law, as a consequence of its Roman law antecedents,
the partnership was a separate legal entity within which the rights of members,
including those who did not actively participate in the business, could be safe-
guarded in a precise fashion.[2] Finally, merchant interest in industry often
occurred as a result of the ownership of a landed estate; exploitation of all the
economic possibilities of properties implied not simply fashionable agricultural
"improvement" but also, in an age of rising mineral rentals and mill-site values,
investment in mining, bleachfields, and cotton firms.

The effect of the deployment of merchant resources on the domestic economy
is less easy to judge. It would be rash, for instance, to conclude that the mercantile
role in industry which has been documented in this article can be taken, without
qualification, to be indicative of a straightforward flow of profits from the tobacco
trade to the domestic sector. The wealth of most of these merchants was not based

Table 6. *The Investment Pattern of Four Glasgow Tobacco Merchants*

Merchant	Date	Summary of financial interests
Alexander Morson	1768	Share in a Boston concern; $\frac{1}{3}$ share in the brigantine *Bell*; £503 13s. in P. & W. Bogle, tobacco importers; £400 in Jamaica concern with Ebenezer Munro; share in a coal and copper mine; £22 18s. 5d. owed him by Neil Jamieson, merchant in Norfolk, Virginia; £100 in insurance venture; share in a plaiding concern with Ebenezer Munro.
Alexander Speirs	1770	Stocks in concerns: "Virginia concern", £55,057 4s. od.; "Maryland concern", £7,410 19s. 9d.; Value of landed pro-perty, £49,050; domestic industry and banks, £18,141 3s. 7½d.; "Occasional transactions", including canal shares, £1,778 9s. 4½d.
William Cunninghame	1790's	Income: John Ferguson & Co. (formerly R. Dunmore & Co.), West India and American merchants, £3,255 6s. od.; land rentals, £3,696 6s. od.; East India stock, £436 5s. 6d.; govern-ment stock, £104 4s. 5d.; bills receivable: £13 os. od.
James Somervell	1791	Shares in various concerns: Somervell, Gordon & Co., £8,503; David Russell & Co., £4,936; money lent on bond to: Findlay, Hopkirks & Co. (tobacco merchants), £1,000; Corbett, Russell & Co. (tobacco merchants), £2,000; Henry Hardie & Co. (linen printers and merchants), £1,000; Muirkirk Iron Co., £1,000; Port Glasgow Ropework Co., £3,000; Tanwork Co., £3,000.

Sources: G.C.A. Register of Deeds, B.10/15/7173, 7174; Speirs Papers, TD131/6/14, States of the Private
Affairs of A. Speirs, Dec. 1770; Sederunt Book of James Somervell, 1791–97, 13; S.R.O. GD 237/151/3
(Copy), State of Mr Dunmore's subjects as on 25 Oct. 1793; GD247/141, Jotting of income of W.
Cunninghame, 2 Oct. 1800.

[1] Devine, loc. cit. (1974).
[2] R. H. Campbell, 'The Law and the Joint-Stock Company in Scotland', in Payne, op. cit. pp. 139–49.

exclusively on returns from American commerce but rested rather on a series of accruals from foreign trade, banking, insurance, land, and government stock (see Table 6). Further, their investments, it would appear, rarely filtered outside the west-central region and do not seem to have played a critical part in the evolution of the important cotton industry. Again, since tobacco firms themselves borrowed from monied groups within Scotland, to facilitate expansion of their businesses, it is a matter of speculation whether the domestic economy gained or lost by the consequent series of complicated credit transactions.[1] What can be said, however, is that merchant industrial investment was very significant in Glasgow and its environs, especially between about 1730 and 1790. Many of the ventures established perhaps might not have evolved if they had not answered specific needs in colonial markets or within the regime of individual traders. Paradoxically, the merchant aristocracy was at least partly responsible for the town's slow metamorphosis from a trading to an industrial centre.[2]

University of Strathclyde

[1] Devine, loc. cit. (1974).
[2] The *Glasgow Courier* commented in 1791, *before* the influx of steam-driven cotton mills into the city, that Glasgow was now "a manufacturing instead of a mercantile town", 8 Sept. 1791.

Part III
France

[11]

The slave and colonial trade in France just before the Revolution

PATRICK VILLIERS

THE production and consumption of colonial products increased considerably during the eighteenth century in the economies of France and the rest of Western Europe. Ernest Labrousse emphasized this in his thesis:[1]

Ce n'est ni le blé, ni le vin, ni le drap ni la toile qui soutiennent la fortune de notre pavillon mais le sucre et le café.

The statistics in money terms of French foreign trade between 1716 and 1772 corroborate such a view, as Table 1, produced by Bruyard, head of the Balance of Trade Office between 1756 and 1781, clearly shows.[2] Exports to the French colonies of America, as well as those of the slave trade, increased faster than other products in foreign trade. The goods coming from the colonies exceeded net imports, but above all – something contemporaries failed to notice – the French export trade to a large extent consisted in reexporting colonial products. Oriented by the mercantilist theory, the statistics of French foreign trade show a credit balance – but can we trust such estimates?

Ernest Labrousse and later Ruggiero Romano pointed out how important such statistical studies, begun in 1713, were.[3] All French merchants had to declare the goods they were exporting or importing at the offices of the *fermes* (customs). Such declarations were made in

---

[1] E. Labrousse, *La crise de l'économie française à la fin de l'Ancien Regime et au début de la Revolution*, 2 tomes (Paris, 1944), tome I, pp. 27–37.

[2] Archives Nationales, Paris, F12 1834 A. This table was established in 1780 by the Sieur Bruyard, who was in charge of the Bureau du Commerce. This source has been also published by Ruggiero Romano, *Documenti e Prime considerazioni interno alla "Balance du commerce" della Francia dal 1716 al 1780*, in *Studi in onore di A. Sapori* (Milan, 1959), pp. 1267–1300.

[3] Labrousse, p. 112; Romano, p. 1271.

Table 1. *French balance of trade, 1716–54, by Bruyard, head of the Balance of Trade Office*[a]

| Year | General trade[b] | | French West Indies[b] | | Trade with Africa |
	Imports	Exports	Imports	Exports	Imports
1716	33,386	47,059	4,484	2,106	—
1717	44,060	52,719	11,191	5,613	—
1718	42,288	71,407	13,445	7,357	—
1719	61,165	84,261	16,325	7,136	—
1720	62,297	158,031	20,884	13,170	—
1721	47,351	69,759	15,345	14,005	—
1722	61,359	90,412	20,949	19,508	—
1723	89,361	150,582	22,042	15,803	—
1724	102,962	91,391	17,852	13,459	—
1725	73,499	102,284	13,021	8,792	—
1726	68,541	95,431	12,901	12,699	—
1727	51,710	87,861	20,223	14,814	1,011
1728	66,554	105,390	17,983	17,926	221
1729	64,469	110,250	19,926	13,696	1,590
1730	70,985	103,741	20,117	9,868	2,302
1731	71,603	111,682	19,442	11,109	3,952
1732	78,647	113,248	18,219	11,951	1,285
1733	68,292	108,640	19,112	13,222	972
1734	60,300	104,227	22,501	10,820	285
1735	66,286	119,313	22,754	15,812	500
1736	75,256	119,773	30,178	17,953	959
1737	76,475	110,699	30,888	14,918	1,141
1738	88,632	126,056	31,824	19,177	1,913
1739	111,030	140,417	37,803	19,427	2,443
1740	112,279	180,265	45,961	21,904	2,421
1741	118,974	184,886	44,551	26,251	3,448
1742	103,615	177,609	50,354	27,408	2,691
1743	117,566	191,130	51,232	24,030	3,775
1744	87,820	148,476	32,307	16,008	1,106
1745	94,096	173,136	31,423	10,263	31
1746	91,584	156,010	21,994	18,442	44
1747	98,704	153,775	29,095	25,962	139
1748	114,496	149,040	20,625	26,428	1,484
1749	149,408	217,890	59,878	27,963	4,597
1750	141,949	213,253	62,034	30,449	3,471
1751	145,815	220,841	48,859	29,317	2,370
1752	166,524	230,915	61,080	47,168	4,840
1753	145,599	244,758	75,428	35,819	4,428
1754	150,230	248,521	76,891	37,436	6,126

[a]"Tabléau géneral contenant la progression annuelle de la valeur intrinsèque des marchandises estrangères de toutes espèces entrées en France comparée avec la valeur intrinsèque des marchandises de toutes espèces sorties pour l'Etranger formant la Balance du Commerce de la France avec l'Etranger depuis et compris l'année 1716, époque du travail ordonné par l'arrêt du Conseil du 29 février 1716.
[b]In thousands of pounds.

212   *Patrick Villiers*

terms of volume. The collectors of customs and their clerks in each big harbor drew up a yearly detailed account in volume for each product and each foreign country. The directors of the Chambers of Commerce then indicated the yearly average price of each commodity. And all the calculations were eventually made in Paris by clerks who wrote the final document under the supervision of the director of the Balance of Trade Office.

E. Labrousse considered that the reliability of this document was already

ce que vaudront les statistiques douanières de la seconde moitié du XIXe siècle les chiffres absolus pêcheront tous par sous-évaluation, mais pourront être retenus au moins comme chiffres relatifs comme exprimant un mouvement à défaut d'un niveau.[4]

In his thesis, published in 1972, Jean Tarrade skillfully used this source again, more particularly studying the way the prices of colonial products were estimated. He estimated that the imports of colonial goods into France were subject to an ad valorem import duty of 4%, and the customs men kept a sharp eye on it. Smuggling, though possible, was limited. But the prices were negotiated every six months. Hence a certain discrepancy arose between the average price agreed upon by the customs men and the real prices. Tarrade also established that the prices were underestimated by at least 20%, and that this probably was true throughout the century. Therefore, the statistics on the imports of colonial goods in France are reliable, taking into account these underevaluations.[5] (Table 2).

These figures show the influence of the war on the foreign trade of France, and especially on the trade with India and the slave trade. Trade with the colonies was greatly dependent on the organization of convoys that would be established after 1780.[6]

The statistics of exports to the colonies and the slave trade are not as reliable as the ones concerning imports. There was no tax on those exports. The elaboration of the export statistics was based on the trust of the trader and the professional competence of the clerks of customs.

From 1763 to 1765, exports to the French West Indies and exports for the slave trade seem to have remained stable. The great historian

---

[4] Labrousse, p. 27.
[5] Jean Tarrade, *Le commerce colonial de la France à la fin de l'ancien Regime, l'évolution du régime de l'Exclusif de 1763 à 1789,* 2 tomes (*Paris* 1972). For comparison, see tome 2, pp. 747–9, tables of the imports and exports of colonial products in weight. Archives Nationales, F12 243–7. Balance du Commerce 1773–8.
[6] Patrick Villiers, *Le commerce colonial atlantique et la guerre d'Independance des Etats-Unis d'Amerique* (New York, 1977).

Table 2. *France: Balance of trade*

Year	General trade	Exports (in *livres tournois*) French West Indies	Africa	Indies
1773	278,951,036	32,850,862	16,387,302	5,520,452
1774	271,489,349	31,131,702	9,786,032	6,522,290
1775	283,072,130	28,220,077	11,915,732	8,834,978
1776	267,124,270	42,541,189	12,603,635	6,341,025
1777	311,544,475	43,338,849	12,536,392	2,952,232
1778	237,561,694	33,247,267	3,423,138	2,352,133
1779	207,635,473	26,832,169	58,152	440,731

General trade (without the French West Indies + Africa + the Indies)

Year	General trade	Imports (in *livres tournois*) French West Indies	Africa	Indies
1773	192,031,856	114,669,107	—	24,383,638
1774	168,397,432	107,040,257	—	20,205,234
1775	161,986,095	101,108,443	—	29,884,148
1776	198,590,264	136,092,942	—	36,214,773
1777	179,500,703	174,612,031	—	1,618,641
1778	175,532,168	178,328,417	—	45,186
1779	175,138,519	32,785,725	—	237,641

General trade (without the French West Indies + Africa + the Indies)

Source: Archives nationales, F 12 243–7, Commerce extérieur, Importations et exportations, pièces diverses.

of Nantes, Gaston Martin, working on the *registres des declarations de retours* of the slave traders, which unfortunately stop just before the American War of Independence, thought that the slave trade from Nantes was at its peak between the Seven Years' War and 1778. Father Rinchon, but mainly Jean Everaert and Jean Meyer, then showed that this was not true. Paul Butel from Bordeaux and Charles Carriere from Marseille confirmed that the colonial and slave trades increased from the War of Independence to the French Revolution.[7] But is it possible to elaborate statistics for all ports and to measure the French exports to the West Indies, knowing that those earlier estimates were made on only a few specific ports?

Statistics are available that allow a comparison between the years before the War of Independence and the years 1784–5 (Table 3).

This document is quite interesting, as it shows the average prices

[7] Paul Butel, *Les negociants bordelais, l'Europe et les Negociants marseillais au XVIIIe siecle*, 2 vols. (Marseille, 1973); Jean Everaert, "*Les fluctuations du commerce negrier nantais, 1763–1792,*" *Cahiers de Tunisie*, Vol. 43 (1963), pp. 37–62; Jean Meyer, *l'Armement nantias dans la deuxième moitié du XVIIIe siècle*, (Paris, 1969).

214   Patrick Villiers

Table 3. *Imports of colonial products to the harbours of Bordeaux, Nantes, Le Havre, Marseille, La Rochelle, and Dunkerque (thousands)*

	1774		1775		1784		1785	
	Quantity	Value	Quantity	Value	Quantity	Value	Quantity	Value
Raw sugar	57,409	15,116	47,749	13,423	55,256	16,768	80,318	26,418
White sugar	87,027	33,752	76,793	32,247	91,945	43,918	15,928	58,119
Coffee	61,945	31,213	64,844	29,511	65,337	50,914	72,478	58,055
Cotton	3,455	5,537	3,743	7,479	4,692	8,487	6,923	15,345
Indigo	13,961	13,147	12,627	9,210	8,600	7,236	16,851	15,114
Cacao	1,260	1,328	1,195	1,369	1,800	1,093	2,532	1,564
Total	213,037	100,697	195,596	93,240	220,653	135,238	279,876	174,618

Source: Archives Nationales, fonds Marine C5 53, f. 35, 28 October 1786. The "total" includes the value or weight of all the imported goods (including goods such as rocou, gayac... Quantities were measured in *livres pesant* (i.e., pounds). Value was measured in *livres tournois* (French money in the eighteenth century).

that had to be retained to go from the information given in volume to the information given in value. Unfortunately, it is only based on the results of goods for the period 1783–4. Those data emphasize the importance of colonial reexports in the French foreign trade.

In addition to these data sources, I demonstrate that by studying the French trading fleet (especially the colonial fleet from 1783 to 1792, with particular attention to the slave ship fleet between 1789 and 1792), we can improve our estimates of French trade. Data on the size and tonnage of vessels in the colonial trade, when properly interpreted, are a valuable new resource.

In 1784, the Maréchal de Castries, minister of the French Navy, wanted to know the consequences of the War of Independence for the French trade fleet. He asked his collaborators for numerous statistical inquiries. The shipbuilding inquiry was studied by Jean Meyer and T. G. A. Le Goff in a definitive paper illustrated with substantial tables.[8]

I briefly present the inquiry about the French trade fleet (Table 4). Before 1778, the Bureau des Classes conducted a yearly survey of trade ships that had sailed and classified them according to their destination and their *département* of origin. The purpose of this inquiry was to know the number of sailors available in case of war. The classification by maritime *département* is proof of this. The *département*

[8] Jean Meyer and T. G. A. Goff, "*Les constructions navales en France pendant la seconde moitié du XVIIIe siècle,*" *Annales E. S.C.*, Vol. 1, (1971), pp. 173.

Table 4. *Distribution of colonial ships (French West Indies)*

Destination	1774	1775	1776	1777
Saint-Domingue[a]	296	278	357	348
Martinique	123	137	116	132
Guadaloupe	67	79	80	42
Cayenne	6	5	15	12
Terre-Neuve	321	340	366	305
Coast of Africa	63	56	55	53
The Indies	27	44	39	18
Total	903	939	1,028	910

was the geographical basis of the census of the sailors. For instance, the *département* of Brest included the Lorient and Nantes port towns.

Some *Etats recapitulatifs* (statistics which were recapitulated yearly) still exist, but most of them are disappointing because they are too vague.

Although the tonnages were missing from these tables, a typology of French ports appears. Bordeaux, Marseille and, to a lesser extent, Le Havre traded with all the islands of the French West Indies and take part in all traffic. Thus, there the slave trade was a marginal activity practiced by only a few specialized shipowners. By contrast, Nantes, La Rochelle, and, on a small scale, Honfleur had a dominating slave trade activity. Only the slave trade allowed them to compensate for their incapacity to obtain cargoes capable of competing in the French West Indies with goods coming from Boreaux or Marseille. However, numerical analysis is too imprecise to explain the details of the patterns.

Castries sought new statistics that were better adapted to the commercial reality.[9]

Monseigneur est le premier ministre de la Marine qui ait désiré qu'il lui soit présenté des états généraux des batiments de commerce existant dans les différents ports et ce n'est qu'en 1784 qu'il en a fait la demande au Bureau de la Direction. Les plus anciens états de cette espèce remis de ce bureau à celui du Commerce Maritime sont en effet du mois de mars de ladite année. . . .

From this inquiry, I was able to establish a first table (Table 5).

However, this inquiry did not give precisely either the tonnages or the destination of the vessels. Fortunately, I have found other in-

[9] Archives Nationales, fonds Marine C5 53, p. 35, October 28, 1786.

216   *Patrick Villiers*

Table 4 *(cont.)*

Ports	Departures to Saint-Domingue				Departures to Martinique			
	1774	1775	1776	1777	1774	1775	1776	1777
Le Havre	40	35	49	41	28	27	20	22
Honfleur	2	—	5	1	—	—	—	—
Cherbourg	4	—	4	3	6	3	8	7
Dunkerque[b]	1	7	14	3	7	1	2	3
Rouen	—	—	—	1	1	—	—	—
Caen	—	—	1	—	—	—	—	—
Nantes	68	61	87	71	2	9	3	5
St. Malo	4	5	5	9	—	1	1	1
Lorient	—	—	—	3	1	1	1	3
Rochefort	4	6	5	9	—	—	1	—
La Rochelle	7	3	4	7	2	2	—	—
Bordeaux	133	128	136	149	46	52	41	49
Bayonne	3	8	6	15	—	4	4	4
Toulon	—	—	1	—	—	—	1	—
Marseille	30	25	39	36	30	35	34	37
Cette	—	—	—	—	123	137	116	132

Ports	Departures to Guadeloupe				Departures to Africa			
	1774	1775	1776	1777	1774	1775	1776	1777
Le Havre	12	18	15	7	13	13	13	15
Honfleur	1	2	4	2	4	2	3	2
Cherbourg	1	3	2	2	—	—	—	—
Dunkerque	—	—	—	—	1	2	—	1
Fecamp	—	1	—	—	—	—	—	—
Nantes	14	10	11	5	14	16	19	21
St. Malo	—	—	—	—	4	3	4	6
Rochefort	1	2	—	—	1	—	—	—
Bordeaux	35	33	47	21	13	11	6	3
Bayone	1	—	1	—	—	—	—	—
Marseille	2	—	—	3	—	—	4	1
Total	296	278	357	346	123	137	116	132

[a]St. Dominguo.
[b]Dunkirk.
Source: Archives Nationales, fonds Marine C4 156, *Etat général des armements faits par le commerce 1774–1777*.

quiries from the Commisaires aux Classes that contain other data. These data are the ones used to establish those aggregate statistics.[10] These inquiries indicate more about the French Maritime trade re-

[10] Ibid., C4 156, August 1783, January 1785, October 1786.

The slave and colonial trade in France   217

Table 5. *Number of trade ships by department*

Year	Brest	Rochef.	Bordeaux	Le Havre	Dunker.	Toulon	Total
1780	1,054	533	589	914	228	1,125	4,443
1781	820	367	480	851	254	1,057	3,859
1784	1,278	493	717	865	403	904	4,660
1785	1,420	512	620	1,001	400	1,301	5,254
1786	1,478	499	542	1,067	383	1,417	5,306

Note: These statistics "were not published during last war, since they would not offer interesting or true data because of the number of ships that used neutral ensigns and did not have French passports.
Source: Archives Nationales, fonds Marine C5 53, p. 35, October 28, 1786.

covery from 1783 to 1787 by *département* and by tonnage. They had to be elaborated each month, but the only ones remaining date from the months of August 1783, January 1785, September 1785, July 1786, and October 1786. I first examine the distribution of the French fleet in terms of activity before studying it from in terms of tonnage. In order to limit data, I present only those of August 1783, January 1785, and October 1786 (Table 6).

The data quoted in Table 6 are to be compared with those established by Poujet, the *commissaire aux classes*, for the inquiry about shipbuiding in France from 1763 to 1786[11] (Table 7).

This table confirms that convoy organization and the neutralization of French ships protected the French trade fleet much more efficiently than they did in the Seven Years War. By 1785, the number of ships reached the level of 1775. The Castries' inquiry did not seem to be carried on after 1786. A table of the French fleet was published in the *Moniteur* of June 29, 1792, and for France indicates 5,535 vessels and a total tonnage of 733,000. This would tend to indicate that the growth of the French fleet had increased after 1786, but at a much slower pace.

These data show that the growth of the French fleet was mostly due to the colonial trade. In fact, from 1785 to 1786, the French fleet increased by 181 vessels, most of them colonial ships. This fact is partly disguised by the data of October 1786. At that time, many colonial vessels were at anchor; this is confirmed by the fact that such a large number of ships was ready to set sail. By comparison, the July 1786 *Etat* indicates 445 vessels in the ports and 697 ships trading with the West Indies.

[11] Ibid., C5 155, *Enquête Pouget*, 1762–86, undated paper.

218   *Patrick Villiers*

Table 6. *Activities of the French fleet from 1783 to 1786*[a]

Département	Total	August 1, 1783 I	II	III
Brest	1,270	259	216	632
Rochefort	453	56	41	356
Bordeaux	694	223	351	120
Le Havre	815	316	188	311
Dunkerque	401	48	166	187
Toulon	887	187	494	206
Total	4,457	1,089	1,556	1,812

I = in the harbor, ready to sail or under construction.
II = colonial trade (boating, Europe) and codfish ship.
III = small coastal ship and coastal fish ship.

Département	Total	In the harbor A	B	Colonial trade Am.	Af.	In.	Boating Grand	Petit
		January 1, 1785						
Brest	1,420	40	220	131	33	34	84	618
Rochefort	512	42	48	23	18	6	11	321
Bordeaux	620	63	122	308	15	27	9	58
Le Havre	1,001	171	126	82	58	3	107	236
Dunkerque	400	106	15	36	2	—	39	94
Toulon	1,301	49	105	176	36	12	481	156
Total	5,254	221	636	756	162	82	731	1,483

A = ready to sail. B = shipbuilding or ship in repair. Am = West Indies. Af = slave trade. In = India + China. Trade with the Levant counts 197 vessels from the *département* of Toulon, 24 of Dunkerque, 21 of Le Havre, and 9 of Brest.
Fishermen were only taken in account in the total.

Département	Total	In the harbor A	B	Colonial trade Am.	Af.	In.	Boating Grand	Petit
		October 1, 1786						
Brest	1,507	132	98	69	41	33	69	701
Rochefort	515	46	54	11	25	3	8	299
Bordeaux	542	63	87	296	32	18	7	20
Le Havre	1,121	139	168	51	43	—	85	376
Dunkerque	376	178	13	17	1	—	27	65
Toulon	1,374	78	88	160	42	18	583	94
Total	5,435	636	508	604	184	72	779	1,455

A = ready to sail. B = shipbuilding or ship in repair. Am = West Indies. Af = slave trade. In = India + China. Trade with the Levant counts 258 ships of the *département* of Toulon, 11 of Dunkerque, 9 of Le Havre, and 7 of Brest.
Fishermen were only taken in account in the total.
[a]These statistics were established by *département*, not by port.

The slave and colonial trade in France   219

Table 7. *Number of trade vessels in France*

Year	1773	1774	1775	1780	1781	1784	1785	1786
Number	4,294	4,651	4,970	4,443	3,859	4,660	5,254	5,306

Table 8. *Departures of colonial vessels, 1783*

Département	Americas		Africa		Indies	
	Number	Tonnage	No.	Tonn.	No.	Tonn.
Brest	76	25,677	41	8,387	22	7,830
Rochefort	17	4,378	15	3,838	3	1,210
Bordeaux	169	48,019	16	3,793	20	7,184
Le Havre	60	11,303	19	2,914	1	412
Dunkerque	16	3,195	3	420	—	—
Toulon	75	19,758	—	722	5	2,405
Total	413	112,330	97	20,074	51	19,041

An *Etat nominatif des navires coloniaux par port et en tonnage* allows us to complete the 1783 data and confirms the growth of the colonial fleet[12] (Table 8).

The second purpose of the 1784–6 inquiry is to give us a distribution of the fleet per tonnage. Again, I have selected January 1, 1783, January 1, 1785, and October 1 1786 (Table 9).

One must have the classification of vessels, according to their activity, tonnage, and departure in order to be able to interpret these data fully. Robert Richard studied the fleets of Le Havre port towns. Studying the *Matricule des navires de commerce,* he succeeded in separating the registered fleet (*flotte inscrite*) from the fleet in trade (*flotte en activité*). The comparisons are made on January 1 of each year,[13] (Table 10). This table confirms the growth of the French fleet and its stagnation after 1788. For the trade fleet, the decline begun in 1790. The colonial trade, and particularly the slave trade, were especially affected.

[12] Ibid., F2 81, *Etat nominatif des batiments armès pour Saint-Dominigue, la Martinique, la Guadeloupe, Cayenne, Tabago, Cote d'Afrique, Indes et Terre-Neuve, année 1783,* undated paper.

[13] Robert Richard, *La flotte de commerce du Havre (1751–1816), étude statistique d'après les archives des Classes de la Marine,* in *Aires et structures du commerce français au XVIIIE siècle* (Lyon, 1975), pp. 201–35.

220   *Patrick Villiers*

Table 9. *Distribution of the French fleet per tonnage, 1783–6*

| Tonnage | Brest | Rochef. | General total, January 1, 1783 | | Dunker. | Toulon |
			Bordeaux	Le Havre		
500+	69	12	88	—	—	4
300–499	101	17	157	22	12	23
100–299	233	47	168	129	144	383
1–99	788	230	192	464	242	439
Total	1,191	306	605	615	398	849

General total: 4,064 ships.

| Tonnage | Brest | Rochef. | General total, January 1, 1785 | | Dunker. | Toulon |
			Bordeaux	Le Havre		
600+	36	12	27	—	1	4
500–599	17	2	72	3	1	6
400–499	45	8	103	7	3	6
300–399	73	15	101	37	9	30
200–299	105	9	115	101	44	100
100–199	174	41	128	226	113	419
1–99	970	425	74	627	229	736
Total	1,420	512	620	1,001	376	1,374

General total: 5,254 ships, 720,000 tons, and 64,800 sailors.

| Tonnage | Brest | Rochef. | General total, October 1, 1786 | | Dunker. | Toulon |
			Bordeaux	Le Havre		
600+	35	10	25	—	—	5
500–599	26	2	60	2	2	8
400–499	44	6	97	10	2	12
300–399	66	16	95	22	9	32
200–299	88	10	106	107	47	119
100–199	206	44	131	258	77	488
1–99	1,042	427	28	722	239	710
Total	1,420	512	620	1,001	376	1,374

Sailing: 4,147 ships, 550,000 tons, 49,500 sailors.

At this point, the problem is to determine precisely the part played by the colonial trade in the whole maritime activity, and then to evaluate the composition of the colonial fleet and its evolution. Statistics for 1783 and those elaborated by Jean Tarrade for 1773, 1783, and 1788 give us a first view of the issue. I have presented 1783 statistics as Jean Tarrade did.[14] (Table 11).

[14] Tarrade, p. 731.

The slave and colonial trade in France 221

Table 10. *Distribution of the fleet of Le Havre,*
1783–92

	Registered		Trade	
	Number	Tonnage	Number	Tonnage
1783	60	7,600	36	3,535
1784	122	17,789	113	16,474
1785	178	30,004	172	29,272
1786	196	33,663	179	31,507
1787	221	36,783	188	31,305
1788	241	40,306	197	33,307
1789	240	39,888	194	33,209
1790	235	40,100	174	29,618
1791	235	40,936	163	28,570
1792	235	40,190	161	26,931

Looking at Table 11, a few conclusions can be drawn.

1. *The importance of the colonial trade in the French maritime activities.* For instance, in 1783 the colonial trade used 509 vessels out of the 1,556 sailing in the colonial trade (*long cours*), offshore and coastal traffic (*grand cabotage*), and cod fishing (*pêche à la morue*), that is, 33% and 15% of the 3,368 boats in use. As for tonnage, the proportion was even higher. In 1788, the share of colonial trade was still increasing.

2. *The general growth of colonial trade* (see Table 12). In 1783, the slave trade was booming because ship owners wanted to meet the demand of plantation owners, as a consequence of the war, but 1788 turned out to be the peak year for slave trading. Colonial trade kept on growing.

3. *Classification of the destinations* (see Table 13). Trade with the *partie française de St. Domingue* increased, and that with Martinique and Guadeloupe improved in spite of questioning of the policy of the *exclusif colonial*. However, Saint-Domingue mostly harbored big vessels sailing from the largest French ports.

4. *Classification of French colonial ports* (see Table 14).

Average tonnage data are often researched by maritime historians, but they are misleading. The distribution of the port fleets may not be accurate. With the help of data from *l'état nominatif de 1783*, I have compiled a table (Tables 15 and 16) showing the distribution by capacity (tonnage) of colonial ships trading with Saint-Domingue.

The distribution in Gans curves of the port towns of Bordeaux and Nantes are very similar. The biggest ships were the most numerous,

Table 11. Foreign destinations of the French fleet, 1773, 1783, and 1788

Foreign destination, 1773

Harbor	St. Domingue		Martinique		Guadeloupe		Guyane		Total American			Africa			General tonnage		
	N	T	N	T	N	T	N	T	N	T	M	N	T	M	N	T	M
Dunkerque	11	1,431	—	—	—	—	—	—	11	1,431	130	—	—	—	11	1,431	130
Fécamp	—	—	1			45 tx	1	150	1	45	—	—	—	—	1	45	—
Le Havre	27	6,005	39			6,205	—	—	67	12,360	184	16	2,459	154	83	14,819	179
Honfleur	3	770	—	—	—	—	—	—	3	770	257	1	90	90	4	860	215
Cherbourg	1	120	7			747	—	—	8	867	108	—	—	—	8	867	108
St. Malo	6	1,570	1	80	1	30	5	430	13	2,110	162	3	630	210	16	2,740	171
Nantes	85	28,025	5	880	11	2,444	1	70	102	31,419	308	29	4,150	143	131	35,569	272
La Rochelle	5	1,300	—	—	—	—	2	380	7	1,680	240	4	600	150	11	2,280	207
Bordeaux	116	30,544	61	15,182	29	6,076	1	300	207	52,101	252	5	813	163	212	52,914	250
Bayonne	6	756	3	444	—	—	—	—	9	1,200	133	—	—	—	9	1,200	133
Marseille	56	8,473	36	8,106	7	1,125	3	500	82	18,294	223	2	345	173	84	18,639	222
Total	296	78,994	106	24,782 +47	48	9,674	13	1,830	510	122,277	240	60	9,087	151	870	131,364	230
						6,997 tx											
M		267		206				141			240			151			230

Windward Islands

222

Continued overleaf

Table 11 (*cont.*)

Harbor	St. Domingue		Martinique		Guadeloupe		Foreign destination, 1783 Tabago		Guyane		Total American			Africa			General tonnage		
	N	T	N	T	N	T	N	T	N	T	N	T	M	N	T	M	N	T	M
Dunkerque	9	2,245	4	690	1	130	1	130	—	—	15	3,195	213	3	420	140	18	3,615	200
Dieppe	1	225	—	—	—	—	—	—	—	—	1	225	225	—	—	—	1	225	225
Fécamp	1	340	1	—	—	—	—	—	—	—	1	340	340	—	—	—	1	340	340
Le Havre	28	4,909	17	2,991	4	740	—	—	—	—	49	8,640	176	14	2,373	—	63	11,013	174
Rouen	1	200	—	—	—	—	—	—	—	—	1	200	200	—	—	—	1	200	200
Honfleur	4	849	—	—	—	—	—	—	—	—	4	849	212	5	54	—	9	1,390	154
Cherbourg	2	385	—	—	—	—	—	—	1	50	4	839	209	—	—	—	4	839	209
St. Malo	1	325	—	—	—	—	—	—	—	—	2	375	187	1	300	—	3	675	225
Morlaix	1	210	—	—	—	—	—	—	1	80	1	210	210	—	—	—	1	210	210
Lorient	1	600	2	370	1	220	—	—	1	80	4	900	225	4	690	—	8	1,570	196
Nantes	62	22,072	—	—	5	1,640	—	—	—	—	70	24,162	345	36	7,497	—	106	31,659	298
La Rochelle	10	2,158	—	—	—	—	—	—	—	—	10	2,158	215	15	3,543	—	25	5,701	228
Rochefort	6	2,150	—	—	—	—	—	—	1	70	7	2,220	358	—	—	—	7	2,220	358
Bordeaux	118	35,354	29	6,880	12	2,650	—	—	2	680	161	45,564	283	15	3,543	—	176	49,147	307
Bayonne	7	2,155	1	300	—	—	—	—	—	—	8	2,455	306	1	250	—	9	2,705	300
Marseille	42	7,615	23	4,773	5	950	—	—	2	260	72	13,618	189	3	722	—	75	14,340	191
Toulon	2	250	—	—	—	—	—	—	—	—	2	250	125	—	—	—	2	250	125
Total	297	82,292	77	16,004	30	6,784	1	130	8	1,120	412	106,200tx		97	20,074tx		509	126,274tx	
M	277		207		226		130		140		257			207			248		

223

Table 11 *(cont.)*

Foreign destination, 1788

Harbor	St. Domingue		Martinique		Guadeloupe		Tabago		Guyane		Total American			Senegal		Africa			General tonnage		
	N	T	N	T	N	T	N	T	N	T	N	T	M	N	T	N	T	M	N	T	M
Dunkerque	10	2,360	12	3,050	2	310	6	1,541	—	—	30	7,261	242	—	—	—	—	—	30	7,261	242
Le Havre	65	15,705	24	5,196	10	1,982	7	1,555	1	110	107	24,548	229	12	1,988	19	4,300	226	138	30,836	223
Honfleur	6	1,110	—	—	—	—	—	—	—	—	6	1,110	185	—	—	10	2,791	279	16	3,904	244
St. Malo	9	2,160	—	—	—	—	—	—	—	—	9	2,160	240	—	—	2	1,364	682	11	3,524	320
Nantes	89	33,378	4	620	6	1,935	—	—	1	105	100	36,028	360	—	—	32	11,113	347	132	47,151	357
La Rochelle	6	3,681	—	—	—	—	—	—	—	—	6	3,681	614	—	—	6	5,065	844	12	8,746	729
Bordeaux	176	54,405	44	11,079	29	9,105	—	—	4	850	253	75,439	298	1	77	12	4,557	380	266	80,073	301
Bayonne	8	1,355	7	1,047	—	—	—	—	—	—	15	2,402	160	—	—	—	—	—	15	2,402	160
Marseille	89	22,935	43	11,514	6	1,385	—	—	3	365	141	36,199	257	—	—	7	1,987	284	148	38,186	258
Divers	7	1,535	2	230	1	150	—	—	—	—	10	1,915	192	1	497	3	1,485	495	14	3,897	278
Total	465	138,624	136	32,736	54	14,867	13	3,096	9	1,430	677	190,753	282	12	2,132	93	33,095	356	782	225,980	289
M	298		241		275		238		159		282			178		356			289		

N = number of trade vessels. M = average of tonnages.

224

The slave and colonial trade in France 225

Table 12. *Number of ships leaving French ports*

Trade with West Indies	1788 compared to 1783	164.3%
Trade with West Indies	1788 compared to 1773	132.5%
Slave trade	1788 compared to 1783	95.8%
Slave trade	1788 compared to 1773	155%
Total trade	1788 compared to 1783	153%
Total trade	1788 compared to 1773	137.2%

Table 13. *Trade with Saint-Domingue and Martinique-Guadaloupe*

	Share of Saint-Domingue		
Number of ships	1773: 58%	1783: 72%	1788: 68.7%
Tonnage	1773: 64.8%	1783: 78%	1788: 72.8%
	Share of the Martinique-Guadeloupe		
Number of ships	1773: 39.4%	1783: 25.9%	1788: 28%
Tonnage	1773: 33.9%	1783: 21.4%	1788: 24.8%

Table 14. *Trade with the West Indies (without the slave trade)*

	1773		1783		1788	
	Number	Tonnage	No.	Tonn.	No.	Tonn.
Bordeaux	40.5%	42.6%	39.0%	42.9%	37.4%	39.2%
Nantes	20.0%	25.4%	16.9%	22.7%	14.8%	18.8%
Marseille	16.1%	14.8%	17.4%	12.8%	20.8%	18.9%
Le Havre	13.1%	9.8%	11.8%	8.1%	15.8%	13.1%
La Rochelle	2.4%	2.0%	2.4%	2.0%	0.8%	1.9%

a consequence of the king's regulations in their favor as well as of convoy navigation during the War of Independence. The ship owners of Le Havre were the victims of their geographical situation. So, later, they preferred to invest in fast, mid-sized ships that they used as privateers and then as slave ships.

The case of Marseille was quite different. Shippers often entrusted their cargoes to their captains in order to avoid the forwarding agents of Saint-Domingue. Too big a ship implied too long a stay in the port of call.[15]

[15] Charles Carriere, *Négociants marseillais au XVIIIe siecle* (Marseille, 1973), pp. 594–602.

226   *Patrick Villiers*

Table 15. *Distribution per tonnage toward Saint-Domingue in 1783*

Tonnage	Bordeaux	Nantes	Le Havre	Marseille
600 tx[a]	4	6	—	1
500–699 tx	11	11	—	—
400–499 tx	18	11	1	—
300–399 tx	30	12	1	3
200–299 tx	26	10	10	14
100–199 tx	15	9	12	16
0–99 tx	14	3	4	8
	118	62	28	42

[a] tx = tonneaux (French tons).

Table 16. *Distribution per tonnage toward Saint-Domingue in 1783*

Tonnage	Bayonne	Rochefort	La Rochelle	Honfleur	Dunkerque
600	1	—	—	—	—
500–599	2	—	—	—	—
400–499	—	3	—	—	2
300–399 tx	1	3	3	1	1
200–299 tx	1	—	3	1	2
100–199 tx	1	—	2	1	3
0– 99 tx	2	—	2	1	1
	8	6	10	4	9

tx = tonneaux (French tons)

Large ships required a very capitalistic commercial organization, because investments were large. Stops in ports of call had to be reduced so that large-scale economies could be justified. The use of large ships also revealed a growing integration between plantation owners, ship owners, and merchants.

The Nantes case differs from that of Bordeaux. Nantes mostly imported raw sugar for Orleans refineries, which were the first in France, whereas Bordeaux reexported 47% of French colonial products.[16]

What was the evolution of the ships' size from 1783 to 1789? To answer this question, the maritime historian can use a surprising source: the *registres de congés (passports) de droits d'ancrage et de balisage* of the accounts of the *Amiral de France's* chancellor. Since 1681, the owner of every ship leaving the French coasts had to buy a clearance

[16] Jean Butel, pp. 212–23, 229–45.

The slave and colonial trade in France 227

Table 17. *Distribution per tonnage of the fleets of Nantes, Bordeaux, and La Rochelle*

					Nantes						
	1773	1780	1781	1782	1783	1784	1785	1786	1787	1788	1789
− 50 tx		2	2	2	2	—	3	1	1	—	1
50–100		10	11	12	6	9	3	4	7	3	—
100–150		9	6	7	9	11	8	4	7	3	6
150–200		4	4	5	9	10	7	8	4	10	11
200–250		2	1	4	8	12	7	9	9	4	3
250–300		2	1	6	12	9	11	10	16	8	9
300–350		4	1	2	14	14	18	11	13	18	20
350–400		5	1	4	10	15	18	14	14	9	11
400–500		6	1	8	13	19	27	23	26	23	31
500–600		7	3	6	6	10	16	17	14	12	22
600–800		2	3	5	4	8	11	12	7	8	8
800 +		—	—	—	—	3	—	1	1	2	2
Total		53	34	61	93	120	129	114	119	107	118

					Bordeaux						
	1773	1780	1781	1782	1783	1784	1785	1786	1787	1788	1789
− 50 tx	2	—	1	2	—		—	1	3	2	—
50–100	4	11	8	12	15		8	7	8	6	15
100–150	11	8	14		12		11	14	12	13	17
150–200	24	15	9	12	18		19	27	22	30	19
200–250	45	11	13	6	19		23	29	24	22	24
250–300	37	7	11	2	13		25	24	20	25	16
300–350	36	18	22	9	14		30	28	21	28	30
350–400	19	19	24	9	20		38	37	34	39	25
400–500	17	16	25	17	27		43	42	34	42	28
500–600	1	3	11	3	8		10	7	9	6	6
600–800	—	1	5	3	2		3	4	1	1	2
800 +	—	—	—	—	—		—	—	—	—	—
Total	196	109	143	87	148		210	220	188	214	182

and pay taxes. He also had to pay anchor and buoy taxes, but most of these registers were lost. Fortunately, most of the *registres de congés* from 1780 to 1789 were preserved. Thus the name of the ship and of the captain, the destination, and the tonnage of the ship were known. From these archives, limiting myself to Bordeaux, La Rochelle, and Nantes, I have established Table 17.

Whatever the port town, the increase of tonnage is indubitable,

228　　　　　　　　　　　　*Patrick Villiers*

Table 17 (*cont.*)

	1773	1780	1781	1782	1783	1784	1785	1786	1787	1788	1789
				La Rochelle							
50–100 tx	2			5	3	3		—	—	2	1
100–150	4			2	—	3		2	—	—	1
150–200	1			2	3	5		—	—	—	—
200–250	1			3	2	4		3	3	2	2
250–300	4			—	—	2		—	—	1	—
300–350	2			5	2	5		2	—	1	
350–400	1			1	1	3		—	—	1	
400–500	—			3	1	3		3	—		2
500–600	—			—	1	1		1	2	2	3
600–800	—			2	—	4		3	2	2	—
800–1000	—			1	—	—		4	2	1	2
1,000 +	—			—	—	—		4	3	3	1
Total	15			24	13	33		22	12	15	12

Source: Archives Nationales, series G5.132, La Rochelle; G5.122, Nantes; and G5.45, Bordeaux.

especially for the over–400 *tonneaux* class. Unfortunately, a thorough study reveals that slave ships changed their tonnage declarations after 1784. Is it necessary to reject any analysis of tonnage from 1784 to 1792? Is it necessary to reject any source about tonnages, taking for granted that if there were a forgery of slaves ships' tonnages, this was also the case for any other kind of ship?

The answer is contained in the analysis of the documents about maritime practices of the eighteenth century.

In spite of the French government's efforts, ships carrying illicit merchandise were numerous in the French West Indies. Smugglers carrying slaves and sailing to Guadeloupe and Martinique were particularly numerous.

Thus, officially, 183 slaves a year would have landed in Martinique between 1775 and 1777. In fact, it was the English ships that provided these French islands with slaves. French shippers complained about unfair competition, and plantations owners accused the ship owners of selling slaves at outrageous prices.

Castries decided to put an end to this situation by regulating the arrival of foreign slave ships with a first act dated June 28, 1783. In

The slave and colonial trade in France   229

the preamble of this act, the number of 19,700 slaves sold in 1776 is quoted and the annual needs are estimated at up to 25,000.[17] Besides, the French slave traders were know to avoid the French Leeward Islands. Consequently, foreign slave ships carrying more than 120 tons and 180 slaves were allowed to sail to these islands for three years on payment of a duty tax of 100 livres per slave. The duty was due to allow a premium of the same amount to the French slave traders laying anchor in the same ports. This measure was accepted by French ship owners, but it had only a small effect.

Its main purpose was to disclose the exact number of slaves brought in by foreigners: (1,180 in 1783, 913 in 1784, 0 in 1785, and 1,683 in 1786) and by the French (205 in 1783, 579 in 1784, 414 in 1785, and 191 in 1786).[18]

Facing this failure and seeking administrative simplification, Castries published a decree approved by the king's council on October, 26, 1784, which was enforced after November 10. The tax of 10 livres per slave introduced in French colonies was suppressed, as well as the *Acquits de Guinée*.

The *Acquits de Guinée* gave an exemption to the slaves traders of half the taxes on colonial goods introduced into France with the product of the sale of a slave cargo. As a counterpart of the suppression of the *Acquits de Guinée*, they received a premium of 40 livres per ton of cargo. Slave ships sailing to Martinique and Guadeloupe received 60 livres and 100 livres if they laid anchor at Cayenne.

This act was much discussed by Castries and Calonne, *Controleur général des Finances*, and especially the problems of tonnage and financial cost. The basis retained by Calonne was an average of 14,365 Africans brought in every year from 1768 to 1777, a yearly ship tonnage of 11,967 tons, and a yearly exemption of 950,636 livres. Dividing 950,636 livres by 11,967 tons gives a premium of 79.4 livres. The slaves shippers protested vigorously.[19]

Castries refused any compromise to modify the premium amount, but he allowed a new measure of ship tonnage on January 28, 1785, followed by another one in 1786, each of them more favorable to the ship owners. These two methods of measuring tonnage misled historians, most of whom believed in a general forgery. This was a mistake, as I demonstrate.

---

[17] Tarrade, pp. 517–20.
[18] Archives Nationales fonds Colonies C8B.18, Martinique, *Etats des noirs francais et étrangers introduits dans la Colonie de 1782 a 1786.*
[19] Tarrade, p. 552.

230 *Patrick Villiers*

Measuring ship tonnage was a usual practice that the Maritime Act of 1681 had recalled:[20]

Tous navires seront jaugés incontinent après leurs constructions par les gardes-jurés ou prudhommes du mêtier de charpentier qui donnent leur attestation du port du batiment laquelle sera enregistreée au greffe de l'Amirauté.

In order to discourage shippers and captains who cheated, the Amiral de France created the position of state tonnage measurer in 1709. The clerk registered the certificate of tonnage measurement and stamped it. This certificate was attested to in every French port and was reported on insurance declarations and on official registers. The ship owners' aim was to diminish their measures of ship tonnage in order to pay less in taxes, but if the ship was sold to the king or particulars, this cheating worked against them. Moreover, when a dispute arose, it was inexpensive to have the tonnage measurer create a new certificate: only two or three livres. The difficulty rested mainly in establishing a clear rule of ship tonnage measurement:[21]

L'usage est de prendre la longueur de tête en tête du dehors de l'étrave au dehors de l'étambot, la largeur au fort, en dehors des préceintes, le creux du maitre-bau sur quille, de faire un produit des trois dimensions et de le diviser par 100. On obtient le port en tonneau.

In fact, the burden tonnage varied by up to 10 percent according to the shape of the ship – whether sharp built or Dutch built. A check of slave ships' tonnage shows that registered tonnage declared on the *Registres de congés de l'Amiral de France* are the same as tonnages declared on the *Registres de de soumission* of La Rochelle. Jean Mettas, in his *Répertoire*, noticed tonnage differences. In each case, they came from the data of the *Archives des Colonies* or private sources, particularly newspapers such as *Les Affiches américaines*. The *Etats de Commerce* established by Customs, such as those of the Nantes port town, did not mention the registered tonnage but the burden tonnage actually used in the journey of the ship coming from the West Indies. Therefore, the important differences found in research are easy to explain.

In the slave ship case, letters written by a French Navy shipwright of Rochefort harbor tell us how three slave ships of La Rochelle were measured (Table 18).

In a note, this shipwright mentioned that the *port en tonneaux de*

[20] Valin, *Commentaire sur l'Ordonnance de 1681*, Livre II, titre X, *Du navire . . .* (La Rochelle, 1766).
[21] Vial du Clairbois, *Encyclopèdie Marine* (Paris, 1783), tome 3, jauge p. 552.

Table 18. *Table about the burden of the ships*
La Fille Unique, *the* Forcalquier, *and the* Comte d'Hector

| | Main measures of the burden | | | | | | | |
	1	2	3	4	5	6	7	8
Fille Unique	116	104	110	31	28.6	19.6	12.5	4
Forcalquier	121.8	106.4	114	33	31.6	19.6	12.9	4.3
Comte d'Hector	108	98	103	27	25	17.3	9.9	4.7

1 = length of the lower deck   5 = breadth molded
2 = length of the keel   6 = depth of the hold
3 = average of the length   7 = depth from the kelson to the first
4 = breadth extream   deck
                                     8 = height of the between decks
(Translation from a dictionary of naval architecture of the 18th century.)

| | Burden when using internal measurement measures | | | General burden when using external measurement measures |
	Cale	Entrepont	Total	Cale + Entrepont
Fille Unique	850 tx[a]	381 tx	1,231 tx	1,455 tx
Forkalquier	786 tx	466 tx	1,247 tx	1,667 tx
Comte d'Hector	458 tx[a]	369 tx	827 tx	1,057 tx

[a]tx = tonneaux (French tons).
Source: Archives du Port de Rochefort, 2G[4] No. 3.

poids (burden weight) was supposed to be 650 *tonneaux* for the *Fille Unique*, 680 *tonneaux* for the *Forcalquier*, and 300 to 350 *tonneaux* for the *Comte d'Hector*.

The study of Amiral de France registers reveals that the *Forcalquier* (also named the *Comte de Forcalquier*) had sailed toward Saint-Dominigue in 1784 with a declared tonnage of 700 *tonneaux* in 1785 as a slave ship with a registered tonnage of 1,350 *tonneaux*, and again in 1787 as a slave ship with a registered tonnage of 1,667 *tonneaux*. In 1788, in Nantes port town, back from the West Indies, it was registered as a 700-*tonneaux* ship.

On the La Rochelle books, the *Comte d'Hector* is registered as a 380-*tonneaux* cargo in 1783 on the G5 *serie*, as a 833-*tonneaux* slave ship in 1785, and as a 1,057-*tonneaux* slave ship in 1788.

The *Fille Unique* is mentioned only once in 1787 as a slave ship of 1,667 *tonneaux*, but it was considered to have a cargo of 650 *tonneaux* on its muster roll in the archives of Rochefort harbor.

232   *Patrick Villiers*

All these data show that the changes of tonnage measurements in La Rochelle are not the result of an accident but come from two successive rules of tonnage measurements.

Ship owners were very sensible. Slave captains crowded the Africans in the area between decks and on the upper deck. The hold of the ship was entirely occupied by the water and the food for the middle passage. First, the shippers were permitted to include the area between decks in the measurement so that the maritime reality would be the same as the measurement rule. Second, the shippers emphasized that partial platforms, which were set on the decks for children and wives, reduced the volume allowed to the crew. As a consequence, the rule of external measurement is definitely the most accurate.

Of course, the government had to pay for the new subsidies resulting from these changes. The premium was paid when the ship left France and the measurement was then registered on the departure book, but on returning from the West Indies, the slave ship, a simple cargo carrier now, adopted cargo tonnage again.

To measure the French colonial fleet accurately, one should use only the measurements written in the *rules de desarmement* of 1785–92 – that is, the roll of laying up of the ship. Unfortunately, these registers are scarcely complete in the archives of French harbors and port towns. But a slave ship often sailed previously as a cargo, so its registered tonnage preceding 1785 indicates its nonslave ship tonnage. A study of the names of the French ships reveals that ships rarely changed names, even when they changed ownership. With the help of a computer, this problem should be soluble. I have tried to do so with handwritten notes for the La Rochelle port town. The result is given in Table 19.

A King's Council Act dated September 10, 1786, allowed, in addition to the subsidy of 40 livres per registered *tonneaux*, a premium of 160 livres per slave sold in the French colonies and 200 livres per slave sold in Saint-Dominigue. Necker, in his *Rapport au Roi*, mentioned that the premium allowed for slaves *"forment un objet de 2,400,000 livres"* The premium seems to have been paid correctly until 1789. In 1790, 105 ships were granted the premium, but only 31 in 1791 and 28 in 1792. The information is quite confusing. It seems that in 1792,

---

[22] Archives du Port de Rochefort, from manuscripts found by M. Boudriot of Paris, 2G⁴, No. 3; Jean Mettas, Serge Daget, and Michele Daget, *Répertoires des Expéditions négrières, Ports autres que Nantes*, (Paris, 1985), tome 2.

The slave and colonial trade in France 233

Table 19. *Slave ships of La Rochelle from 1783 to 1789*

Year	Name of Ship	Slave tonnage[a]	Cargo tonnage[b]	Estimated slaves[c]	Slaves carried[d]
1783	Marie-Louise	150	150	—	200
	Hirondelle	200	200	—	358
	Joli	350	350	—	403
	Belle Pauline	300	300	—	575
	Colombe	160	160	350	357
	Industrie	60	60	120	67
	Bonne Société	300	300	450	342
	Iris	60	60	60	—
	Euryale	300	300	—	400
	Utile	55	55	—	—
	Thetis	180	180	300	185
	Nisus	350	350	650	—
	Aimable Louise	350	350	700	577
	Nouvel Achille	400	400	800	380
	13 Cantons	500	500	700	520
	Elise	38	38	120	—
	Comte d'Hector	380	380	700	736
1784	Reine de Golconde	350	350	—	—
	Pauline	350	350	—	448
	Cigogne	160	160	—	—
	Iris	400	400	—	966
	Union des 6 freres	200	200	—	—
	Trois Frères	300	300	600	600
	Cerf-Volant	100	100	—	—
	Bellecombe	300	300	—	500
	Alerte	16	16	—	—
	Aurore	300	300	—	476
	Meulan	580	580	—	687
	Clameur ou Railleur	316	316	—	500
	Plaisanterie	18	18	—	—
	Caraibe	150	150	—	—
	Mercure	190	190	—	160
	Concorde	215	715	—	—
	Follette	50	—	—	—
1785	Aimable Suzanne	450	180	350	375
	Ebène	350	—	300	280
	Rosalie	280	—	399	370
	Joli	500	350	450	433
	Marquis de Voyer	700	300	500	605
	Lutin	179	—	—	194
	Comte de Forcalquier	1,350	700	376	138
	Concorde	375	215	—	376
	Argus	203	—	—	280
	Comte d'Hector	833	380	600	800
	Loudunois	792	400	300	—
	Duc de Normandie	446	240	—	459
	Reverseaux	1,179	—	—	425
	Fille Unique	1,232	—	600	—

234   *Patrick Villiers*

Table 19 (*cont.*)

Year	Name of Ship	Slave tonnage[a]	Cargo tonnage[b]	Estimated slaves[c]	Slaves carried[d]
1786	Cigogne	493	—	—	400
	Réparateur	780	300	—	410
	Cacique	199	—	—	78
	Diamant	402	—	—	286
	Ville de Basle	441	150	—	300
	Aurore	800	300	400	—
	Prevost de Langristin	1,540	700	—	240
	Comte de Puysegur	1,253	600	—	370
	13 Cantons	1,021	500	—	440
	Plutus	807	450	—	525
	Comte d'Estaing	536	200	—	355
	Aunis	1,581	760	—	718
	Reine de Podore	316	150	—	118
	Bonhomme Richard	1,646	700	—	518
	Railleur	897	316	—	635
	Bien Aimee	681	300	—	316
	Reine de Golconde	831	—	—	251
	Amitie	781	300	—	224
	Comtesse de Puysegur	625	340	—	400
	Tigre	711	360	—	359
	Desiree	975	500	—	367
1787	Laboureur	795	350	—	—
	Victoire	827	350	—	300
	Bon Francais	1,519	—	—	334
	Nouvelle Betsy	529	200	—	342
	Comte de Forcalquier	1,667	650	—	779
	Bon Père	581	280	—	—
	Meulan	1,229	580	—	541
	Nouveau Joly	670	—	—	533
	Solide	810	—	—	242
	Frères	302	—	—	120
	Réparateur	734	300	—	514
1788	Duc de Normandie	517	240	—	429
	Aimable Suzanne	534	—	—	464
	Comte de Puysegur	1,253	600	—	540
	Trois Soeurs	609	—	—	205
	Comte d'Hector	1,057	380	—	672
	Desire	175	—	—	506
	Tigre	700	300	—	450
	Reverseaux	1,524	—	—	700
1789	Ville de Basle	447	150	—	155
	Bon Père	584	280	—	363
	Cigogne	809	—	—	409
	Nouvelle Betsy	529	200	—	353
	Meridien	92	—	—	—
	Duc de Normandie	517	240	—	376
	Sartine	1,259	600	—	450
	Victoire	827	—	—	288
	Deux Amis	402	—	—	—

Continued overleaf

The slave and colonial trade in France   235

Table 19 (*cont.*)

Year	Name of Ship	Slave tonnage[a]	Cargo tonnage[b]	Estimated slaves[c]	Slaves carried[d]
1790	*Comte de Puysegur*	1,253	600	—	500
	Comte de Forcalquier	1,667	650	—	530
	Bon Citoyen	92	—	—	—
	Réparateur	723	350	—	360
	Revanche	795	300	—	—
	Saint-Jacques	1,288	500	—	—
	Pauline	790	350	—	450
	Alcyon	—	—	—	—
	Bonhomme Richard	1,646	750	—	545
	Marie-Elisabeth	289	110	—	41
	Neptune	695	—	—	—
	Joly	670	—	—	—
	Reverseaux	1,524	—	—	—

[a] Registered tonnage from the Amiral de France's registers Archives Nationales, series G5.
[b] Registered tonnage in the *Registres de Soumission* de la Rochelle.
[c] Number of slaves estimated by the ship owners at the departure from La Rochelle.
[d] Number of slaves sold in the West Indies.[22]

at least 3,077 slaves were introduced into Martinique and 1,598 into Saint-Domingue.[23]

The 1791 budget did not plan any credit for the premium, but on the ship owners' demands, the *Comite des Finances* in March 1792 estimated the whole premium at 2,815,000 livres. Finally, the Assembly voted on August 16, 1792, the payment of the past due premium from January 1791 to August 16, 1792. The government offices were in no hurry to pay. Following the ship owners' claims, the premium was paid until July 1793: fifty-three vessels received 919,377 livres by virtue of the act of *40 livres par tonneau de jauge*. The premium for introducing slaves amounted to 795,120 livres, of which 319,000 was for Saint-Domingue. On July 27, 1793, the question was raised in the National Assembly. Bishop Gregoire vehemently intervened and

[23] In Jean Vidalenc, "La traite des nègres en France au début de la Révolution," *Annales historiques de la Révolution francaise*, (1957), p. 62.

236 *Patrick Villiers*

stated that the premium should not be paid any longer, anticipating the law of the Convention pronouncing the abolition of slavery on February 15, 1794.[24]

[24] Archives Nationales, F12 1653, F12 1654; Patrick Villiers, *Traite des Noirs et Navires négriers* (Paris, 1985), pp. 113–22.

[12]

TRADITIONS AND CHANGES IN FRENCH ATLANTIC TRADE BETWEEN 1780 AND 1830.[*]

by

P. BUTEL

I

The Rapid Expansion of the West Indies

In the history of relations between Europe and the Americas at the end of the eighteenth century, a study of the commercial trends which stimulated activity on the French Atlantic front reveals the spectacular rise of the 'Jewel of the West Indies', the French half of Santo Domingo, immediately prior to the slave revolt in August 1791 and the maritime war of 1793, when the burning of plantations and the threat to safety on the seas destroyed the base upon which it rested. The French Windward Islands, Martinique and Guadeloupe, French Guyana and Tobago, a recently acquired pioneer island, were certainly far from inactive in trade, as they, like Santo Domingo, provided sugar, coffee, cotton and indigo which were then redistributed in France and to an even greater extent in Europe as a whole. The Greater Antilles were, however, the main driving force behind trade. Santo Domingo drew the largest number of French ships, varying between 550 and 600 per year in 1787 and 1788. These figures include both 'direct' shipping plying regularly between the Caribbean and the homeland by the most direct and therefore shortest and most profitable route in terms of time, and the trading ships which put in for long periods on the coast of Africa. In the region of 480 ships used the regular direct trade routes to deliver food, flour, wine, salted meat and oils which were indispensable for feeding the planters and their workforce and also equipment such as sugar mill wheels, boilers and various iron fitments which were needed to run the plantations. In addition to these goods, the same ships would also bring the colonists, who were keen to keep up with the latest fashions, articles such as carriages, saddles, handkerchiefs, shoes, fine quality shirts, mirrors, fine wines, fruits preserved in brandy and meat conserves. They made a name for transporting food, clothing and planters' equipment. Over a hundred vessels exporting, cotton fabrics, sheets, armaments and brandy to the coast of Africa, supplied Santo Domingo with about 28,000 slaves per year between 1786 and 1789.

[*]This article has been compiled from information used in a report to the International Economic History Congress at Caracas, July 1983. It has been translated from the French by Hilary Owen, Terra Nova Translations (Nottingham), to whom the Editors are deeply grateful.

A large number of coasters either extended this trade with France or competed with it, providing a link between the French Cape or Port-au-Prince and Jamaica, Spanish America and also North American ports. A great many cargoes of valuables, shipped from French ports as goods intended for private sale, disappeared on the Spanish Main. This was the largest single area of shipping for the Windward Islands and Martinique in particular where Saint-Pierre Harbour often provided an anchorage for schooners and brigantines of low tonnage which were well suited to weaving up and down the coasts between Trinidad and Cartagena, engaged in smuggling.

Martinique and Guadeloupe were also open to North American trade which kept their plantations constantly supplied with slaves. French traders had little to do with these islands, in practice. They were obliged to meet the increasing demand from Santo Domingo and kept their market open to the shipping firms of New York and New England. These firms used ships of low tonnage which either filled up with slaves from the great depots of the Caribbean – Jamaica, Saint-Eustace and Curação – or took them captive on the coast of Africa. The French Windward Islands, on the other hand, received between 130 and 140 ships per year from France, sailing direct to Martinique and a further fifty or so to Guadeloupe. It is worth noting with regard to the black slave trade that the Spanish American markets, which were expanded in 1789 by the decision to open officially certain ports to foreign trade, were a fairly formidable competitor to the markets of Martinique and Guadeloupe.

The Wealth of Colonial Produce

Before the French Revolution, sugar and coffee carried most weight in the balance of trade, in terms of both volume and value. France received about 95,000 tons of sugar, of which over 71,000 tons came from Santo Domingo, and over 39,000 tons of coffee, about 34,000 of which were sent from the Greater Antilles[1]. West Indian sugar reached a value of 90 million *livres*, and coffee came close to 88 million. The value of cotton goods unloaded came to less than 22 million, which is less than 10% of the total value of West Indian produce.

It is important to note the subtle way in which the density of West Indian trade depended upon the development of the plantation economy, if one's analysis is confined to French imports alone and is further limited within this context to sugar, coffee and cotton. In fact, a large proportion of the commodities produced were directed towards foreign markets, either illicitly or under perfectly legal conditions following the partial lifting of *L'Exclusif* – the Trade Monopoly – in 1784. French merchants were aware of these trade developments and in the 1780s they voiced their resentment at loosing considerable profits as a result of direct links being established between Europe and the colonial markets. French Atlantic trade felt under threat from falling profits. The French failed to follow the

---

[1] The volumes and values from 1788 were drawn from Page, *Traité d'Économie Politique et de Commerce* (Paris, An IX), the interest of which M. Pluchon has kindly indicated. The statistics accord with the series found in Archives Nationales, F12. 1835 and Colonies, F2 B6.

commercial initiative of English and American shipowners who reduced the time which ships spent anchored in West Indian ports and cut the size of crews, enabling them to make gains in productivity on a scale that their rivals never matched[2]. As French ports faced the crisis of the revolution they were, without doubt, not as prosperous as they were generally thought to be.

Sugar production in Santo Domingo should be estimated above the 71,000 tons sent to France if smuggling is taken into account. Part of the island's sugar production was sold directly to North American or European ports through Danish, Dutch or British warehouses. The Virgin Islands provide a good illustration of the scale on which smuggling took place. This group of twelve to fifteen small islets, with 'arid soil scarcely capable of feeding its population of a thousand whites and about 9,000 blacks' used, according to Page, to ship some 35,000 tons of sugar prior to the French Revolution[3]. In 1788 the French islands exported rum and molasses to the value of five million *livres*. 1,245 North American ships weighing around 90,000 tons in total imported the molasses and also defied prohibition laws by exchanging sugar, coffee and cotton goods for flour, salted meat and dried fish which were vital commodities on the plantations.

Sugar, coffee and cotton were not the only products supplied by the plantations, although they predominated in shipments. On account of its small volume and high value, indigo remained a product prized by all dealers who were aiming for high returns on the sale of their products in Europe. In 1788, France received 555 tons of indigo to the value of more than 10.4 million *livres*. Indigo was also much in demand for its beautiful blue colour used in the dyeing of fabrics and was not infrequently re-exported on the Swiss and German industrial textile markets. France re-exported about 330 tons of it. Bordeaux provides an indication of how the indigo trade was thriving alongside coffee and sugar. In 1788 it took the largest share in the re-exportation of indigo, handling 186 tons which constituted over 56% of all shipments abroad. In the same year, this port in the Gironde had exported 49% and 53% of the sugar and coffee sold abroad. These four products, sugar, coffee, cotton and indigo enabled France to retain the upper hand on the Northern European and Mediterranean markets in spite of increasing British competition, in the sugar trade at least, in the 1780s. French commerce overall was at its most successful on the foreign markets where 157 million of the 218 million *livres* of colonial products imported were then re-exported.

Under the heading 'miscellaneous', the French balance of trade registers certain irregular shipments amounting to a total value of over 8 million *livres*. It is possible to glean some idea of what these were from the cargo lists of the ships which entered the ports. Figuring prominently on these lists are leather goods from the Santo Domingo coast, which made up the bulk of shipments made by the first French to settle in the Greater Antilles in the seventeenth century, the famous

---

[2] James F. Shepherd and Gary M. Walton, *Shipping, Maritime Trade and the Economic Development of Colonial North America* (Cambridge, 1972), p.76; Jean Meyer, 'Notes et informations', *Revue française d'histoire d'Outre-Mer*, LXVI (1979), 466.
[3] Although emphasised by Page, the role of the Virgin Islands does not appear to have been fully appreciated. It represents a transfer of the smuggling trade outside the ports open to foreign commerce since 1784 at Santo Domingo.

buccaneers. The value of annatto, another plant used for dyeing and of spices such as ginger and cassia used for medicinal purposes was, however, considerably higher. Campeachy wood which was formerly used as a dyeing agent and had, in the previous century, been the object of one of the busiest Caribbean trades also figures on the cargo lists. In the area around a port like Bordeaux, the industries of Aquitaine (such as drapery in Agen and Nérac) used indigo, Pernambucco wood or campeachy. The tanneries of these industrial centres worked the leather produce of Santo Domingo. Many ships transported mahogany beams which served as ballast on account of their weight, and these were used to make the sumptuous furniture which was highly popular with the upper classes of the towns.

Feeding the plantations

In order to acquire these products, the ports could either ship foodstuffs or consumer goods, or supply the plantations with slaves. Whilst returns from the Caribbean islands were concentrated upon certain major products, shipments from Europe varied considerably in order to meet the diverse demands of the plantation economy.

In 1788, France shipped more than 16,400 tons of flour to the West Indies, although the requirement far exceeded this amount. In 1786 and 1787 the port of Bordeaux alone had loaded 20,000 and 18,000 tons of flour bound for the West Indies and the export levels of 1788 seem fairly low. In fact, only the importation of North American flour made good the net deficit and, owing to the low prices in force at the time, flour from Philadephia and New York became a powerful competitor to French flour. Where the payment for European cargoes was concerned, the sale of flour was something that ships' captains came to dread. It was slow which meant spending more time in port and it interfered with the owners' turn around schedules for the ship. It was also one of the main factors contributing to the build up of planters' debts as the captains were obliged, in order to get rid of the flour, to agree to long periods of credit for the local population. However, from the seventeenth century onwards, these shipments were a driving force behind the commercial agriculture of Aquitaine and the food industries of the region. By the end of the Ancien Régime, around 9,000 tons were regularly delivered to Bordeaux by the 39 millers of the Agen area and the Montauban millers shipped comparable quantities. The growth of these exports to the West Indies was accompanied by a rapid development in ship-fitting which enabled practically all ships to carry in their holds the high quality flour which was so popular amongst the planters. After 1815, in spite of the loss of Santo Domingo, the Trade Monopoly was upheld which meant that the outlets of Martinique and Guadeloupe were still open to flour.

Salted meat, along with flour, was for a long time one of the products in most demand in the Caribbean colonies. In 1685 the *Code Noir* had stipulated that slave masters should feed their work force with manioc, salted beef and salted fish. In fact, although this obligation was reinforced on several occasions it was far from being adhered to on a regular basis, certainly as far as salted meat was concerned. Gabriel Debien has shown that salted beef formed a far larger proportion of the slaves' diet in the seventeenth century than it did in the eighteenth. Nonetheless, the shipping of salted meats did provide the foundation of a major trade. In fact, despite Colbert's efforts in this field, French agriculture did not succeed in obtaining a product of satisfactory quality. Throughout the entire eighteenth century, shipowners used meats from abroad, and in particular salt beef from Ireland, to keep the plantations supplied. From 1727 to 1741 they were even authorized to load ships bound for the West Indies in Ireland itself. As was the case with flour, a smuggling trade which the merchants complained of, very soon doubled French shipping figures. This type of trade was at its most prevalent in Martinique and on the south coast of Santo Domingo where North American ships were in a hurry to unload salted meats and exchange them for sugar and coffee, which was illegal until the partial lifting of the Monopoly in 1784. In 1788, according to Page, the French shipped just under 6,000 tons of salted meat to the West Indies, 3,580 tons of which was beef. In 1787 Bordeaux sent almost 3,000 tons, 1,700 tons of which was beef. At the end of the Ancien Régime it still constituted a sizeable element of trade and was run from Bordeaux by a merchant colony with a character very much its own, namely the Anglo-Irish community. These merchants were able to allow the ship owners long periods of credit, often more than twelve months, on salted meats which they had sent from Waterford or Cork.

This salted meat trade had been well established in Bordeaux for a long time. We are confidently informed by the Chamber of Commerce in 1715 that 'salted beef from Ireland has always provided the commercial base upon which trade with America rests as it is used to feed the negroes'. Throughout the century the exportation of Irish products developed considerably as it was boosted by the rapid growth of the sugar and subsequently coffee plantations of Santo Domingo. In 1769 it was, according to L. Cullen, 73% higher than it had been between 1717 and 1720[4]. In 1770 Bordeaux took in over 5,000 tons of salt beef from Ireland, some of which, it should be noted, never actually reached the West Indies as it was used to feed a constantly increasing fleet of merchant seamen. In the 1770s between two thirds and three quarters of Irish beef exports were absorbed by English colonies and France. Levels of demand on the transatlantic markets actually reached a peak on the eve of the American War of Independence. Previous conflicts had had fairly limited effect on trade bound for the West Indies because, in spite of British embargoes, products still reached the planters through neutral fleets such as the Dutch one. The embargo appears to have been far more drastic during the American War of Independence. The Irish market began to contract in spite of the demands of their Navy and the troops. In the 1780s there was a marked increase in direct supplies from North America and L. Cullen concludes that the old Irish salted meat markets had dwindled and even disappeared in 1800. The Irish prosperity which had been so closely linked to the rapid growth of the plantations failed to survive the crisis; at least this was certainly the case with Santo Domingo. After 1815, the volume of exports came to no more than a quarter to a third of what it had been in its heyday during the 1770s.

---

[4] Louis M. Cullen, *An Economic History of Ireland since 1660* (London, 1971), p.53.

The *Code Noir* put planters under an obligation to give their slaves salted fish if there was no salt meat. The colonists of the West Indies seemed able to depend for their supplies on the produce of the French fisheries of the Great Bank of Newfoundland. In 1788, French fish production was estimated at about 262,000 hundred-weight of dried cod, worth 7 million *livres*. In the same year French ports shipped salted fish worth just under five million *livres* to the Caribbean (this total also includes livestock, although their value was quite low). The figures for these shipments from France should also include the cargoes which shipowners were able to send direct from fishing zones in the West Indies.

The market could not, in fact, have been adequately supplied without the aid, once again, of North America. In 1788 the North Americans are believed to have exported produce worth seven million *livres* from their fisheries and Page emphasizes the fact that seven-elevenths of these exports went to French or colonial ports. There is an official note to the effect that in 1787 goods worth over five million *livres* entered the warehouses of Santo Domingo which were open to trade from the United States and, at the Saint-Pierre warehouse in Martinique, import figures stood at over 2.3 million *livres*. In its early stages, the American War of Independence seemed to threaten the existence of a trade which was vital to the planters. A captain from Bordeaux, who had put in at Saint-Pierre noted on 20 May 1776 that flour and cod were becoming very scarce 'since the New England War'[5]. This shortage did not in fact last very long and on 18 December 1776 a merchant in Port-au-Prince was surprised to see North American trade picking up again: 'there are ships coming in from that part of the world every day'. In spite of the encouragement which the government of Louis XVI gave the French fishing industry, in this area, as in others, the islands, especially Santo Domingo, depended heavily on American imports.

It is important to point out that these merchants who, when sitting *en masse* in their home Chambers of Commerce protested violently against the opening of the islands to foreign trade, did not scruple to try and take advantage of it when the opportunity arose. This attitude emerges strongly in the correspondence of the Bordeaux merchant, Labat de Sérène. Immediately after the lifting of the Trade Monopoly in August 1784, a move which the Chambers of Commerce could not condemn harshly enough, Jean-Pierre Labat de Sérène planned to send ships loaded with unrefined sugar, coffee and cocoa, all of which were prohibited products, from Martinique to the coast of America. One of his agents in Saint-Pierre, where merchants showed the greatest ingenuity in evading the rules, stated that in spite of the risks involved it was advisable to 'be on good terms' with the coasters carrying prohibited goods which could be placed at the bottom of the hold and then covered over with authorized merchandise. Goods of this kind were loaded along the coasts outside the ports. The safest way of doing this was to fake shipments to the islands of Saint-Pierre and Miquelon. None of the new regulations which attempted to put an end to smuggling amounted to anything more than 'ineffectual scare tactics'. Ships could go to Charleston, which was busier on the trading front than Baltimore and then take on freight for France.

---

[5] Archives départementales de la Gironde, 7 B 1449, correspondence of Jacques Grenouilleau, ship-owner.

The high buying season in Baltimore was Christmas when tobacco was at its cheapest, best and most abundant. Boston was considered to be too far north and goods were 10% dearer there. Even if it was not possible to store everything at the bottom of the hold, smugglers devised the idea of placing prohibited goods in rum barrels all of which could then be passed off as containing rum. It is not difficult to see why one of the ships in question was called *Doctor Pangloss*. Everything was for the best in the world of trade. Inevitably, the interests of the international merchant community did not fit in with those of the state. The practices outlined above flagrantly disregarded regulations and war. Other cases could be quoted, such as the Jewish shipping company of Bordeaux, David Gradis and Sons, which used the services of fellow Jews based in London and Saint-Eustace, at the time of the American War of Independence, to keep the plantations of Martinique supplied with Irish beef which had officially been hit by the embargo.

The rise of the West Indian market had stimulated the development of food industries such as flour in South-Western France. Although it did not, on the other hand, permit the expansion of 'home-grown' meat exports and the French fisheries were not able to meet the demands of the markets, there was one product shipped to the Caribbean which underwent considerable development. Wine and its substitute brandy undoubtedly profited from the prosperity of the colonies. It is therefore not entirely surprising, given the way in which viticulture spread inland, that wine was nearly always a principal element of cargoes from Bordeaux, La Rochelle and Nantes. Wine, at a total value of 6.7 million *livres*, easily headed the list of 'food' shipments to the French West Indies in 1788 with flour, at a value of 5.7 million *livres*, ranking well behind it. The majority of the cargoes consisted of Bordeaux wine. They amounted to a total value of 4.8 million *livres* and a total volume of over 330,300 hectolitres as against 114,300 hectolitres of other wines. The hold on West Indian markets was particularly evident where French wines were concerned and this was especially true of Guyana where, at the beginning of the century, the West Indies only provided a small outlet for the wine growers. In 1723, this market scarcely made up 10% of Bordeaux's exports, which was seven times smaller than the Dutch market. In the 1770s, when colonial trade was at its peak, the shipping of Bordeaux wine to the West Indies was already approaching the volume it reached at the end of the Ancien Régime, that is over 270,000 hectolitres or 40% of the total Bordeaux wine trade. The colonies were the best foreign market at that time as they bought greater quantities than either Holland or the Hanseatic ports. The wines came from all over Aquitaine and from the vineyards of Gaillac and Cahors in particular. Shipowners, however, tended to acquire estates in the area around Bordeaux which was closer to their own firms and kept them supplied with the best cargo wines. Wines were an essential element of these cargoes. On certain ships, as in the case of the *Basse Pointe*, which was owned by David Gradis and Sons and bore the emblem of the owner's plantation in Martinique, the 1,359 hectolitres taken on board in September 1786 were worth 36,766 *livres* and represented almost 20% of the total value of the cargo.

Foodstuffs such as flour, salt meat, fish and wines were vital to the planters and their work force and to colonial towns. The significance of these towns should not be underestimated as the consumption there of products such as wine and flour was relatively higher than that of the plantations. The only town on the French Cape, at Santo Domingo, had a population of about 20,000 in 1788, the number of houses and inhabitants having tripled in less than half a century. Port-au-Prince had a population of over 10,000 at that time. According to Moreau de Saint-Méry, over 2,200 tons of flour were consumed per year on the French Cape[6]. Assuming that consumption levels were comparable in Port-au-Prince, these two towns must have absorbed over 3,000 tons of flour, that is slightly less than 20% of the total shipped by France to the West Indies.

Fashion and clothing

The plantations, and probably to an even greater extent the towns, were particularly keen to get hold of consumer goods. Sheets, and especially fine quality cloth, lingerie and hosiery for the well-to-do and the planters, coarser linen cloth for the slaves, shoes, silk stockings and handkerchiefs were all articles which pandered to the coquetry of the Creole people. Moreau de Saint-Méry gives a better picture than anyone of how the population of the French Cape was drawn to these items sold privately and displayed at the White Market every Sunday: 'jewellery, shoes, hats, haberdashery, crockery, pottery, old iron and ... monkeys or parrots .... the market starts at about seven o'clock and lasts until midday. It's the done thing to take a stroll around the White Market even if you're not going to buy anything.' Apart from the vivid description, these markets also give a better idea than food sales of the tight hold which the world of the plantations and colonial towns had on national economies. The importance to the British economy of the rapid expansion which took place in the Irish and Scottish linen industries is already well known, as these expanded to meet the growing requirements of the continental American and West Indian markets.

Products from Bohemia, Silesia, Brittany, Venice and Birmingham passed through Atlantic ports and converged on these privileged areas of commerce. In 1788, out of goods worth over a total 76 million *livres* exported from France to the West Indies, textiles exceeded 34 million placing them way ahead of foodstuffs which amounted to less than 29 million *livres*. 'Utility' cloth, worth over 127 millions, was easily the leading export. As early as the seventeenth century, Breton cloth had enjoyed considerable success on the Spanish American market following its exclusion from the English market. It remained a favourite amongst West Indian consumers in the following century. In the port of Bordeaux alone, the exporting of white linen cloth reached a value of 6 million *livres* in 1787. The exportation of muslin from France and India was bordering on one million. Bordeaux merchants shipped silks worth 400,000 *livres*. Hosiery, especially Cholet handkerchiefs, was very much in demand and Bordeaux shipped 1.6 million *livres* of it. In order to supply these very varied consignments, buyers focused on all areas of production in France and abroad. White linen from Maine,

[6] Moreau de Saint-Méry, *Description de la partie française de Saint-Domingue* (Philadelphia, 1797), II, 493. He indicates that at the French Cape twenty-five bakers used 70 barrels of flour a day, at 180 lbs per barrel, a total of 12,600 lbs a day.

conversation chairs and cotton cloth from Rouen, hosiery from Troyes and Cholet, Sedan sheets, lace from Le Puy, silks and ribbons from Lyons and Saint-Étienne, made up the extremely wide range from which West Indian trade gained its profits.

Owing to their high value and minimal bulk, these goods formed the basis for seamens' private dealings and were often brought on credit by merchants who could not afford a share in a whole cargo or the expense of fitting their own ships but who could earn a substantial amount in this kind of trade. These merchant adventurers in Port-au-Prince, the French Cape and Saint-Pierre in Martinique would make use of relations in the locality whose knowledge of the markets was the key to the success of their dealings. High quality foodstuffs, potted goose leg, baskets of anisette, fruits preserved in brandy, crates of capers and cheeses, bottles of vintage wine, saveloy and beef stew all went to satisfy the voracious Creole appetite. Moreau de Saint-Méry notes on this point, 'the corruption of taste induced by heat means that salted meat, ham, goose leg, beef stew and sausage have become the staple diet.' Handkerchiefs from Saumur and Cholet, ladies' and gentlemens' silk stockings, fine quality shirts, weapons, pistols and guns from Saint-Etienne testified to the value placed on appearances which was so important on the islands.

The value of these goods intended for private sale was far from insignificant. A private cargo worth 10,000 to 15,000 *livres*, or even more, would ensure the most profitable returns in indigo or piastres. Certain Portuguese Jewish companies seem to have made a speciality in this area of sales, not only to the French colonies but also to the ports of Spanish America. Salomon Raba, one of the founders of the great Bordeaux company, informs us that, 'The Spanish bought fine quality goods such as silks, cambric, lace, velvet, gold and silver braid and silk stockings from us'[7]. Jacob Azevedo, one of his rivals, noted in a letter of 1771 that the Raba company was sending a great deal of the quality clothing such as twill and silken breeches and silk dressing gowns, which were popular with the colonists, along with a large number of gilt decorations, all of which was shipped as private cargo and brought in large profits. In fact, the Raba Company, which was set up in Bordeaux in 1765 and subsequently established a subsidiary on the French Cape with a capital liability of 80,000 *livres*, found itself holding assets of over 4.3 million *livres* less than twenty years later in 1783. This fortune made Raba one of Bordeaux's leading companies. More than 20-22% of the profits were made from private sales which figure appears to be well above what came in from cargoes or ship-fitting. Profits were also maintained by Spanish merchandise such as cocoa from the coast of Caracas, indigo from Guatemala and piastres. Although, according to Ch. Carrière, the Jews of Marseilles were no more than a 'marginal group with apparently limited means at their disposal', in Bordeaux and Nantes, as in Port-au-Prince and the French Cape, their communities were very active. Bordeaux in the 1780s possessed over 150 Jewish households. Their close links with communities in Amsterdam, London and Curaçao enabled them to make use of a solidarity network which was indispensable to business proceedings.

---

[7] Raba private archives, *mémoir* on his life by Salomon Raba; see Gérard Nahon, 'Un Portugais se penche sur son passé: la note didactique de Benjamin Raba', *Hommage à George Vajda*, ed. Peeters (Louvain, 1980), p.526.

An Increasing Number of Men

The private sale of goods was a common starting point for 'upstarts' who came to the Indies to make the fortune that had eluded them at home. A vast influx of men doubled, in effect, the movement of goods linking the homeland to the colonies. Natives of Bordeaux were particularly numerous as they had crossed the Atlantic in the 1780s. In Bordeaux, as in the other ports, the 'American' group tended to be extravagant with the money they had made on the plantations or in West Indian business. Available information relating to the period between the American War of Independence and the Revolution is unfortunately rather incomplete, although it is possible to make a few estimates. Passengers sailing from Bordeaux numbered 120 in 1780, 160 in 1781 and 84 in 1782. The war seems to have slowed crossings considerably despite the use of a detour via Ostend, but the movement of passengers picked up again in 1783 when 951 people set sail. In 1784 there were 630 passengers in the first eight months of the year increasing to 1,013 in 1787. Figures such as these are particularly useful in assessing movements in the closing years of the Ancien Régime. A distinct increase emerges in relation to preceding decades. In the period from 1767 to 1776 a total of 7,829 passengers set sail for the Americas. Forty years earlier between 1727 and 1736 the number of departures only amounted to 2,215. J. P. Poussou has counted almost 31,000 passengers departing from the port of Bordeaux alone between 1713 and 1787[8]. These numbers certainly do not compare with those of the following century when emigrants keen to leave for North and Latin America were crowding into the French ports. In 1837, 1838 and 1839, Bordeaux witnessed the departure of 2,028, 2,379 and 1,398 passengers, 43% of whom were bound for Central America. From Le Havre, on the other hand, almost 100% of departures, that is an average of about 7,500 emigrants in each of those three years, were bound for North America. The degree of movement in the eighteenth century was certainly lower than this and it is difficult to arrive at any definite conclusions as to its real significance[9]. It is certainly not acceptable to interpret this movement merely in terms of emigration. Many of the passengers were planters on the way back from a trip home with their families. The figures also include tradesmen and merchants who had been on business trips to Paris or the ports, and there were even quite a few large number of slaves who had been to France to learn a craft or who were travelling with their masters. There were also a few free coloured people who had taken a trip to France and were returning to the West Indies.

It should be pointed out that these 'official lists' take no account of stowaways nor of the large numbers of deserting officers and sailors who emigrated to the West Indies during the long periods that the ships put into port.

Although genuine emigrants do not seem to have constituted the majority of passengers, there definitely were some, and quite a wide choice of careers was open to them on arrival. They could be private traders, would-be merchants, lawyers, medical practitioners, surgeons, law officers who would not have to pay

---

[8] Arch.dép.Gironde, 6 B 57-58, registres des passagers, 1780-7. Thanks are due to my colleague and friend Jean-Pierre Poussou for providing the number of passengers from 1713-87.
[9] Maurice Lévy-Leboyer, *Les banques européennes et l'industrialisation internationale dans la première moitié du XIXe siècle* (Paris 1964), p.287 for the emigrants in 1837-9.

expenses as in France, craftsmen whose know-how was always at a premium on the plantations and in the towns, and in many instances there were young men aged between twenty and twenty-five who had no particular speciality to offer but found the unknown exercized a certain appeal. Hilliard d'Auberteuil protested against the immigration of these people without trades or professions considering them to be a danger. Some of them managed to obtain posts as assistant managers on the plantations or book-keepers in tax offices or commercial firms. Many of them, however, remained unemployed and made up the groups of 'Poor Whites' who inhabited the very unruly towns and were willing to get involved in the revolts of 1790[10]. Following P. Pluchon it is possible to trace a certain antipathy towards them on the part of the colonies. In his *Plan de Constitution pour la Colonie de Saint-Domingue*, Ch. de Chabanon asks, 'How often do we see people in the West Indies who have been forced out of their own country by their dissolute behaviour, vice and even crime? What a long list we could make of deserting sailors, cheap-jack traders and lower middle class folk, in a word "poor whites" whose dissolute and debauched behaviour with black and half-caste women makes them quite intolerable everywhere!' In taking this attitude the colonists chose to forget, perhaps, that many of them owed their own fortunes to the efforts of an ancestor who had chosen the American Eldorado, or what he had taken to be such, in preference to the more humble conditions of his homeland.

It is very important to take into account the fact that many people's wealth certainly was founded upon decisions originally made for apparently dubious reasons. Apart from the Raba family, the Bordeaux merchants who were so powerful during the 1780s, an obvious example is Jacques Mesplès, that humble merchant's clerk who was uprooted from his family at the age of twelve to serve a merchant's apprenticeship in various towns of South West France and left Bordeaux as an apprentice in the merchant navy at the age of nineteen in the middle of the Seven Years War in 1761: 'My modest wages did not satisfy my need to earn money and so I had the idea of going over to the West Indies'. Such statements prove that he was definitely induced to leave France by the appeal of making a fortune overseas. As was often the case with characters like Mesplès, he deserted his ship as soon as he arrived in Port-au-Prince, and with the assistance of a 'relation', since friends or relations from the same town or village played a major role in helping immigrants to start up, he obtained merchandise worth 1,400 *livres* on credit and then successfully concluded his first 'private deal'. Mesplès sent for his brother to join him, his private sales continued and prospered and the profits went into indigo and cotton which Mesplès then went to sell personally in Paris and at Beaucaire fair. Following his return to Santo Domingo, he made two more trips to Europe and in 1770 he began a career as a shipowner in the West Indies. He then increased his business dealings by making sizeable investments in real estate which led to his involvement in the building of Port-au-Prince theatre round about 1777. The deserter of the 1760s had become one of the town's leading citizens with a sum of over 1.6 million *livres* at his disposal although he had started out with a mere 1,400. In 1782, the *nouveau riche* Mesplès even attempted to add patriotic glory to his notoriety in business by trying to persuade the authorities to

---

[10]P. Pluchon, *Histoire des Antilles et de la Guyane* (Toulouse, 1982), p.185.

agree to a plan of campaign against Jamaica[11].

There was, indisputably, a 'movement of men' between France and the Caribbean. Of course, they did not all depart in the obscure circumstances of deserting sailors. Some were drawn by the cultural development of the colonial towns. In July 1784, four architects, aged between 32 and 40 years old, announced that they were going to leave Bordeaux for the French Cape. The spectacular growth of urban development in this particular town was connected with immigrants such as these. Also in 1784, four dancers set sail from France probably intending to perform in the shows which were held every Sunday, Tuesday and Thursday and crowded out with locals as Moreau de Saint-Méry observes. He emphasizes 'the Creoles' passion' for tragedy and comedy and their craze for dancers.

The West Indies and the Enlightenment

Do ideas follow the movements of men? It is undeniable that knowledge did travel across the Ocean. Moreau de Saint-Méry, who was an excellent chronicler of events in Santo Domingo, takes careful note of how the first collections of literature were set up on the French Cape allowing the locals to subscribe to journals and buy books. He quotes two Swiss, one of whom was from Geneva, as having assisted in this matter. Printers and booksellers began to send to Santo Domingo their first editions, and even newspapers such as the *Affiches Americaines* which dealt basically with business and legal news. Journals such as these had as many as 1,500 subscribers, as did the *Affiches Americaines* in 1788.[12] The *Cèrcle des Philadelphes*, founded in 1784 received official recognition on 17 May 1789 when it was awarded the title of The French Cape Royal Society for the Sciences and the Arts. At that time it had 40 resident members.

It is difficult to gauge exactly how far this culture did penetrate a colonial environment which was more interested in making a rapid fortune than in anything else. In a daybook belonging to a Bordeaux merchant bookseller there is a reference in 1790, not only to numerous works by Rousseau and Voltaire being sold to the town's merchants, but also to the shipment of two crates of books worth 825 *livres* to a inhabitant of Dondon in Santo Domingo. There is no further information available, however, about books being sent to this West Indian planter[13], though it seems highly likely that this was far from being an isolated example. It could be postulated that books, like other forms of merchandise, provided the basis for a thriving trade between the French Islands and Spanish possessions. This was very probably the case. R. Darnton has pointed to the difficulties which the editors of the *Encyclopédie* encountered, despite using Flemish staging points in Ostend, or Italian ones in Turin and Genoa, in trying to get their works into Spain and Portugal[14]. Spanish booksellers lived in fear and

[11] Arch.Nat., Outre-Mer, fonds dit de l'Indemnité de Saint-Domingue, note manuscrite de Jacques Mesplès.
[12] Moreau de Saint-Méry, op. cit., I,323.
[13] Arch.dép. Gironde, 7 B 1450, registres, Ducot, marchand-libraire.
[14] Robert Darnton, *L'aventure de l'Encyclopédie* (Paris, 1982), p.238.

trembling of the Inquisition and were not prepared to run any risks. It is possible to conclude from this that the Caribbean smuggling trade favoured the circulation of books in Spanish America rather than in the homeland. In the latter, the Abbé Raynal was translated in 1784 and an edition of the *Histoire des Deux Indes* was published in Madrid. These works could hardly do other than encourage American colonists to believe that prosperity came through the freedom of trade and agriculture[15].

II

The Transformation of Trade during the Revolution and the Empire.

The slave revolt in Santo Domingo in August 1791 and the maritime wars during the Revolution and the Empire put an end to a Golden Age in West Indian Trade, although it did not seem quite so golden to many French merchants. Quite a few of them within the ports were aware of the internal problems of commerce and in particular of increasingly strong foreign competition. They blamed this competition for their falling profits and doubtless failed to realize that powerful innovative measures were really called for in order to make their ventures pay. When innovation did receive the support of the law, as had been the case when the Monopoly was lifted in 1784, they simply called for protection through a return to the old structure of the privileged market. During the turmoil of the Revolution when sugar mills of the Greater Antilles ground to a halt and ships ceased to cross the Atlantic, their sole desire was to return to times past during which they had prospered for so long. This remained the attitude they took when peace was restored in 1815.

The violence of the revolution considerably weakened trade. The plantations were ruined by the slave revolt and danger abounded at sea. It is, however, worth qualifying the impression this picture gives. Santo Domingo was not so cut off from Europe as is generally claimed. Sometimes French merchants used British and American staging posts so that some trade with the Greater Antilles remained possible, although it was certainly carried out under very difficult conditions. Coffee production, in particular, did remain, quite high as it depended less on the huge working parties of slaves which had been broken up by the revolt. A few planters sought refuge in Jamaica and Cuba, which was just emerging as a large sugar producing island, and continued their business there. Martinique which was occupied by the English for most of the Revolution, restored in 1802 and then reoccupied by the British in 1805, was also able to keep production going. Guadeloupe remained firmly under the control of the Republic in the form of Victor Hughes and managed, until the naval war of the Empire, to maintain a far from insignificant position in French markets.

The main point of interest does not, however, lie in the fact that some merchants of Bordeaux or Nantes made efforts to keep up trading links and occasionally met with success. It is far more important to observe how the North

---

[15] Victor-Louis Tapié, *Histoire de l'Amérique Latine* (Paris, 1945), p.26.

Americans and the English took a hold in the West Indies, and to note the transformation of trade which accompanied this development.

Vain Hopes

Although the French business world had connections with American companies which were often quite effective, the French do not seem to have been genuinely aware of the economic 'revolution' which was taking place or, more specifically, of the major roles which New York and London had to play in this. In 1815, when the Lesser Antilles were surrendered to the France of Louis XVIII, the sole intention of the French traders was to resume their former relations with the colonies within the framework of a fully restored Monopoly and they hoped to regain a foothold in Santo Domingo. As far as the latter was concerned there appears to have been a powerful current of opinion which historians have not, perhaps, taken sufficiently into account. If one attempts to compile a register of everything published between 1800 and 1810, containing some reference to the restoration of Santo Domingo, a whole series of works would emerge which appeared amongst the 'best-sellers' of the day, or at least this would be the case in the ports and their surrounding areas. They all concentrate on ways of regaining possession of the Greater Antilles and re-establishing peace there. The colony's history of disasters is used to insinuate that it would be in the interests of the State to allow the former colonists to recover their properties. These colonists, experiencing a kind of mass psychosis and obliged to take refuge in Kingston, Jamaica, address their complaints to the home Chambers of Commerce in 1814. This indicates that the plantations had suffered total ruination. No effort was made to understand the real motive of the black rebel slaves. 'The negro's idea of liberty is the right to do nothing.' If possession of the island were regained 'a great many ships would soon set sail for the colonies from Bordeaux, Marseilles, Nantes, La Rochelle, Le Havre, Dunkirk and other home ports loaded with territorial and manufacturing goods .... in order to trade them at a profit as they used to do in the old days, for the invaluable commodities which come from our mountains and plains.'[16]

These colonists, faithful to the doctrine which they themselves had helped to weaken by opening more and more ports to foreigners (after all there was even an English 'covered market' on the French Cape), could not see beyond the possibility of re-establishing direct links, protected by a Monopoly, between the homeland and its recovered colony, even though trade between the two had undergone a complete transformation.

---

[16] A Lunan, *Exposé de l'état actuel des choses dans la colonie de Saint-Domingue par les colons réfugiés à la Jamaïque* (Kingston, 1814).

Cuba and the New Plantations

It is impossible to stress too highly the magnitude of the American breakthrough in the West Indies, immediately after the War of Independence. This breakthrough was intensified during the Revolution and the Empire, although it began long before either of these events. The first trade centre outside the French islands, which the companies of Baltimore, Philadephia and New York used, was undoubtedly Havana. The 'English' occupation of this port in 1762 established the necessary links with North American merchants. By 1780 these merchants had founded companies and their business expanded considerably at the time of the Santo Domingo Revolution. The rise of sugar prices in Europe which followed the revolution gave an added incentive to these new ventures. In addition to this, in 1792 and 1793, French planters in Santo Domingo were beginning to withdraw to the nearby island of Cuba taking their capital and their slaves with them[17].

Production in Cuba amounted to no more than 12,000 tons of sugar between 1786 and 1789. Its annual average between 1790 and 1799 came to nearly 19,000 tons, in 1800-1809 it rose to 31,500 tons and in 1810-1819 it reached the level of 37,000 tons. It should be noted that it was largely as a result of new developments on the world market after 1820 that it soared to over 60,000 tons in 1820-1829[18]. Cuba reached a production level comparable to Jamaica at the beginning of the nineteenth century. The island owed this rapid expansion in sugar growing both to the influx of Santo Domingo planters who brought their technology and their slaves and also to the fact that their produce entered the markets via North American traders. The number of American ships docking in Havana in 1796 totalled 150 which represented 27% of the port's shipping. In 1800 there were 604 vessels, representing 78% of the shipping. Cuban sugar exports to the United States rose to about 28,000 tons at that time.

The coffee trade also underwent considerable development at the end of the eighteenth century and the beginning of the nineteenth in the Santiago region of Cuba, resulting once again from the settlement of both white and mulatto colonists leaving Santo Domingo, especially following the failure of the Leclerc expedition in 1803. In 1800, Cuba was already exporting over 1,350 tons to the United States and these shipments doubled in 1806 rising to over 2,300 tons[19]. The settlement in Cuba of refugees from Santo Domingo played a large part in this development. A. Yocau estimates the number of white colonists from Santo Domingo who came under the jurisdiction of Santiago in Cuba at over 2,600 and the number of free mulattos at 1,891 in 1808. The progress made in coffee production was not, however, comparable to the sugar boom which the island enjoyed. In 1801, the

---

[17] A. Yocau, L'émigration des colons français de Saint-Domingue au cours de la Révolution, Université de Bordeaux III, thèse de troisième cycle, 1973, p.286.

[18] H. S. Klein, 'The Cuban Slave Trade, 1790-1843', *Revue française d'histoire d'Outre-Mer*, LXII (1975), 70.

[19] The refugee planters from Santo Domingo also developed the production of coffee on Jamaica from the 1790s; in 1795, according to Seymour Drescher, *Econocide, British Slavery in the Era of Abolition* (Pittsburgh, 1977), p.88, Jamaica exported three times more coffee than Martinique.

United States which was the only neutral transporting country at that time, imported in the region of 19,000 tons of coffee (including produce from Santo Domingo) from the French Indies. Between 1804 and 1805, when Santo Domingo had been devastated by another war of independence, the Americans were still importing about 12,000 tons from the French islands. American imports into Cuba were still considerably lower than this. It should be pointed out that this French colonial produce represented barely a third of what their production levels had been in 1788.

The decision to open the Spanish American ports to the free trading of slaves had, in 1789, been a powerful contributory factor in the rapid growth of new plantations and the North American trade which kept them supplied with provisions and labour. H. S. Klein underlines the close parallel between the growth of Cuban sugar exports which stood at around 147% between 1790 and 1819, and the progress made in Cuban slave imports, which increased by 578% over the same period, growing at an even faster rate[20]. The Americans were not, however, the only ones to profit from the development of this market and all the major trading powers had some share in it. The slaves, unloaded at Havana numbered 5,041 per year in the decade 1790-1799. During the first two decades of the nineteenth century this number rose to an annual average of 5,295 and 11,797[21]. There was a distinct increase in the early 1790s and the 1800s, followed by a fairly marked shift in levels of importation. They did not experience a rapid rise again until 1810 as the high entry levels paved the way for the second Cuban sugar boom in the 1820s. These fluctuations should be considered in relation to the problems encountered by neutral trade, especially between 1807 and 1810. Klein has also shown that the Americans were unusual in importing slaves mainly from the Caribbean repositories of Jamaica, Saint-Eustace and Dominica. The use of this inter-Caribbean network distinguishes American traders from their English and Spanish rivals who tended rather to import from the coast of Africa[22]. According to Anstey the Americans brought 41,730 slaves directly from Africa to Cuba between 1791 and 1810 and 18,720 to the rest of Spanish America during that period. Cuba was thus clearly the main import centre for American traders in the Caribbean[23].

The Rise of the Americans

The United States had profited from the opening of Spanish American ports to foreign trade (this opening had coincided with Cuba's first boom in sugar production) and from the naval war between France and Great Britain. From 1793 onwards the conflict had forced the French Indies to depend on foreign traders. The Americans, who transported colonial products from the French and Spanish colonies and sold them indispensable food and consumer goods in return,

---

[20] Klein, art, cit., p.69.
[21] ibid., p.70 after the estimates of Humboldt.
[22] ibid, p.74.
[23] R. Anstey, 'The volume of the North American Slave-Carrying Trade from Africa, 1761-1810', *Revue française d'historie d'Outre-Mer*, LXII (1975), 64.

could hardly fail to get involved in this profitable line of shipping in spite of a powerful current of public opinion moving for the abolition of this trade. Anstey sees a close link between these movements. The tonnage of American goods grew between 1789 and 1806 to over eight times its previous volume, whilst American coffee exports rose from 500 tons to 17,500 tons between 1791 and 1794. Finally the Anglo-Spanish War in 1796 provided the Americans with even greater opportunities to intervene in trade. They, along with the Danes, remained the only neutral nations who could offer to carry out transactions in relative safety[24].

A report written in November 1799 by a Bordeaux merchant at a time when American trade was suffering an embargo in France, recognized the importance of American shipping which 'was flourishing and has gone on to fare even better during the early years of the war because we have been able to trade indirectly with our colonies by sailing under the American flag.'[25] It should be emphasized that some American companies who took advantage of the increased scope in shipping set up in Bordeaux, Nantes and Bayonne. There were also conversely, traders from France or of French origin who settled on the American side of the Atlantic between New York and Charleston and who were often partners in West Indian companies or who had trading posts in Cuba, Santo Domingo or Guadeloupe. Although these links took root before the Santo Domingo revolution they were certainly strengthened as a result of it. Merchants or planters from the Greater Antilles withdrew to the coast of America. E. H. Schell has studied the network of Dutilh, who had a brother Jean Dutilh living in Jamaica. Etienne Dutilh joined the Wachsmuth firm in Philadelphia and prospered in business there until his death in 1810[26].

The Atlantic coast of the United States was essential as a staging post in the 'indirect' shipping which linked France to its possessions in the West Indies. In Europe two different zones were available to Franco-American commerce. The north European ports, mainly Hamburg, were used to store colonial commodities and were also kept supplied by British commerce. The northern coast of Spain from Corunna to San Sebastián was frequented by American ships because merchandise could quite easily be dispatched from there to Bordeaux and Paris via Bayonne[27]. As a result of blockage, relations between companies on either side of

---

[24] ibid, p.58. Seymour Drescher, op. cit., p.72 shows that the English also profited in the 1790s from the needs of the Antilles, calculating that annually more than 40,000 slaves were landed by their traders. The restrictive legislation of 1799 (obligations to provide a minimum space on board ship for each negro transported) slowed down this expansion, but English capital could be invested under a neutral flag. The Slave markets of Jamaica, Surinam and Trinidad were still very important in 1806 on the eve of the abolition of the slave-trade by the English.

[25] Paul Butel, *La croissance commercial bordelaise dans la deuxième moitié du XVIIIe siècle* (Lille, Atelier des thèses, 1973), I, 148-9.

[26] Ernest H. Schell, 'Stephen Dutilh and the challenge of neutrality: the French trade of a Philadelphia merchant, 1793-1807', *Conference on Franco-American Relations, 1765-1815* (Eleutherian Mills Historical Library, October 1977). P. Butel, *Les négociants bordelais, l'Europe et les Iles au XVIIIe siècle* (Paris, 1974), p.46 for the example of the firm of Pierre Changeur installed at Baltimore. In 1804 the American market was the second largest customer of Bordeaux with more than 7 million *livres* of imports.

[27] Cottons from Lisbon, one of the main centres of neutral trade, were transported by carts

the Atlantic tended to fluctuate. Consequently, in the spring of 1797 the crisis in Franco-American relations caused Etienne Dutilh to concentrate more on trade with India and China and also on direct trade with Cuba and the American ports. Two years later, Dutilh used Spanish staging posts to ship tobacco and sugar to France. El Ferrol, Corunna and San Sebastián were the ports where he had agents. These ports, where the goods captured by pirates were sold, also provided warehouses for colonial commodities such as sugar and cotton from Brazil and merchandise relating to the black slave trade or to European trade in the West Indies, cloth from Brittany and Silesia, *'baptistes'*, silk stockings and watches, all of which were articles 'fit for Vera Cruz and Caracas'. African and West Indian trade was still undertaken in Spanish America. In addition to the shipment of West Indian coffee and sugar, Etienne Dutilh also loaded his ships with campeachy wood from Central America and cocoa from Caracas. French firms retained their reputation by shipping valuables, vintage wines, Lyons silks and high quality cloth. Some French shipowners took advantage of the neutral position afforded by the American flag and continued in the midst of the war to ship standard cargoes in which food and equipment made up the largest part of the tonnage. On 13 August 1804 a Bordeaux shipowner named Charles Fieffé loaded an American brig which he owned with wine, flour, oil, and boilers for the sugar mills. It was bound for Santo Domingo[28].

On a micro-economic level these diverse companies convey some ideas of how business in France under the Directory and to an even greater extent under the Consulate and the early days of the Empire was consistently deluded about the situation in the West Indies and America[29]. Periods of peace or negotiation meant, in effect, that all the merchants could resume traditional maritime trade and enjoy a return to their former prosperity. During these periods the produce from new trading companies set up in Paris and the main ports flourished, bringing together bankers, merchants or former Santo Domingo planters. The existence of an American circuit doing trade in cotton and cloth from India and of a rival British circuit helped to feed these ambitions which were, however, less and less founded on realities. L. Bergeron has analysed the relatively effective policies of men like Oberkampf and Ternaux who led the French markets in prints and cotton. Spanish America continued to provide outlets for these manufacturers with the assistance of American staging posts. Bayonne emerged as a place of primary importance in controlling access to this market, on account of its relations with Cádiz, Oporto and Lisbon. Nevertheless, this type of trading remained speculative and prices fluctuated wildly from one extreme to the other. Places either experienced serious shortages or glutting, as occurred in Lisbon which

---

from Bayonne to Paris: see Paul Butel, Charles Fieffé, *armateur et commissionaire*, contribution à la négoce bordelais sous la Révolution et l'Empire, Université de Bordeaux III, thèse de troisième cycle, 1967 (ed. Hachette, microfiches, 1973), pp.144-9.
[28] ibid., p.131
[29] Louis Bergeron, *Banquiers, négociants et manufacturiers parisiens du Directoire à l'Empire* (Paris, 1975), ii.724 well analyses how this business world was seized 'by feverish hope' when peace negotiations led it to believe in a return to 'normal conditions'; ibid., p.478 for the American textile circuit; p.535, for the establishment of Ternaux in the world of international commerce and p.658 for Oberkampf and exports.

amassed 60,000 bales of cotton at the end of 1807, only to suffer shortages in spring 1808 causing cotton prices to rocket.

Commercial trade was doubled by trade supplying the government which was equally open to any prospects the Atlantic afforded. The ambitions of Ouvrard provide a good case in point. In 1804 he wanted to transfer to Europe metals accumulated in Mexico which could then be converted into cash and he even went so far as to secure a commercial monopoly with Spanish America in the autumn of that year. The declaration of war between England and Spain ruined this particular venture. Even politicians were closely involved in these business speculations, and men such as Fouché and Tallien stood out in this respect at the end of the Directory. All trade carried out under these conditions remained extremely shaky as it depended heavily on foreigners and France's most positive gain during this period lay in industrial developments which centred on continental exchanges.

The presence of American merchants on both the Caribbean and European fronts prevented French colonial trade from being completely stifled. It did not, however, bring about any basic modifications in major commercial trends. Although certain tensions existed, the North Americans remained closely involved in British interests. In New York on 6 July 1797, the French merchant Michel Olive voiced his disappointment at the signing of the Anglo-American Trade Treaty. 'The English have never been totally eradicated from this country and their power is still on the increase ... they get carried away by England's power ... they are constantly indebted to their homeland's former glories and yet they use it to acquire such huge advances on goods that they fear circumstances might force English merchants to engage rather less freely in the shipping of products which they hold onto for a long time and which are one of their principal sources of finance.'[30] French merchants adhered to a traditional concept of trade, the foundations upon which the wealth of colonial trade under the Ancien Régime had been built, namely respect for the Monopoly and the use of foreign trade for illicit dealings if necessary.

III

The Impossibility of Returning to Traditional Prosperity

New Channels of Trade

After 1815 the colonial Ancien Régime appeared to have been restored. France regained its West Indian properties, Martinique and Guadeloupe and theoretically at least, the right to recover Santo Domingo. However, even allowing for the fact that the Greater Antilles had effectively been lost, the situation was not the same as it had once been. The French took only a very minor part in trade with Spanish America which had been so important to commercial

---

[30] Archives municipales de Bordeaux, Papiers Monneron, fonds privée, correspondance.

Traditions and Changes in French Atlantic Trade 143

dealings in the West Indies in 1788. For many products and for textiles in particular, New York became an indispensable intermediary. Silk from Lyons, fine quality muslin from Tarare and bombazine from Cambrésis, which had an outlet in Latin America, all passed through New York[31]. Breton and Flemish cloth shipped to America throughout the eighteenth century was replaced overseas by articles made in Belfast and Dundee. The Germans exported their Silesian *'platilles'* and their Dresden china. Their cloth was reputed for its 'sound quality' and British articles stood out as a good bargain. The French did relatively little business outside their own colonies.

Within the shipping business the Americans competed fiercely with the English because their cargoes were reasonably priced and their trade was flexible. In the Caribbean during the 1830s American ships numbered about 1,800 to 2,000, making up 53% of the tonnage in Haiti and Puerto Rico and 43% of the ships entering Cuba. In 1826 there were four times as many American ships as British in Vera Cruz (400 as against 95). There were also a great many, between 200 and 300, in the little harbours of the Spanish Main[32] Distance was a factor which worked in America's favour. 1,250 miles lay between Cuba and New York, whereas 5,000 miles separated Cuba from England.

Within Europe, London and to a lesser extend Hamburg took the lead in relations with the Caribbean. The redistribution of colonial commodities in Europe practically disappeared from ports such as Bordeaux and came to centre on the warehouses of London. Stettin, which had been one of Bordeaux's major customers before 1793, no longer bought its sugar there. Although ships continued to link the Baltic ports with Bordeaux, they carried only wine and brandy from Guyana and were no longer loaded with West Indian goods. It was London that supplied Stettin with up to 40% of its sugar. The same trend emerged in Saint Petersburg and the Danish ports.

The development of the West Indies had stimulated and unified French maritime dealings in the Atlantic. Even the fishing vessels sent to the Newfoundland Banks were, to an extent, integrated into West Indian trading channels, as they sent a proportion of the catch to the West Indies so that the profit was absorbed back into France in the form of colonial commodities. The wars of the Revolution and the Empire and to an even greater degree, transformations in Atlantic trade, the growing influence of London as the main storage point between Europe and the Americas and, finally, the impact made by North American trade, caused the French, who had lost Santo Domingo, to experience a drastic reduction in their shipping levels, which was perhaps exaggerated by the Bordeaux merchant, D. Johnston, in 1833 but did occur:

'With the exception of the territorial resources which Paris and northern Europe still draw upon, all that we once owned and which made us so properous has been virtually abandoned since it was impossible to sell it .... our advertising is limited. Our warehouses are almost totally empty and still. Bordeaux has already become a third rate trading port and is going further downhill.'[33]

---

[31] Lévy-Leboyer, op. cit., pp.146-50.

[32] ibid., pp.225 et seq. for the American entrepôt trade and their penetration into the Caribbean.

[33] ibid, p.260

An Erratic Decline

The overall decline in activity is reflected in the general movement of fleets. A 200,000 ton colonial fleet of about 700 ships in 1788 may be contrasted with the 108,000 tons of shipping per year which linked France under the July Monarchy (1835-1840) with all her American and Asian colonies[34]. Colonial imports declined very irregularly depending on the product and more specifically on the port. In 1835 sugar was shipped at a rate of 33,000 25,000 and 8,000 tons to the ports of Le Havre, Marseilles and Bordeaux and 20,740 tons entered Nantes in 1831. In 1788 sugar was imported into these ports at a rate of 9,000, 25,000 and 30,000 tons respectively, making a total of 89,000 tons. At the beginning of the July Monarchy, import levels rose to almost 86,000 tons. This amount may not seem radically different from that which was attained immediately prior to the French Revolution but it should be borne in mind that produce from Réunion in the Indian Ocean contributed to this and that sugar cane production in Guadeloupe increased quite considerably from 1820 onwards at the expense of coffee. Of all the ports which grew up around the plantation boom, Bordeaux was the hardest hit by the decline in shipping and the near extinction of its re-exportation trade to northern Europe. Nantes also suffered a decline in the sugar business in spite of progress made in the refining industry. Marseilles and Le Havre, on the other hand, were doing well, though the improvement was linked to major developments in consumption at home whereas re-exportation was on the decline. The export of refined sugar, which rose to over 15,000 tons in 1832 owing to the institution of subsidies, subsequently declined significantly and remained over two thirds lower than the Dutch re-exportation levels.

As far as the coffee trade was concerned, Le Havre, Marseilles and Bordeaux received 7,000, 4,500 and 1,860 tons in 1835. Nantes imported 890 tons in 1831. All the ports were hit by the decline in this area. In 1788 Bordeaux ranked first importing over 16,000 tons, followed by Le Havre with over 10,000 tons and then Marseilles and Nantes receiving 6,000 and 4,700 tons respectively. The loss of Santo Domingo where plantations had expanded a great deal in the latter half of the eighteenth century was not offset by imports from new producers in Cuba and Brazil. Once again, the loss of northern European markets made a considerable impact.

The reputation of Le Havre in the 1830s was based on cotton. The French market received just over 48,000 tons between 1835 and 1838. Le Havre imported in the region of 33,000 tons and its progress was particularly evident in the period following the Restoration (6,000 tons in 1820-24) and especially after the end of the Ancien Régime as 1,300 tons were imported in 1788. The growth of the cotton industry under the First Empire, initially around Paris and then in the north and east of France after 1815, explains why Le Havre held the position it did. A transformation in trade also occurred in this area. In 1788 the French Indies and Santo Domingo in particular were the main suppliers. After 1815 it was the North American market which supplied most of the market.

---

[34] ibid., p.247.

It would, however, be inaccurate to paint too black a picture of French trading activities in the Caribbean and Spanish America in the 1820s. English merchants were settling in increasing numbers in Cartagena, La Guayra and Mexico. The French were supplanted, however, on account of various political blunders and errors in their basic methods. M. Lévy-Leboyer has demonstrated a tendency towards change after 1825 with a new generation of merchants departing for South America. It is most important to note that the situation in France was highly uneven. Bordeaux was quite definitely on the decline whilst Le Havre and Marseilles were faring considerably better.

Conclusions

Having occupied a privileged position on the markets of the Americas, French trade was suddenly confronted with British and American competition to which it was forced to submit as it proved unable to regain the dynamism which had been its distinguishing feature during the eighteenth century. It did undoubtedly benefit when the Monopoly was restored in the West Indies but the loss of Santo Domingo dashed all hopes of any genuine return to times past. Time does not stand still. During the revolts and the Revolutionary and Imperial wars the Atlantic markets in Europe and the Americas came increasingly under the control of Great Britain and the United States. French business men were victims under the Directory, the Consulate and the Empire of delusions created by wild fluctuations in the overall economic climate. The chance of a return to the underlying structures of the past seemed feasible on various occasions, a particular case in point being the frenzied hope which accompanied the temporary reoccupation of Santo Domingo. But the point of no return had been reached. New producing companies had emerged and cotton, the raw material of an industry still thriving in France, was becoming America's most attractive product. Nonetheless, it would be impossible to overstate the importance which the American world still held for France after 1815, as it remained a focus of attention for a great many fortune seekers.

Université de Bordeaux III

Part IV
The United States

[13]

Explorations in Economic History 13, 397–422(1976)

Economic Change after the American Revolution: Pre- and Post-War Comparisons of Maritime Shipping and Trade*

JAMES F. SHEPHERD

Whitman College

AND

GARY M. WALTON

Indiana University and University of California, Berkeley

I. INTRODUCTION

In 1775, restrictions implemented by both the British and the American governments eliminated all direct and legal trade between the revolting 13 colonies and Great Britain and her loyal possessions. One cost of the American Revolution from the viewpoint of historians was the lapse in quantitative information on commodity trade and shipping. Not until August, 1789 did the American government take up where British officials had left off in the collection of data on shipping and trade at North American ports. Customs data for South Carolina and Pennsylvania for several years in the 1780's provide some clues to changes in the external economic relations of these states before the adoption of the Constitution, but for the most part there is a lack of sufficient statistical evidence with which to obtain a reasonably sound overall view of overseas trade and shipping for the period from 1775 to 1790. The lack of quantitative information for these years is most unfortunate, for few periods are more deserving of scholarly interest.

Of course, the levels of wartime commerce moved with the changing fortunes of war. By mid-1775 acute shortages were already felt, not only for war-related goods such as powder, flints, muskets, and knives, but also for other items like salt, shoes, woolens, and linens. To procure arms and ammunition, Congress authorized limited trade late in 1775 with the foreign West Indies, and unrestricted trade to any foreign area was allowed the following spring. Consequently, France, Spain, The Netherlands, and their American possessions became important trading partners of the revolting

*Earlier drafts of this paper have been presented to the Johns Hopkins University History Seminar on the Atlantic Economy, to the Berkeley–Stanford Economic History Workshop, to the University of Pennsylvania Economic History Seminar, to the Indiana University Economic History Seminar, and to the 49th Annual Meetings of the Western Economic Association. We are grateful to the participants at these events, who offered advice and encouragement. We also wish to thank Lawrence A. Harper, Robert L. Sexton, Gloria L. Main, Jackson Turner Main, and Gordon Philpot for comments and suggestions on an earlier version of this paper. Lastly, we are grateful to Albert Fishlow and Roger L. Ransom, who judiciously and nonanonymously acted as referees of this paper. Responsibility for any remaining errors rests solely with the authors.

colonies. Despite these new ties, the lowest levels of trade were reached in 1776 and 1777. These were years in which the British maintained an effective though incomplete naval blockade of American ports.[1] The main central ports from southern New England to Philadelphia were blockaded for most of the War, especially before 1778. Boston remained open after mid-1776, and it was a stronghold of American trade and privateering for the remaining years of the War. In addition the southern ports were open off and on until Savannah was taken in December, 1778, and Charleston in May, 1780; but these centers of trade generated little activity until commercial bonds with Europe were strengthened. Moreover, although some trade continued at British-occupied ports, such as New York, the levels of trade were low, especially for exports.

From a casual policy of open ports to foreigners, the American colonies came to sign formal treaties of commerce. The first such alliance was with France in 1778, and from this date until early 1782 American *wartime* commerce was at its zenith. Paralleling and reinforcing the rise of French–American commerce was the growth of trade with Spain and The Netherlands, especially after they entered the war against England in 1779 and 1780, respectively.

The Dutch were particularly active as carriers of tobacco from the Chesapeake, and the Dutch island of St. Eustatius took on the characteristics of an entrepôt in the Caribbean. In fact, the lively trade there contributed to Britain's decision to declare war against The Netherlands late in 1780. Pre-War commercial contacts between New England and Spain were maintained throughout the War, although normal trade between Spain and the colonies was on a reduced level, especially in fish, salt, and wine. Nevertheless, Spain was a center for the sale of captured prizes by American privateers, and similar to the Dutch island of St. Eustatius, Spanish Cuba became an important trade center in the Caribbean, particularly for Philadelphia and Baltimore merchants.

The revolting colonies suffered heavy losses at sea in 1782 as a result of the new southern deployment of the Royal Navy, which seized American vessels trading in the Caribbean. This reinforced the earlier effect of the British conquest of St. Eustatius, which severed trade with that important entrepôt in 1781. In general, British naval action was much more intensive in the last year of war, which brought insurance costs and risks at sea to an all-time high. Accordingly, the wartime flow of goods in and out of the colonies probably peaked before 1782.

Although direct firsthand evidence is lacking, there can be little doubt that wartime trade was considerably below pre-War levels. First, available quantitative evidence on earlier periods of conflict in North America shows

[1]For an interesting account of British blockades and their similar dislocating effects on the economies of Continental Europe during the Napoleonic Wars, see Crouzet (1964).

that wartime brought about sharp reductions in commerce, especially exports. For instance, the official values of colonial exports from 1751 to 1755 were over 40% higher than during the following 5 years of war (*Historical Statistics*, 1960, p. 757). It should be emphasized that this decline was precipitated *without* legal restrictions and blockades, effects that tended further to reduce exports during the American Revolution. Second, it could be expected that trade would be directly affected by the great reduction in shipping activity and the higher risks and costs of shipping that resulted from British blockades and naval action. It must be remembered that the export trades, especially in southern staples, were largely carried by British vessels before the war. The absence of British shipping plus the diversion of American ships from freight carriers to privateers greatly reduced the supply of ships for commerce. French, Dutch, and Spanish shipping activity only partly compensated for these reductions. In addition, the loss of ship sales to England, and the loss of bounties on particular colonial products, such as indigo and naval stores, depressed production for export. Even the coastal trade fell off because of the lack of ships, the blockades, and the embargoes imposed by the individual colonies. It should not be overlooked that the sharp rise in ocean freight rates affected the delivered cost of colonial exports, which were goods typically of low value relative to their bulk, proportionately more than imports. Third, transaction costs and uncertainty were increased, and exchanges were made more difficult to negotiate because of the hyperinflation brought about by wartime finance. The general level of prices in the colonies rose at an unprecedented rate, increasing several hundred times from the beginning of the War to the withdrawal of Continental currency and the return to hard money in 1781. Lastly, the flood of imports entering North America, especially from Britain, when peacetime trade resumed, demonstrates the deprivation that the War imposed on American consumers.[2] Clearly wartime trade was substantially below normal peacetime levels; but because the degree of decline will never be known precisely, disagreement on the magnitudes of wartime trade undoubtedly will persist.

---

[2] In addition to this indirect evidence we know that because of the reduced level of imports into the colonies, American resources were channeled into import-competing industries and economic self-sufficiency increased in the 13 colonies. Examples of such adjustments abound. For instance, Bezanson notes the increase of artisan workshops in and around Philadelphia. She also states that the putting-out system became general early in the War, especially in spinning for the textile plants. By the middle of 1776, 4,000 women were reputed to be employed in their homes under this system in the Philadelphia vicinity alone (see Bezanson, 1951, p. 17). The use of cereals in making beer, whiskey, and other alcoholic beverages lessened dependence upon imported wines and West Indian rum, as well as upon domestically produced rum made from imported molasses. Further evidence on external trade reduction during the 1770's and 1780's is reflected in the evidence on slave imports (see Fogel and Engerman, 1974, p. 25). Also, see Jensen, 1958, pp. 219-220.

Similarly, disagreement on the health of the new United States economy after the War has abounded, both among contemporary observers and among historians. For instance, Tench Coxe contended that affairs reached ". . . a very disagreeable condition by the year 1786."[3] Benjamin Franklin, on the other hand, upon returning from Europe, said that perhaps the state of the economy was ". . . less gloomy than has been imagined."[4] Historians, too, have voiced sharp differences of opinion. Curtis Nettels has painted a picture of a commercial depression,[5] whereas Merrill Jensen has called the period ". . . one of extraordinary economic growth."[6] The reasons for such differences of opinion again have stemmed from the lack of any overall statistical picture of output and trade for the United States during the 1780's.

Clearly, the Confederation period was one of change and readjustment. The new nation was forced to adjust both to peacetime conditions and to being outside the British Empire. The latter fact meant that the United States was subject, as any other foreign country, to British mercantilist restrictions. The impact of these adjustments had differing effects upon the several regions and the various trades. Gordon Bjork, who has recently examined the American economy of the 1780's, has stated:

> There are three separate considerations which might lead one to expect economic difficulties during the period: (1) The war wrought widespread disorganization and damage to the productive capacity of the economy. (2) The loose Confederation which preceded federal union allowed states to regulate interstate commerce. Because Hamilton argued in the Federalist Papers that a federal union was necessary to promote internal commerce, it has been said that the absence of federal union during the period constricted internal commerce. (3) The exclusion of the former colonies from the mercantilist system of the British Navigation Acts meant that certain markets for American exports were closed. The loss of these commercial privileges caused Lord Sheffield to prophesy commercial doom for the former colonies, and Thomas Jefferson lamented the exclusions and prohibitions at great length.[7]

Bjork's study was an attempt by a "new" economic historian to construct a quantitative view of the economy during the formative years of the New Nation. The purpose of the present paper is to give an alternative statistical perspective to developments which took place between the colonial years and the time of the adoption of the Constitution. The procedure followed is to use the statistical information on trade and shipping from the American Inspector-General's Ledgers[8] for the years 1768 through 1772 as a benchmark to compare with customs data for the years 1790–1792.[9]

[3]Quoted from Bjork, 1964, p. 541.
[4]Quoted from Bjork, 1964, p. 541.
[5]Nettels, 1962; see especially Chaps. 3, 4.
[6]Jensen, 1958, p. 423.
[7]Bjork, 1964, p. 542.
[8]Great Britain, Public Record Office, Customs 16/1.
[9]*U.S.A.S.P.*, 1832.

Before presenting this new statistical view of the comparative patterns and composition of trade, and of the magnitudes of trade, a critical evaluation of Bjork's evidence and analysis is presented in Section II. The statistical portrayal then follows in Sections III, IV, and V. Finally, a summary and conclusions are briefly set forth in Section VI.

II. THE PERIOD OF CONFEDERATION: FRAGMENTARY EVIDENCE

It has now been more than a decade since Bjork first presented his quantitative picture of the external economic relations of the United States for the 1780's. His attempt to give a quantitative assessment of economic change during this critical decade was an important break with previous studies of the period; earlier inquiries had been limited primarily to qualitative evidence. In contrast to these earlier investigations, Bjork boldly offered "hard numbers" to buttress his analysis. Two pillars of evidence form the basic structure of Bjork's study. The first pillar comprises estimates of exports derived from the customs-house returns of individual states. To obtain current values of trade Bjork valued the customs-house export quantities with average annual prices of the major staple commodities of the relevant ports. His account of the foreign trade of the 13 states is reproduced here in Table 1. As is evident from the table, only information from South Carolina and Pennsylvania exist for many years in the 1780's.

Of particular interest are the aggregate estimates at the bottom of Table 1. These should be viewed with extreme caution, if not total skepticism. They have been constructed by assuming that the total trade of the 13 states paralleled the trades of South Carolina and Pennsylvania, and that the partial returns for these 2 states from 1784 to 1788 remained in constant proportion to total trade, 1790–1792. By this procedure these aggregates suggest a rather severe business cycle that bottomed out in 1786 and 1787; generally, they support the pessimistic views of Coxe and Nettels quoted above in Section I.

As Fishlow (1964) has noted, several flaws mar Table 1's aggregates. First, the trade of only two states was observed. These two states were important ones, to be sure, but a mere 31% of total trade in 1790–1792 is too small a proportion of the total, even appropriately adjusted, to give a convincing view of total trade. Second, the adjustment procedure using constant shares of 1790–1792 is directly at odds with the observations for 1786 and 1788, which indicate that South Carolina's exports exceeded rather than were lower than Pennsylvania's exports for each year. Bjork's selection of 1790–1792 weights therefore bestows greater importance to Pennsylvania's trade than would result if he had used weights from other years. Third, other evidence used by Bjork on British trade with the United States shows an increase in trade from 1784 to 1785 rather than a decline of 25% shown in his

TABLE 1

Bjork's Estimates of Exports by State 1784-1792

(in $000)

State	1784	1785	1786	1787	1788	1789-90	1790-91	1791-92	Average proportion of trade by states (percentage) 1790-92
Georgia							491	459	2.4
South Carolina	2,148	1,892	2,303	2,717	2,551		2,693	2,428	12.9
North Carolina			506				525	528	2.6
Virginia							3,132	3,553	16.8
Maryland						2,028	2,240	2,624	12.2
Delaware							120	134	0.6
Pennsylvania	3,725	2,509	2,059	2,142	2,427	3,511	3,436	3,821	18.2
New Jersey							27	23	0.1
New York					1,925	2,000	2,505	2,536	12.7
Connecticut							710	880	4.0
Rhode Island							470	698	2.9
Massachusetts				1,588	1,969		2,520	2,888	13.6
New Hampshire							143	181	0.8
Official total value of exports, in $000						17,450	19,012	20,753	
Ratio estimate of total value of exports in $000,000	18.9	14.2	14.4	14.4	15.5	17.5			

Source: Bjork, 1964, p. 548.

ECONOMIC CHANGE AFTER AMERICAN REVOLUTION   403

aggregates (Bjork, 1964, p. 550). Similarly, the estimates of United States trade to France and to Holland do not support the view of an extended depression in trade. Instead, the mid-1780's appear as years of modest advance (see Buron, 1932; and Kohlmeier, 1925).

Since Great Britain, France, and The Netherlands were major overseas trading partners of the United States, and exports to these countries formed more than one-half of total United States trade, Bjork's portrayal of a nationwide depression in 1786 is questionable. Similarly, as Table 1 shows, South Carolina apparently did not suffer the sharp drop in trade experienced by Pennsylvania. Perhaps the more pessimistic portrayals of a nationwide depression in 1786 reflected in Bjork's estimates of total trade have resulted from too much concentration on Pennsylvania.

Aside from these shortcomings, Bjork's Table 1 does not permit direct comparisons with trade of the later colonial period. For instance, no adjustment was made to show exports in real terms, nor was any evidence on total real exports from the late colonial period presented. Moreover, no adjustment was made for population growth. Were real per capita exports higher in the 1780's than in the early 1770's? Because Bjork's estimates are given in isolation, their usefulness has been severely limited.

By comparison, Bjork's second pillar stands more sturdily. It shows estimates of the terms of trade for the years 1770–1775 and 1784–1792. This evidence, reproduced here in Table 2, nicely complements and increases the usefulness of his estimates of the current value of exports in Table 1. If exports in the late colonial period were not significantly different from those in the 1780's, then the improved terms of trade between these periods signified an increase in total U.S. import capacity. Whether or not the increase occurred in per capita terms was left unanswered, however.

Also, the finding of relatively constant import prices, 1770–1775 to 1784–1792, with higher export prices between these periods is not free of bias. Similar to the export aggregates of Table 1, Bjork weighted his export price series by the share of commodities in total exports for the years 1790–1792. It is quite possible that the 1770–1775 weights would substantially alter this favorable terms of trade picture. For instance, favorable markets abroad for wheat and flour and breadstuffs in 1791 and 1792 give these items unusually large weights. In contrast, tobacco was no longer the leading export in 1790–1792 (in current prices), and its price was weighted less than it would have been with an earlier selection of weights. As suggested by Fishlow, these and other alterations would leave the terms of trade higher in the 1780's than in the early 1770's, "but with considerable difference in magnitude." [10]

In any case, without making the proper link between the evidence given in

[10] Fishlow, 1964, p. 563. For a more complete account of these and other criticisms of Bjork's study, see Fishlow (1964, pp. 561–566).

TABLE 2
Bjork's Import and Export Prices and the Terms of Trade

Year	Import price index A	Import price index B	Composite import price index	Export price index	Terms of trade
1770	123	98	110	69	63
1771	108	100	104	75	72
1772	103	102	102	83	81
1773	114	104	109	78	72
1774	115	100	108	73	68
1775	123	96	109	70	64
1784	109	98	103	115	112
1785	101	101	101	106	105
1786	98	104	101	97	96
1787	97	105	101	92	91
1788	94	103	99	87	88
1789	94	105	99	87	88
1790	100	100	100	100	100
1791	107	99	103	92	89
1792	120	99	110	86	78

Source: Bjork, 1964, p. 554.
Notes: Import price index A is a Laspeyres index (1790 = 100) composed of U.S. prices for tea, coffee, sugar, salt, molasses, Madeira wine, rum, and Russian duck. Import price index B is also a Laspeyres index (1790 = 100) based on British prices for blue cloth, common shoes, stockings, and hats modified to take into account changes in the rate of exchange between sterling and the dollar. Indices A and B are given equal weight in the composite index.
   The export price index is a Laspeyres index composed of 14 commodities accounting for 86.8% of the value of total exports in 1790.

Tables 1 and 2, and without the necessary adjustments of the estimates, one is left uncertain about the comparable conditions of trade between the periods, especially in real per capita terms. It would appear from the evidence that quite possibly conditions were worsening, particularly from a longer-run perspective when the early 1770's are compared to the early 1790's. Table 1 suggests little improvement in the absolute levels of total trade, 1784–1792, and Table 2 suggests that by 1790–1792 the more favorable terms of trade enjoyed in the early and mid-1780's had been dissipated. To investigate more thoroughly this possible worsening of conditions, we now turn to newly assembled evidence on aggregate U.S. maritime trade and shipping.

III. PRE- AND POST-WAR COMPARISONS: PATTERNS AND COMPOSITION OF AMERICAN EXPORT TRADE

   In contrast with the 1780's, the early 1790's offer the possibility of a much more systematic comparison with pre-War trade. This results from the availability of customs data which the new American government began to

ECONOMIC CHANGE AFTER AMERICAN REVOLUTION 405

collect in August 1789. With this evidence, the patterns, magnitudes, and composition of foreign trade for the years 1790–1792 can be compared with the statistical picture of trade in 1768–1772.

An interval of 17 years between these records of trade is appropriate for giving perspective to the longer-run effects of independence. Of course, changes in trade were a persistent feature of pre-Revolutionary America, and some of the changes to be noted were a consequence of pre-War trends. The West Indian trade, for example, increased in relative importance over the entire 18th century. Consequently, though independence was an important factor in altering trade patterns and magnitudes, it is impossible to isolate the impact of independence from earlier trends and changes which would have occurred had the 13 colonies remained within the British Empire. The effects of the adoption of the Constitution and the emergence of a stronger central government had important consequences for the United States economy, especially over the longer run.[11] Still, one would expect that the basic economic structure of the country, and the patterns of its foreign trade in the early 1790's, was shaped more importantly, first, by a resource base and the existence of an Atlantic economy which were the heritage of earlier years; and second, by modifications brought about by recovery and independence, and the consequent readjustments which took place in the 1780's. Beginning in 1793, however, the situation pertaining to the country's external economic relations changed as the major European powers entered into the Napoleonic Wars. Because the effects of this conflict were so great, any changes which had been brought about by the War and independence would be obscured by the effects of the Napoleonic Wars on American trade.

Thus, to begin this comparison of American overseas trade, the annual average values of exports from the 13 colonies to major overseas areas in 1768–1772 are compared with those values from the United States in 1790–1792,[12] in Table 3. In order to make the values comparable, the dollar values from 1790–1792 have been converted to pounds sterling, and to 1768–1772 prices.[13]

[11]Important shorter-run consequences followed from such actions by the federal government as the funding of the national debt and the assumption of the state debts.

[12]The fiscal years in the customs records were August 1789, through September 30, 1790; October 1, 1790, through September 30, 1791; and October 1, 1791, through September 30, 1792. The first customs year thus contained from 13 to 14 months, but this should have only a slight upward bias on the 3-year averages.

[13]There are certain factors that make the values in Table 3 less than perfectly comparable. For example, export values to the Canadian colonies are not available for 1768–1772; Florida and Louisiana are included in the trade with the foreign West Indies in 1790–1792 (they were not included for 1768–1772); and legal trade with other areas, such as the East Indies, did not exist in 1768–1772. Nevertheless, these qualifications are minor and the broad patterns of trade with overseas areas can be contrasted. (See footnote 17 for a discussion of the computation of real values.) Note that a "national" or overall export price index is used to compute real values

TABLE 3

Average Annual Exports to Overseas Areas: The 13 Colonies, 1768-1772, and the United States, 1790-1792[a] (Thousands of Pounds Sterling; 1768-1772 prices)[b]

Destination[c]	1768-1772	Percentage of total	1790-1792	Percentage of total
Great Britain and Ireland	1616	58	1234	31
Northern Europe	—		643	16
Southern Europe	406	14	557	14
British West Indies ⎱	759	27	402	10
Foreign West Indies ⎰			956	24
Africa	21	1	42	1
Canadian colonies	— [d]		60	2
Other	—		59	1
Total	2802	100	3953	100

Source: Average annual exports for 1768-1772 are taken from Shepherd and Walton (1972, pp. 94-95); and exports for 1790-1792 are taken from *U.S.A.S.P.* (1832).

[a] The annual average exports for 1790-1792 are taken from export values given in the source for the following periods: (1) various days in August, 1789, to September 30, 1790; (2) October 1, 1790 through September 30, 1791; and (3) October 1, 1791 through September 30, 1792.

[b] Values for 1790-1792 were converted to pounds sterling and 1768-1772 prices on the basis of a Paasche price index implicit in the calculations of real values of the more important commodity exports in Table 4. This implicit Paasche index is 4.924, which includes the exchange rate between sterling and dollars, and the change in the average level of prices of those exports (listed in Table 4) between 1768-1772 and 1790-1792 (see footnote 17 for a discussion of the exchange rate and changes in the general level of export prices). This index stems from revaluing the quantities of those annual average commodity exports in 1790-1792 with average prices of the same commodities exported in 1768-1772 (Table 4).

[c] Northern Europe includes continental European countries north of Cape Finisterre. Southern Europe includes Spain, the Canary Islands, Portugal, Madeira, the Azores, the Cape Verde Islands, Gibraltar and other Mediterranean ports in Europe (except French ports). The Foreign West Indies includes the Swedish, Danish, Dutch, French and Spanish Caribbean possessions, and Florida and Louisiana. Africa includes North Africa, the west coast of Africa, and the Cape of Good Hope. The Canadian colonies include the British American colonies, including Newfoundland and the British fisheries; and St. Pierre, Miquelon, and the French fisheries. Other destinations include the East Indies, the northwest coast of America, and unknown destinations.

[d] Not available.

of 1790-1792 exports destined for each overseas area. An error is committed using this estimation procedure because of the different mix of commodities going to each overseas area. The share of tobacco was larger in exports to Europe than in total exports to all overseas areas. The price of tobacco decreased relative to flour. As a result, the use of an overall export price index tends to understate the real value of exports to Europe and to overstate the real value of exports going to the West Indies (to which flour was a relatively more important import than tobacco). Such errors could only be avoided if separate indexes were prepared for the trade with each overseas area. The same problem occurs below on the American side when we estimate exports by colony/state and region.

From Table 3, it is clear that by 1790 the United States had taken advantage of its new freedom to trade directly with other northern European countries. The major part of this trade was with France and the Netherlands, and the major commodity exported to these countries was tobacco, though exports of rice, flour, wheat, and Indian corn (maize) were important.[14] The establishment of this trade with northern Europe, however, did not preclude the major share of American exports from reverting to Great Britain, though pre-War levels of exports to Britain were not reached by 1790–1792. The reversion of much of American foreign trade to Britain probably occurred soon after the War ended.[15] The reasons for this have long been discussed by historians.[16] Many of the imports desired by Americans were found in greatest variety and at the best price and quality there. British woolens, Irish linens, and the vast array of hardwares of British manufacture are examples. British merchants, too, through a common language, established contacts, and a knowledge of American markets, regained a competitive edge over French and Dutch merchants after the War. Still, the emergence of a large direct trade with other northern European countries must stand as a major consequence of independence.

By 1790 trade with the West Indies had surpassed its relative pre-War role, and trade with southern Europe, which had been severely disrupted by the War, had just regained its relative position. The major difference after the War is one not shown in Table 3 because a precise breakdown between exports to the British and foreign West Indies is not available for 1768–1772. Before the Revolution, trade with the British West Indies had been greater than with the foreign islands. By 1790 the situation was reversed. The exclusion of American shipping from the British West Indies after the War was a major factor. Undoubtedly, this shift is overstated by the statistics. Many American ships clearing for foreign islands went illegally to British Caribbean areas. Also, in the 1780's Saint Eustatius remained an entrepôt from which British islands were supplied, as it had during the War. Consequently, any conclusions about changes in the important West Indian trade brought by independence must be tentative. It would appear, however, that the United States was shifting towards increased trade with non-British areas of the Caribbean during the 1780's. The War and independence must have played a part in such a shift; but this trend had been going on before the Revolution, and was likely only accelerated by independence and restrictions upon American shipping.

The changes in the composition of trade that accompanied these changing

---

[14] The late 1780's and early 1790's appear to have been times of poor crops in Europe. Demand for American foodstuffs may have been abnormally high as a result.

[15] See Bjork, 1964, p. 550, for evidence on British–American trade during the 1780's.

[16] Johnson, 1915, pp. 125–127; Gray, 1933, pp. 599–602.

TABLE 4

Annual Average Exports of Selected Commodities from the 13 Colonies, 1768-1772, and the United States, 1790-1792

Commodity	Thirteen Colonies, 1768-1772			United States, 1790-1792		
	Quantity (1)	Value (thousands of current pounds sterling) (2)	Value (thousands of dollars; 1790-1792 prices) (3)	Quantity ^a (4)	Value (thousands of current dollars) (5)	Value (thousands of pounds sterling; 1768-1772 prices) ^e (6)
Beef ^b	26,036 bbl	51	209	60,457 bbl	367	159
Pork ^b				29,741 bbl	285	
Bread	38,634 tons	410	2,534	3,823 tons	221	712
Flour				63,256 tons	4,178	
Cotton	29,425 lb	1	7	163,822 lb ^c	41 ^c	8
Fish, dried ^d	308,993 quintals	154	740	375,619 quintals	900	187
Flaxseed	233,065 bu	42	189	352,079 bu	286	64
Grain:						
Indian corn	839,314 bu	83	424	1,926,784 bu	974	191
Rice ^e	140,254 bbl	311	1,971	129,367 bbl	1,818	287
Wheat	599,127 bu	115	654	998,862 bu	1,090	192
Indigo ^f	547,649 lb	113	567	493,760 lb	511	101
Iron:						
Bar	2,416 tons	36	195	300 tons	24	4
Pig	4,468 tons	22	116	3,667 tons	95	18
Livestock: ^g						
Cattle	3,433	21	63	4,861	89	29
Horses	6,048	60	240	7,086	282	71
Naval Stores:						
Pitch	11,384 bbl	5	21	7,279 bbl	13	3
Tar	90,472 bbl	34	135	68,463 bbl	102	25
Turpentine	19,870 bbl	9	42	51,194 bbl	108	24
Oil, whale	3,841 tons	46	212	1,826 tons ^h	101	22
Potash	1,381 tons	35	134	4,872 tons	472	123

Rum, American	342,366 gal	22	132	441,782 gal	170[i]	28
Tobacco	87,986 hhd	766	3,093	110,687 hhd	3,891	964
Wood Products:						
Pine boards[k]	38,991 M ft	70	228	45,118 M ft	264	81
Staves and headings[l]	21,585 M	65	275	31,554 M	401	95
Total, above commodities		2,471	12,181		16,683	3,388
All exports		2,802			19,465	

Source: See Table 3.

[a] Five commodities (bread, flour, flaxseed, rice, and whale oil) were given in different units in the two sources; see Table 3). The following amounts were recorded in the *U.S.A.S.P.* (1832), and the following ratios have been used to convert to equivalent units for purposes of comparison.

Commodity	Amounts recorded in *U.S.A.S.P.*	Conversion equivalencies
Bread	85,644 bbl	1 bbl = 100 lb
Flour	722,923 bbl	1 bbl = 196 lb
Flaxseed	50,297 casks	1 cask = 7 bu
Rice	113,196 tierces	1 tierce = 600 lb = 1.1429 barrels (of 1770)
Whale oil	460,114 gallons	1 ton = 252 gal = 8 barrels

Tons of bread and flour were interpreted as long tons of 2240 lb. Sources for these conversions have been several. The reader may wish to see *Historical Statistics* (1960, Chap. Z); Cole (1938, p. x); Gray (1933, p. 610); and Shepherd and Walton (1972, p. 206).

[b] Quantities of beef and pork were given in barrels in both sources for the two periods. However, Cole (1938, p. x) states that barrels of beef averaged 225 pounds and pork 217 pounds until 1789, and 200 pounds thereafter. No adjustments were made in the quantities of barrels for beef and pork in this table, but the appropriate adjustment, based upon these weights (as stated by Cole) were made in computing the value of 1768–1772 exports in 1790–1792 prices, and the value of 1790–1792 exports in 1768–1772 prices.

[c] The source listed the 1790 quantity of cotton exports as 2027 bales, and the 1790 value as $58,408. No attempt was made to convert the 1790 quantity to pounds. Consequently, the average quantity and value of cotton exports shown in this Table are for 1791 and 1792 only. The average value of cotton exports for 1790–1792 was $46,733.

[d] Dried fish was recorded in quintals in both the American customs records, 1768–1772, and the *U.S.A.S.P.* (1832) for 1790–1792. The latter source, however explicitly states for 1791 that these quintals were hundred weights of 112 pounds. Cole (1938, p. x) states that quintals of dried codfish were 100 pounds during both these periods. This raises the possibility that in the 1768–1772 records, quintals were 100 pounds, and 112 pounds in the 1790–1792 source. In view of the lack of any other evidence bearing upon this question, however, no adjustment was made of the quantity data for dried fish exports for either period.

continued

TABLE 4—*Continued*

e Rice exports for 1790 and 1791 may be understated because one quarterly return for 1790, and two consecutive quarterly returns for 1791 (April 1–September 30), for Charleston, South Carolina had not been submitted, according to the source (*U.S.A.S.P.,* 1832). The source gave the following annual data on rice exports.

	Quantity (tierces)	Value ($)
1790	100,845	1,753,796
1791	96,980	1,503,190
1792	141,762	2,197,311
Average 1790–1792	113,196	1,818,099

If rice exports in 1790 and 1791 were as large as in 1792 (162,014 barrels of 1770 valued at 359,000 pounds sterling in 1768–1772 prices), then annual rice exports in the early 1790's would have averaged more than in 1768–1772.

f With regard to indigo exports for 1792, the source stated: "There is reason to believe that an error of clerkship has arisen in some of the returns of indigo, as the quantity shipped in the several years last past has been much greater, on a medium, than 371,442 pounds." The source gave the following data on indigo exports.

	Quantity (lb)	Value ($)
1790	612,119	537,379
1791	497,720	570,234
1792	371,442	425,558
Average 1790–1792	493,760	511,057

Consequently, annual indigo exports in the early 1790s may have averaged more than in the years, 1768–1772. Indigo exports averaged 554,920 pounds and $553,807 in 1790–1791 (115,000 pounds sterling in 1768–1772 prices).

g Livestock, especially cattle, probably was overvalued in the 1768–1772 source. In view of the small amounts involved, no attempt was made to correct the values in this Table.

h The 1790 quantity of whale oil exported was given as 15,765 barrels. It was assumed these were barrels of 31.5 gallons.

i The average quantity of American-produced rum exports is for 1790 and 1791 only. Exports in 1792 were not given in the source.

j Tobacco exports were given in both hogsheads and pounds in the source for 1769–1772. The average weight of a hogshead in these years was 1,015 pounds per hogshead.

k The quantities of pine boards are given in thousands of feet. The average quantity of exports for 1790–1792 included both pine boards and plank. The 1790 quantity did not distinguish pine from oak and other boards and plank. Pine boards and plank were 94% of all boards and plank exported in 1791 and 1792. In view of the probable small amounts involved, no adjustment was made to the 1790 quantity and value of boards and plank exported.

l The quantities of staves and headings are given in thousands.

patterns of trade can be seen in Table 4.[17] Though not all commodity exports are listed, those that comprised the major proportion of the value of exports are given (over 88% in 1768-1772, and over 85% in 1790-1792). Contrary to popular belief, the great pre-War staple, tobacco, was no longer the single most valuable export by the early 1790's in terms of current values, though tobacco exports came to exceed pre-War levels and reached an all-time high in 1790-1792.[18] Tobacco production may have equaled or perhaps exceeded pre-War levels by the mid-1780's.[19] Higher prices of tobacco in the later 1780's together with higher levels of output resulted in modest recovery in the tobacco-producing areas of Virginia and Maryland, as well as stimulating the Piedmont region of North Carolina into which tobacco production was spreading.[20]

This appears not to have been the case for the other important southern staples of rice and indigo, however, and the export trade of South Carolina may have actually fallen from 1768-1772 to 1790-1792 (also, see Table 5). This conclusion must be qualified because of incomplete customs returns from that state for 1790 and 1791 (see Table 4, footnotes *e, f*; Table 5, footnote *d*). Nevertheless, even when noting this qualification, exports of the lower south surely did not increase to the extent they did from other regions,

[17]In order to compare the magnitudes of trade as well as the composition, the real values of those commodities listed in Table 4 were computed in two ways. First, 1768-1772 exports were valued using the average dollar prices implicit in the quantities and values of the same commodities exported in 1790-1792 (column 3). Second, 1790-1792 exports were revalued in the same way, using implicit average sterling prices from 1768-1772 (column 6). Thus, there are two comparisons of real values that may be made. These two comparisons are equivalent to revaluing 1790-1792 exports by a Paasche price index, which provides a lower limit to the change in prices between the two periods, and a Laspeyres price index, which provides an upper limit to the change in prices. The Paasche index is 4.924 and the Laspeyres 4.930 (1768-1772 = 100), hence the ambiguity in the price level change is very small. It should be noted that these two index numbers include the exchange rate between sterling and the dollar, as well as the change in the level of export prices. The usual exchange rate between the U.S. dollar and sterling was $4.44 = £1 (Nussbaum, 1957, p. 32) after the U.S. dollar was established in the Coinage Act of 1792. The same exchange rate had earlier prevailed for Spanish dollars in circulation. Consequently, if this rate can be used to convert dollars to sterling, the Paasche index becomes 1.109 and the Laspeyres 1.110 (1768-1772 = 100). Hence, export prices rose on the average about 11% from 1768-1772 to 1790-1792. This price level change can be compared to the Warren-Pearson price index (*Historical Statistics*, 1960, p. 116). Taking a simple average of the Warren-Pearson index numbers for 1768-1772 and 1790-1791 (1792 is not given), the price index for 1790-1791 is 1.105 (1768-1772 = 100) very nearly the same as our Paasche and Laspeyres indexes from Table 4. For 1789-1791 (remembering that the 1790 fiscal year covered part of 1789), the Warren-Pearson price index yields a price index for 1789-1791 of 1.098 (1768-1772 = 100). Had we used the Warren-Pearson price index to compute real values, by chance, our results would have been nearly the same. The results indicate that the real value of exports increased by about 37% from 1768-1772 to 1790-1792.

[18]Robertson, 1973, p. 115; Bjork, 1964, p. 544. The 1790-1792 exports of tobacco valued in 1768-1772 prices exceeded the value of flour exports, however. Current values of flour were higher due to the increase in its price relative to tobacco between the two periods (see Bezanson, 1951, pp. 332-342).

[19]Gray, 1933, p. 605.

[20]Tobacco prices fell, however, in 1791 (Gray, 1933, p. 605).

or keep pace with the rise in population (see Table 5, footnote *d*). Higher rice prices offset to some extent the lower quantity of rice exports in 1790–1792, but indigo fell in both quantity and value. The decline in indigo production, however, was not to the very low levels that some have attributed to the loss of the British bounty and the encouragement of its production by the British in the West Indies after the War.[21]

Naval stores were other exports largely produced in the southern colonies. Average annual exports of these commodities in 1790–1792 were mixed compared with 1768–1772; but their total value was about the same in both periods, and small relative to tobacco, rice, and indigo. Though average annual exports of cotton increased by over five times from 1768–1772 to 1790–1792, the overall value of cotton exports was still relatively small before Whitney's invention of the cotton gin in 1793.

The most outstanding feature of Table 4 is the dramatic increase in the export of foodstuffs like barreled meats (beef and pork), bread and flour, Indian corn, and wheat. Because these were the more important commodities in the West Indian trade, the increase in their share of total exports should come as no surprise. These trends were under way before the Revolution occurred, however, and the shift into grain production in the upper south in the later colonial period is well known.[22] To repeat, then, not all of this increased export of foodstuffs can be attributed to independence.[23]

One sharp reversal in exports clearly due to independence was the impact of the prohibitive duty on whale oil imports imposed by the British in 1783. New England's whaling industry suffered as a result.

Overall, there was an increase in the real value of exports of about 37% from 1768–1772 to 1790–1792, assuming that the customs data upon which these comparisons have been based are reasonably accurate.[24] Did this increase in real exports keep pace with population? What were the regional effects of these changes? It is to these questions that we now turn.

IV. COMMODITY TRADE: REGIONAL AND PER CAPITA TRENDS

Comparisons of per capita values of exports from the individual colonies and states, and major regions, disclose further interesting changes in the American economy. These comparisons are shown in Table 5 in real terms

---

[21]See, for example, Thomas, 1965, p. 628. Indigo production did decrease greatly after 1792, however, due to competition with the West Indies for British markets (Gray, 1933, pp. 610–611). It is possible that indigo exports began to decline in 1792, and that this was the reason for the lower figure in the customs returns of this year (see Table 4, footnote *f*).

[22]Klingaman, 1969, pp. 268–278.

[23]Increased demand for foodstuffs from Europe due to poor crops in the late 1780's and early 1790's has been noted above in footnote 14. To the extent such demand came from northern continental countries, independence allowing direct trade with these countries would have been a factor.

[24]The implicit Paasche quantity index from Table 4 is 1.3696, and the implicit Laspeyres quantity index is 1.3711 (1768–1772 = 100).

TABLE 5

Average Annual Exports from Colonies and Regions of the 13 Colonies, 1768–1772;
and States and Regions of the United States, 1791–1792[a]
(Thousands of Pounds Sterling; 1768–1772 Prices)[b]

	1768–1772			1791–1792		
Origin	Total exports	Percentage of total	Per capita exports[c]	Total exports	Percentage of total	Per capita exports[c]
New England						
New Hampshire	46	2	0.74	33	1	0.23
Massachusetts	258	9	0.97	542	14	1.14
Rhode Island	81	3	1.39	119	3	1.72
Connecticut	92	3	0.50	148	4	0.62
Total, New England	477	17	0.82	842	22	0.83
Middle Atlantic						
New York	187	7	1.15	512	14	1.51
New Jersey	2	—	0.02	5	—	0.03
Pennsylvania	353	13	1.47	584	16	1.34
Delaware	18	1	0.51	26	1	0.44
Total, Middle Atlantic	559	20	1.01	1127	30	1.11
Upper South						
Maryland	392	14	1.93	482	13	1.51
Virginia	770	27	1.72	678	18	0.91
Total, Upper South	1162	41	1.79	1160	31	1.09
Lower South						
North Carolina	75	3	0.38	104	3	0.27
South Carolina	455	16	3.66	436	12	1.75
Georgia	74	3	3.17	97	3	1.17
Total, Lower South	603	22	1.75	637	17	0.88
Total, all regions	2802	100	1.31	3766	100	0.99

Sources: See Table 3 for sources of export data. Population data used to compute per capita exports were taken from *Historical Statistics* (1960, pp. 13, 756).

[a] The annual averag. exports for 1791–1792 are taken from export values given in the source for the following periods: (1) October 1, 1790, through September 30, 1791; and (2) October 1, 1791, through September 30, 1792. Note that Table 5 differs from Tables 3 and 4 in that average exports are computed for only 2 fiscal years, 1791 and 1792, rather than 3 years, 1790 through 1792. This is because exports were not given by state or region of origin in the source for fiscal year 1790.

[b] See Table 3, footnote *b*.

[c] The population of Maine was included with that of Massachusetts for computing per capita exports in 1768–1772 and 1791–1792. The population of Vermont was included in that of New England for computing the regional per capita exports of that region, but Vermont's population was not allocated among the other New England colonies and states for computing per capita exports of the individual colonies and states for 1768–1772 and 1791–1792. Per capita exports are given in pounds sterling.

[d] Because of incomplete returns from Charleston, South Carolina, for 1790 and 1791, and errors which may have affected the returns for indigo (see Table 4, footnotes *e* and *f*), exports from South Carolina and the lower south may be understated in this table. If rice exports had been as great in 1790 and 1791 as in 1792 (for which a full year's returns presumably exist), then total exports from South Carolina and the lower south would have been greater by 77,000 pounds sterling. If indigo exports had been as high in 1792 as they averaged in 1790–1791 (see Table 4, footnote *f*), then total exports from South Carolina would have been greater by about 9000 pounds sterling. Additional exports of 86,000 pounds sterling from South Carolina would have resulted in per capita exports for the state of 2.10 pounds sterling in 1791–1792, and per capita exports for the lower south of 0.99 pounds sterling.

in order to adjust for inflationary effects and sterling–dollar exchange. It is clear that the increase in real exports from 1768–1772 to the early 1790's was due almost entirely to increased exports from New England and the Middle Atlantic regions. Compared to pre-War proportions among the regions, therefore, overseas trade gained slightly in relative importance to the northern regions, and especially to the Middle Atlantic states. It might be noted that this occurred despite the depressed economies of Pennsylvania and New Hampshire, which suffered because of the falling off in shipbuilding and the lumber trade.

As indicated by the fall in per capita exports, the export trade of the southern regions did not keep pace with a growing population. Though the export trades of these regions just about regained their pre-War absolute levels of exports by the early 1790's, per capita exports were significantly below pre-War levels. In contrast, and with the exceptions of New Hampshire, Pennsylvania, and Delaware, the export trades of the northern states increased relatively more than their populations. In particular, exports from New York boomed, reflecting the increased agricultural output of that state. This contrast among the states makes generalization difficult, if not impossible. Clearly, the decline of more than 25% in real per capita exports between 1768–1772 and 1790–1792 hides as much as it reveals. Moreover, the fall in per capita export values for the south was likely the result of a slowing in the growth of demand for southern staples rather than the direct consequence of market alterations stemming from independence and new economic and political alliances. It should be emphasized that it was the export trade in southern staples which was stagnating—not the aggregate size of the southern economies. Population growth and settlement were rapidly taking place; but this vigorous growth was in the western parts of the original southern states, and in the future states of Kentucky and Tennessee, rather than in the older staple-producing areas. Soon there would be a great new southern staple; but, at this moment in the early 1790's, the older staples were beginning to fall into eclipse.

This discussion also illustrates the fact that the new United States, like the 13 colonies, did not comprise a single, integrated national economy. Political and social, rather than economic, ties primarily bound the new nation together.

V. SHIPPING FLOWS AND INVISIBLE EARNINGS

Paralleling the growth of commodity trade was the growth of mercantile and shipping activities which had been so important to New England and the middle colonies before the War. Although tonnage statistics of vessels clearing American ports are not available, there is information on tonnages of entering vessels after 1789. Alexander Hamilton described this entering shipping as "vessels employed . . . in the import trade of the United States . . ." (*U.S.A.S.P.*, 1832, p. 50). Table 6 compares these tonnage flows with ones from before the War. According to the *American State Papers*, the total tonnage of shipping entering U.S. ports in the years 1790–1792 averaged about 587,000 tons per year. Due to a change in the definition of tonnage measurement between 1768–1772 and 1790–1792, however, the tonnage data from the *American State Papers* are not comparable with those from the pre-War years.[25] This relationship has been investigated by McCusker (1967), Walton (1967), and French (1973), who found that pre-1786 registered tonnage was substantially less for any vessel, on the average, than post-1786 measured tonnage (based upon the 1773 formula). To account for this change of definition, all tonnages taken from the *American State Papers* have been multiplied by correction factors of 0.75, 0.65, and 0.55 to obtain tonnage ranges comparable with the registered tonnage of 1768–1772. This range of correction terms is used because the relationship between registered and measured tonnage varied systematically by size category of ships (Table 6, footnote *a*).

Because American vessels typically were smaller—certainly smaller than British vessels—an appropriate comparison of pre-War American-owned tonnage is most likely with the range set forth by columns (4) and (5). For comparisons of foreign-owned tonnages, however, column (6) should most likely be compared to the range specified by columns (8) or (9) because foreign vessels were normally larger.

What does this comparison of tonnage flows suggest about shipping earnings before and after the Revolution? Existing estimates are based upon evidence pertaining to the volume of American-owned tonnage and average earnings per ton.[26] Unfortunately, evidence on average earnings per ton for 1790–1792 is scanty and incomplete. There are no data on utilization of shipping capacity for this period, nor do freight rate series for U.S. shipping routes exist. Rates in the Baltic timber trade declined about 30% from 1770–1790 (Nor'h, 1965). Consequently, one is led to conclude that any increase in shipping earnings must have come from an increase in the volume of American-owned shipping engaged in overseas trade.

Table 6 does support the view that there was a considerable growth of shipping volume between these periods. Not only did the absolute amount of tonnage increase with all areas, but as shown in Table 6 the proportion of American-owned shipping increased in all overseas trades except for the important West Indies trade. Here the British restrictions on American shipping precluded direct legal trade with the British islands. Of course, American ships may have gone illegally to the British islands, or American

[25]See Walton, 1967; French, 1973.

[26]The estimated average annual shipping earnings for 1768–1772 (Shepherd and Walton, 1972, p. 128) are less than half the estimated shipping earnings for the United States in 1790–1792 of 6.5 million dollars (North, 1960, p. 600). The 1768–1772 estimate employs data on tonnage flows into and outward from the American colonies. The 1790–1792 estimate is based upon the stock of American-owned tonnage.

TABLE 6

Annual Average Shipping Tonnage^a (by American and Foreign Ownership)^b Entering Major Regions^c of the 13 Colonies, 1768–1772, and the United States, 1790–1792, from Foreign Areas (in Hundreds of Tons)^c

| | American-owned | | | | | Foreign-owned | | | | |
| | 1768–1772 | 1790–1792 | | | | 1768–1772 | 1790–1972 | | | |
	(1)	(2) (Unadjusted)	(3) (0.75 of (2))	(4) (0.65 of (2))	(5) (0.55 of (2))	(6)	(7) (Unadjusted)	(8) (0.75 of (7))	(9) (0.65 of (7))	(10) (0.55 of (7))
Overseas area of origin: American region of destination										
Great Britain & Ireland										
New England	95	165	124	107	91	45	36	27	24	20
Middle Atlantic	104	207	155	135	114	61	213	160	138	117
Upper South	34	180	135	117	99	349	346	260	225	190
Lower South	22	59	44	38	32	200	155	116	101	85
Total	256	611	458	397	336	655	750	563	488	413
Northern Europe										
New England	—	108	81	70	59	—	9	6	6	5
Middle Atlantic	—	106	80	69	58	—	38	29	25	21
Upper South	—	109	82	71	60	—	102	77	66	56
Lower South	—	34	26	22	19	—	51	38	33	28
Total	—	358	268	232	197	—	200	150	130	110
Southern Europe										
New England	58	143	107	93	79	11	8	6	5	4
Middle Atlantic	90	207	155	134	114	29	85	64	55	47
Upper South	21	92	69	60	51	43	47	35	30	26
Lower South	6	21	16	14	12	25	19	15	13	11
Total	176	462	347	301	254	108	160	120	104	88

ECONOMIC CHANGE AFTER AMERICAN REVOLUTION 417

West Indies										
New England	437	938	703	610	516	18	134	100	87	74
Middle Atlantic	183	374	281	243	206	35	370	278	241	204
Upper South	97	230	172	149	126	62	294	220	191	162
Lower South	56	337	253	219	186	130	341	256	222	188
Total	774	1879	1409	1221	1033	246	1139	854	740	626
Africa, Total	—	8	6	5	4	20[b]	5	4	3	3
Canadian Colonies, Total	—	21	16	14	12	—[d]	207	155	134	114
Other, Total	—	48	36	31	26	—	27	20	17	15
Total from foreign areas										
New England	590	1389	1042	903	764	74	280	210	182	154
Middle Atlantic	378	923	692	600	508	125	815	611	530	448
Upper South	153	622	467	404	342	459	808	606	525	444
Lower South	84	453	340	294	249	370	585	439	380	322
Total	1205	3387	2540	2202	1863	1028	2488	1866	1617	1368

Sources: For 1768–1772, Shepherd and Walton (1972, pp. 118–119); and for 1790–1792, *U.S.A.S.P.* (1832, pp. 51–63, 206–216, 254–263).

[a] The tonnage data for 1768–1772 are based upon the pre-1786 measure of registered tonnage used to record the size of British vessels. After 1786 British vessels were required to register on the basis of the 1773 formula for measured tonnage. The relationship between pre-1786 registered tonnage, and the measured tonnage calculated from the 1773 formula, has been investigated by McCusker (1967), Walton (1967), and French (1973). In the samples observed by French pre-1786 registered tonnage for the same ships averaged approximately 25.45% less than their post-1786 measured tonnage. However, as noted by French, the relationship between registered and measured tonnage differed from ship to ship, and varied systematically by size classification of ship. The difference tended to be larger for smaller ships; registered tonnage was approximately 43 to 45% less than measured tonnage for ships ranging from 51 to 150 registered tons, and 30 to 32% less for ships in the range of 151 to 250 registered tons (French, 1973, p. 440). Therefore, in order to present a probable range within which 1790–1792 tonnage estimates comparable to the 1768–1772 data fell, we have presented three different sets of estimates, the tonnage data from the *U.S.A.S.P.* (1832) were multiplied by correction factors of 0.75, 0.65, and 0.55 to obtain the 1790–1792 tonnage estimates in columns (3)–(5) and (8)–(10).

Actual reporting years for the 1790–1792 data were October 1 of the preceding year through September 30 of the stated year. Tonnage returns for three states, Rhode Island, New Jersey, and North Carolina, were incomplete for 1790 due to the fact that these states did not ratify the Constitution before October 1, 1789. Average annual estimates of tonnage entering each of these three states were based upon 1791 and 1792 data only.

continued

TABLE 6—*Continued*

In some instances the totals for a state differed from the detailed data due to errors of addition. In all cases, the detailed data were accepted. It should be noted that the aggregation of tonnage in the above table differs substantially from the aggregation given in the source (*U.S.A.S.P.*, 1832, p. 250), where the average annual American-owned tonnage entering the states during 1790–1792 was 375,601 tons (unadjusted) compared with the figure for American-owned tonnage of 338,700 tons in this table. The average annual foreign-owned tonnage estimated was nearly the same (247,994 from *U.S.A.S.P.*, p. 250, compared with 248,800 in this table). The difference may be due (or partly due) to the fact that the aggregation in the source (*U.S.A.S.P.*, p. 250) pertains to the *calendar* years, 1790 through 1792, and not to the fiscal years beginning with October 1, 1789, through September 30, 1792.

[b] Tonnage was recorded in the *U.S.A.S.P.* (1832), the source of the 1790–1792 data, by place of ownership. In a very few instances, tonnage was indicated to be jointly owned by foreign and U.S. residents. These observations were classified as foreign-owned tonnage in this table. The breakdown between colonial and foreign-owned tonnage for 1768–1772 was not given in the American customs records. Estimates therefore were made on the basis of ownership data taken from samples of recorded entries of ships from naval office lists of various colonial ports; see Shepherd and Walton (1972, pp. 122–123). Evidence to estimate the ownership of the annual average of 1,974 tons entering the colonies from Africa was incomplete. Consequently, this tonnage was listed in the table as being all foreign-owned, though some unknown proportion unquestionably was owned in the colonies. The largest part of this tonnage (an annual average of 1440 tons) entered the lower south, and probably the greatest part of this was British-owned.

[c] The major foreign areas are defined in Table 1, footnote c, except that Florida and Louisiana were included in the "other" category in this table. The "other" places of origin included China, the East Indies, the South Seas, Bourbon and Mauritius, and Florida and Louisiana. The data were available to present regional breakdowns for Africa, the Canadian colonies, and "other" places of origin, but it was not deemed worthwhile because of the small amounts of tonnage involved. Definitions of regions are given in note *c* to Table 2.

[d] Not available.

[e] Tonnage for regions may not add to totals because of rounding.

goods may have been reexported from the foreign islands, but the consequence of the restrictions seems to have been an increased relative importance of foreign-owned shipping (nearly all British).

A comparison of American-owned tonnage inflows in 1768–1772 (column (1)) with the probable range of American-owned tonnage inflows in 1790–1792 (columns (4) and (5)) in Table 6 suggests that American-owned tonnages did increase perhaps by 50–80%. It may well be that the growth of foreign and American-owned tonnage inflows approximated the 80% increase of United States population between these two periods, and that per capita shipping earnings varied little. Of course, such comparisons and conclusions depend upon the tonnage correction factor selected in Table 6; but even the most conservative estimates suggest substantial growth in shipping volume. The regional patterns, too, conform to those discussed earlier. The northern colonial regions clearly experienced greatly increased shipping activity. Tonnage entering the southern regions in the early 1790's was greater (even by the most conservative estimates in Table 6), but the increases were relatively smaller than for the northern regions.

In summary, it seems probable that in the early 1790's shipping earnings and mercantile profits had recovered from the doldrums of the 1780's. This recovery, though not dramatic, was important to the maintenance of the strong commercial base of the New England and Middle Atlantic regions, and to the recovery from the troublesome years of the 1780's.

VI. SUMMARY AND CONCLUSIONS

In conclusion, what were the important consequences of the American Revolution and independence on American maritime trade and shipping? It led to the beginnings of direct trade with northern European countries other than Britain. During the 1780's these countries became markets of moderate importance for American products which no longer had to be routed through Great Britain. Trade with southern Europe recovered and regained its relative importance, while the West Indian trade became relatively more important. Had not British restrictions been placed upon American shipping to the West Indies, this trade would have been even greater. Together with the relative decline of trade with northern Europe went a relative decrease in the importance of the traditional southern staples. Because these trends had existed before the Revolution, however, such changes cannot be attributed solely to the War and independence.

Certainly, the War itself led to lower levels of trade and increased self-sufficiency for the country. This increase in American self-sufficiency persisted into the 1780's as the United States adjusted to independence. Not only does the direct evidence upon trade support this conclusion, but the evidence of declining agricultural productivity in Pennsylvania (Ball and Walton, 1976, p. 100) over this period indicates that economic improvement was interrupted by War and readjustment which necessitated greater self-sufficiency. Many examples of increased domestic manufacturing activity exist, as well.[27]

Whether one views the years between 1768–1772 and 1790–1792 as a period of economic stagnation, or decline and then recovery, it is apparent that these were years of economic difficulty and perhaps depressed living standards for the New Republic. The new evidence presented here is not consistent with the perspectives given by Jensen (1958), who asserts that "by 1790 the U.S. had far outstripped the colonies of a few short years before" (p. 218); or "by 1790 the export of agricultural produce was double what it had been before the war. American cities grew rapidly . . ." (p. 224).[28]

Total exports were 37% above their pre-War level by the early 1790's, but this was far short of the 80% increase in population increase for the period. Overall, the United States economy of the early 1790's does not appear to have been a prime example of export-led growth. The relative overall importance of foreign trade was declining, both in export values per capita, and most likely as a share of per capita income. For the American colonies, and the United States before the Civil War, such a large fall in per capita export values was an unusual peacetime experience. These changes were noticeably different by region, however, and great caution must be taken when dealing with trade in the aggregate. The southern decline of exports relative to population was sharp; the New England states (except for New Hampshire) and New York more than fully recovered from trade disruptions, but overall there was a significant decline in the relative importance of foreign trade. All this was to be drastically changed, however, by two events that occurred in 1793: the beginning of the Napoleonic Wars, and Eli Whitney's invention of the cotton gin; but the dramatic consequences of these events could not have been foreseen in 1792—or in 1775.

In closing, it is important to note that the commercial base that had developed in the United States before 1790 played a crucial role in the ability of the new nation to take advantage of economic possibilities which arose in following years. The development of this commercial base, especially in New England and the Middle Atlantic regions, stood in sharp contrast to the lack

---

[27] Jensen, 1958, pp. 219–227. One might also wonder if the failure of the population of the three largest cities (Philadelphia, New York, and Boston) to keep pace with general population growth is also indicative of a greater reliance on domestic production. Philadelphia increased from about 40,000 to 42,500 from 1775 to 1790, New York from 25,000 to 33,000, and Boston from 16,000 to 18,000 (Bridenbaugh, 1955, p. 216; Jensen, 1958, p. 116). Baltimore, on the other hand, more than doubled in population between these dates. This slower growth of these northern cities does not seem consistent with the greater growth of overseas trade of the northern regions. Obviously, however, many other factors would influence their growth.

[28] Jensen's comments seem more appropriate for the Middle Atlantic region than representative of the overall state of the economy. Nevertheless, they are too optimistic even for this region.

of similar developments in other colonies in Latin America and elsewhere. Surely this was an important aspect of the differential economic success of North America. United States prosperity in trade and shipping during the period of the Napoleonic Wars was to come and go, but the nation would soon embark upon an irrevocable course of industrialization and a path of development that would result in material standards of living undreamed of in 1790.

REFERENCES

Ball, D. E., and Walton, G. M. (1976), "Agricultural Productivity Change in Eighteenth-Century Pennsylvania." *Journal of Economic History* **36**, 102–117.

Bezanson, A., *et al.* (1951), *Prices and Inflation during the American Revolution: Pennsylvania, 1770–1790.* Philadelphia: University of Pennsylvania Press.

Bjork, G. C. (1964), "The Weaning of the American Economy: Independence, Market Changes, and Economic Development." *Journal of Economic History* **24**, 541–560.

Bridenbaugh, C. (1955), *Cities in Revolt: Urban Life in America, 1743–1776.* New York: Knopf.

Buron, E. (1932), "Statistics on Franco-American Trade, 1778–1806." *Journal of Economic and Business History* **4**, 571–80.

Cole, A. H. (1938), *Wholesale Commodity Prices in the United States, 1700–1861: Statistical Supplement.* Cambridge, Mass.: Harvard University Press.

Crouzet, F. (1964), "Wars, Blackade, and Economic Change in Europe, 1792–1815." *Journal of Economic History* **24**, 567–588.

Fishlow, A. (1964), "Discussion." *Journal of Economic History* **24**, 561–566.

Fogel, R. W., and Engerman, S. L. (1974), *Time on the Cross: The Economics of American Negro Slavery.* Boston: Little, Brown.

French, C. J. (1973), "Eighteenth-Century Shipping Tonnage Measurements." *Journal of Economic History* **33**, 434–43.

Gray, L. C. (1933), *History of Agriculture in the Southern United States to 1860.* 2 Vols. Washington, D.C.: Carnegie Institute of Washington.

Jensen, M. (1958), *The New Nation: A History of the United States during the Confederation, 1781–1789.* New York: Knopf.

Johnson, E. R., *et al.* (1915), *History of Domestic and Foreign Commerce of the United States.* Washington, D.C.: Carnegie Institute of Washington.

Klingaman, D. (1969), "The Significance of Grain in the Development of the Tobacco Colonies." *Journal of Economic History* **29**, 268–78.

Kohlmeier, A. L. (1925), "The Commerce of the United States and the Netherlands, 1783–1789." *Indiana University Studies* **12**, 3–47.

McCusker, J. (1967), "Colonial Tonnage Measurement: Five Philadelphia Merchant Ships as a Sample." *Journal of Economic History,* **27**, 82–91.

Nettels, C. P. (1962), *The Emergence of a National Economy 1775–1815.* New York: Holt, Rinehart and Winston.

North, D. C. (1965), "The Role of Transportation in the Economic Development of North America," in *Les grandes voies dan le monde, XVe–XLXe siecles.* Paris: SEVPEN.

North, D. C. (1974), *Growth and Welfare in the American Past,* 2nd ed. Englewood Cliffs, N.J.: Prentice-Hall.

Nussbaum, A. (1957), *A History of the Dollar.* New York: Columbia University Press.

Robertson, R. M. (1973), *History of the American Economy,* 3rd ed. New York: Harcourt Brace Jovanovich.

Shepherd, J. F., and Walton, G. M. (1972), *Shipping, Maritime Trade, and the Economic Development of Colonial North America.* London: Cambridge University Press.

Thomas, R. P. (1965), "A Quantitative Approach to the Study of the Effects of British Imperial Policy Upon Colonial Welfare: Some Preliminary Findings." *Journal of Economic History*, 25, 613–638.

United States, *American State Papers* (1832), Class IV, *Commerce and Navigation*, Vol. VII. Washington, D.C.: Gales and Seaton. [Cited as *U.S.A.S.P.* (1832).]

United States, Bureau of the Census (1960), *Historical Statistics of the United States, Colonial Times to 1957*. Washington, D.C.: U.S. Government Printing Office, Chap. Z. [Cited as *Historical Statistics* (1960).]

Walton, G. M. (1967), "Colonial Tonnage Measurement: A Comment." *Journal of Economic History* 27, 392–397.

[14]

EXPLORATIONS IN ECONOMIC HISTORY 17, 6–25 (1980)

The Role of Exports in American Economic Growth during the Napoleonic Wars, 1793 to 1807*

CLAUDIA D. GOLDIN

University of Pennsylvania

AND

FRANK D. LEWIS

Queen's University

AMERICAN PER CAPITA INCOME GROWTH BEFORE 1840

Research on American economic growth before 1840 has produced a disparate picture. The various estimates contained in works by David (1967), Gallman (1971, 1972a, 1972b), North (1966a, 1974), and Taylor (1964) are on the whole contradictory. Data for the pre-1800 period are inconsistent with those for later decades, and there are disagreements on estimates for identical years. There are many problems in determining the correct interpretation of growth over this period. The data are few and necessitate simple economic models. Unfortunately models that emphasize different sectors frequently yield quite diverse results. North's framework of export-led growth, for example, is at variance with David's which relies on sectoral change in the economy. A composite view of the 130 years from 1710 to 1840 cannot at present be constructed from the research of North concerning the 1793 to 1807 period, of David for the 1800 to 1840 period, and of Gallman and Taylor for 1710 to 1840.

Economic growth during several key decades appears responsible for most of the disagreement about growth during the entire pre-1840 period. One of these critical eras is that from 1793 to 1807, the period of American

*The authors acknowledge the helpful comments of Stanley Engerman and Neil Bruce and those of the participants at the MSSB Conference on Exports and Growth, especially Donald McCloskey and Knick Harley. Requests for reprints should be sent to Claudia D. Goldin, Department of Economics, University of Pennsylvania, Philadelphia, Pa. 19104.

6

neutrality in shipping. North and Taylor view this decade and a half as a high point in per capita income. The favorable trade conditions produced by the Napoleonic Wars greatly benefited American shipping, and, according to North and Taylor, the export sector pulled the entire economy rapidly along. The current dollar value of exports quintupled from 1790 to 1807. Reexports also increased as the United States skirted the 1756 Rule of War by carrying goods to its own ports and then reshipping to others. Net exports plus net freight earnings more than doubled in constant (1790) dollars over this 17-year period (see Appendix, Table A2). The export sector in the United States was aided considerably by these changes, but their effect on the rest of the economy is more speculation than fact.

The data produced by various studies of pre-1840 growth are given in Table 1. In several instances the original source did not give an exact figure, and numbers that are liberal interpretations have been bracketed. All estimates have been indexed to $96 for GNP per capita in 1840 and have been expressed in 1840 dollars facilitate comparison.[1]

Several contradictions are apparent in this table. For example if Taylor is correct that the economy boomed around the turn of the 19th century, then David's 1800 to 1840 growth rate is too high. North's export-led growth theory implies a severe drop in income from about 1774 to 1793 if it is to be consistent with both the David figures for 1800 to 1840 and those of Gallman for 1710 to 1774.[2] There could not have been a "substantial increase in productivity"[3] during the 1793 to 1807 period and average annual growth of 1.1% from 1800 to 1840 without a decline in income during an earlier period. The minimum rate of annual decline given by the Gallman and North figures in Table 1 is −0.53%, and the maximum decrease in income implied by these figures is −1.32% per year. These are substantial decreases in per capita income and rival any produced by the various depressions and wars in American history. But they are not necessarily accurate representations of economic history and hinge on rapid export-led growth during the period of American neutrality.

Evidence from several independent sources does support the conclusion of an economic depression in the post-Revolutionary War period. A decrease in per capita income is implied by Shepherd and Walton's (1976) per capita export figures which drop sharply from 1768–1772 to 1791–1792. Ball and Walton's (1976) index of total factor productivity in agriculture declines from 1775 to 1790, and the data ascribed to Gallman yield a per capita GNP figure for 1805 compatible with a 6 to 9% decline in productivity for the period 1774 to 1805.

[1] R. Gallman, unpublished national income estimates, p. 5.
[2] North's most recent position is stated in his *Growth and Welfare*, 2nd ed. (North, 1974, pp. 83–86).
[3] North (1974), p. 72.

8   GOLDIN AND LEWIS

We have called the statement that the American economy was spurred
along by export growth from 1793 to 1807 the "North–Taylor"
hypothesis. It has been previously questioned by David who dismissed it
on both theoretical and empirical grounds.[4] The economy, according to
David, was not open enough for any but a drastic change in export
demand to have had a large impact on total income. In addition, the
method of valuing exports and imports at base year prices implies that an
improvement in the terms of trade, such as was experienced after 1793,
would be accompanied by a decline in measured income, not an increase.[5]
Furthermore, David's own data are inconsistent with a substantial improvement in income during this period.

North's and Taylor's assertions about export-led growth lack an
explicit framework. David's counterargument applies only to the period
after 1800 and uses a procedure that generates just a first approximation to
the full impact of the foreign trade sector. The theory of export-led growth
applied to the period 1793 to 1807 has not been tested formally. Our paper
will fill this gap by measuring the impact on income of improvements in
the foreign sector from 1793 to 1807. We will also construct estimates of
per-capita income growth for the period of American neutrality.

AN EVALUATION OF EXPORT-LED GROWTH: 1793 TO 1807

A Simple Computational Method: The Terms of Trade Effect

The thesis that growth was export-led during the period of American
neutrality can be evaluated by observing the economy's performance in
the absence of the more favorable trade conditions. By imposing on the
economy from 1796 to 1807 its 1793 foreign sector position the resultant
decline in income can be measured.[6] The more simple the method chosen
to analyze this problem, the more variables are held constant and therefore the more hazardous its use. A conceptually simple, but somewhat
incomplete, analysis holds the terms of trade constant at their 1793 value.
A more complex method holds the levels of export demand and import
supply at their 1793 values. The terms of trade effect is discussed first to

----

[4] David (1967), pp. 188–194.

[5] This follows because an improvement in the terms of trade implies a decrease in the ratio
of exports to imports. David discounts this argument and applies a terms of trade approach
(David, 1967, p. 190). We also employ this method but only as a first approximation of the
full impact of the foreign trade sector.

[6] We could test, for example, how much higher incomes would have been in 1810 had
favorable trade conditions continued. However, North's writings state that 1793 to 1807
were highly prosperous years in terms of the previous period. For example, North has stated
that the "period [1793–1807] stands out as an extraordinary era in economic well being as
compared to the earlier period or even to the period of peace after 1814" (North, 1967, p.
389). This is the assertion that is being tested.

EXPORTS IN AMERICAN ECONOMIC GROWTH, 1793–1807   9

TABLE 1
American per Capita GNP before 1840, for selected years 1710 to 1840
(1840$)

Year	(1) David	(2) Gallman	(3) North	(4) Taylor
1710		46–61		45
1774		61–71		90
1793			[55]^a	[74]^a
1800	62		62	
1805		63–76		[90]^a
1810	59			
1820	65			
1830	81			
1840	96	96	96	96

^{a} Numbers in brackets are those implied by the author and have not been explicitly stated. See *Sources and Notes* for their derivation. Due to rounding errors calculations based on these estimates may not conform exactly.

Sources and Notes. Column (1): David (1967), pp. 151–197. We have expressed the data in his Table 8 (p. 184) in 1840 prices with a per capita GNP in 1840 of $96 and have used his variant II, for which his $\gamma = .511$. The figure of $96 for per capita GNP in 1840 is from R. Gallman (unpublished national income estimates, p. 5).

Column (2): Gallman (1972b), pp. 22–24, 28–29; Gallman (1972a); p. 208; Gallman (1971); Jones (1975). Gallman's range of estimates for NNP per capita in 1774 extends from $60 to $70. We have converted this to GNP using Jones' wealth estimates and assuming a 1% rate of depreciation to buildings and a 3% rate to equipment. The GNP per capita range for 1710 was obtained from Gallman's NNP estimates using the assumption that the ratio of GNP to NNP was identical to that computed for 1774. The 1805 figure of $63 was calculated from Gallman's estimate of the increase in per capita factor inputs from 1805 to 1840 and his estimate of the increase in agricultural total factor productivity. (We assume that the rate of growth of nonagricultural productivity was equal to Gallman's estimate for that in agriculture.) We have also incorporated in the $63 figure the effect of changes in the industrial allocation of the labor force. The upper bound figure of $76 for the same year directly follows from Gallman (1972b, p. 29). This range of $63 to $76 is consistent with Gallman's statement (Gallman, 1971) that "David's per capita GDP estimates for [1790 to 1820] must be too low" (p. 79). Note that Gallman's estimate of a 14% increase in per capita factor inputs from 1774 to 1805 implies a decline in productivity of between 5.7% applying both upper bound estimates and 9.3% applying the lower bound estimates for that period.

Column (3): North (1966a, 1974). In the first edition (1966) of *Growth and Welfare* North stated that "in 1799 per capita incomes were extraordinary and may have been almost as high as they were half a century later" (p. 73). He is more cautious in the revised edition and attempts to reconcile his theory concerning the 1793 to 1807 period with David's estimates (1974, p. 84). Although North contends in both editions that "[t]here can be no doubt that the years 1793 through 1807 were extraordinarily prosperous for the American economy" (1974, p. 72), he neither pinpoints the level of income nor estimates its growth during this period. We have ascribed the David estimate of $62 for 1800 to North on the basis of the discussion in the 2nd ed. of *Growth and Welfare*. Assuming that "extraordinarily prosperous" implies, at a minimum, the average rate of growth which David estimated for 1810 to 1840, U.S. per capita income would have grown at 1.6% per year from 1793 to (say) 1800 and would have been $55 in 1793. This figure has been bracketed because it is not

10   GOLDIN AND LEWIS

clarify the more general method of imposing on the 1796 to 1807 economy
its 1793 foreign sector position.

The terms of trade, the ratio of the price of exports to imports, rose
dramatically from 1793 to about 1798 and though they fell after 1798 they
remained well above their 1793 level (see Table 2). In a mere decade the
young country had considerably increased its foreign purchasing power.
These trading ratios were the most favorable the United States would
experience for many decades. Their effect on income can be derived by
assuming no improvement in the terms of trade after 1793 and computing
the implied percentage drop in income. Under the less favorable conditions the country could purchase fewer imports with the given quantity of
exports. The results of this exercise, summarized in Table 2, indicate that
income would have fallen about 2.27 to 5.20% below the values achieved
at various dates. Income would have been lower by 3.40% annually, on
average, had the terms of trade returned to their less favorable 1793 level.

*A More Complex Method: The Effect on Income of a Change in Export
Demand and Import Supply*

The terms of trade method generally has severe limitations. It assumes
that the volume of exports is insensitive to changes in the terms of trade
and is complicated by an index number problem—the price of imports is
assumed fixed. This method provides a good approximation for small
changes in the terms of trade but could generate highly misleading results
for larger ones. Rather than rest our conclusions on a possibly faulty
analysis we have derived a more accurate but more complex method. It is
a procedure that measures the impact on both producer's and consumer's
surplus of changing the levels of export demand and import supply. We
test the sensitivity of our results to the elasticities of supply and demand

---

explicitly stated by North. Note that this picture is inconsistent with North's previous view
that per capita income was so high in 1800 as to be unrivaled for half a century.

   Column (4): Taylor (1964), pp. 427–444. These numbers were constructed according to
Taylor's verbal description of growth from 1710 to 1840. Taylor conjectured that "[d]uring
the Revolutionary War, productivity fell off and remained relatively low during the Confederation period. Then it appears to have risen rapidly during the 1790's so that *by the first five
or six years of the new century the average level of living was about where it had been in the
early 1770's*. Conditions continued good to 1807, but thereafter embargoes, non-intercourse
acts, and the War of 1812 definitely depressed living standards. A brief expansion following
1814 ended with a sharp reaction in 1819–20. A period of slow growth followed in the
twenties, giving way to rapid improvement in the thirties. *By 1836–1840, the level of living
had, I believe, risen to (or somewhat above) the average reached in 1770–1774 and 1799–
1804*" (p. 437, our italics). He also "[hazarded] the opinion that *the average level of living
about doubled in the sixty-five years before the Revolution*" (p. 437, our italics). The 1793
figure was obtained by allowing a rapid rate of growth of 1.6% per year from 1793 to 1805. A
more rapid rate would serve to lower that figure.

TABLE 2
The Effect on Income of a Return to the 1793 Terms of Trade,
for selected years 1796 to 1807

Year	Terms of trade (1793 = 100)	Effect on income[a] (negative percentage)
1796	144.1	4.94
1798	180.2	5.20
1800	129.8	2.48
1803	124.7	2.76
1805	124.3	2.27
1807	121.1	2.52

[a] The terms of trade effect is the change in the quantity of imports that can be purchased with the given quantity of exports at the 1793 terms of trade. The change in income is

$$\Delta Y = \left[\frac{p_x^{1793}}{p_m^{1793}} - \frac{p_x^i}{p_m^i} \right] p_m^i Q_x^i.$$

where p_x^i, p_m^i = price of exports, imports in year i; p_x^i/p_m^i = terms of trade in year i; Q_x^i = quantity of exports in year i; ΔY = change in income. The change in relative income is

$$\frac{\Delta Y}{Y} = \frac{p_x^i Q_x^i}{Y} \left[\frac{p_x^{1793}/p_m^{1793}}{p_x^i/p_m^i} - 1 \right].$$

where $\Delta Y/Y$ is the relative effect on income of a return to the 1793 terms of trade, and $[p_x^i Q_x^i/Y]$ is the ratio of the value of exports to income.
Sources. North (1966a), p. 229; Appendix, Table A4.

and to assumptions about the employment of factors of production. The calculation is performed in two stages. The first determines the effect on income of a change in the level of export demand, holding the level of import supply constant, and the second, the effect on income of a change in the level of import supply, holding the level of export demand constant. The results are summed to get the total impact of returning the economy to its 1793 trade position.

The effect on economic growth of an increase in export demand will be larger if an economy begins from a position of unemployed resources. The exogenous shock then leads to the employment of previously idle factors, and the increase in income is the full product of the factors and not merely their marginal increase to total income. It is important therefore to determine whether the analysis of the period 1793 to 1807 should assume full employment or unemployment in the absence of the more favorable trade conditions.

Information on the economic situation during the period of the Confederation is scanty. Agricultural goods and other primary products dominated the economic scene and fully 85 to 90% of labor was involved in their cultivation and production. There has been considerable debate on the strength of the economy during this period and on the severity of the economic depression following the Revolutionary War. But even if the long-run effects of the war were minor, the foreign trade sector must have experienced a difficult initial transition. Export demand declined precipitously after independence with real per capita exports falling about 30%.[7] The export sector probably did experience periods of idle capacity during the early years of the new republic. One recent text has stated that "contemporary accounts are filled with citations of idle ships, shuttered warehouses, and unemployed sailors. The gloom spread back from the docks as sail makers, insurance agents, and nearby farmers saw the shrinking demand for their supporting services." [8] Although some capital in the export industry could not be transferred to other sectors, its labor probably did not remain unemployed for long. It is difficult to imagine an agricultural economy sustaining substantial labor unemployment in the nonfarming sector.

The hypothetical economy of unchanged foreign trade conditions could assume either a full employment economy or one of unemployed resources, and there is no clear-cut evidence to support either proposition. Two sets of assumptions are therefore employed in the analysis. In an economy of full employment, factors released from the export sector shift to other sectors and resources drawn into imports are taken from alternative uses. In an economy experiencing unemployment, resources do not shift to productive uses and are valued at a zero opportunity cost. The assumption of unemployed resources in the export sector produces a larger estimate of the effects of improved export trade conditions than that of fully employed factors. The rise in income from a shift upward in export demand includes the full opportunity cost of the resources drawn into exports. To bias our results in favor of export-led growth, we compute the import side only under the condition of full employment. Resources shifting into import-substitute production are assumed to be drawn from alternative uses and not from a pool of unemployed factors. The two assumptions on the export side result in two estimates (higher and lower) of the impact of more favorable trade conditions and are combined with the one (upwardly biased) assumption on the import side.

The estimate on the export side, given the assumption of full employment, can be described with reference to Fig. 1, in which (A) refers to home production and consumption. The decrease in export demand lowers price in the home market (from p_x to p_x'), reducing producer's surplus (by $p_x'ECp_x$) and raising that of consumers (by $p_x'BAp_x$). The net result, ignoring the issue of distribution, is a loss of $ABEC$. This can be seen in a parallel fashion with reference to (B) of the same figure. The S_x function is the excess supply schedule for exports, derived from the domestic relationships in (A). The decrease in export demand (D_x to D_x') reduces price

[7] See Shepherd and Walton (1976).
[8] Gunderson (1976), p. 104.

EXPORTS IN AMERICAN ECONOMIC GROWTH, 1793–1807   13

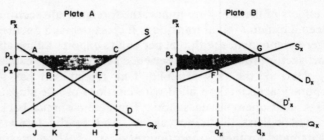

FIG. 1. The effects on income of a change in the demand for exports under full employment. D = U.S. demand curve for the export commodity; S = U.S. supply curve of the export commodity; D_x = world demand curve for U.S. exports; D'_x = hypothetical world demand curve for U.S. exports (what demand would have been in 1796 to 1807 had the less favorable 1793 trade conditions prevailed); S_x = excess U.S. supply curve of the export commodity; q_x = quantity of U.S. exports prior to change in demand; q'_x = quantity of exports under hypothetical conditions; p_x = actual price of U.S. exports; p'_x = hypothetical price of U.S. exports.

(p_x to p'_x) and quantity (q_x to q'_x), and depresses income by $p'_x FG p_x$, (identical to $ABEC$ by construction of S_x).

Under the assumptions of a constant elasticity of supply of exports (γ) and a constant elasticity of foreign demand for exports (ϵ), the area $ABEC$ can be represented by

$$\Delta Y^f_e = \frac{S_x p_x^{\gamma+1}}{\gamma+1}\left[\left(1 + \overset{*}{D}_x\right)^{(\gamma+1)/(\gamma+\epsilon)} - 1\right] \quad \text{for } \epsilon \neq \infty,$$

and (1)

$$\Delta Y^f_e = \frac{S_x p_x^{\gamma+1}}{\gamma+1}\left[\left(1 + \overset{*}{p}_x\right)^{\gamma+1} - 1\right] \quad \text{for } \epsilon = \infty,$$

where ΔY^f_e = the change in income caused by a shift in the demand curve for exports assuming full employment of factors, D_x = level of demand for exports, S_x = level of supply of exports, and an asterisk (*) over a variable denotes the relative change in that variable from its actual to its hypothetical value.[9] The relative, not the absolute, change in income is more

[9] This can be derived as follows. Assume export demand can be represented by

$$Q_x = D_x P_x^{-\epsilon}, \tag{a}$$

and export supply by

$$Q_x = S_x P_x^{\gamma}. \tag{b}$$

It follows from (a) and (b) that in equilibrium

$p_x = (D_x/S_x)^{[1/\gamma+\epsilon]}$ and from Fig. 1 that

$$p'_x/p_x = (D'_x/D_x)^{[1/\gamma+\epsilon]}. \tag{c}$$

Area $p'_x FG p_x$ is given by

$$\Delta Y^f_e = \int_{p_x}^{p'_x} S_x P_x^{\gamma} dP_x$$

or

$$\Delta Y^f_e = \left[\left(S_x p_x^{\gamma+1}\right)/\gamma + 1\right]\left[\left(p'_x/p_x\right)^{\gamma+1} - 1\right]. \tag{d}$$

Substituting Eq. (c) into Eq. (d), and noting that $\left[D'_x/D_x = 1 + \overset{*}{D}_x\right]$ yields Eq. (1).

appropriate for this analysis, and it can be expressed similarly as

$$\frac{\Delta Y_e^f}{Y} = \frac{\lambda}{\gamma+1} \left[\left(1 + \overset{*}{D}_x\right)^{(\gamma+1)/(\gamma+\epsilon)} - 1 \right] \quad \text{for } \epsilon \neq \infty,$$

and   (2)

$$\frac{\Delta Y_e^f}{Y} = \frac{\lambda}{\gamma+1} \left[\left(1 + \overset{*}{p}_x\right)^{\gamma+1} - 1 \right] \quad \text{for } \epsilon = \infty,$$

where Y is total income, and λ is the ratio of the value of exports to total income, measuring the "openness" of the economy.

The assumption of unemployed resources results in a larger income effect from a change in export demand than that given by Eq. (2). The change in income is now the full increase in the value of exports, equal to the entire shaded area $[p_x'Fq_x'q_xGp_x]$ in Fig. 2. Resource opportunity costs are assumed to be zero in this case, and an overestimate of the gain in income from a shift in the demand for exports probably results.[10] The derivation of this area is similar to that for the lower bound estimate and can be expressed by

$$\Delta Y_e^u = p_x'q_x' - p_xq_x. \quad (3)$$

where ΔY_e^u = the change in income caused by a shift in the demand curve for exports assuming unemployment of factors. The relative change in income generated by a shift in the demand curve for exports is

$$\frac{\Delta Y_e^u}{Y} = \lambda \left[\left(1 + \overset{*}{D}_x\right)^{(\gamma+1)/(\gamma+\epsilon)} - 1 \right] \quad \text{for } \epsilon \neq \infty,$$

and   (4)

$$\frac{\Delta Y_e^u}{Y} = \lambda \left[\left(1 + \overset{*}{p}_x\right)^{\gamma+1} - 1 \right] \quad \text{for } \epsilon = \infty.$$

Equations (2) and (4) can help answer historical questions only when estimated with data and four values are required to compute the relative change in income. Two of these, $\overset{*}{D}_x$ and λ, can be estimated from data for 1796 to 1807, and, for lack of direct information, the other two, ϵ and γ, have been assigned several feasible values. The ratio of the value of exports to income (λ) ranges from 10 to 16% and is given in the Appendix (Table A4). Estimates of $\overset{*}{D}_x$ for three values of ϵ (2, 5, and ∞) are listed in Table 3. The values for $\overset{*}{D}_x$ and λ are then used to evaluate Eqs. (2) and (4) for two values of γ (1 and 3), and Table 4 lists the results.

The data in Table 4 report the relative drop in income were there no

---

[10] The assumption of unemployed resources adds the area $[q_x'FGq_x]$ to the decrease in income resulting from a fall in export demand. This is actually an overestimate of the true effect because it includes the increased value of exportables consumed domestically (given by $AJKB$ in Fig. 1). The true impact should only include area $EHIC$, the decrease in factor payments to inputs released from export production. Therefore our measure necessarily overstates the change in income by $AJKB$, and a further upward bias results from assuming that factors are fully unemployed.

EXPORTS IN AMERICAN ECONOMIC GROWTH, 1793–1807   **15**

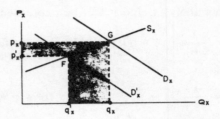

FIG. 2. The effects on income of a change in the demand for exports under unemployment. Notation is the same as in Fig. 1.

expansion in the demand for U.S. exports after 1793. For example, assuming $\epsilon = 2$ and $\gamma = 1$, income would have been between 1.86 and 3.72% less in 1796. Estimates of the change in relative income for the entire gamut of the assigned ϵ and γ values can also be read from this table. To illustrate, income in 1803 would have been between 1.35 and 4.67% lower had the export trade sector not improved from its 1793 position.

These estimates cannot be used to assess the thesis of export-led growth without considering the import side as well. The analysis to this point provides only part of the picture because the price of imports has been artificially held constant. Import prices fell substantially during this

TABLE 3

The Hypothetical Percentage Change in the Levels of the Demand for Exports and the Supply of Imports, for selected years 1796 to 1807

Year	$\epsilon = 2, \psi = 1^a$		$\epsilon = 5, \psi = 4^a$		$\epsilon = \infty, \psi = \infty^a$	
	$\overset{*}{D}_x$	$\overset{*}{S}_m$	$\overset{*}{D}_x$	$\overset{*}{S}_m$	$\overset{*}{p}_x$	$-\overset{*}{p}_{m_t}$
1796	32.5^b	42.9	64.0	64.2	18.9	16.8
1798	45.7	4.9	90.2	9.3	43.6	1.6
1800	19.1	27.1	50.8	45.2	15.3	10.0
1803	45.8	39.4	66.5	49.6	14.8	6.3
1805	39.8	49.3	61.0	59.0	13.5	7.5
1807	53.4	62.4	64.3	72.3	8.5	10.7

^{a} Under the assumption of balanced trade: $\epsilon = \psi + 1$. See, for example, Mundell (1968), p. 25.

^{b} All values are negative.

Sources. Appendix, Table A1, Columns (2) and (3); Table A2, Column 3; and Table A3, Column 2.

Notes.

$$[1+\overset{*}{D}_x] = [D_x^{1793}/D_x^i] = [p_x^{1793} \cdot q_x^{1793}/p_x^i \cdot q_x^i] [p_x^{1793}/p_x^i]^{\epsilon-1} \quad (\epsilon \neq \infty).$$

The "i" superscripts indicate the appropriate year. Similarly

$$\left[1 + \overset{*}{S}_m\right] = \left[S_m^{1793}/S_m^i\right] = \left[p_{m_t}^{1793} \cdot q_m^{1793}/p_{m_t}^i \cdot q_m^i\right] \left[p_{m_t}^{1793}/p_{m_t}^i\right]^{1-\psi},$$

under the assumption of a constant supply elasticity ($\psi \neq 0$).

16 GOLDIN AND LEWIS

period, reinforcing the effect on the export side. The initial *ceteris paribus* assumption can be remedied by considering the effect on income of shifting the import supply curve back to its 1793 position. The method used is similar to that applied to the export sector with the additional complication of an import tariff.

The effect on income of a change in import supply can be illustrated with reference to Fig. 3. The shift in the supply of imports from S_m to S'_m (in plate B) increases the price paid by consumers from p_m to p'_m and decreases quantity demanded from q_m to q'_m. This reduces consumer's surplus by $p_m CDp'_m$ (in (A)), increases producer's surplus by $p_m BAp'_m$, and results in a net income loss of $ABCD$ ($=p'_m EFp_m$). There is also a change in tariff revenues, from $[p_{m_t} p_m FG]$ to $[p'_{m_t} p'_m EH]$, and the full impact on income is a loss of $[p_{m_t} GFEHp'_{m_t}]$. The relative loss in income can be represented by

$$\frac{\Delta Y_i}{Y} = -\Pi \left| \left(1 + \overset{*}{S}_m \right)^{(\eta - 1)/(\psi + \eta)} - 1 \right| \left(\frac{1 + t\eta}{1 - \eta} \right) \qquad \text{for } \eta \neq 1, \psi \neq \infty,$$

and $\qquad\qquad\qquad\qquad\qquad\qquad\qquad\qquad\qquad\qquad\qquad\qquad\qquad$ (5)

$$\frac{\Delta Y_i}{Y} = -\Pi \left| \left(1 + \overset{*}{p}_{m_t} \right)^{1 - \eta} - 1 \right| \left(\frac{1 + t\eta}{1 - \eta} \right) \qquad \text{for } \eta \neq 1, \psi = \infty,$$

TABLE 4

The Effect on Income of a Return to the 1793 Export Demand Level, for selected years 1796 to 1807

Year	$\epsilon = 2$		$\epsilon = 5$		$\epsilon = \infty$	
	$\gamma = 1$	$\gamma = 3^a$	$\gamma = 1$	$\gamma = 3$	$\gamma = 1$	$\gamma = 3$
1796	[1.86, 3.72]^b	1.09	[2.33, 4.66]	1.61	[2.76, 5.53]	2.29
1798	[1.95, 3.91]	1.13	[3.13, 6.26]	2.01	[3.98, 7.96]	2.62
1800	[0.71, 1.42]	0.42	[1.13, 2.25]	0.81	[1.52, 3.05]	1.30
1803	[2.33, 4.67]	1.35	[2.12, 4.25]	1.47	[1.91, 3.82]	1.65
1805	[1.66, 3.33]	0.97	[1.56, 3.13]	1.09	[1.46, 2.92]	1.27
1807	[2.89, 5.77]	1.65	[2.10, 4.20]	1.46	[1.18, 2.35]	1.08

^{a} The effect of unemployed resources is computed using only the smaller values for η and γ because of an upward bias imbedded in our method, see footnote 10. The area $q'_x FGq_x$ in Fig. 2, the additional income loss under unemployment, overestimates the true loss. It includes not only the value of factors leaving export production but also the amount by which consumers gain because of lower export prices. There is a similar upward bias on the import side because we implicitly exclude the value of factors of production attracted into import substitute goods, given their increased price. These two biases can be ignored only if the volumes of exportables domestically consumed and importables domestically produced are small. But an elasticity of import demand of 4 and one of export supply of 3 implicitly constrain these values to be large. These elasticities would then be much too high to represent those of the total demand and supply curves. The analysis of unemployed resources is therefore confined to the case of $\eta = 2$ and $\gamma = 1$.

^{b} Numbers in brackets give the full employment and unemployment estimates, respectively, all expressed as a negative percentage.

Sources. Table 3; Appendix, Table A4.

EXPORTS IN AMERICAN ECONOMIC GROWTH, 1793–1807   17

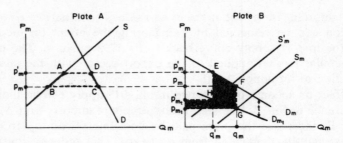

FIG. 3.   The effects on income of a change in the supply of imports. D_m = excess demand curve for import commodity, excluding the tariff; D_{m_t} = excess demand curve for import commodity, including the tariff; S_m = supply curve of imports; S'_m = hypothetical supply curve for imports; S = domestic supply for the import commodity; D = domestic demand for the import commodity; q_m = actual quantity of imports; q'_m = hypothetical quantity of imports; p_m = actual price of imports, including the tariff; p'_m = hypothetical price of imports, including the tariff; p_{m_t} = actual price of imports, excluding the tariff; p'_{m_t} = hypothetical price of imports, excluding the tariff.

where ΔY_i = the change in income caused by a shift in the supply curve of imports, η = the (constant) elasticity of demand for imports, ψ = the (constant) elasticity of supply of imports, S_m = the level of supply of imports, t = the average ad valorem tariff rate, and $\Pi = p_m q_m / Y$.[11]

Values for $\overset{*}{S}_m$, Π, t, η, and ψ are required to evaluate Eq. (5) and thereby determine the change in relative income from shifting the import supply curve. The ratio of the value of imports to income, Π, and the average tariff rate, t, have been tabulated in the Appendix (Table A4), and the hypothetical percentage change in the import supply level, $\overset{*}{S}_m$, is given in Table 3. Equation (5) has been calculated for two values of η (2

[11] Equation (5) can be derived as follows for $\psi = \infty$. Assume import demand can be represented by:

$$Q_m = D_m P_m^{-\eta},$$

and the import supply function by

$$Q_m = S_m P_m^{\psi},$$

where D_m = the level of demand for imports. The tariff drives a wedge between the demand and supply price of imports, so that in equilibrium:

$$p_m = (D_m/S_m)^{[1/\psi+\eta]}(1+t)^{[\psi/\psi+\eta]}.$$

Area $p_{m_t}GFEHp'_{m_t}$ in Fig. 3 is given by

$$\Delta Y_i = -\int_{p_m}^{p'_m} [D_m P_m^{-\eta}]dP_m + (p'_m - p'_{m_t})q'_m - (p_m - p_{m_t})q_m.$$

Noting that $p'_m = (1+t)p'_{m_t}$ and that $p_m = (1+t)p_{m_t}$ we have

$$\Delta Y_i = -p_{m_t}q_m [(S_m/S'_m)^{[1-\eta/\psi+\eta]} - 1] \cdot [1+t\eta/1-\eta].$$

Substituting $\left[S'_m/S_m = 1 + \overset{*}{S}_m\right]$ and $\left[\Pi = p_{m_t}q_m/Y\right]$ gives Eq. (5).

TABLE 5
The Effect on Income of a Return to the 1793 Import Supply Level,
for selected years 1796 to 1807[a]

Year	$\psi = 1$		$\psi = 4$		$\psi = \infty$	
	$\eta = 2$	$\eta = 4$	$\eta = 2$	$\eta = 4$	$\eta = 2$	$\eta = 4$
1796	3.08	2.05	2.84	2.29	2.60	2.67
1798	0.22	0.17	0.22	0.21	0.21	0.26
1800	1.40	1.04	1.33	1.21	1.27	1.50
1803	2.38	1.72	1.66	1.50	0.92	1.11
1805	3.18	2.21	2.18	1.88	1.10	1.29
1807	5.17	3.49	3.58	3.01	1.80	2.07

[a] Expressed as a negative percentage.
Sources. Table 3; Appendix, Table A4.

and 4), and the results are presented in Table 5. These figures are all based on the assumption of full employment to bias our results in favor of an export-led growth thesis.

The results of the two calculations, that on the export and that on the import sides, are summed to conform to the equilibrium conditions $\epsilon = \psi + 1$ and $\eta = \gamma + 1$, implied by balanced trade.[12] Table 6 is constructed according to that procedure and gives the total effect on income of a return to 1793 trade conditions. The assumptions of infinitely elastic foreign demand and supply curves ($\epsilon = \psi = \infty$), and fairly large values for the domestic demand and supply elasticities ($\eta = 4$, and $\gamma = 3$), produce a decline in income ranging from 2.56% (1805) to 4.96% (1796). The values for other years tightly group around 3% and range from 2.76 to 3.15%. Had there been no change in the foreign sector from 1793 and 1807, per capita income would have been reduced by approximately 3%. Using David's figure of $62 for 1800 (see Table 1), these values imply that income per capita would have been about $60 in 1800 had the foreign sector remained at its 1793 position. Favorable trade conditions in 1800 relative to 1793 increased per capita income by slightly less than $2.

These estimates are strikingly similar to those obtained with the simpler terms of trade analysis (see Table 2), although the more sophisticated procedure has enabled sensitivity tests with regard to employment assumptions and parameter values. The similarity of the two methods is a consequence of the comparatively small change in the terms of trade and the low share of national income generated by export production. The change in the terms of trade, with the exception of the initial years, was less than 30%. More importantly, the export sector was always a small part of the full economy, producing only about 12% of total product.

[12] See, for example, Mundell (1968), p. 25. These conditions partially account for our choice of values for ϵ, η, γ, and ψ.

TABLE 6

The Total Effect on Income of a Return to the 1793 Levels of Export
Demand and Import Supply, for selected years 1796 to 1807[a]

Year	$\epsilon = 2, \psi = 1$[b]		$\epsilon = 5, \psi = 4$		$\epsilon = \psi = \infty$	
	$\eta = 2,$ $\gamma = 1$[b]	$\eta = 4,$ $\gamma = 3$	$\eta = 2,$ $\gamma = 1$	$\eta = 4,$ $\gamma = 3$	$\eta = 2,$ $\gamma = 1$	$\eta = 4,$ $\gamma = 3$
1796	[4.94, 6.80][c]	3.14	[5.17, 7.50]	3.90	[5.26, 8.13]	4.96
1798	[2.17, 4.13]	1.30	[3.35, 6.48]	2.22	[4.19, 8.17]	2.88
1800	[2.11, 2.82]	1.46	[2.46, 3.58]	2.02	[2.79, 4.32]	2.80
1803	[4.71, 7.05]	3.07	[3.78, 5.91]	2.97	[2.83, 4.74]	2.76
1805	[4.84, 6.51]	3.18	[3.74, 5.31]	2.97	[2.56, 4.02]	2.56
1807	[8.06, 10.94]	5.14	[5.68, 7.78]	4.47	[2.98, 4.15]	3.15

[a] Expressed as a negative percentage.
[b] Under the assumption of balanced trade $\epsilon = \psi + 1$, and $\eta = \gamma + 1$.
[c] The second term in brackets is the impact on income assuming that factors leaving export production would be unemployed.
Sources. Tables 4 and 5.

Income Growth from 1793 to 1807 and the Role of the Foreign Sector

Changes in the foreign sector from 1796 to 1807 probably did not lead to substantial growth in per capita income. This analysis has suggested that income would have been 3% lower had Napoleon not blessed America with the war in Europe. But even though a more favorable foreign sector did not result in enormous growth rates, changes in foreign trade could still have been the major source of growth during the period. Estimates of per capita income growth for 1793 to 1807 are required to assess this notion.

We have used Gallman's (1972b) estimate of the increase in the per capita supply of inputs and the data from Table 6 on the effect of the foreign sector to compute per capita income growth. The supply of factor inputs per capita grew by 14% from 1774 to 1805,[13] and we employ two alternative assumptions concerning the time path of growth over these three decades. The first is that the per capita supply of factors in 1784 was equal to that in 1774 and then increased at a constant rate from 1784 to 1805. The second estimate constrains the 1793 level to equal that in 1774 and then allows it to increase at a constant rate.[14] The former assumption implies that there was no net increase in inputs during the Revolutionary War. It yields a lower bound estimate of input growth from 1793 to 1805. The latter assumption implies that there was wartime destruction of

[13] Gallman (1972b), p. 24.
[14] We assume that the rate of increase in per capita factor inputs between 1805 and 1807 equalled that between 1795 and 1805. The decline in productivity implied by Gallman's figures has been allocated to the period before 1793; this implies no change in factor productivity from 1793 to 1807. See Table 1, *Sources and Notes* (2).

20   GOLDIN AND LEWIS

TABLE 7
Estimates of the Average Annual Rate of per Capita Income Growth
between 1793 and selected years ($\epsilon = \psi = \infty$)

	Lower bound[a]		Upper bound[a]	
Year	(1) $\eta = 2, \gamma = 1$	(2) $\eta = 4, \gamma = 3$	(3) $\eta = 2, \gamma = 1$	(4) $\eta = 4, \gamma = 3$
1796	2.49	2.35	2.97	2.83
1798	1.49	1.22	1.97	1.69
1800	1.03	1.03	1.51	1.51
1803	0.92	0.91	1.39	1.38
1805	0.84	0.84	1.32	1.32
1807	0.84	0.86	1.32	1.33

[a] The lower and upper bounds result from different assumptions about the time path of input growth from 1774 to 1805. See text for an explanation.

Sources. Gallman (1972b), p. 24; this paper, Table 6.

Notes. The growth rate of per capita income is computed as

$$\overset{*}{Y} = [(1+\overset{*}{F})^n/1+X]^{1/n} - 1,$$

where

$\overset{*}{Y}$ = average annual growth rate in per capita income,
$\overset{*}{F}$ = average annual growth rate in per capita factor inputs,
X = proportional effect on income of a return to the 1793 levels of export demand and import supply,
n = number of years between 1793 and the selected year.

resources that required 9 years to rebuild. There is some empirical basis for accepting the upper bound estimates, but both are used for purposes of comparison.[15] The values implied by these two assumptions are 0.63% (lower bound) and 1.10% (upper bound) for the growth in per capita factor inputs from 1793 to 1805. They are combined, in Table 7, with the effect on income of a return to the 1793 foreign sector conditions to yield estimates of per capita income growth from 1793 to 1807.

These results indicate that the rates of growth achieved during this period were low with the exception of a fairly rapid increase in income between 1793 and 1796. They are generally less than the David estimate of 1.6% for 1810 and 1840. But even though the rate of growth was modest, the foreign sector contributed significantly to the growth that did occur. Of the 1.03 to 1.51% rate of increase in per capita income from 1793 to 1800, the foreign sector accounted for 0.40 percentage point per year or from 27 to 39% of the total. The entire period 1793 to 1807 appears to have

[15] Ball and Walton compute a decline for 1775 to 1790 in their index of total factor productivity for all variants of their analysis except three, for which it remained the same. See Ball and Walton (1976), Table 7, p. 112.

TABLE 8

Hypothetical Average Annual Rate of per Capita Income Growth between
1793 and selected years ($\epsilon = \psi = \infty$; $\eta = 2$, $\gamma = 1$)[a]

Year	Labor and capital attracted to the export sector are unemployed		Capital attracted to the export sector is unemployed	
	Lower bound[b]	Upper bound	Lower bound	Upper bound
1796	−0.31	0.16	0.33	0.80
1798	−0.19	0.28	0.37	0.84
1800	0.40	0.88	0.56	1.03
1803	0.43	0.90	0.56	1.04
1805	0.50	0.97	0.59	1.06
1807	0.54	1.01	0.60	1.07

[a] This assumes no change in the levels of export demand and import supply.

[b] The lower and upper bounds result from different assumptions about the time path of input growth from 1774 to 1805. See text for an explanation.

Sources. Gallman (1972b), p. 24; this paper, Table 7.

Notes. The hypothetical growth rate in per capita income is computed as

$$\overset{*}{Y} = [(1+\overset{*}{F})^{\eta}(1+y)]^{1/\eta} - 1,$$

where y = difference between the proportional effect on income assuming unemployment of factors and assuming full employment. The impact of capital alone is computed by multiplying y by an estimate of capital's factor share (0.32).

experienced the slightly lower growth rate of 0.84 to 1.33% per year with the foreign sector contributing about 0.22 percentage points.[16]

Growth in income is also estimated from 1793 to selected years from 1796 to 1807 under the hypothetical (unfavorable) trade conditions. The assumption of unemployed resources is used to bias the results in favor of a larger impact from trade. Table 8 gives both the extreme case of unemployed capital and labor, and an intermediate case of employed labor but induced capital formation.[17] Whereas it seems possible that some capital would have been idle during this period, it is unlikely that labor would have been. The results in Table 7 can be combined with those in Table 8 to illustrate the degree to which the economy was stimulated by its neutral trade position during the Napoleonic Wars. The per capita income growth rate would have been between 0.60 and 1.07% had trade not expanded (given employed labor and induced capital). It was between 0.84 and 1.32% under the more favorable conditions. Therefore the im-

[16] The impact of the foreign sector in 1807 is quite sensitive to the assumed values of ϵ and ψ. If $\epsilon = 5$ and $\psi = 4$, the effect of the foreign sector increases from 0.22 percentage point per year to 0.42 percentage point per year. Our upper bound estimate of the rate of growth in per capita income between 1793 and 1807 becomes 1.52% per year.

[17] The multiplier effects of the unemployed labor and capital are assumed to be zero. This is reasonable given the predominance of the agricultural sector in the economy.

22   GOLDIN AND LEWIS

proved trading conditions led to an increase in the per capita income growth rate of about a quarter of a percentage point.

CONCLUDING REMARKS

The shipping and export industries in the United States received a considerable fillip from America's neutral position during the Napoleonic Wars. The expanded powers and reach of the American merchant industry have been imaginatively described and romanticized. One author, for example, has written of the period:

> Almost the whole carrying trade of Europe was in American hands. . . . The merchant flag of every belligerent, save England. disappeared from the sea. It was under our flag that the gum trade was carried on with Senegal, that the sugar trade was carried on with Cuba, that coffee was exported from Caracas, and hides and indigo from South America. From Vera Cruz, from Carthagena, from La Plata, from the French colonies in the Antilles, from Cayenne, from Dutch Guiana, from the isles of France and Reunion, from Batavia and Manila, great fleets of American merchantmen sailed from the United States, there to neutralize the voyage and then go on to Europe. They filled the warehouses at Cadiz and Antwerp to overflowing. They glutted the markets of Emden and Lisbon. Hamburg and Copenhagen, with the produce of the West Indies and the fabrics of the East.''[18]

North and Taylor have expanded this legend by adding the export sector's role in the growth of the entire economy. Not only did exports and shipping increase, but the whole economy was thrust forward.

The period of American neutrality loses much of its legendary importance when confronted with statistical analysis. The results of both the terms of trade model and the more complex supply and demand framework demonstrate that changes in the foreign sector increased the rate of per capita income growth from 1.07 to about 1.32% (see Tables 7 and 8). The buoyant foreign sector increased growth by about one-quarter of a percentage point or slightly more than 25% of hypothetical growth, using the upper bound measure. These numbers become 0.60 and 0.84% using the lower bound estimates, implying an approximately equal absolute effect of one-quarter of a percentage point, although the relative impact on growth (40%) is much greater.

Our reinterpretation of the period of American neutrality enables a more accurate computation of the pre-1840 growth experience. Assuming that per capita income in 1805 was $65 (a figure consistent with Gallman's critique of David) and that the per capita income growth rate from 1793 to 1805 was about 1.08% (the average of the estimates in Table 7), income in 1793 would have been $57. This implies an average annual decline in per

---

[18] J. B. McMaster (1976), *A History of the People of the U.S.* (New York: Appleton, Vol. III, p. 225), quoted in H. E. Krooss and C. Gilbert (1972), *American Business History* (Englewood Cliffs, N.J.: Prentice–Hall, pp. 79–80).

EXPORTS IN AMERICAN ECONOMIC GROWTH, 1793–1807   **23**

capita income of −0.34% from 1774 to 1793 (allowing $61 for per capita income in 1774) and results in a more realistic set of data for the pre-1840 period. The critical periods for further study appear to be the years of the Revolution, the period of Confederation, and the early history of the Republic under the Constitution.

Even though the increase in trade during the period from 1793 to 1807 did not dramatically increase incomes, we have not assessed its longer range effects. Impressive changes took place during these 14 years—the major port cities grew, towns developed in the hinterland, shipping tonnage expanded substantially, corporate chapters increased, and the banking and commercial sectors widened. The period of neutrality may not have greatly spurred income but, to paraphrase Curtis Nettels, it may have led to the emergence of a nascent national economy.

REFERENCES

Ball, D. E., and Walton, G. M. (1976), "Agricultural Productivity Change in Eighteenth-Century Pennsylvania." *Journal of Economic History* **36**, 102–117.

David, P. (1966), "Technical Appendices to U.S. Real Product Growth Before 1840: New Evidence, Controlled Conjectures." Research Center in Economic Growth, Stanford University, Memorandum No. 53-A. Mimeograph.

David, P. (1967), "The Growth of Real Product in the U.S. Before 1840: New Evidence, Controlled Conjectures." *Journal of Economic History* **27**, 151–197.

Gallman, R. (1971), "The Statistical Approach: Fundamental Concepts as Applied to History." In G. R. Taylor and L. F. Ellsworth (Eds.), *Approaches to American Economic History*. Charlottesville: The University Press of Virginia.

Gallman, R. (1972a), "Changes in Total U.S. Agricultural Factor Productivity in the Nineteenth Century." *Agricultural History* **46**, 191–210.

Gallman, R. (1972b), "The Pace and Pattern of American Economic Growth." In L. Davis *et al.* (Eds.), *American Economic Growth: An Economist's History of the U.S.* New York: Harper & Row. Chap. 2.

Gunderson, G. (1976), *A New Economic History of America*. New York: McGraw–Hill.

Jones, A. H. (1970), "Wealth Estimates for the American Middle Colonies, 1774." *Economic Development and Cultural Change* **18**, 1–165.

Jones, A. H. (1975), "Revised Table and Source Notes on Colonial Wealth for Census Bureau Publication." Mimeograph.

Mundell, R. (1968), *International Economics*. New York: MacMillan Co.

North, D. C. (1966a), *The Economic Growth of the United States, 1790–1860*. New York: Norton.

North, D. C. (1966b), "The United States Balance of Payments, 1790–1860." In National Bureau of Economic Research, *Trends in the American Economy in the Nineteenth Century*. Conference on Research in Income and Wealth, Vol. 24. Princeton, N.J.: Princeton Univ. Press.

North, D. C. (1969), "Early National Income Estimates of the U.S." *Economic Development and Cultural Change* **9**, 387–397.

North, D. C. (1974), *Growth and Welfare in the American Past: A New Economic History*. Englewood Cliffs, N.J.: Prentice–Hall, 2nd ed.

Shepherd, J. F., and Walton, G. M. (1976), "Economic Change after the American Revolution: Pre- and Post-War Comparisons of Maritime Shipping and Trade." *Explorations in Economic History* **13**, 397–422.

24   GOLDIN AND LEWIS

Taylor, G. R. (1964), ''American Economic Growth Before 1840: An Exploratory Essay.''
Journal of Economic History **24,** 427–444.

APPENDIX

TABLE A1
Price Indexes, for selected years 1793 to 1807

	Wholesale price index (1790 = 100)	Export price index/ wholesale price index (1793 = 100)	Import price index/ wholesale price index (1793 = 100)
1793	113.3	100.0	100.0
1796	162.2	123.3	85.6
1798	135.6	177.2	98.4
1800	143.3	118.0	90.9
1803	131.1	117.4	94.1
1805	156.7	115.6	93.0
1807	144.4	109.3	90.3

Sources. Historical Statistics, p. 116; North (1966a), pp. 221 and 229.

TABLE A2
The Value of Exports and Net Freight Earnings of the U.S. Carrying Trade,
for selected years 1793 to 1807

Year	(1) Value of exports[a] (thous. current $)	(2) Net freight earnings of the U.S. carrying trade (thous. current $)	(3) Value of earnings from exports and the carrying trade[b] (thous. 1790 $)
1790	19,905	5,900	28,805.0
1793	24,360	11,900	32,003.5
1796	40,764	21,600	38,448.9
1798	28,527	16,600	33,279.5
1800	21,841	26,200	33,524.8
1803	42,206	23,700	50,271.5
1805	42,387	29,700	46,003.2
1807	48,699	42,100	62,880.2

[a] The value of exports is net of the value of reexports.
[b] Column (3) = $\{[$Column (1) + Column (2)$]$ / Column (1) of Table A1$\}$.
Sources: North (1966a), pp. 221 and 249; this paper, Table A1, Column (1).

EXPORTS IN AMERICAN ECONOMIC GROWTH, 1793–1807   25

TABLE A3

The Value of Imports for Consumption and Customs Duties,
for selected years 1793 to 1807

Year	(1) Value of imports for consumption (thous. current $)	(2) Value of imports for consumption (thous. 1790 $)	(3) Customs duties (thous. current $)
1793	30800	27184	4255
1796	56636	34917	6568
1798	37552	27693	7106
1800	44122	30790	9081
1803	52073	39720	10479
1805	72346	46168	12936
1807	85097	58931	15846

[a] Column (2) = [Column (1)/Column (1) of Table A1].

Sources. Historical Statistics, p. 712; North (1966a), p. 228; this paper, Table A1, Column (1).

TABLE A4

The Ratios of the Value of Exports and Imports to Income and the
Average Tariff Rate (Computation of λ, Π, and t)
for selected years 1796 to 1807

	1796	1798	1800	1803	1805	1807
National income (thous. 1790 $)[a]	238,019	284,839	310,261	360,840	397,056	435,245
λ: $(p_x q_x/Y)$	0.1615	0.1168	0.1081	0.1393	0.1159	0.1445
Π: $(p_{m_i} q_m/Y)$	0.1467	0.0972	0.0992	0.1101	0.1163	0.1354
t^b	0.1160	0.1892	0.2058	0.2012	0.1788	0.1862

[a] The gross national product (Y) figure for 1800 is estimated by assuming that per capita Y grew at the same rate between 1800 and 1840 as did David's estimate of per capita gross domestic product (GDP). Per capita Y between 1793 and 1807 is assumed to have grown at the same rate as did David's estimate of per capita GDP over the period 1810 to 1840. Our results are not very sensitive to changes in these assumptions.

[b] The average tariff rate, t, is the ratio of customs duties received by the federal government to the value of imports for consumption. Imports for consumption rather than total imports are used because reexported goods were subject to duty rebates.

Sources. David (1967), p. 184; R. Gallman, unpublished national income estimates, p. 5; *Historical Statistics,* pp. 7 and 115; this paper, Table A2, Column (3).

[15]

INTERNATIONAL ECONOMIC FLOWS—1815-1860

The Statistical Evidence

The quantitative data to analyze America's international economic relations during these years may be conveniently organized and analyzed under four separate headings: the balance of payments, the terms of trade, the flows of immigrants, and the acquisition of land.

I

While the quality of the data in the balance of payments from 1815 through 1819 is similar to that for the earlier period, after 1820 there are important improvements and the data are far more reliable.[1] During this period our international economic relations were the subject of extensive discussion, and there are many direct estimates of the various components, as well as qualitative evaluations, against which to check the figures and their significance.

As a percentage of the value of exports, tobacco, rice and lumber products declined during this period. Wheat and flour were erratic, being 16 per cent of exports from 1816 to 1820 but declining thereafter until the last fifteen years, when they increased slightly. Manufactures were a slightly declining percentage of exports in the 1830's and thereafter showed a modest gain. Cotton, of course, dominated the export trade. It constituted 39 per cent of the value of exports from 1816 to 1820, and increased to 63 per cent of total export values from 1836 to 1840. Thereafter it dropped somewhat,

---

[1] See the introduction to my study, "Balance of Payments," *loc. cit.*, for an evaluation of the quality of the data.

75

76   *1815-1860*

but the level continued high—over half of the value of exports
for the remaining years to the Civil War. Chart I-VIII shows the

CHART I-VIII

Value of Total Exports and Cotton Exports: 1815–1860
(in Millions of Dollars)

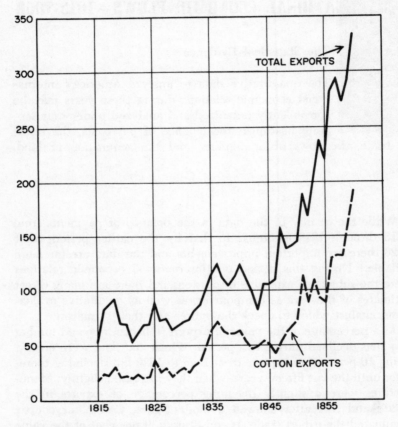

Source: Appendix I, Table A-VIII.

value of total exports and the value of cotton exports from 1815
to 1860.

The value of exports showed little increase in the 1820's but expanded rapidly from 1831 through the ensuing boom. After a decline during the depression of the early 1840's, the value of exports increased during most of the period up to 1860. Several years of extraordinarily high export values (in comparison to the secular trend) reflected special circumstances, such as the cotton speculation in 1825 and the Irish famine in 1847.

The United Kingdom alone took almost half of our exports, with France taking an additional 12 to 17 per cent (based on five year averages). The West Indies, which had been a major market for American exports and took 19 per cent in the years 1821 to 1825, were a continually declining percentage thereafter, being only 7 per cent in the five years preceding the Civil War.

After exports, the next most important credit in the balance of payments was shipping earnings. Unlike the earlier period when they accounted for perhaps a third or more of total international credits, in this period they were never more than about 10 per cent of credits and were actually a decreasing percentage throughout. The revival of navigation laws and foreign competition, as well as the expansion of the cotton trade, resulted in American shipping being confined primarily to our export and import trade and engaged less in trade between foreign countries. Foreign shipping was increasingly important from 1845 to 1860, presaging our transition from creditor to debtor status in this sphere during the war years. United States and foreign shipping earnings in our international accounts are shown in Chart II-VIII.

The funds that immigrants brought with them were an important credit in the last fifteen years of the period under study, when the first great wave of immigration occurred. Over 90 per cent of the immigrants were from Britain, Ireland or Germany. There was a striking difference in their well-being; the Germans were relatively prosperous while the Irish were desperately poor, with little left after their passage money. Approximately two-thirds of them came in American ships, providing an additional credit in the United States account.[2]

The three items discussed above—exports, shipping earnings, and

----

[2] See Section III of this chapter for a discussion of the significance of immigrant fares. My study on the United States balance of payments provides further discussion of this subject, and Appendix III in this study summarizes the quantitative data on immigrant funds.

78   *1815-1860*

CHART II-VIII

Net U.S. Shipping Earnings and Earnings of Foreign Ships Carrying U.S.
Imports: 1815–1860
(in Millions of Dollars)

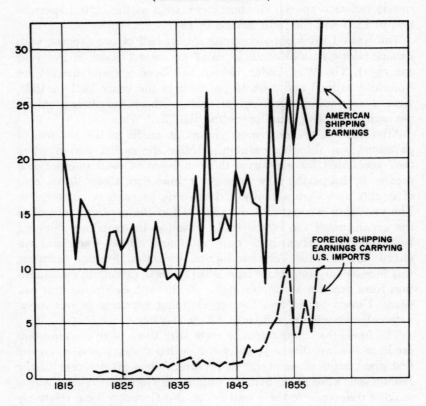

Source: Appendix T, Table B-VIII.

immigrant funds—comprise the net credits on current account of
the United States balance of payments during this period.

Imports were the major debit item. There were two major classes
of imports, manufactured goods and tropical (or semitropical)
goods such as coffee, tea, sugar, and cocoa. Manufactures were the
most important, with textile imports (cotton, wool, silk, and linen)
comprising a third or more of the value of this sector. Iron and

International Economic Flows—1815-1860   79

steel imports assumed increased importance during the first big railroad boom in the early 1850's.

Import values were more volatile than exports, rising more rapidly in periods of expansion and dropping more precipitously in times of slower growth. Their value is shown in Chart III-VIII.[3] Britain was the major source of imports, accounting for somewhat more than a third. France supplied another 9-18 per cent (again based on five year averages). Cuba and the West Indies accounted

CHART III-VIII

Value of Imports: 1815–1860
(in Millions of Dollars)

Source: Appendix I, Table C-VIII.

---

[3] It should be noted that the value of imports shown here differs from the official figures in that it makes an allowance for undervaluation from 1832-1860. See "Balance of Payments," *loc. cit.*, Appendix B, for a discussion of the basis for the allowance.

80   *1815-1860*

for most of the tropical goods, which reached a high of 28 per
cent of imports from 1821–1825 and a low of 17 per cent from
1851–1855. Among invisible items, immigrants' remittances and
tourist expenditures were the major net debits. The former grew

CHART IV-VIII

Immigrants from the United Kingdom: 1844–1860. Graphed with a Three-
Year Lag Against Remittances to the United Kingdom: 1847–1863

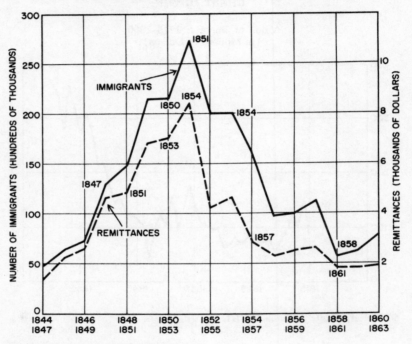

Source: *Appendix I, Table D-VIII.*

rapidly during the wave of immigration after 1845. These remittances were primarily for passage money to bring over relatives
and friends, and most of them went to Ireland. They bear an

interesting relationship to immigration, which is illustrated in Chart IV-VIII. Remittances to the United Kingdom moved directly with the volume of immigration from there three years earlier. The most plausible explanation for this close relationship is that it took Irish immigrants approximately three years to save passage fares for friends and family in Ireland.

The flow of specie during this period served both as a mechanism of adjustment between the price levels of the United States and foreign countries (particularly the United Kingdom), and in the 1850's as another export industry which financed a large import surplus and helped sustain the expansion of that decade. Specie flows were particularly important in relating the monetary systems of the United States and the United Kingdom. When domestic price levels diverged significantly, the resulting flow of specie tended to lead to international price readjustment in a fashion to be expected by monetary theorists. Chart V-VIII shows specie flows against an index in which United States wholesale prices (Warren-Pearson) are divided by British wholesale prices (Sauerbach index) to illustrate this relationship. It is clear that after the discoveries of 1848 gold plays an additional role, and is in effect another export commodity as well as an inflationary influence upon United States and foreign prices.

Interest and dividends were a continuous debit item in our balance of payments. Not only did the amount vary with the level of foreign debt and of the interest rate, but it was strongly affected on two occasions during this period by repudiation of debts—1816–1818, and 1841–1845. Chart VI-VIII presents the interest upon foreign indebtedness.[4]

The balance of trade of the United States was generally unfavorable. Chart VII-VIII not only illustrates the fact that imports exceeded exports for all but a few years (primarily the 1840's), but also shows the greater volatility of import values. Long swings are also evident in both exports and imports.

The balance of payments (see Appendix I for complete balance)

---

[4] Cf. "Balance of Payments," loc. cit., for a discussion of the method of estimating the interest change.

82   *1815-1860*

reveals three periods of capital inflow, one of outflow, and a period
in which there is little net movement. The years 1815–1818, 1832–
1839, and 1850–1857 were periods of significant foreign borrowing.
The 1840's were a decade of debt repudiation and return of securities to America, while the 1820's show relatively little net capital

CHART V-VIII

Quotient of United States Wholesale Price Index (Base 1830) Divided by
English Wholesale Price Index (Base 1830). Graphed against
Specie Flows: 1815–1860

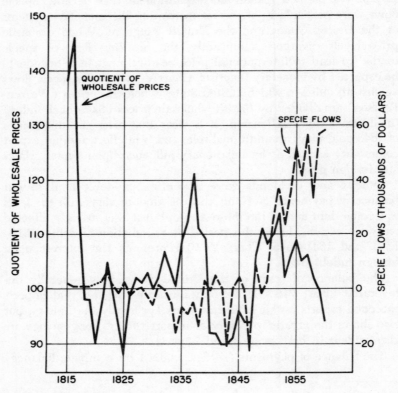

Source: Appendix I, Table E-VIII.

International Economic Flows—1815-1860   **83**

movement. Chart VIII-VIII shows the residual of the balance of payments [5] and illustrates the long swings that characterize its movement.

The resulting aggregate foreign indebtedness of the United States shows a substantial increase in the three periods of capital inflow, with the most significant rate of increase occurring during the pe-

CHART VI-VIII

Interest and Dividends on Foreign Indebtedness: 1815–1860
(in Millions of Dollars)

Source: *Appendix I, Table F-VIII.*

---

[5] It should be pointed out that the residual of the balance of payments and net capital movements are the same thing only under certain assumptions about the figures and inclusiveness of the component parts. For a discussion of this, see the text of my study on the United States balance of payments.

84   *1815-1860*

CHART VII-VIII

Value of Imports and Exports of the United States: 1815–1860
(Figures from "U.S. Balance of Payments, 1790–1860.")

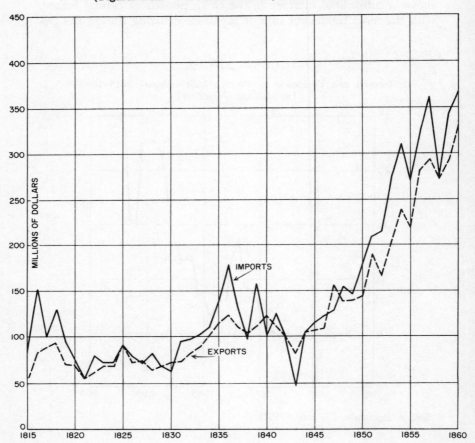

Source: Appendix I, Tables A-VIII and C-VIII.

CHART VIII-VIII

Residual Balance of Payments: 1790–1860
(in Millions of Dollars)

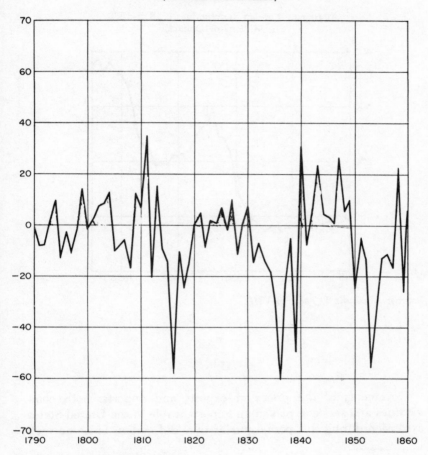

Source: Appendix I, Table G-VIII.

86   *1815-1860*

riod 1832–1839.[6] Our aggregate foreign indebtedness is presented
in Chart IX-VIII.[7]

CHART IX-VIII

Aggregate Foreign Indebtedness: 1815–1860
(in Millions of Dollars)

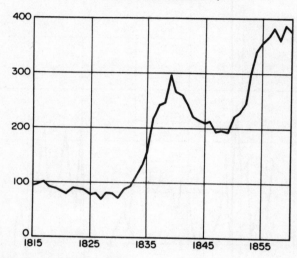

Source: *Appendix I, Table H-VIII.*

II

Movements of the prices of exports and imports, both commodities and services, played an important role in the United States
expansion during this period just as they did earlier. Since no such

---

[6] We were repudiating debt while incurring it from 1816-1819. See Appendix
A, "Balance of Payments," *loc. cit.*

[7] See Appendix C, "Balance of Payments," *loc. cit.*, for independent direct
estimates of aggregate indebtedness as corroboration of the figures in Chart
IX-IX.

International Economic Flows—1815-1860   87

indices exist, the manner in which they were developed for this study is treated in detail in Appendix III; the results of the study are summarized here.

CHART X-VIII

Export Price Index and the Price of Cotton: 1815–1860
(Base 1830)

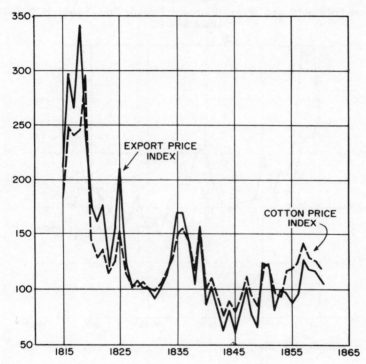

Source: Appendix I, Table I-VIII.

The export price index is dominated by the price of cotton, as Chart X-VIII indicates. In general, export prices declined substantially from the 1818 peak throughout the 1820's, with the exception of 1825, when a short-lived speculation in cotton occurred. The

88   *1815-1860*

1830's witnessed a surge in export prices which began in 1831–1832 and extended, with a break in 1837–1838, to 1839. The price decline in the 1840's was not so severe as that which followed the boom of 1818. The sharp rise in 1847 resulted from the demand

CHART XI-VIII

Export Price Index and Warren-Pearson Wholesale Price Index: 1815–1860
(Base 1830)

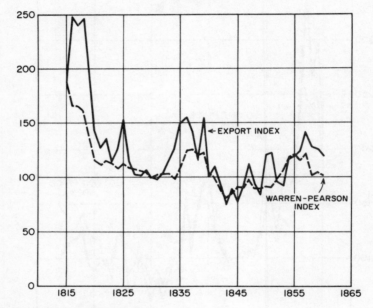

Source: Appendix I, Table J-VIII.

for wheat due to the Irish famine. The irregular rise in the 1850's reflected another period of expansion in the American economy. Prices of exports were more volatile than domestic goods, as a comparison of the export index with the Warren-Pearson wholesale price index in Chart XI-VIII indicates. Export prices fell more

International Économic Flows—1815-1860   89

rapidly from 1818–1830 and rose more in periods of expansion, particularly that of the 1830's. The volume of exports was far steadier, as Chart XII-VIII indicates. It does show that there was considerable price elasticity in the demand for exports, since years

CHART XII-VIII

Volume Index, U.S. Exports: 1815–1860
(Base 1830)

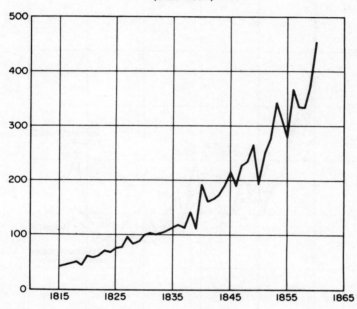

Source: Appendix I, Table K-VIII.

with a sharp price break (1819, 1838, 1840, 1853) were periods of significant increases in export volume.

The import price index and its separate components are shown in Chart XIII-VIII. The overall index shows a fairly persistent downward trend until the end of the 1840's. Manufactures fell significantly in the years after 1815, but manufactured goods fell even more sharply between 1815 and 1830. The fall of raw material and food prices was not large in the early period, but after 1820 they fell almost as much as manufactures. All of our import prices

CHART XIII-VIII

Import Price Index and the Indices of its Component Parts: 1815–1860

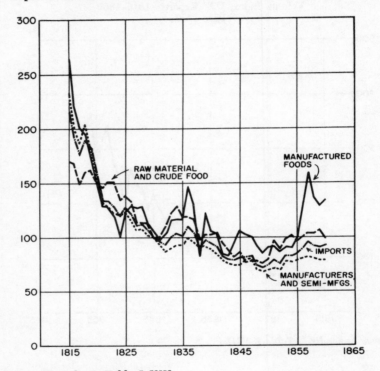

Source: Appendix I, Table L-VIII.

fell during the period. The overall index shows no such spectacular rises during the surges in the United States expansion as occur in the export price index. Increased import values meant an increased volume of imports, and little of the increased demand was ab-

sorbed by price increase. Chart XIV-VIII shows the deflated value
index for the period.

CHART XIV-VIII

Real Value of Imports (Deflated Value Series)
(in Thousands of Dollars)

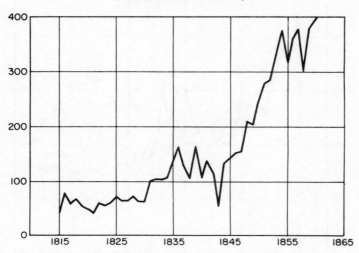

Source: *Appendix I, Table M-VIII.*

A comparison of the export and import price indices illustrates
the marked difference in their behavior, Chart XV-VIII. The resultant net barter terms of trade, Chart XVI-VIII, not only show
that the secular trend was towards improvement in the terms of
trade, but also demonstrate that, in expansive periods of the economy, the terms of trade became extremely favorable. This is particularly true from 1815–1818 and 1831–1839. The correspondence
between changes in the terms of trade and in the international flow
of capital (as indicated by the residual of the balance of payments) is striking. Until 1845 (and less so thereafter), almost every
movement of the terms of trade was paralleled by a reverse move-

CHART XV-VIII

Export and Import Price Indices: 1815–1860
(Base 1830)

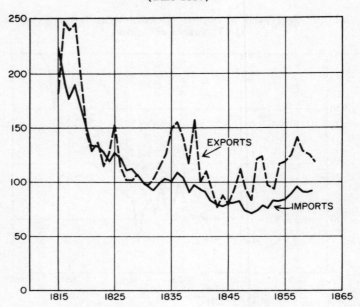

Source: Appendix I, Table N-VIII.

CHART XVI-VIII

Terms of Trade: 1815–1860
(Base 1830)

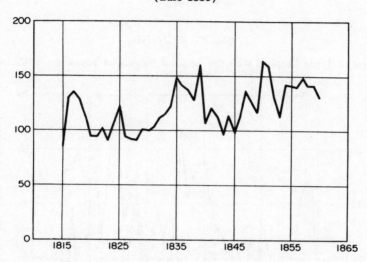

Source: *Appendix I, Table O-VIII.*

ment in the residual in the balance of payments, as Chart XVII-VIII shows. There was increased capital inflow when the terms of trade became more favorable and decreased inflow or actual outflow when they became relatively less favorable.

CHART XVII-VIII

Terms of Trade Graphed with the Residual Balance of Payments: 1815–1860
(Base 1830)

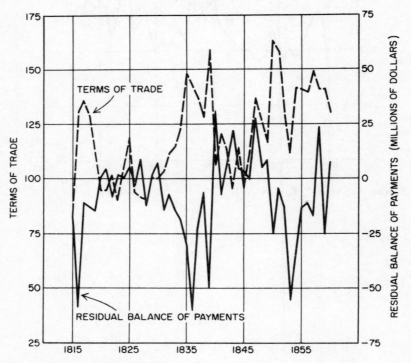

Source: *Appendix I, Table P-VIII.*

Are movements of the terms of trade significantly affected by the price behavior of non-commodity items? The price behavior of the

International Economic Flows—1815-1860   **95**

non-commodity items is at times divergent from commodity trade, but the magnitudes are relatively small, and the overall effect is not great. Freight rates fell dramatically during these years, particularly during the early period, and the price of shipping fell more

CHART XVIII-VIII

Freight Rate Index, U.S. Exports: 1815–1860
(Base 1830)

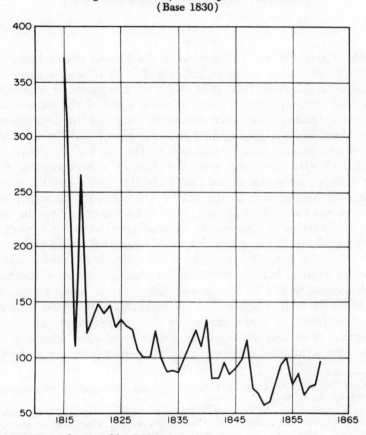

Source: Appendix I, Table Q-VIII.

than that of exports, as Chart XVIII-VIII shows. On the other hand, the price of capital showed no significant drop and actually rose in the 1850's (see Appendix I). However, neither of these two dampening effects on the terms of trade would be very large.

III

Official statistics on immigration to the United States begin in 1820. Contemporary accounts indicate that there was a surge of immigration between 1816–1818. Niles cites a figure of 30,000 in 1817, and contemporary description made much of the large number of immigrants in the years before the onset of the depression.[8] Even after 1820 the immigration data are poor,[9] and the absolute figures are unquestionably inaccurate. The results as shown in Chart XIX-VIII show the general behavior of immigration, the long swings with surges in the 1830's and the 1850's, and the small volume of immigration in the 1820's. Undoubtedly an important factor in the gradual secular increase of immigration was the decline in obstacles to movement: national restrictions, and, particularly significant as far as this chapter is concerned, ocean transport costs. Voyages from Europe had historically been made partly empty or even in ballast, reflecting the smaller volume of finished goods carried to this country in contrast with the bulky goods exported by the United States. The immigrant trade provided a lucrative opportunity to make money on the westward passage, and immigrant fares may be considered here as another freight rate. Their very substantial decline during the period is shown in Table

---

[8] *Niles' National Register*, 75 Vols. (Baltimore, Philadelphia, Washington: 1811-1849), XIII, 35-36.

[9] For a critique see Marian Davis, "Critique of Official United States Immigration Statistics," Appendix II, Vol. II of *International Migrations*, Walter F. Willcox, Ed. (New York: National Bureau of Economic Research, 1929-1931).

International Economic Flows—1815-1860   **97**

7. Although the pull of differential real income and employment was the fundamental cause, the decline in the cost of steerage passage did implement the movement.

As pointed out above, the origin of immigrants during this period was primarily from Ireland, England, and Germany, with all other countries together accounting for only 10 per cent of their number. Equally interesting is the changing composition of immigrants by occupation. While the figures here are rough (since they include

CHART XIX-VIII

Immigration to the United States: 1815–1860

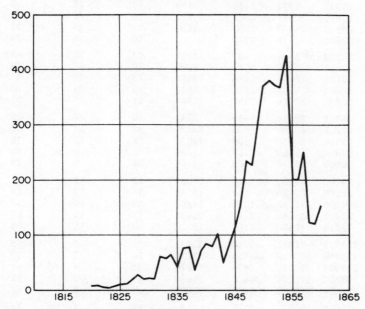

Source: Appendix I, Table R-VIII.

returning Americans), they do show a declining portion of merchants and skilled people, and a rising proportion of unskilled labor (Table 7).

1815-1860

TABLE 7

IMMIGRANT ORIGINS AND OCCUPATIONAL DISTRIBUTION

Year	Total	Alien Arrivals			Occupation as Percentage of Total Arrivals		
		Irish	English	German	Labor	Merchants	Mechanics & Farmers
1820	8385	3974	1782	948	9%	25%	31%
1	9127	3388	1036	365	8	27	31
2	6911	2421	856	139	9	31	24
3	6354	1908	851	179	8	33	27
4	7912	2606	713	224	8	38	24
5	10199	5857	1002	448	10	29	32
6	10837	6032	1459	495	11	29	29
7	18875	10971	2521	425	18	21	31
8	27382	14047	2735	1806	21	19	31
9	22520	8331	2149	582	20	28	22
1830	23322	3105	733	1972	12	25	41*
1	22633	7639	251	2395	10	27	44
2	53179	16665	944	10168	13	18	46**
3	58640	8648	2966	6823	13	15	33
4	65365	33724	1129	17654	14	14	51***
5	45374	29350	468	8245	15	20	55
6	76242	43156	420	20139	29	11	55
7	79340	39810	896	23036	28	12	55
8	38914	17860	157	11369	18	20	55
9	68069	34172	62	19794	22	16	58
1840	84066	41704	318	28581	22	12	63
1	80289	53723	147	13727	28	13	55
2	104565	71542	1743	18287	33	10	53
3	52496	24542	3517	11432	23	14	57
4	78615	46460	1357	19226	29	12	54
5	114371	61942	1710	33138	32	10	56
6	154416	70626	2854	57010	28	6	62
7	234968	124880	3476	73444	32	4	62
8	226527	142631	4455	58014	43	3	52
9	297024	207162	6036	60062	45	3	50
1850	310004	169533	5276	63168	38	5	54
1	379466	266257	5306	71322	48	7	42
2	371603	161351	30007	143575	44	7	48
3	368645	165130	28867	140653	48	7	42
4	427833	105931	48901	206054	37	7	53
5	200877	51877	38871	66219	39	13	45

*Large per cent not stated this year
**Missing quarter
***Large per cent not stated this year

Source: Bromwell, William J., History of Immigration to the United States, (New
York: Redfield 1856).

International Economic Flows—1815-1860   99

IV

Chart XX-VIII illustrates graphically the territorial expansion of the economy during this period. The most striking aspect of this chart is not the addition of Louisiana, which has always been accorded the role of almost doubling the size of the country, but

CHART XX-VIII

United States Territorial Expansion: 1790–1860
(in Millions of Square Miles)

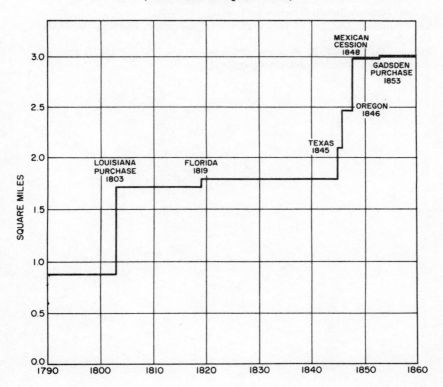

100   *1815-1860*

the even greater increase in territorial expansion which occurred
in three short years between 1845 and 1848. More than 1.2 million
square miles were added to the country's territorial boundaries,
including California, which was quickly exploited for its discoveries
of gold.

References

DAVIS, MARIAN, "Critique of Official United States Immigration Statistics," II,
    Appendix II of *International Migrations*, 2 vols., Walter F. Willcox, ed. New
    York: National Bureau of Economic Research, 1929-30.
Niles' National Register, 75 vols. Baltimore, Washington, Philadelphia: 1811-
    1849
WARREN, G. F. AND F. A. PEARSON, *Wholesale Prices for 213 Years, 1720 to
    1932*. Ithaca: Cornell University Press, 1932.

[16]

THE CAUSES OF COTTON–PRICE FLUCTUATIONS IN THE 1830's

Peter Temin *

THE IMPORTANCE of cotton cultivation to the antebellum United States is beyond doubt. The precise extent of this importance may be debated, but no one can doubt the widespread influence of cotton — the most important single crop in the country, the primary source of foreign exchange, and the source of explosive political controversies over slavery and tariffs. There have been several attempts to describe the market for cotton, most of which have centered on the decade of the 1830's, when the rapid rise in cotton prices is thought to have stimulated the land boom of 1835–1836 and to have accentuated the effects of President Andrew Jackson's celebrated fight with the Second Bank of the United States.[1]

The purpose of this paper is to re-examine the structure of the market for American cotton in this period and to argue that previous analyses — which explain fluctuations in the price of cotton by changes in the supply curve of cotton — have failed to present an accurate picture of the market. This error derives chiefly from the failure of previous investigators to consider explicitly the identification problem present in the analysis of any market. Its correction necessitates a reconsideration of the aggregate fluctuations of the 1830's and the roles of Jackson and Biddle therein.

The course of cotton prices has been recounted many times, but an explanation of their movements more often than not has been lacking. The following quotation from Gray's classic study of antebellum Southern agriculture is entirely typical:

Prices began to improve in the late Spring of 1832–33, and the following Fall the market opened at 18 cents, but with increasing receipts declined rapidly to less than 10 cents. The latter part of the year, however, there was some improvement, which continued steadily throughout 1834–35. This was the beginning of a period of four years of high prices, accompanied by frenzied speculation in cotton, land, and slaves, culminating in the panic of 1837.[2]

The events being described are simple enough. The price of cotton, which had been ten cents or less per pound for the years 1826–1832, rose to more than 15 cents in 1835 and 1836, fell below ten cents in 1838 and again in 1840 and following years.[3] This temporary rise in the price must have resulted from a change either in the behavior of the demand or in the supply of cotton, but Gray's description does not tell us which one. As the quantity of cotton produced was rising steadily throughout this period, and as the trend of cotton prices was not strong, either the supply and demand curves were shifting outward or were very elastic. A change in the behavior of one of the curves therefore would consist either of a temporarily different rate of expansion or of a temporary inelasticity.

The separation of demand and supply influences is necessary to an understanding of the price movements. It is also particularly relevant to an understanding of the 1830's in general because the functional separation implies a geographical separation as well. The supply of cotton was determined by conditions within the United States, and if the price rise and fall in the 1830's derived from shifts of the supply curve, then the instability may be said to have been American in origin. The demand for cotton, on the other hand, was determined largely outside the United States, over four-fifths of the American cotton crop

* I would like to thank Franklin M. Fisher for his many helpful comments on earlier drafts and Donald Cimilluca and Lawrence Herron for their assistance with the calculations. The research for this paper was supported by the National Science Foundation and the Sloan Research Fund, M.I.T. All responsibility for errors and omissions, of course, is mine.

[1] R. C. O. Matthews, *A Study in Trade-Cycle History: Economic Fluctuations in Great Britain, 1833–1842* (Cambridge, England: University Press, 1954), 52; and W. B. Smith, *Economic Aspects of the Second Bank of the United States* (Cambridge: Harvard University Press, 1953), 32.

[2] L. C. Gray, *History of Agriculture in the Southern United States*, II (Washington: The Carnegie Institution, 1933), 699.

[3] Ibid., 1,027. The prices are for short staple cotton in New Orleans, and the years cited are calendar years in contrast to the "crop years" used by Gray.

being exported in eight out of the ten years of the 1830's.[4] Smith and Cole, in their classic study of antebellum fluctuations, suggest that "foreign influences" were important in the "crisis of 1837." [5] Changes in the foreign demand for cotton represent one possible avenue of foreign influence on the American economy.

The first serious attempt to resolve this problem was that of Matthews. He listed three possible hypotheses to explain the rise in cotton prices:

1) rise in the world demand for cotton, i.e., a more than usual rise in the demand curve,

2) exhaustion of cotton-growing capacity established during the land boom of 1818, i.e., a temporary inelasticity in the normally elastic supply.

3) monetary inflation in the United States without any pressure on supply or demand in real terms.

Matthews proceeded to choose among these hypotheses in two distinct ways. He first observed that the rate of growth of cotton production was roughly the same during the period of rising cotton prices as it had been during the preceding decade of falling prices. Then he observed that ". . . this would seem to imply that shifts on both the demand and the supply side played some part in bringing about the observed result." In other words, Matthews assumed that neither the supply nor the demand curve for cotton was perfectly inelastic. A more than usually rapid shift of *one* curve would then have meant a movement along the other and a consequent change in the rate of change of production. The steadiness of the growth of output accordingly indicated that either a combination of hypotheses one and two or the alternative of hypothesis three must have been operative.

Matthews' second approach to this problem was to reject the first hypothesis on the grounds that ". . . there is no evidence of any such increase [in demand], nor is there any particular reason why one should have been expected." This left the choice between hypotheses two and three, which Matthews did not feel obliged to make since his main interest was Britain, not the United States. It was enough for him to establish that ". . . the source of the disturbance lay in the United States, and Britain was a passive recipient of its consequences." [6]

These two approaches can be synthesized by noting that the conclusion of the first is to choose hypotheses one and two *or* hypothesis three, while the conclusion of the second is to choose either hypothesis two or three. The second approach thus makes the choice left by the first. It rules out hypothesis one and consequently a combination of hypotheses one and two. The first approach then makes the choice left at the end of the second by its exclusive choice of hypothesis three. The two approaches taken together therefore select hypothesis three as the explanation of the price rise.

This hypothesis, however, will not explain the rise in the price of cotton. Four-fifths of the American cotton crop was regularly exported. The price of cotton therefore was primarily an export price, i.e., a price paid by foreign importers for American cotton. There is no reason why this external price should have risen as a result of a banking expansion in America. In addition, cotton prices rose relative to other prices in the United States, and this change in *relative* prices cannot be explained by the hypothesis of a general inflation of bank credit.[7] Clearly, we must begin again.

The preceding paragraph has shown only that Matthews' third hypothesis is not tenable. We are left with the choice between an expansion of demand, an exhaustion of supply capacity, and a combination of the two. These possibilities represent different resolutions of the identification problem implicit in this analysis. This does not seem to have been recognized explicitly in the literature, and previous authors have been content to treat only the identification problem explicitly.

Douglass C. North maintained that the sev-

[4] United States Department of Agriculture, Bureau of Statistics, Circular 32, "Cotton Crop of the United States, 1790–1911" (Washington, D.C., 1912); U.S. Bureau of the Census, *Historical Statistics of the United States, Colonial Times to 1957* (Washington, D.C., 1960), 547. The proportion was 79 per cent in the other two years.

[5] W. B. Smith and A. H. Cole, *Fluctuations in American Business, 1790–1860* (Cambridge: Harvard University Press, 1935), 73.

[6] R. C. O. Matthews, op. cit., 52–54. It is not clear whether Matthews saw that he was approaching this problem along two independent lines.

[7] L. C. Gray, op. cit., 1,027; and W. B. Smith and A. H. Cole, op. cit., 158.

COTTON-PRICE FLUCTUATIONS

eral short-lived rises in the price of cotton in the antebellum era were due to a periodic exhaustion of cotton-growing capacity. In his words:

During each period of expansion, millions of acres of new land were purchased from the government for cotton production. Once this land had been cleared and a crop or two of corn planted to prepare the soil, the amount of cotton available could be substantially increased, and the supply curve of cotton shifted very sharply to the right. With the depressed cotton prices that followed such expansion, a good deal of this land was devoted to alternative uses . . . . The result is that the supply curve of cotton . . . was highly elastic over a range of output which included all the available land that had been cleared and readied for crop production and was suitable for cotton . . . . When the growth of demand for cotton finally brought all this potential capacity into production, a further increase in demand resulted in substantial price increases as the supply curve became increasingly inelastic.[8]

There are two problems with this model, one of which was noticed by Matthews in his discussion. According to North, the price rise in the 1830's was caused by a temporary decrease in the elasticity of supply. During the 1820's an expanding demand curve intersected the supply curve along its elastic portion, resulting in an increasing quantity of production without an increase in price. In the 1830's, the demand curve intersected an inelastic part of the supply curve, resulting in a rise in price. This rise in price, however, represented a movement along the demand curve as well as the supply curve. If the demand curve was not completely inelastic and if it did not expand more rapidly in the 1830's than in the 1820's, then the quantity produced would have expanded less rapidly in the 1830's than in the 1820's. As this did not happen, either the demand for cotton was perfectly inelastic or the demand shifted outward more rapidly in the 1830's than in the 1820's.

The economic history of the early nineteenth century is built on the assumption of an elastic demand for cotton textiles The only study which actually attempted to compute a price elasticity of demand estimated it as being between one and two, and no one denies that the fall in the price of cotton textiles led to a

great increase in output.[9] If the fall in the price of cotton textiles led to an increase in output, it would not matter whether this fall came from increased efficiency in cotton mills or from a fall in the price of cotton. If the demand for cotton textiles was elastic, the demand for raw cotton therefore could not have been perfectly inelastic. Consequently, the implication of North's model is that demand expanded more rapidly in the 1830's than in the surrounding decades. North's neglect of demand and his attribution of the price rise solely to supply influences are therefore unwarranted.

The other problem with North's model concerns its "testibility." In order to test the existence of the temporary inelasticity of supply North emphasizes, a variable representing cotton-growing capacity must be used. When production reached full capacity, the elasticity of supply is supposed to have fallen. Only if we know when this event took place can we observe the relevant elasticities. The variable that appears in North's exposition as a measure of capacity is the quantity of cotton-growing land. There is no objection to this on theoretical grounds, but we do not have data on the quantity of actual or potential cotton-growing lands.

The variable that is cited in place of the quantity of land is, therefore, the volume of federal land sales.[10] This volume is taken to be the addition to cotton-growing capacity, ignoring the problems raised by speculative buying of land and state sales of Indian lands. These problems are not trivial, for not all land purchased from the federal government was immediately brought under cultivation, and land was sold by states and speculators as well as by the federal government. But even if the quantity of land available were a good measure of capacity, additions to this quantity would not necessarily indicate an exhaustion of capacity, i.e., a *decrease* in the elasticity of supply. We may illustrate this point by describing two polar situations, each consistent with high prices and large land sales.

[8] D. C. North, *The Economic Growth of the United States, 1790–1860* (Englewood Cliffs: Prentice-Hall, 1961), 71–73.

[9] The estimate is for the United States. R. B. Zevin, "The Growth of Cotton Textile Production After 1815" (to be published).

[10] D. C. North, op. cit., 73–74.

In the first, capacity has been exhausted, leading to sales of land to create new capacity. In the second, demand has risen, raising prices (by a movement along a less than infinitely elastic supply curve) and generating an expansion of capacity in response to higher profits. The first is North's model, but since the second is equally consistent with the data, it cannot be said that the volume of land sales indicates an exhaustion of capacity. Other indices of capacity may be found, but until they are, North's supply curve remains unidentified and his model untestable.

Jeffrey Williamson attempted to sidestep this problem by constructing an index (actually two similar indices) of what he called "excess supply." The ". . . indices are measures of the difference between the five-year moving averages of rates of change of United States cotton quantum produced and rates of change in British demand indices." The "British demand indices" are estimates of the rates of change of the value of British textile production and cotton exports.[11] The "excess supply" indices are therefore differences between rates of change of a *five-year moving average of a quantity series* and rates of change of *annual value series*. They are consequently extremely difficult to interpret. In particular, how do we know they measure supply rather than demand? If British production or exports is taken to represent demand (setting aside the objections to such a procedure) and American production to represent supply, then a comparison of the annual rates of change of demand with the average rate of change of supply would seem to show the temporary excesses and deficiencies of demand, rather than those of supply. Clearly, the indices are not unambiguous measures either of demand or supply. Williamson has ignored the identification problem implicit in any treatment of supply and demand, and his tests consequently do not illuminate North's model.

As the neglect of demand in this model can be justified only on the implausible assumption of a perfectly inelastic demand curve and since it does not seem to be testable with the existing data, we turn our attention to an alternative explanation of the events of the 1830's Abandoning the search for a variable that will identify shifts in the supply curve due to the exhaustion of cotton-growing capacity, we now look at the demand side. Can we, in opposition to Matthews, find reasons why the demand for cotton should have risen more rapidly in the 1830's than in the 1820's? We proceed by specifying a model of the cotton market and submitting it to empirical test.

As we are primarily interested in explaining the movements of the New Orleans price of cotton, we begin with it. The first part of our hypothesis is that the American price of cotton fluctuated with the British price, i.e., that there was a "world price" of cotton. Three factors could have led to a systematic divergence between the American and British prices. First, the British tariff on raw cotton changed over this period. Second, increased efficiency in ocean shipping may have decreased the Anglo-American price differential. Third, the decrease in the weight of gold in the American dollar in 1834 may have represented a devaluation of the dollar, increasing the American price and thereby decreasing the differential between the two cotton prices.

We may test the influence of these three factors by regressing the American cotton price, P_A, on the British cotton price, P_B, on the British tariff, F, and on time, t. If the first factor was important, the former term will be significantly less than zero. If either of the latter two were important, the latter will be. The regression for 1820–1859 is as follows (where the standard errors of coefficients are given below them and D.W. is the Durbin-Watson statistic): [12]

$$P_A = 1.60 + 1.52 \, P_B - 2.85 \, F - .04 \, t.$$
$$\quad\quad\quad (.17) \quad\quad (2.32) \quad (.05)$$
$$R^2 = .77, D.W. = 2.1 \quad\quad\quad\quad\quad (1)$$

The coefficient of the tariff has an appropriate sign, but it is not significantly different from zero and we may neglect its influence. Similar-

[11] J. G. Williamson, *American Growth and the Balance of Payments, 1820–1913* (Chapel Hill: University of North Carolina Press, 1964), 38–40.

[12] The data on the American cotton price come from L. C. Gray, op. cit., 1,027, dated a year later than in Gray to bring them into harmony with the British price. This price comes from B. R. Mitchell and P. Deane, *Abstract of British Historical Statistics* (Cambridge, England: University Press, 1962), 491, and the tariff was computed from it and the data in L. C. Gray, op. cit., 695.

COTTON-PRICE FLUCTUATIONS

ly, there is no evidence of a changing differential between the two prices, and we can ignore changes in freight rates and the gold content of the dollar. Finally, the two prices are highly correlated, showing that the condition in each market was quickly communicated to the other.

This is hardly surprising since Britain was the primary market for American cotton and America was the principal source of supply for the British cotton industry.[13] Accordingly, the second part of our hypothesis is that we may consider demand conditions in Britain and supply conditions in America, making the connection through the size of the American cotton crop and the price linkage shown in equation (1).

Turning to the demand side, we hypothesize that the price of cotton in Britain was affected by three variables. The size of the American cotton crop certainly had an impact. The secular rise in British — and possibly world — population and income should have affected the price. Temporary fluctuations in the level of British income also should have affected the price. Without accurate indices of the latter two variables, however, proxies have to be used. The secular rate of growth of British income has been estimated only for decade averages over 30-year periods, and the use of a time trend does not represent any loss of accuracy for our 40-year period.[14] Fluctuations in income represent a more difficult problem, for our knowledge about short-term movements in income is limited. Nevertheless, for this period primary emphasis must still be given to the harvest. When harvests were good, food was cheap, and income rose. Mathews chronicled the plentiful harvests of 1832–1834 and gave them credit for helping to initiate the recovery of general prosperity. Parry Lewis was even more positive in a recent book: "There is little doubt that the immediate cause of the upswing in 1833 was the good harvest."[15] While the influence of

the harvest was surely on the wane by the middle of the century, we may introduce a variable for it into the regression to see if it is significant. The variable to be used here is the price of bread in London. (The time trend will offset any trends in the price, making it a proxy only for temporary fluctuations.)

The function being described is a composite of the demand curve in Britain, a market-share equation explaining the proportion of the American crop exported to Britain, and a function explaining the change in stocks in Britain. The composite form will be used as the data necessary to identify the individual functions are not in existence, but its parameters obviously cannot be interpreted as pure demand elasticities. On the other hand, since it is partly a demand curve it must be framed in terms of relative prices, and we may exploit the function's assumed logarithmic form to express it as follows:

$$\log P_B = a_0 + a_1 \log Q + a_2 t + a_3 \log B + \log R + u, \qquad (2)$$

where Q is the size of the American cotton crop, B is the deflated price of bread in London, and R is the Rousseaux price index for Britain.

The price of bread and the overall level of British prices are beyond the concern of this inquiry, but the size of the American cotton crop clearly is not. If this variable responded to the level of the then current price — whether American or British — we would have a simultaneous determination of price and quantity. But how could the relevant year's price affect that year's crop? The cotton was planted in the previous year, and the weather determined the size of the crop without reference to the price There are only two ways in which the current price could have affected the quantity sold. First, farmers could have reduced the size of the crop by not harvesting it. There is no indication that this was a widespread practice. Many of the expenses of raising cotton, such as the maintenance of slaves, were fixed costs, and many others preceded knowledge of the price at which the cotton could be sold.· As these expenses were sunk costs, the price of cotton had only to exceed

[13] See the sources cited in footnote 4 and B. R. Mitchell and P. Deane, op. cit., 179–80. About 80 per cent of British consumption came from the United States, and about 60 per cent of American production was used in Britain.

[14] P. Deane and W. A. Cole, *British Economic Growth, 688–1959* (Cambridge, England: University Press, 1962), 70.

[15] R. C. O. Matthews, op. cit., 30, 206; and J. Parry Lewis, *Building Cycles and Britain's Growth* (New York: St. Martin's Press, 1965), 76.

the extra cost of harvesting to bring it onto the market. Second, farmers could have held stocks of cotton which they ran down when prices were high and built up when prices were low. There is no evidence that farmers held such stocks. There were stocks of variable size in England, but these stocks had passed through the market and been counted as part of the crop. The accumulation of stocks was a market transaction, and it therefore appears as an increase in the demand rather than a reduction of the supply. As a result, there is no way in which the current price could have influenced the supply of cotton.

This argument does not exclude the price of the previous year as an influence on the supply of cotton, and we should include it in the supply equation. In addition, a variable allowing for the expansion of supply over time is needed. As was stated above, there are no variables suitable for expressing temporary variations in the supply curve. Instead, we assume that cotton-growing capacity was determined by the quantity of labor, not the quantity of land. Land could be purchased from the government throughout the antebellum period at essentially constant cost. If we assume that there was an upper bound to the amount of land a given number of workers could farm efficiently, then the speed at which new land could be settled would depend on the rate of growth of the potential labor force, i.e., the Southern population. The Southern population is known only at decade intervals, between which it grew at the steady rate of between two and three per cent.[16] As a time trend would be used for interpolation in any case, there is no loss of accuracy in using a time trend directly. The supply curve is therefore:

$$\log Q = b_0 + b_1 \log P_{A,-1} + b_2 t + v. \qquad (3)$$

Finally, we express the link between the American and British prices of cotton in a form embodying the conclusions drawn from equation (1) and compatible with the form of equations (2) and (3):

$$\log P_A = c_0 + c_1 \log P_B + w. \qquad (4)$$

As the resultant system of equations is not

[16] *U.S. Historical Statistics*, 12.

simultaneous, we may estimate the coefficients by ordinary least squares. The results for 1820–1859 are: [17]

$$\log P_n = -1.28 - .71 \log Q + .03\, t$$
$$ (.18) \qquad (.01)$$
$$ - .94 \log B + \log R \qquad (5)$$
$$ (.23)$$
$$R^2 = .70,\, D.W. = 1.6$$

$$\log Q = 5.37 - .05 \log P_{A,-1} + .06\, t \qquad (6)$$
$$ (.09) \qquad\qquad (.002)$$
$$R^2 = .96,\, D.W. = 1.8$$

$$\log P_A = .36 + 1.02 \log P_B. \qquad (7)$$
$$ (.09)$$
$$R^2 = .78,\, D.W. = 2.1$$

The coefficients in these equations all have appropriate signs, and the only one not significantly different from zero is the coefficient of the lagged price in equation (6) The lack of significance of this coefficient means that there is no evidence that the size of the cotton crop in the United States was at all responsive to the price. As a result, the fluctuations of the cotton price may be decomposed in exceedingly simple fashion. The supply of cotton was determined by the growth of Southern population and random factors i.e., the weather, which affected the price of cotton only as the size of the crop deviated from its trend value. All other fluctuations in the cotton price then came from changes on the demand side. We have not explained all the deviations in demand by our equations, but if our specification is correct, the unexplained deviations that do not derive from the error in equation (6) are deviations in demand.

This decomposition of the price fluctuations has been done for 1833–1841, encompassing the price movements that motivated this inquiry. The results are shown in table 1, where each entry in the first column is the ratio of the American cotton price to its long-term

[17] Three characteristics of the results should be noted. First, the R^2 for equation (5) is the R^2 for the unconstrained regression for log P_B, in which the coefficient of log R is not significantly different from one. The R^2 for the regression of the logarithm of the deflated price of cotton is .60. Second, the high R^2 of equation (6) shows that log Q and t are highly correlated. Since both variables appear in equation (5) this multicollinearity means that the prediction interval fans out widely for values of log Q far from its mean. Third, the coefficients of equation (5) do not change significantly between 1820–1845 and 1845–1859. $[F(4,32) = 1.5.]$ The underlying data and computations are available and can be obtained by writing to the author.

COTTON-PRICE FLUCTUATIONS 469

469

TABLE 1. — FACTORIZATION OF RATIO OF COTTON PRICE TO ITS TREND BY CAUSE

	Total Ratio (1)	Supply of Cotton (2)	British Harvest (3)	Other British Demand (4)	British Price Level (5)	American Demand (6)
			Factors Due to:			
833	.93	1.01	1.01	1.26	.92	.78
834	1.05	.96	1.11	1.17	.97	.86
835	1.47	.98	1.26	1.22	.97	1.00
836	1.46	.95	1.21	1.16	1.07	1.02
837	1.29	.95	1.09	.95	1.03	1.26
838	.88	.85	.94	1.26	1.04	.86
839	1.23	1.06	1.02	.95	1.14	1.04
840	.79	.82	1.00	.97	1.13	.88
841	.93	1.00	1.05	.86	1.07	.97

ources:
olumn (1): Antilog of the error of a regression of log P_A on t.
olumn (2): Antilog of the error of a regression of log Q on t times (1.02) (−.71).
olumn (3): Antilog of the error of a regression of log B on t times (1.02) (−.94).
olumn (4): Antilog of the error of equation (5) times (1.02).
olumn (5): Antilog of the error of a regression of log R on t times (1.02).
olumn (6): Antilog of the error of equation (7).

rend. These ratios have been factored accord-
ng to the source of the deviation from one,
he factors being shown in the other columns
f table 1.[18] The entries in the second column
re the factors due to fluctuations in the
American cotton harvest. They, and they
lone, show in the influence of shifts in the
upply curve. It is clear that the effect of
upply was to depress the price through the
oom of the 1830's, this factor being less than
ne through 1838. The cotton crop was larger
han its long-term trend value in these years,
nd the greater supply acted to *reduce* the
rice.

If a restriction in the supply of cotton did
ot cause the price to rise, what did? The re-
naining columns of table 1 may be used to
nswer this question. The American price
id not deviate from the British price during
he boom, nor did the overall British price
evel rise above its long-term trend. Instead
he British demand for cotton rose in 1834
nd 1835 as a result of the favorable harvests
n Britain. We have thus accumulated evi-
lence to support Lewis' contention that good
arvests sparked the boom of the 1830's.
The unexplained demand for cotton was also
igh in these years, but it shows no trend from

[18] The possible influence of lagged price on the size of the
otton crop has been neglected in the derivation of table 1,
simple time trend being substituted for equation (6).

1833 to 1835 when the price of cotton was
rising sharply.)

In 1836, another favorable harvest continued the support for cotton prices, although the
harvest was not as good as in the previous
few years. By 1837, the harvest was no longer
abundant and accumulated stocks had been
exhausted, causing the price of bread to rise
and the demand for cotton to fall.[19] The
British price fell, and the American price followed at a slower pace. (Note the large entry
in the last column for 1837.) The American
price continued its fall in 1838, falling relative
to the British price which remained stationary
as a result of offsetting forces. The American
harvest of 1837 was bountiful and the British
harvest was not, but these depressing influences were offset by a rise in the demand for
cotton not explained by our regressions.

The transitory rise in the price of cotton
in 1839 is conventionally attributed to the efforts of Nicholas Biddle. In conjunction with
his bank — The United States of Pennsylvania,
the successor to the Second Bank of the
United States — he bought and held large
stocks of cotton. There is some confusion
about his motives, but the view most often
seen is that he was attempting to corner the
market, raise the price, and thereby lift the
United States out of its depression.[20] It was
presumably due to Biddle's operations that
the American price rose relative to the British
price in 1839, but this engineered rise in the
demand was not the sole influence raising the
price. Of equal importance was the short cotton harvest of 1838 which had an inflationary
impact on the price of cotton equal to that of
Biddle's actions. (Compare the second and
sixth columns of table 1.) Similarly, the end
of Biddle's efforts coincided with — or perhaps
was caused by — the good cotton crop of 1839
which helped to depress the price of 1840.
While Biddle should not be forgotten, the

[19] R. C. O. Matthews, op. cit., 30, chronicles the harvest.
[20] L. H. Jenks, *The Migration of British Capital to 1875*
(New York: Alfred A. Knopf, 1927), 88–98; Fritz Redlich,
The Molding of American Banking: Men and Ideas, I
(New York: Hafner Publishing Co, 1951), 133; W. B.
Smith, op. cit., 195–202, 216, and 220; and B. Hammond,
*Banks and Politics in America, from the Revolution to the
Civil War* (Princeton: Princeton University Press, 1957),
467–68, and 503. See R. C. O. Matthews, op. cit., 62, for
a contrary view.

story of his efforts does not tell the whole tale.

We may conclude this telling of the tale by reiterating three conclusions that have emerged in the course of the discussion. First, there is no evidence — either in the steady growth of cotton production itself or in the other data that are available — of an exhaustion of cotton-growing capacity in the antebellum period, much less of a *periodic* exhaustion. The hypothesis of price rises based on periodic exhaustion of capacity accordingly should be abandoned. With it goes the explanation of "long swings" in American cotton prices generated by the changing elasticity of the supply of cotton.[21]

Second, the primary cause of the rise in the price of cotton in the years prior to 1836 was the rise in demand in Britain deriving from a series of good harvests. Not all British cotton goods were consumed at home, and there were presumably other factors influencing the

[21] D. C. North, op. cit., 11–14; and J. G. Williamson, op. cit., 40–41.

demand for cotton, but the rise in the home demand was the most systematic inflationary factor.[22] While the discussion here has not explored the implications of this finding, it is probable that the United States acted in the 1830's as an amplifier of changes in Britain, not as an independent oscillator. This conclusion, of course, is opposed to Matthew's and North's views of the period.

Finally, the much publicized activities of Nicholas Biddle after the crisis of 1837 must be seen in the context of rapidly fluctuating harvests. The price would have risen in 1839 and fallen again in 1840 without his help. His actions may have magnified these movements, but they did not create them.

[22] In particular, the American demand for British textiles was not large enough to have had an important inflationary impact. Only 11 per cent of British cotton exports went to the United States in 1831–1835, and the proportion for 1836–1840 (seven per cent) was even smaller: J. Potter, "Atlantic Economy, 1815–60: the U.S.A. and the Industrial Revolution in Britain," in L. S. Pressnell, ed., *Studies in the Industrial Revolution* (London: University of London, 1960), 258.

Name Index